Religion, Economics, and Politics in FATA-KP

Washington College
Studies in Religion, Politics, and Culture

Joseph Prud'homme
General Editor
Vol. 15

The Washington College Studies in Religion, Politics, and Culture series
is part of the Peter Lang Humanities list.
Every volume is peer reviewed and meets
the highest quality standards for content and production.

PETER LANG
New York • Bern • Berlin
Brussels • Vienna • Oxford • Warsaw

Religion, Economics, and Politics in FATA-KP

The Enduring Challenges of Merged Tribal Districts in Northwestern Pakistan

Edited by
Tahir I. Shad and Syed Hussain
Shaheed Soherwordi

PETER LANG
New York • Bern • Berlin
Brussels • Vienna • Oxford • Warsaw

Library of Congress Cataloging-in-Publication Data

Names: Shad, Tahir I., editor. | Soherwordi, Syed Hussain Shaheed, editor.
Title: Religion, economics, and politics in FATA-KP: the enduring
challenges of merged tribal districts in Northwestern Pakistan /
edited by Tahir I. Shad and Syed Hussain Shaheed Soherwordi.
Description: New York: Peter Lang, 2021.
Series: Washington College studies in religion,
politics, and culture; vol. 15 | ISSN 2151-7010
Includes bibliographical references and index.
Identifiers: LCCN 2020050006 (print) | LCCN 2020050007 (ebook)
ISBN 978-1-4331-6478-1 (hardback) | ISBN 978-1-4331-6479-8 (ebook pdf)
ISBN 978-1-4331-6480-4 (epub)
Subjects: LCSH: Federally Administered Tribal Areas (Pakistan)—Economic
conditions. | Federally Administered Tribal Areas (Pakistan)—Politics
and government. | Federally Administered Tribal Areas (Pakistan)—Social
conditions. | Federally Administered Tribal Areas (Pakistan)—Religion.
Classification: LCC DS392.F43 R45 2021 (print) | LCC DS392.F43 (ebook) |
DDC 954.91/1053—dc23
LC record available at https://lccn.loc.gov/2020050006
LC ebook record available at https://lccn.loc.gov/2020050007
DOI 10.3726/b14996

Bibliographic information published by **Die Deutsche Nationalbibliothek**.
Die Deutsche Nationalbibliothek lists this publication in the "Deutsche
Nationalbibliografie"; detailed bibliographic data are available
on the Internet at http://dnb.d-nb.de/.

The hardcover edition was published in 2021.
This paperback edition was published in 2022.
ISBN 978-1-4331-9843-4 (paperback)

© 2021, 2022 Peter Lang Publishing, Inc., New York
80 Broad Street, 5th floor, New York, NY 10004
www.peterlang.com

All rights reserved.
Reprint or reproduction, even partially, in all forms such as microfilm,
xerography, microfiche, microcard, and offset strictly prohibited.

This book is dedicated to my children, Laiba, Abdullah and Aleena Soherwordi.
—Syed Husain Shaheed Soherwordi

This book is dedicated to the loving memory of my parents,
Iqbal Mohammed Shad and Fazal Bibi Shad, and my father-in-law,
Rajabali Hussain. They have been my inspiration and strength.
—Tahir I. Shad

Table of Contents

Illustrations ix
Tables xi
Foreword xiii
Acknowledgments xv

Chapter One: Introduction and Overview 1
    Tahir Shad and Syed Hussain Shaheed Soherwordi

Chapter Two: The Economic Implications of the Federally Administered
    Tribal Areas' (FATA) Merger with Khyber Pakhtunkhwa 7
    Syed Hussain Shaheed Soherwordi

Chapter Three: Economic Development in FATA: A Strategic Perspective of
    Pakistan's Foreign Policy 23
    Noor Shah Jahan

Chapter Four: The Socioeconomic Profile of the Federally Administered
    Tribal Areas 63
    Noreen Naseer

Chapter Five: Religion and Politics in FATA 79
    Fazal Wahid

Chapter Six: From Jihad to Salam in Pursuit of Political Change: A Perspective Based on Qur'ānic Sources — 93
Muqtedar Khan and Tahir Shad

Chapter Seven: Indigenous Economics and the Role of Women in Economic Development of Federally Administered Tribal Areas — 105
Zainab Azmat

Chapter Eight: Women Empowerment Through Livestock Management: A Strategy for Achieving the Sustainable Development Goals (A Case Study of Mohmand Agency of Federally Administered Tribal Areas) — 121
Shaista Naz and Noor Paio Khan

Chapter Nine: Exposure to Violence, Human Capital, and Market Development: The Case of FATA — 135
Muhammad Nasir

Chapter Ten: Education and Socioeconomic Development of FATA: Challenges and Opportunities — 153
Sajid Ali

Chapter Eleven: Economic Development in the FATA and Impediments to Progress — 169
Amina Khan

Chapter Twelve: Assessing the Potential for Food Self-Sufficiency on Fragmented Farms in FATA — 179
Shahnaz Akhtar, Sher Ayaz and Muhammad Sabir Afridi

Chapter Thirteen: Accelerating Economic Development of Federally Administered Tribal Areas via Improved Transportation and Communication: A Way Forward — 197
Muhammad Sabir Afridi

Chapter Fourteen: Employment and Economic Development in FATA — 219
Saeed Ahmed

Chapter Fifteen: Justification for Construction of Dams: An Economic Viability of the Jabba Dam in FATA — 233
Zalakat Khan Malik and Asfandyar

About the Authors — 269
Contributors — 271
Index — 279

Illustrations

Figure 3.1:	The Pakistan–Afghanistan Border Tribal Area	25
Figure 3.2:	Northern Portion of Pakistan–Afghanistan Border	26
Figure 3.3:	Southern Portion of Pakistan–Afghanistan Border	27
Figure 3.4:	Pakistan's Federally Administered Tribal Areas	28
Figure 5.1:	War Report: Week Ten	86
Figure 7.1:	Percentage of Population by Age, Group and Gender	109
Figure 8.1:	Theoretical Framework of Livestock's Contribution to Rural Livelihoods	126
Figure 9.1:	Terrorist Incidents 2001–2006	138
Figure 9.2:	Terrorist Incidents 2007–2012	139
Figure 13.1:	Agencies and Frontier Regions in FATA	198
Figure 13.2:	Existing and Proposed Highways in the FATA Region	209
Figure 13.3:	Railways in the FATA Region	211
Figure 13.4:	Airport Locations in the FATA Region	212
Figure 13.5:	Post Office Locations in the FATA Region	213
Figure 13.6:	Landline and Broadband System in the FATA Region	213
Figure 13.7:	Points of Interest in Each Agency of the FATA Region	214
Figure 13.8:	Radio Stations in the FATA Region	215
Figure 15.1:	Map of the Proposed Jaba Dam in Khyber Agency, Pakistan	235
Figure 15.2:	NPV and BCR over the Entire Life of the Jabba Dam	241

Tables

Table 4.1:	School, College, and University Statistics (for Both Girls and Boys)	64
Table 4.2:	Access to Basic Facilities	66
Table 4.3:	Land Used for Agriculture in the FATA	67
Table 4.4:	Wheat	67
Table 4.5:	Rice	68
Table 4.6:	Grains	68
Table 4.7:	Livestock in FATA	68
Table 4.8:	Industrial Units Established in the FATA	70
Table 4.9:	Industrial Statistics in FATA (2010)	71
Table 4.10:	Minerals in FATA	72
Table 4.11:	Minerals Extracted from FATA (2006–2008)	73
Table 4.12:	FDA Funds Allocated to the Development of the FATA	75
Table 8.1:	Contribution of Livestock to Rural Livelihood in the Study Area	129
Table 8.2:	Empirical Results of Chi-square Test Showing Women's Role in Rural Livelihoods by Managing Livestock	130
Table 8.3:	Empirical Results of Simple Linear Regression Analysis Showing Women's Role in Rural Livelihoods by Managing Livestock	131
Table 9.1:	Comparison of Health Indicators in FATA and KP	139

Table 9.2:	Descriptive Statistics	143
Table 9.3:	Impact of Violence on HAZ	145
Table 9.4:	Impact of Violence on HAZ: Robustness	147
Table 9.5:	Impact of Violence on HAZ: Heterogeneous Effects	148
Table 10.1:	Primary Net Enrollment Rate of Pakistan	157
Table 10.2:	Want for a Male Child by FATA Parents	158
Table 10.3:	Want for a Female Child by FATA Parents	158
Table 10.4:	Services That Government Should Provide to Residents of FATA	159
Table 10.5:	FATA Education Statistics	160
Table 10.6:	"In and Out" of School Children in FATA	160
Table 10.7:	Provincial and National Education Scores of FATA	161
Table 10.8:	Educational Index-District Ranking	161
Table 10.9:	Learning Levels of FATA's Students (English)	162
Table 10.10:	Learning Levels of FATA's Students (Urdu/Pashto)	162
Table 10.11:	Learning Levels of FATA's Students (Arithmetic)	162
Table 12.1:	Descriptive Statistics of Output and Input Used in the Study Area	185
Table 12.2:	ANOVA and Model Fit Information	186
Table 12.3:	Regression Results	186
Table 13.1:	Spending as a Percentage of the Total Annual Developmental Program	205
Table 13.2:	Airports in and around FATA	207
Table 15.1:	Economic Parameters for the Jabba Dam in FATA	240

Foreword

That human beings are prone to tribalistic tendencies is well documented in human history. Indeed, the nature of our identity is determined by how we view ourselves as individuals and groups relative to others. In this formation, we choose to select characteristics that identify ourselves as separate or similar to others. These choices are often an accident of history as much as they are of the politics of remembering and forgetting. In today's world, these challenges are being more acutely felt in an era of neoliberal global capitalism, the on-going fragmentation of nation-states that are retreating into ethnic nationalism or cultural chauvinism, and when questions relating to Islam and Muslims are at the forefront in the minds of policymakers, tribal leaders, activist and community groups, and for the people in the region in general. In this heady mix of a global society facing significant shifts to the tectonic plates that had aligned the twentieth-century world order, South Asia is undergoing a series of economic, political, religious, and cultural uncertainties, and no less than the territory of the FATA-KP region.

In the past years, relations between Afghanistan and Pakistan have remained complex, fraught with inconsistencies, and laden with external agitations and influences. In particular, the space between Afghanistan and Pakistan, known as the FATA-KP region, contains many sensitivities facing the two countries separated by the quest for stability, recognition, and acceptance. This territory has experienced intense militarization from the Pakistani perspective and new Islamist extremism problems because of the rise and eventual demise of the Taliban in the region. The emergence of the Taliban created consternation for the many different ethnic and linguistic cleavages, with many forced to endure systematic targeting as part of attempts to standardize a strict form of Islam, in the process erasing local cultures, replacing it with an oppressive regime that took Afghanistan into the dark ages. It also happens to be one of the most geographically picturesque places on the planet, one that I was able to see for myself when I was able to visit Mingora and Kalam in 2012, shortly after the Pakistan Army managed to defeat the Taliban.

Because of numerous political and economic challenges facing this region of South Asia, the FATA-KP area has faced limited opportunities for economic development and growth. It has received little or no physical investment of capital in the area. As a result, it has left numerous communities locked out of opportunities, with the perennial risk of returning to ethnic and tribal conflict—a consistent reminder of what could easily go wrong. Approximately five million people in the region represent significant challenges for numerous actors. With the official political and territorial merger between FATA and Khyber Pakhtunkhwa in 2017, new opportunities are potentially opening up. This book helps to identify some of the primary issues for policymakers working to determine a series of social, political, economic, and cultural developments in the region. However, the tribal code remains essential for community relations, and it will be essential to tackle these contestations, too. As a net exporter of risks due to this region being unstable, underdeveloped, and mired in perennial conflict, there remain weighty questions. This has had particular implications for Pakistan in the past, given the Af-Pak border's porous nature.

In light of these issues and questions, this book is a much-needed contribution that is a significant attempt to determine deep insights into the specific policy needs for the FATA-KP region. It explores history, politics, and economics, assessing the impact of unification in 2017 for the region in the future. The book argues that economic development is the only way forward for the region, but geopolitical tensions across the wider South Asian region remains a thorny subject. It also pays detailed attention to specific political and religious issues unique to the area, which is the central focus of this collection of expert essays and papers, all with the specific aim of determining a deeper foundation for policy development.

Tahir Abbas FRSA
Institute of Security and Global Affairs
Leiden University
The Hague
November 2020

Acknowledgments

The idea for this book came from Prof. Syed Hussain Shaheed Soherwordi at the University of Peshawar, Pakistan, following a conference organized by the Center for FATA (Federally Administered Tribal Areas) Studies in January 2017, at the University of Peshawar, entitled *Economic Currents and Opportunities for Economic Development in FATA*. Papers presented at the conference form the core of this publication.

No major undertaking can be successful without the support of your home institution and colleagues. We would like to acknowledge here the support provided by The Institute for Religion, Politics, and Culture at Washington College, Chestertown, MD, USA, and the Center for FATA Studies (CFS), University of Peshawar, Pakistan.

Dr. Muqtedar Khan from the University of Delaware was instrumental in introducing us to each other and encouraging us to publish this book. Our deepest gratitude goes to him for his ideas, critique, and suggestions throughout the duration of this project. We would also like to acknowledge and thank Dr. Joseph Prud'homme for incorporating this publication into his series on Religion and Politics with Peter Lang Publishing. We have been fortunate to have friends with whom we could share both the fruits and the burdens of rewriting and editing process. Our thanks to Dr. Tahir Abbas, Dr. Melissa Deckman, Dr. Christine Wade, Dr. Andrew Oros, Dr. Daniel Premo, Dr. Shakeel Ahmed, Akhtar Amin, Dr. Syed Fazal-e-Hadi, Yousaf Rahim, Haroon Shinwari, Riaz Afridi, Dr. Gary

Ador Dionisio, Dr. Kamran Bokhari, Dr. William Kruvant, Omer Hayat and Charito Kruvant for their camaraderie, constant support and encouragement.

Several people played a key role in the production of this book. Special thanks to Ms. Teresa Abney for all her hard work, along with Julia Jakus, Arif Khan, Dr. Fazal Wahid, Zara Shad, Zahir Shad, Zaffar Shad, Shadia Shad, and Sabahat Shad for helping with the research. We would like to thank everyone from the Peter Lang Publishing team who helped us throughout the process, especially Ms. Meagan Simpson and Mr. Abdur-Rahman.

Finally, this book may not have been possible had it not been for the advice, encouragement, and support given to us by our respective families.

For Tahir Shad- his wife, Dr. Aziza Shad, was always by his side, providing him with invaluable feedback, motivation, especially when unexpected challenges cropped up, threatening this publication's timeline. My Children Zain Shad, Zaamin Shad and Zeeshan Shad were invaluable in encouraging me to finish the project when it seemed like a uphill struggle.

For Hussain Shaheed Soherwordi- his sister, Sajida Sahar and brother Dr. Syed Masoom Ali as well as his profound friend, Rashid Chughtai were instrumental in supporting his academic endeavors through every thick and thin.

Over and above, all contributors deserve our appreciation for forming the subject material of the book. We are immensely grateful to them for looking at the tribal areas (a neglected region in the past) of the KP with progressive narratives. Their research work pushed us to rethink what we thought we knew and hence we brought drastic changes in our already existing narratives. Thus, editing this book was an education process for us as editors.

Editing this collection of research work was harder than we thought and more rewarding than we could have ever imagined. We hope it is of benefit to all-policy-makers, scholars, members of civil society, and especially our students in the US and Pakistan alike.

          Tahir I Shad   **Syed Hussain Shaheed Soherwordi**

CHAPTER ONE

Introduction and Overview

TAHIR SHAD AND SYED HUSSAIN SHAHEED SOHERWORDI

Pakistan's Frontier Region (FR) has been at the forefront of the War on Terror since 2001. The Federally Administered Tribal Agencies (now known as merged Tribal Districts) are a critical geostrategic area for Pakistan. This work highlights key economic, political, and religious issues in the FATA-KP region in order to identify means to eradicate ongoing conflicts and integrate the region within mainstream Pakistani society. The first step to achieving integration was taken on May 24, 2018, when the National Assembly of Pakistan passed the Federally Administered Tribal Areas (FATA) Reform Bill, which merged FATA with the adjacent Khyber Pakhtunkhwa (KP) province. Nevertheless, this region faces significant challenges on the road to peace and stability. The analyses in this work discuss the past and present condition of the FATA-KP region with two guiding questions in mind. Firstly, why is the FATA-KP region more unstable than the rest of Pakistan? Secondly, how can stability be improved in the FATA-KP region? Digging deeper into these questions, the authors explore the mechanisms now hindering this region from development and good governance.

This work provides a unique Pakistani perspective and understanding of a region that has not been studied extensively to date. A road map to the region's development and stability is provided in the following chapters.

The designation of the FATA-KP was the bequest of British imperial power, and, though they have long departed, the region itself is a lingering legacy of the former British presence in 1901. Over the last 100+ years, significant global developments have ricocheted into the fragile region with a destructive echo. Since the separation of Pakistan and India (1947), the rise and fall of the Cold War (1947–1991), the Soviet-Afghan War (1979–1989), the invasion and annexation of Kuwait by Saddam Hussein's Iraq (1990), the Afghan Civil War and the emergence of the Taliban (1992–1996), the U.S. invasion of Afghanistan (2001) and Iraq (2003), the birth of *Daesh* (also known as the Islamic State of Iraq and Syria or ISIS) and an incalculable expansion of technology, globalization, the fragile FATA territory have been unable to lift itself into the modern era. Situated along the volatile eastern Afghanistan-Pakistan border, the FATA's legislative stagnancy has resulted in a situation far more dangerous than development doldrums.

This project analyzes the FATA's geopolitical, socioeconomic, and sociopolitical stability with respect to both domestic and international security perspectives. It is clear that the FATA must be integrated into the main body of Pakistan if there is any hope of increasing the socioeconomic profile of the tribal regions. Increasing development opportunities despite geopolitical insecurities is essential. Herein, we argue that simply addressing the challenges posed by terrorism, extremism, and religious tensions with only military means are not enough. Military overtures must be complimented, and eventually exchanged for economic development so that the region can weather the perennial volatility it faces.

The Federally Administered Tribal Area (FATA) is a "geographical belt," comparable in many ways to a buffer zone. This tribal region is located in the northwest part of Pakistan, lying between the provinces of Khyber Pakhtunkhwa to the north and east, Baluchistan to the south, and the neighboring country of Afghanistan to the west. The territory is almost exclusively inhabited by Pashtun tribes. The FATA consists of seven Tribal Agencies and six Frontier Regions (FDA, 2007–2014). Although the Pashtun tribes residing in the FATA bear some commonalities, there are prominent ethnic and cultural differences as well. Therefore, developing a singular, flat model and expecting it to fit all of the unique agencies and tribes would be an impractical approach for the economic development of the region.

For this reason, this project proposes a series of phased economic development reforms that can guide FATA's transition as an integrated territory within the rest of Pakistan. These reforms can and should encourage dimensions of indigenous economic practices, women's empowerment, the education system, food security, subsistence agriculture, and transportation and communication infrastructure where possible. These improvements can be implemented in 10+ year plans designed to organize a committed effort to develop and integrate FATA with the rest of Pakistan.

Particularly over the past two decades, the residents of FATA have been subjected to ever-higher levels of collateral turmoil. These rigors are layered on top of existing economic hardships and low employment opportunities. Notoriously the most impoverished region in Pakistan, stability in FATA oscillates between a perpetual state of domestic insecurity that ranges from "tenuous" to "dire" in direct relation to the fluctuation of violence, warfare, and terrorism.

Throughout this work, stability and security are studied in three major categories. *Geopolitics* thematically encompasses the analyses on domestic security, international security, terrorism, FATA's history of conflict, and warfare in general. *Economic Development* in all its forms (financial capital, human capital, and natural resource capital) is explored predominantly in socioeconomic terms. Doing so emphasizes aspects of local empowerment such as increasing women's involvement in economic activities (particularly rural, indigenous women) or developing better food self-sufficiency strategies. Supporting education as well as transportation and communication infrastructure also falls within this analytical category.

Because the region's most profitable market is dominated by illicit trade and trafficking, a significant consideration is given to the nature of the black market. How can these markets be minimized? Creating employment opportunities in legitimate industries is the most logical place to start. In line with socioeconomic development, one study discusses the nature of prenatal and postnatal violence upon human capital, in terms of individuals' long-term ability to become self-fulfilled and self-sustaining citizens who can contribute to society. Ways to support indigenous economic practices are presented as a potential means of promoting environmentally sound development initiatives. *Religion and Politics* also play a significant role in the history of conflict within the region. Within this project, it is discussed in terms of moving away from *Jihad* and toward *Selam*. Policy perspectives are posed and considered from local, regional, and international points of view as well.

Typically, the international level of analysis focuses on military overtures, whereas regional and local levels are more likely to prioritize education, infrastructure, and development. While this project situates FATA in the international scheme for the sake of context, all policy recommendations are suggested with a mind to regional and local concerns. No initiative, regardless of its stance, will be effective in the FATA until relentless poverty is attended to.

Although the FATA meets every criterion for immediate attention, the sheer immensity of the situation (among other factors) has dissuaded both definitive action and firm policy implementations. However, there is no room for continued neglect. The fact that this suffering region has been generally quantified as the epitome of "backwardness" by many sources makes it all the more imperative to address, or—at a bare minimum—begin to discuss the volume of issues present in the Federally Administered Tribal Agencies. It is a question of priority and resource allocation. Pakistan has been all too eager to flaunt its nuclear capabilities to the world, but how does it justify the large portion of its citizens who do not have toilets attached to their home, access to clean water, or the fact that, as a nation, it has failed miserably to meet the Millennium Development Goals? The latter reality is much less bragged about.

As you will soon read, the FATA is not only a region at the mercy of the insecurity in the international system but also a primary exporter of instability itself. More than a corridor for extremism and trafficking between the East and the West, the tribal agencies are a known epicenter where terrorism flourishes due to limited rules of law. Likewise, in the wake of minimal opportunities for social mobility, joining extremist groups or engaging in illicit trade is often seen as one of the few means to social mobility. However, with the military operation called Operation Zarb e Azb, the security situation in the tribal belt has improved to a greater extent.

Certain issues like lack of funds or their mismanagement pose another set of challenges that are affecting the smooth implementation of the reforms' agenda. However, the allocation of three percent of the National Finance Commission (NFC) award for Tribal Areas' reconstruction has been approved. Similarly, the four provinces of Pakistan to partake in FATA's reconstruction by contributing a share of their developmental funds have further expedited the reforms' agenda.

The protracted armed conflict in Afghanistan has a debilitating impact on FATA since it lies on the Pakistan-Afghanistan (Af-Pak) border. The porous nature of the border, as well as displacement of FATA tribesmen and Pakistani Taliban militants on both sides of the border, becomes an important enabler of conflict in the region, which is exploited not only by the militants but also by drug traffickers, gun runners, and contraband smugglers, thereby sustaining the illegal economy in FATA. The China Pakistan Economic Corridor (CPEC) is also viewed by regional states as an effort by China to play the role of a regional hegemon. But the weak institutional and socioeconomic structure in FATA leaves the region very weak to absorb the shocks of instability and the corresponding geostrategic maneuvering in Afghanistan.

All the challenges and perceived negative outcomes of the proposed FATA reforms need to be mitigated by well-thought-out strategies that are adequately planned and executed in both short-term (5 years) and long-term (10 years) by the Government of Pakistan.

This collaborative project hopes to bring definitive action one step closer, which begins by highlighting aspects of the FATA's society where resources could most effectively be invested. An effective policy design paired with a strong follow-through can evoke positive strides toward the mainstreaming of this region within the main body of Pakistan.

Building a Base for Policy Recommendations

This book is composed of a collection of professional perspectives. Their collaboration is, in many forms, a protest against institutionalized economic inertia, political abuse, and administrative neglect that the FATA has suffered since its conception. The following seeks to cast a light on how the circumstances in the FATA are not only relevant from a humanitarian perspective but essential to the concerns of domestic and international security perspectives as well. Instability in this region has a global spillover-effect, with consequences that cannot be mopped up so "easily" as the mess was made. Integrating the FATA with the main body of Pakistan would increase government presence (as in rules of law, annual data inclusion, subsidies, etcetera) and also allow this region to reap the benefits of legislature already in place elsewhere in Pakistan but which could be highly effective in the FATA as well. Resuscitating the FATA's economy would increase political stability in the region. In turn, normalizing both of these aspects would reduce the proliferation of extremism. Proper economic development would also lessen the need to engage in trafficking, thus transforming, little by little, illicit business into mainstream economic activities.

In sum, by consolidating both geopolitical and socioeconomic insights, this collaborative project aims to influence more appropriate future policies in the tribal districts of northwestern Pakistan.

CHAPTER TWO

The Economic Implications of the Federally Administered Tribal Areas' (FATA) Merger with Khyber Pakhtunkhwa

PROF. DR. SYED HUSSAIN SHAHEED SOHERWORDI
Chairman, Department of International Relations
University of Peshawar

Introduction

The FATA is situated along Pakistan's northwestern border with Afghanistan. It is a wedge of rugged mountainous terrain, dotted with sparsely populated valleys, home to a dozen Pukhtoon tribes and hundreds of clans and sub-tribes. This mountainous land, hitherto known as the Federally Administered Tribal Areas (FATA), was made up of seven "political agencies" and six smaller zones. These smaller agencies were called "Frontier Regions (FR)" and essentially separated the tribal agencies from the rest of the Khyber Pakhtunkhwa (KP). On three sides, the FATA was bounded by the "settled" districts of the province. The Durand Line forms Pakistan's western border. In the 19th century, the area held great strategic importance, serving as a buffer between the British colonial government of India and Tsarist Russia. Starting with the 1979 Soviet invasion of Afghanistan, the turmoil and instability across the Durand Line spilled over into the FATA.

The FATA had remained one of the most insular and isolated corners of the country cut off from the mainstream of Pakistani society. Increasingly impoverished and marginalized, the people of FATA became easy prey to terrorist elements. The overall subpar economic situation of the region reflected the lethargic governmental policies that governed it. This coupled with overall economic decline in the country due to the after-effects of the global war on terror (Nasr, 2014). The FATA's economy was chiefly pastoral, with agriculture practiced in a few fertile valleys. The local economy operates on an informal basis and is largely undocumented as few laws provide for the regulation of economic activity.

Most households are engaged in primary-level, subsistence agriculture cultivation, and livestock rearing. Others are involved in business and trading. If these options are not available, they find employment in the small-scale commercial and industrial sectors. Those unable to earn a living at home migrate to other parts of the country or travel abroad in search of work. Women take an active part in agricultural activities, collect fuelwood and fetch water, and do so in addition to attending to household work as well as other family duties (Ahmed, 2013).

The FATA in Retrospect

After the creation of Pakistan, Quaid-e-Azam Muhammad Ali Jinnah was quick to realize the importance of the FATA. In 1948, while speaking in Peshawar to a grand *jarga* of the Tribal Areas, he declared:

> "Keeping in view your loyalty, help, assurances and declarations we ordered, as you know, the withdrawal of troops from Waziristan as concrete and definite gesture on our part—that we treat you with absolute confidence and trust you as our Muslim brethren … Pakistan has no desire to unduly interfere with your internal freedom… We want to put you on your legs and self-respecting citizens to have the opportunities of fully developing and producing what is best in you and your land… I agree with you that education is absolutely essential, and I am glad that you appreciate the value of it. It will certainly be my constant solicitude and indeed that of my Government to try to help you to educate your children, and with your cooperation and help we may very soon succeed in making great progress in this direction." (Ahmed, 2013)

The untimely death of Jinnah, however, left his aspirations for the FATA unrealized. The children of FATA would neither be properly educated, nor would they be provided full economic opportunities to capitalize on what was best within them and their land. The chaos in Afghanistan was matched by political and social turmoil in Pakistan throughout the 1980s and 1990s. When, in the wake of post-9/11 politics, the Pakistan Army entered the FATA in 2003, the final *nail in the coffin* was hammered.

The U.S. Invasion of Afghanistan: A Strategic Nightmare for Pakistan

After the United States' intervention in Afghanistan in 2001, some very stark realities emerged in the region. These realities had and continue to have serious repercussions for Pakistan. First, the fleeing Al-Qaeda operatives from Afghanistan found shelter in the adjoining tribal area (FATA) of Pakistan (mainly Waziristan) and received warm sympathy from their Muslim brethren in the region. Secondly, the U.S. war against the Taliban regime aroused the hatred of the tribal people against the U.S. forces in Afghanistan, and they directed their canons against the security forces of Pakistan on the plea that the government of Pakistan is the ally of the U.S. Thirdly, the U.S. presence in Afghanistan was exploited by the anti-Pakistani elite in Afghanistan; thus they warmly welcomed Indian influence in Afghanistan. This represented a serious geopolitical threat to Pakistan as the Indian missions in Afghanistan started supporting the militants in FATA (who had taken up arms against Pakistan). Collectively, these developments led to the erosion of the political-administrative system in the FATA; the arrival of the Pakistan armed forces in the FATA rendered the Political Agent (PA) and his authority useless.

Excessive explosions in FATA and government installations were detrimental for the rule of law. Further, the excessive assassination of the *Maleks* and tribal elders by the militants created a political vacuum which was filled by the extremists. Such extremists were militants intoxicated by waging Holy War against the infidels (the U.S.) and its allies (armed forces of Pakistan) (Aziz, 2013).

Thus, the U.S. effort to state-build in Afghanistan ultimately resulted in the dismantling of state institutions in the FATA. Adding insult to the injury was the ever-increasing Indian influence in Afghanistan. This posed an "East-West" threat scenario for Pakistan. Furthermore, the porous border between Pakistan and Afghanistan was used by the militants who were carrying out terrorist attacks against the U.S. in Afghanistan. As *to and fro* movement became frequent across the Durand Line, the U.S. started drone strikes against these elements on Pakistan's soil. This situation put Pakistan in a quandary. On the one hand, it was supporting the U.S. in its war on terror, and on the other hand, it was the victim of the U.S. drone strikes. Pakistan could receive neither the U.S. applaud nor the support of its own population, and it was sustaining a huge economic loss in the process (Yusufzai, 2015).

Destruction of the Tribal Code and the Need for a New System

The destruction of the Tribal Code devolved the situation throughout the region. Scores of tribal elders had been killed, so *jarga* was incapable of settling conflicts. In the absence of an effective political administration and in the presence of the military, FATA's situation deteriorated. Religious zealots carried the sway, and the old system of Pukhtoonwali almost vanished. The FATA's former structure of governance had long gone. In its place, the Government of Pakistan sought to carve out a new system to replace the old one. In this context, the future of the FATA became a question of worldwide debate. The deficit of trust between the central government and the people of FATA had grown beyond proportion. The situation became so uncertain that it was no longer the *system* of governance that was of importance for the FATA people, but the very *existence* of the FATA itself. Bringing the FATA into the mainstream national political arena would be an uphill task, but it seemed to be the only option. The drivers of the transformation of FATA's structure needed to be selected with extreme caution; the process ensued relentlessly (FRC, 2009).

Economics of the FATA's Merger with Pakhtunkhwa

After the Government of Pakistan announced the merger of the FATA with the province of Khyber Pakhtunkhwa (KP), a mixed reaction was evinced by the people of FATA. Even so, the vast majority of the people have welcomed this development. A variety of economic potential exists in the tribal areas given the population, land, geography, and vicinity of the Afghan border. If mainstreamed, this can be mutually beneficial for both the FATA-KP and Pakistan.

Economic Potential of FATA

The economic potential of the agency (now called the tribal district) is covered in the succeeding lines:

Bajaur Agency. The major source of the economy has been agriculture. Traditionally, the majority of this population depends upon subsistence agriculture. However, what they produce is not sufficient to sustain the complete population, which means that grain and other necessities must be imported from other parts of the country. The second most major economic input has been cattle ranching. It is still common in all the highland country, and people involved in this profession typically live a nomadic life shifting their abode in search of pastures per the severity of the weather. Minerals including iron and copper are also found in the Agency, but these can only be mined in certain areas. A few villages exist, which are wholly employed and dependent upon this profession. Inferior cotton carpets and shawls are also made in these areas; several families sustain themselves through this livelihood. Forests have been another major source of income and have contributed to the overall revenue generation of the area. The *Deodar Forest* of the valley is a famous source of income to thousands of people. Although these are protected by the Forest department, certain rights have been secured by the local population to sustain their livelihoods.

Mohmand Agency. The Mohmand country comprises barren hills, and a little of fertile alluvial plains are available between the *doab* of the rivers. There, they produce grass, dwarf palm, firewood, and charcoal. Though meager, this is just enough to sustain the population. The majority of the population relies on trade through Khyber Pass from Afghanistan. In recent years, traditional commodities have been replaced by the smuggling of drugs, weapons, and other electronic items within the Afghan transit trade which passes through Khyber Pass.

Khyber Agency. The Khyber Pass is the great northern route from Afghanistan into Pakistan, while Kurram and Gomal Passes form intermediate communications. Agriculture has been the major source of sustenance besides trade. A limited cottage industry of gun manufacturing also exists in the Bara area of Khyber Agency. Nowadays, smuggling through the Afghan transit trade route is the mainstay of the economy along with drug trafficking and gunrunning. Cattle farming continues to be a tradition which supports the tribes in Khyber Agency. The Mullagori marble deposits are one of the largest marble deposits in the world. Other mineral deposits in the Khyber Agency include soapstone, limestone, dolomite, ciliate, silica sand, barite, mica, and graphite. Soapstone is the second most important mineral of Khyber Agency. With only a few industrial units of significance, the Khyber Agency has a very low industrial base. There are also other small silk processing units at Alam Gudar Bara, which serve as a cottage industry (Khan, 2008).

Orakzai Agency. This agency is named after a tribe inhabiting the northern slopes of the Samana range and the adjoining valleys of Tirah. The major source of income is, as per other areas of the Khyber Agency, agriculture. However, a small industry of gun manufacturers also exists in the area. Over the last two decades, poppy cultivation and drug smuggling have gained momentum in these areas as well.

Kurram Agency. Wherever water is available, the soil is highly productive, agriculture is the major profession. Major crops of the region include maize, wheat, rice, barley, and clover. Apples, pears, grapes, cherries, pomegranates, and peaches also grow in abundance and are one of the highest income sources. It is said that famine is unknown in Kurram. Forests of Blue Pine and Chinar contribute to the economy of the agency a great deal (IPRI, 2012).

North Waziristan Agency. The agency consists of large and fertile valleys. These valleys are irrigated by the Kurram, Tochi and Gomal Rivers, respectively. The lands of the valley are extremely rich and able to grow heavy crops of maize, rice, sugar cane, and wheat. Although agriculture is the backbone of their economy, smuggling also brings a significant amount of cash into the agency. Forests of Mulberry, *chinar*, willow, *gurgura* and wild olive are also abundant on the slopes of the mountain. These can potentially be exploited to bring increased finances to the area. Fruit orchards of apples, apricots, and peaches contribute to the economy of the agency as well. Cattle farming is also a major source of livelihood in the agency.

South Waziristan Agency. The lands which lie close to numerous streams are well cultivated; however, the extent of their production does not provide enough grain for the whole population. The land is so fertile that wheat, barley, rice, maize, and millet (the chief crops) are often cut when green for fodder, and grow so well that the same varieties spring up once again before the final harvest. Fruit orchards of apples and peaches also contribute to the economy of the area. The chief mineral product is iron, which is found and smelted in many places, especially in the hills above Makin. Forests include wild olive, *gurgura*, and dwarf palm trees. Mats and ropes are made of the dwarf palm by the men, and the women weave rough cloth from wool and blankets from goat's hair. Cattle farming is also very common in many tribes in the area, especially the *Ghilzai Powindas*. Trade has also been a famous profession in the area due to the link through Gomal Pass. It still continues, albeit with an amalgamation of smuggling. In certain areas of the agency, poppy cultivation has also been popular.

Economic Implications for Pakistan

The merger of FATA with Pakhtunkhwa will have its economic implications. The following is recommended to hasten the pace of development work in FATA and to boost its economy enough that it is brought in line with the settled areas of Pakistan:

Development Plan. The Central Government should allocate funds and provide loans to tribesmen organizations and individuals. Such loans should be provided on minimal markup rates, and private and public sectors should be encouraged to assist the tribal organizations to develop viable and resource-generating economic ventures of their own.

Share in National Finance Commission (NFC) Awards. The NFC Award is based on the population of each province. Since the government's drive is to bring the FATA into the national mainstream, it is imperative that the region be included in the NFC Awards as a separate entity for some time to come in order to bolster its infrastructure (Firdous, 2017).

Transparent Financial Management. A system of transparent financial management should be evolved with the participation of the public. The authority of the auditor general should be extended to the FATA, and proper audit of accounts of all government departments should be carried out.

Trade Sector. The international efforts for reconstruction in Afghanistan, and opening up of trade routes to Central Asian Republics (CARs) offer great economic opportunities for Pakistan. Potentially, this could spell up to one billion dollars of annual trade. Creating environments conducive to trade will greatly improve the economic situation. The following measures will help in this regard:

Open Trade Routes—Formal trade routes between Pakistan and Afghanistan should be opened on priority, for example, the Ghulam Khan Route between Miranshah and Khost.

Relax Customs Regulations—Relaxed customs regulations will encourage the legalization of informal (smuggling) trade. Doing so would allow for increased regulation of such trade.

Tribal Chamber of Commerce—The establishment of a Tribal Chamber of Commerce would enable the tribal traders to have better interaction with the national and international markets.

Tribal National Bank—An institution should be present in the FATA which can provide financial services, counseling, and planning services necessary to free the tribesmen from the isolated "economic island" within which they have been living for centuries.

Agriculture Sector. Supporting the agriculture sector can provide a substantive base for economic development. The following measures are recommended in this regard:

- Adopt the "pocket area" approach to focus on the production of specific crops in identified production zones.
- Improve water management practices by introducing efficient water use technologies. This will be helped by constructing small dams, ponds, and reservoirs.
- Reclaim cultivable wasteland through dry land agriculture. Introduce biopesticides.
- The irrigation network needs to be developed by the construction of small dams, check dams, and channels.
- A land settlement system should be evolved on modern lines.

- Processing facilities should be provided to ensure proper packing and canning of fresh and dry fruit for international markets.
- Model fish farms should also be constructed to encourage locals to adapt to the modern systems of enhancing their income.

Forestry Sector. The forestry sector needs to be explored for economic improvement in the area. The following steps are recommended to be undertaken:

- Launching of a conservation campaign for the forests.
- Encouraging plantation of new trees by the provision of free saplings.
- Establishment of checks to moderate the smuggling of timber to Afghanistan.
- Modernization of the timber industry in the area.
- Provision of assistance to locals for olive grafting and plantation of oaks and chilgoza pines.

Live Stock Sector. The following steps are recommended in this regard:

- Improve access to services, including animal health services.
- Increase the number of female livestock extension workers.
- Make feed and fodder widely available.
- Improve the condition and productivity of rangeland, in collaboration with research institutions and the forest department.
- Introduce new species of fodder, in collaboration with research institutions, farmers, tribes, and herders.
- Enhance livestock rearing and ranching through breed improvement.
- Set up marketing facilities for farmers.
- Improve rural infrastructure and access to markets.
- Declare "pocket areas" for dairy production. This could be facilitated via linkages to the agricultural industry for marketing and delivery services.
- Ensure that savings and credit services are available to support micro-enterprises and on-farm income-generation activities.
- Enable farmers to improve marketing by providing useful information.
- Mobilize local communities and establish links with both public and private sector services. This would be most needed for technical assistance and other inputs.
- Encourage and support the establishment of livestock and poultry-based industry.
- Develop a database, carry out resource mapping, and set up an information system to assist in planning and monitoring.
- Conduct research on animal nutrition and breed improvement.

- Raise awareness about the importance of the sector in terms of livelihood security, and lobby for adequate funding.
- Establish new veterinary hospitals and artificial insemination centers.
- Set up government-subsidized livestock markets.
- Provide incentives in the form of easy loans.
- Establish food processing facilities for the canning of meat.

Minerals Sector. The FATA possess great potential within their accessible mineral resources. In order to increase productivity in the mining sector and improve the quality of the product, the following strategies should be adopted:

- Set up a legal framework which would govern mining activities. Such a framework would encompass leasing, outline dispute resolution mechanisms, and regulate the industry.
- Increase the productivity of mines by adopting modern methods to boost quality and reduce wastage.
- Introduce new technologies through joint ventures based on public-private partnerships.
- Maintain a healthy workforce by improving safety. Develop emergency evacuation procedures.
- Improve the quality of human resources through intensive training.

The following needs to be done to improve the situation in this sector:

- Encourage tribesmen either in joint ventures or lease agreements with public and private sectors.
- The whole of FATA needs to be brought under geological survey mapping.
- Special funds should be allocated for mineral exploration and development on modern lines.

Industrial Sector. There is great potential available for the development of certain industries in the area which can and should be capitalized upon by both the public and private sector. These include:

- Construction material (including cement).
- Decorative material, such as wood and marble products.
- Defense-related industries, such as small arms and ammunition manufacturers.
- Public and private sectors should be encouraged to set up small-scale industries.
- Establishing clusters or "pockets" in industrial pacts should be explored as an option.

- Set up training centers within functioning industrial units. For example, this could be applicable for enterprises such as marble processing, mining, light engineering, or footwear manufacturing.
- Organize local artisans into trade guilds to promote the best possible practices. Such guilds would promote standardization and quality control.
- Set up a regulatory authority responsible for formulating investment-friendly policies. This can be done by increasing dialog with stakeholders.
- Strengthen infrastructures in the region, such as by improving roads, electricity, and the water supply.
- Hold a regular dialog with local tribes to promote investment.
- Short-term mining courses should be arranged by the Mining Department at the Peshawar University of Engineering and Technology.

Tourism Sector. Recommendations in this regard are as follows:

- Develop tourist facilities. Provide services at selected locations.
- Facilitate private-sector involvement.
- Promote areas that have already witnessed some degree of tourist activity.
- Encourage and ease inter-agency exchange visits and tours.
- Research the cultural and natural heritage of the area and make this information widely available.

Infrastructure Development. The following measures are recommended:

- Rehabilitate roads for better connectivity to strategic locations.
- Construct new roads in remote or underdeveloped areas to generate economic opportunities and improve security.
- Build new bridges and rehabilitate damaged bridges.

Good Governance. Good governance is a key prerequisite for achieving the goals set out in the economic development of the FATA. Ensuring that the governance system is participatory, supported by a robust legal framework with active public consultations will make a world of difference in decades to come.

Law and Order. Another basic prerequisite for socioeconomic development is human security. While this is, of course, a critical issue for the people's quality of life, security is equally important to service providers and government officials who travel to and work in the area. To this end, the following is recommended:

- Reinforce the Frontier Corps with more human resources, modern equipment, mobility, intelligence, higher salaries, and training in counterinsurgency.
- Properly train, better equip, and reform the FATA police and Khasadar Force.

- Fence and equip the Pak-Afghan border with monitoring sensors in Afghanistan. Designate selected crossing places.
- In a phased manner, handover of areas to FC and local Law Enforcement Agencies.

Conflict Resolution. The people of FATA have long been accustomed to using violent means for settling conflicts between the members of different tribes and clans. Although an indigenous mechanism for conflict resolution already exists in the form of the *jarga*, there is a need to find ways to prevent conflict from occurring in the first place. Thus, it is worth exploring the possibility of a set of rules and regulations, arrived at by mutual consensus, that would serve as a basic charter or code of conduct for peaceful coexistence (Shinwari, 2010).

Private Sector Participation. The private sector has to play a crucial role in achieving the targets of economic development in the FATA. The government must improve the framework and conditions for the development of the private sector. Doing so would encourage public-private partnerships.

Budgetary Allocation. Each year, the Federal Government sets aside a block allocation, known as the Annual Development Program (ADP). This is intended to be used exclusively for development expenditures. This allocation, disbursed according to the province, region, sector, or project, is part of the federally funded Public Sector Development Program (PSDP). The FATA receives an annual share of ADP funding. In addition to the ADP, the PSDP provides separate funds for programs and projects in various agencies and FRs and contributes to donor-assisted initiatives. Sector-specific allocations from the ADP are made at the Civil Secretariat FATA, based on priorities and needs. Although the development budget is not intended to finance salaries or recurrent liabilities, in practice, this is often the case. Insufficient allocations for repairs and maintenance, meanwhile, mean that some of these costs are also met through the development budget.

Analysis

Any strategy in the erstwhile FATA could be effectively evolved and meaningfully implemented if the said tribal structure is somehow overthrown as it cannot be reformed at this moment. The foremost measure in diluting the tribal structure is to have such physical and social structures in place in the FATA that could effectively lead the process of social change there. These physical and social structures could take root and thrive only in a conducive environment. Since no such environment exists there, it has to be introduced from scratch. This could most effectively be done by establishing some cities in the tribal belt of Pakistan. These cities should have well-laid infrastructures and well-protected and delimited boundaries in order to effect change in tribal areas rather than getting *tribalized*. The foundations of these proposed cities in tribal areas could obviously not be implemented immediately within industries due to location problems and the total non-existence of industries there. However, these cities could be made fully functional and economically viable through the service sectors like education, transportation, construction, telecommunication, and media.

The growth of the service sector (instead of the industrial sector) could save crucial time available for developing the FATA. This could certainly be done through an evolutionary process as well. The gradual development of these sectors would make the cities self-sustaining. The newly established mega-towns would decidedly draw educated, skillful people not only from FATA but also from outside. Thus, they would evolve a work and need-based professional environment. As such, the social milieu is always impersonal and individualistic in orientation; it directly clashes with the highly personalized and collective tribal social structure (Ahmed, 2013). Social change may be brought about by bringing together educated and skillful professionals. The proposed "new cities" could be catalytic for the social change much-needed in FATA that must culminate in transforming the social complexion of the tribesmen and women. This change could be maintained and sustained. It even has the potential to *snowball* once the evolving social institutions of the modern family, liberal education, non-subsistence, mass production economy, secular political affiliations and above all by the non-tribal religious institutions begin to reshape.

In the would-be cities of FATA (with its professional, non-agrarian and somewhat urban environment), the incoming hitherto tribal families would have to sever their links and bonds to survive in the new social settings. Overthrowing the tribal identities and bonds indeed would be indispensable for the families to be functional in the new setting of the city. This foundation of a new family that is nuclear in a structure having parents and their children or at the most grandparents could be laid, if the new cities in FATA and their planners and governors can manage the situation where a large number of such tribal families could be implanted in these proposed cities.

This would be a Great Leap Forward, using China's Mao Zedong term for his "Cultural Revolution" (1966–1976) in dismantling the tribal structure. On the one hand, the hitherto tribal families would be no longer under the collective decision-making of their clans and tribes; on the other hand, children of these new families would have a completely new environment to socialize in. This socialization in a generation's time would significantly dismantle the tribal structure in FATA provided all other elements move in the desired direction. Children undergoing their socialization in a non-tribal and hence non-violent and tolerant milieu would be more likely to be open-minded in their outlook, modern in their perspective, and have a higher degree of tolerant social behavior.

This would significantly curtail the level of extremism in the tribal society, which, by that time, as expected would no longer be a tribal one (Ayaz, 2013).

Only within such proposed new cities in FATA could one expect to have educational institutions which would have the capacity to educate the tribesmen. However, for these educated institutions to function in an ideal manner, the majority of the teachers have to be brought in from elsewhere. Once such educational institutions are operational, children of the re-settled tribal families in these cities could be introduced to standardized formal education (which would have no linkage to tribal values). Likewise, tribeswomen could also enroll in courses for educational and training purposes. Thus, galvanizing half of the tribal population to contribute to the demolishing of the old tribal structure in which it now has no say, let alone control. As far as tribeswomen are concerned, the relative urban social setting of the proposed cities could help them redeem their personalities, social roles, and rights in several ways. The existing tribal structure does give women unrivaled respect, but it is essentially due to the Pakhtun social code and traditions rather than tribal edifice. The decadent tribal structure and the radical control-taking attitude, on the other hand, have almost ostracized women in recent decades (Caroe, 2000).

The FATA's economy can be described by the terms: *subsistence*, *agrarian*, *amorphous*, *undocumented*, and *unregulated*. Every tribal family (and clan) produces its own on the very small landholdings and raises domestic animals for meat and milk. The State does not have any role in the tribal economy. Thus, tribesmen justifiably pay no taxes and hence have no sense of belonging or responsibility to the state. This leaves the tribal economy highly susceptible to criminalization and radicalization. Likewise, it is no coincidence that criminality and smuggling mafias have manipulated the conditions in the FATA for their own ends. Infamous for bringing the proverbial kegs of ill-gotten wealth, the tribal areas have consistently been a main financial source and lifeline of clerical extremist and terrorist outfits and their activities (Khan, 2015).

The institution of modern politics could only develop within the ambit of conducive, tolerant social and physical structures. Modern politics is a great vehicle of change and is instrumental in the democratization of society. At the moment, tribal structures are incompatible with modern politics. Therefore, the proposed cities in FATA could offer an introductory platform for political players and political parties to organize their activities formally. Only through politicization will the power-political vacuum in the tribal areas be efficiently filled by genuine actors representing the needs of the community. Otherwise, the present political power edifice in the FATA will continue to be dominated by corrupt state officials and clerical parties. The Taliban would strengthen further, and thus, these problems would continue to multiply. Without an urban foundation, all attempts to extend the stipulations of the Political Parties Acts to the tribal areas, as announced by

President Zardari recently, would be a futile exercise. Moreover, cities with their peculiar culture tend to serve as sanctuaries for intellectuals, liberals, and dissenting voices. This is indeed important in the context of prevailing conditions in the tribal areas.

Land settlement has never before been carried out in the FATA, and the lack of it has been one of the biggest sources of "blood feuds" in the tribal belt. By carrying out land settlements and establishing the ownership rights of the individuals, nearly half of these issues would be resolved. This will prove to be one of the greatest agents of change in the tribal belt (Khan, 2015).

Conclusion

The future of FATA may be tailored as per the vision of Quaid-e-Azam Muhammad Ali Jinnah as he foresaw in 1948. The initiation of the merger process and the corresponding reforms were, no doubt, a swim upstream. Keeping in view the volatile nature of the FATA at present and its past record of being resistant to modernity, one could feel disappointed. However, such harsh situations demand hard solutions and even harder work. By appreciating the realities on the ground and triggering the aforementioned agents of change in FATA, we can expect to create a meaningful and sustainable change for the better. In this region, which has become the subject matter of a vast number of international strategists and analysts these days, a better future for the posterity of FATA's people will be within sight. After these catalytic elements are set in motion, FATA's future will be set on a track for transformation. Bringing the FATA back into the fold of Pakistan is the direst need of the time.

Bibliography

Ahmed, A. (2013). *Thistle and Drone: America's War on Terror or War on Tribal Islam*. Lahore: Vanguard Books.

Ayaz, E. (2013). *Peace and Development in FATA through Economic Transformation*. Islamabad: FATA Research Centre.

Aziz, L. G. (2013). *Ye Khamoshi Kahan Tak*. Islamabad: Seven Spring Publishers.

Caroe, O. (2000). *The Pathans*. Karachi: Oxford Press.

FATA Research Centre. (2009). *Extremism and Radicalization: A Study on the State of Governance in FATA*. Islamabad: FATA Research Centre.

IPRI Factfile. (2012). *FATA: A Profile of Socio-Economic Development*. IPRI Fact File.

Khan, A. (2015, June 13). *Civil Servant*. (F. Wahid, Interviewer).

Khan, A. M. (Summer 2008). *The Dispensation of Justice in Federally Administered Tribal Areas (FATA) of Pakistan: Its Applications and Analysis*. Central Asia, No. 62, Area Study Centre (Russia, China and Central Asia), Pakistan: University of Peshawar.

Nasr, V. (2014). *The Dispensable Nation: American Foreign Policy in Retreat*. New York: Anchor Books.

Shinwari, N. A. (2010). *Understanding FATA: Attitude towards Governance, Religion and Society in Pakistan's Federally Administered Tribal Areas*. Islamabad: Community Appraisal and Motivation Programme, Vol. IV.

Yusufzai, R. (2015, June 10). Peshawar Bureau Chief. *The Daily News*. (F. Wahid, Interviewer).

CHAPTER THREE

Economic Development in FATA: A Strategic Perspective of Pakistan's Foreign Policy

DR. NOOR SHAH JAHAN
Department of International Relations, University of Peshawar

Introduction

One of the most complex dimensions within South Asian politics is Pakistan's foreign policy intentions, both in the Federally Administered Tribal Areas (FATA) and in Afghanistan. Forever volatile, both regions have seen limited gains. While Pakistan often blames the United States for the creation of the Taliban, the Abbottabad Commission Inquiry Report leaks prompted a more extensive debate. Is the nature of U.S.–Pakistani relations tactical or strategic? For the U.S. establishment, the Pakistani perspective of reality is as difficult to grasp the complex behavior of Pakistani foreign policymakers. This chapter examines the creation of jihadi groups, how these groups developed such deep ties with Pakistani Inter-Services Intelligence (ISI), and the tortured strategic U.S.–Pakistan relationship. It also analyzes how these countries became locked in a deadly embrace, paradoxically as both patrons and victims of terrorists' global jihad.

Superficially, Pakistan's foreign policy intentions are associated with their governmental declarations. Their behavior speaks otherwise. Since the Soviet Union's intervention in Afghanistan, Pakistan's foreign policy behavioral pattern counter-intuitively disregarded its own policy declarations. Rather, its operational behavior compensates for these marked inconsistencies with threats or coercive persuasion against non-state actors. The mainstreaming of FATA demands economic development through civilian surge and the consolidation of the military gains. This chapter presents an overview of economic, and social developments in FATA from the strategic perspective of Pakistan's foreign policymakers, and analyzes how the motivations embedded in Pakistani declaratory policy and exhibited in behavior on the Afghan front merely covered a ploy for attempting a complex operational high-risk strategy of mixing the umbrella of nuclear deterrence, compellence, and completely misunderstood guerrilla war in Kashmir. To prevent the growing outreach and strength of the Taliban in the region hinges on the rule of law and terrorist-free frontiers and the restoration of peace in Afghanistan and on cultivating peaceful relations among the regional countries. Ultimately, this chapter concludes that the behavior of Pakistani policymakers looks more backward than forward by "carving" geopolitics is unsustainable than strategically leaning toward progressive geo-economics.

At times, the intentional, declaratory and operational aspects of Pakistan's foreign policy are well defined. At other moments, only one or two of these are articulated or self-evident. Still, in other cases, they do not overtly announce them and keep their interests and intentions vague and pursue them through a variety of clandestine means. This study examines the strategic perspective of Pakistan's foreign policy by focusing on economic, social, and political dimensions. Special attention is devoted to studying the ongoing fight against militants as well as their nexus with criminals and the Pakistani state. Through critical analysis, this study aims to cut through the common assumptions and pitfalls that obstruct our understanding of the strategic, albeit shortsighted role of the intelligence service. In this, we must inevitably look at the impact of the ISI's failure after gambling on the outcome of guerrilla jihad in Afghanistan and Kashmir, highlighting the collapse of the Taliban's regime in Afghanistan as well as its impact on the region. Lastly, this study examines Pakistan's counterterrorism strategy and how it is viewed by regional and extra-regional states.

Geography of the Pakistan–Afghanistan Tribal Area

The geography of the Pakistan–Afghanistan border tribal areas is as diverse as it is forbidding. The landscape is composed of towering mountain ranges, narrow valleys, desert plains, and rocky, barren wastelands. Topography alone prohibits the creation of an identifiable border. In itself, this is geo-politically cumbersome. In the southern section, the border areas begin on the tropical floor of the subcontinent and push northward into the three great mountain ranges of Central Asia: the Himalaya, Pamir, and Hindu Kush. Part of the border lies in the range of monsoon belt of South Asia, but it receives comparatively little rainfall. In this space, some 40 million Pashtuns manage to make a tough living. There exist two established border-crossing points: Torkham, in the north at the end of Khyber

Pass, and Chaman in the south, through which the bulk of legal cross-border traffic transacts on a daily basis. These are manned by the Pakistani Customs Service and Levies. About twenty other border-crossing routes are also manned by customs officials, *Khassadars*, and Levies.

The northern section of the border extends from the Pamir mountain range pass at Mintaka in the Wakhan Corridor to the Gomal River in Paktika Province on the Afghan side of the border and South Waziristan on the Pakistani side. This section of the border stretches 1,025 kilometers long. It includes the northern Hindu Kush region, the Safed mountain range, southeast of Kabul, and the western region of Peshawar, as well as the border crossing point at Torkham. The northernmost segment of the border contains the Afghan provinces of Badakhshan, Nuristan, Kunar, Nangarhar, Paktia, Khowst and Paktika in the south.

Figure 3.1: The Pakistan–Afghanistan Border Tribal Area. *Source*: U.S. Department of State (2007)

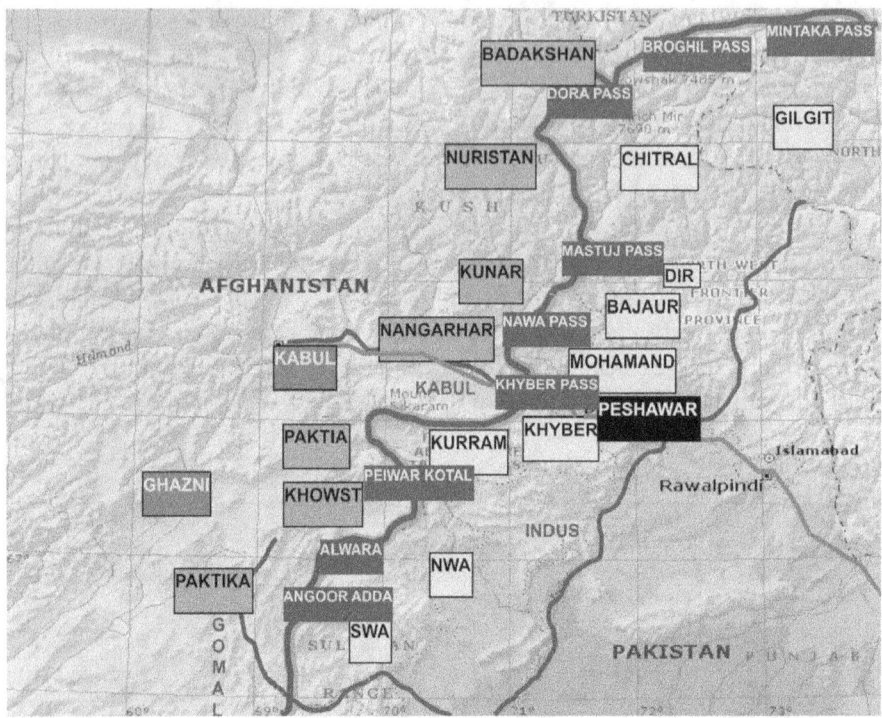

Figure 3.2. Northern Portion of Pakistan–Afghanistan Border. *Source*: Senior Pakistani official interview (Interviewed by Johnson and Mason, Rawalpindi, Pakistan, March 12, 2007)

All seven Federally Administered Tribal Agencies of Bajour, Mohmand, Khyber, Orakzai, Kurrum, North and South Waziristan are on the Pakistani side of this border.

The Federally Administered Tribal Area runs from north to south along the northern section of the border and forms a wedge between Afghanistan and Khyber Pakhtunkhwa. Approximately four million people live in this region, virtually all of whom are Pashtuns. The 1200-kilometer-long southern section of the Pakistan-Afghanistan tribal border stretches from the Gomal River to the Iran-Pakistan border at Robat. On the Pakistani side of this sits the largest but least populated province of Baluchistan. On the Afghan side, from east to west, lie four provinces: Zabul, Kandahar, Helmand, and Nimroz.

For centuries, these tribal areas have fascinated observers, beginning with the British East India Company of 1,000 officials known as "The Governor and Company of Merchants of London trading to East India." On a charter requested

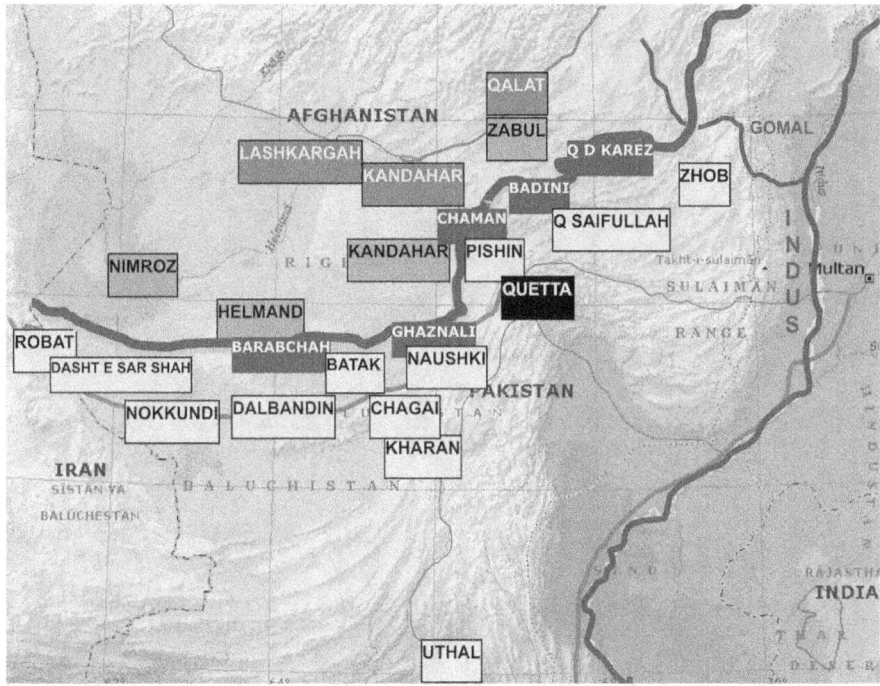

Figure 3.3. Southern Portion of Pakistan–Afghanistan Border. *Source*: Senior Pakistani official interview (Interviewed by authors, Rawalpindi, Pakistan, March 12, 2007)

by Queen Elizabeth, they explored the region in the late eighteenth century. Generations of Victorian explorers, administrators, and soldiers followed these initial explorations. While they could neither penetrate nor subdue it, they developed complex mythology about Pashtun border tribes as warriors and worthy adversaries, as Rawlinson pointed out. During the nineteenth century, at the height of its imperial power, Great Britain tried and failed to subject the Pashtuns to state authority. A century of British fascination and amateur anthropology inspired romantic theories about the region and its people. Some even linked the Pashtun peoples' genealogy with the lost tribe of Israel, as expressed in Rudyard Kipling's (1901) novel, *Kim*, which obscured social reality. The resistance of the tribes and the British Empire's struggle to control them prompted the latter to adopt a "masterly inactivity" border policy. With regard to the debate about the origins of the Pashtun people, it is generally believed that tribes of their forefathers settled them about 1,000 years ago from Ghor and Pashtun tribes who formerly inhabited the FATA. They are descendants of Karlan, who include Afridi, Daur, Zadran, Ketran, Mehsud, Mohmand, and tribes of Wazir.

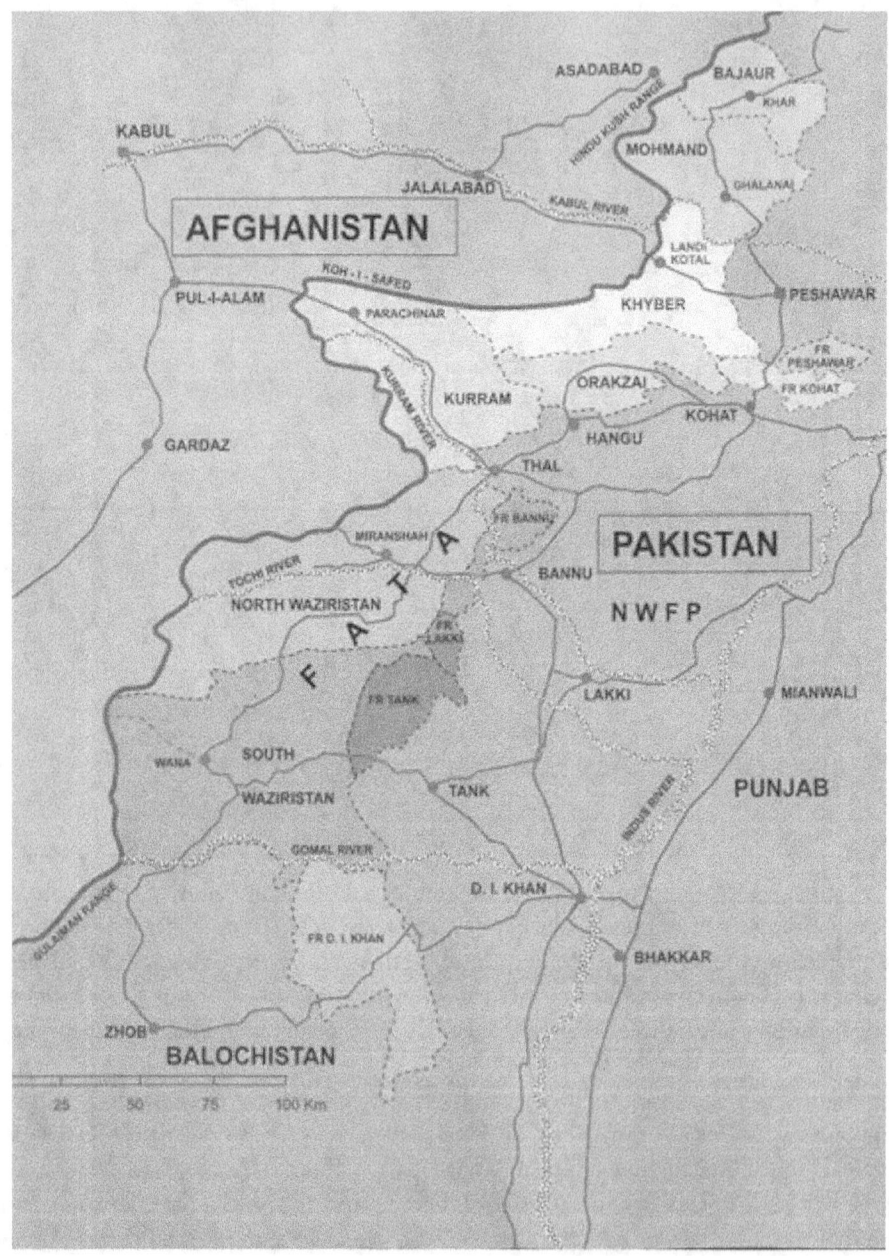

Figure 3.4. Pakistan's Federally Administered Tribal Areas. *Source*: Federally Administered Tribal Areas (FATA), http://www.fata.gov.pk/

The mainstreaming of the FATA is a "hot topic" which lends itself to the question: In an environment of tribal conscious and tribal culture, *is this possible?* The answer is not yet clear, but discussing this subject allows us to shift the focus from conflict to cooperation, and from bargaining to mutual assistance. Ever-changing regional and international preferences, as well as power politics, rewrite the limits on what actions weak states can pursue. In this environment, policymakers attempt to navigate the situation in and around the tribal areas. However, first, it is necessary to explain the conceptual framework of this analysis and the underlying insights which guide it.

A Conceptual Framework of Analysis

A researcher must properly organize their anthology of data by sorting these diverse "raw materials." In other words, a researcher must make intelligible sense of otherwise unintelligible data. Only by gathering facts and describing the events and concepts within a convenient and systematic framework of analysis can one depict the general pattern of behavior in democratic processes of a country's foreign policy decision-making and implementation process.

However, developing an organizational system is more than relating data to general propositions. The most important question would be where the researcher must first focus their attention on the scale: On which level should this analysis take place? Should it be on the level of the international system, the state, or the individuals' level? In groundbreaking research on the causes of war, Kenneth N. Waltz developed the above three levels of analysis, providing a clear framework of analysis with which to analyze foreign policy. In his 1961 article, J. David Singer highlights the importance of the two most employed levels of analysis: that of the international system and the nation-state.

Situating one's analysis at the international level can offer a broad and inclusive understanding of the environment, but it can also obscure the role and impact of a particular state on the system itself. This level of analysis accepts a high degree of uniformity in states' foreign policy behavior, which is unrealistic. Further, references are not made to individual actors or ideologies within states. At this level, a state's foreign policy behavior is conceived to be guided by rational and purposeful action, rather than a permanent pattern of reactions to an international environment which is viewed as external. Further, the focus of analysis is restricted to the interactions of international relations. Out of necessity, attention is limited to particular situational components of the system. This perspective considers nation-states, their policy objectives, and the limitations of their situational environment on an international scale.

Throughout this study, state behavior is not only examined in reference to the external environment (as it would be in a strictly international level environment), but also about the specific domestic conditions that affect policy decisions. "Policy outputs," so to speak, can include the declaration of wars, the establishment of alliances, containment initiatives, imperialistic overtures, diplomatic maneuvers, coercive persuasion, engagement, and an innumerable number of other actions. These measures are pursued as a result of the pressures of domestic political structures, or ideologies, elites, the political culture of the state, or a combination of these elements.

At the state level of analysis, the behavior of the state is primarily examined by focusing on the goals, motivation, and role of domestic structures and the conditions' influences and impact on its foreign policy orientation toward the external environment. At this level of analysis, the diverse characteristics of any given state are focused, resulting in an analysis entirely preoccupied with national problems demanding the attention of state policy. Over-emphasizing the domestic differences may distort reality in a way that leads to an ethnocentric explanation, in which virtues are attributed to one's own nation and vices to others.

In the next level of analysis, the focus shifts to a lower and more partial level of analysis by concentrating on the action and behavior of individuals or groups of individuals. Per the usual approach of a diplomatic historian, the state foreign policy behavior is identified with individual policymakers. Subsequently, these insights are defined by "action" or the purposes of such policies. How and why did these policymakers make certain choices rather than alternative courses of action? The means by which states utilize their resources and capabilities to the attainment of their selected objectives in the name of the state is of vital interest. Particular attention is given to the study of ideologies, motivations, perceptions, and individuals' power, values, and authority based on legitimacy or otherwise its absence, and the dominant positions influencing policy decisions.

Given that all these dynamics set limits upon the policymakers, which level of analysis is the most significant? Singer points out that there is no overriding sense of preference of one level over the other. Likewise, in this study, all three levels of analysis are employed with equal weight.

FATA: Economic and Social Development

Since Pakistan's independence in 1947, its northwestern provinces have been neglected. No worthwhile economic or infrastructural development has touched the region in over half a century. The vestiges of the former colonial system, which was based on the patronage of tribal *Maliks* (elders) with a stipend system, still linger in the FATA. The failure to integrate the FATA into mainstream Pakistan falls heavily on the shoulders of policymakers who exploited it as a strategic base from which they could influence events in Afghanistan. Ideally, mainstreaming the FATA territories would begin with proper legislation, as the Prime Minister reiterated at the groundbreaking ceremony of *Kurram Tangi Dam* on Friday, March 3, 2017.

The Pak-Afghan Transit Trade Agreement (ATTA) was signed in Kabul on March 2, 1965, by Afghanistan and Pakistan to promote trade between the two countries and to extend transit facilities for goods imported and exported by Afghanistan through the port of Karachi. These facilities are exempt from Pakistani duties or customs tariffs. On paper, these goods and exports are destined for Afghanistan; however, in practice, key provisions of the agreement are frequently violated by the smuggling of goods. Once these goods reach Afghanistan, they are either parceled into smaller consignments and distributed in Afghanistan, or they are smuggled back into FATA's markets and in settled areas of Pakistan for resale. The exact volume of unregulated trade is not known; however, the estimates vary from $2 to $4 billion.

In 2005, the governments of Afghanistan and Pakistan saw it fit to revise the 1965 Afghan Transit Trade Agreement, and both countries proposed a new revised treaty. In November 2008, Afghanistan submitted a draft of the agreement to Pakistan, and it was approved with its input in March 2009. The revised Afghanistan–Pakistan Transit Trade Agreement (APTTA), consisting of fifty-eight articles, with two annexures and four protocols, came into force in February 2010. Historically, the domestic Pakistani manufacturing sector has suffered due to the smuggling of goods from Europe via Dubai and Karachi to Pakistan. As a result of complaints about the negative impact of unregulated goods in the Pakistani manufacturing sector, the government banned items with the highest perceived susceptibility to smuggling. Initially, the list covered 24 commodities, but these shriveled to six by the 2000s and have since been reduced further to three commodities: cigarettes, cooking oil, and auto parts.

Over the last 40 years, tribal society patterns have changed. In the 1970s, tribal people began migrating to Karachi and the Gulf region in search of jobs. The *Dubai chalo* ("go to Dubai") phenomenon became even more attractive to the younger generation of tribal people when the Federal Government made it easier to acquire passports. This affected the traditional socioeconomic and political fabric of the people; members of once minor lineages were now able to generate new wealth. Fazal Rehim Marwat argues that the "Dubai phenomenon" attracts tribal youth, particularly those from North and South Waziristan. He also noted that in 2010, more than half of the about 350,000 Pakistani *Pushtroon* belonged to FATA. In the 1980s, the rise of smuggling and the growing inflow of remittances increased further wealth in the lower middle class, particularly the dis-empowered. New inequalities affected the social structure—a resurgence of dependence on land as the greatest source of power.

Z.A. Bhutto introduced quotas providing for the educational institutions in FATA that would benefit the children of the *Maliks* who live in cities outside the FATA region. He also established educational institutions in FATA, among them the Cadet College in Razmak, which opened in 1978. The pattern of politics was changed with the introduction of a universal adult franchise in the FATA in 1996. Previously under the 1973 Constitution, only some 37,000 *Maliks* and a handful of other tribal elders were entitled to cast a vote on behalf of the tribal people. A functioning local government was long overdue, but it was not until 2002 that the Local Government Regulations was signed (and thus officially approved) by President Pervez Musharraf. Per the regulation, 70% percent of the agency councilors were elected. The remainders were chosen by the Political Agent, who was to act as Chairman of the Agency Councilors. Among 397 Agency Councilors, only 19 seats were reserved for women.

As a result of the Soviet invasion of Afghanistan, an influx of refugees fled to neighboring Iran and elsewhere. The majority of them ultimately took refuge in Pakistan's tribal areas, Khyber Pakhtunkhwa and Baluchistan. Pakistan's historical support for the cause of Jihad in Afghanistan was instilled through the more than three-decades-long Afghani crisis. This crisis has been a major reason for the sheer number of weapons in tribal society, the drug as well as the "Kalashnikov (AK-47) culture," and the smuggling of goods. Each of these elements contributed to the decline of law and order and the escalation of domestic political and economic pressures, unemployment, and human trafficking, among other transnational crimes. This affected the very fabric of tribal society in such a way that it has partly contributed to the Talibanization of tribal and Pakistani society. The selfsame tribesmen who fought a long brutal jihad against Russia then joined forces with the Taliban in combating the warlords during the civil war that ensued after that.

The FATA is believed to be the epicenter of drug trafficking and opium cultivation. The region is riddled with small-scale heroin factories that supply heroin to the rest of Pakistan and abroad as well. Because no law exists, which allows for an independent audit of the Political Agent's collected money in the form of different punitive actions from the tribal peoples, this system lends itself to the unmitigated corruption of officials and misappropriation of funds.

The World Bank identified four categories of players challenging tribal elites. The first group is composed of traditional landowning—pro-administration *Maliks* who are interested in "milking the system." Second, the newly rich traders, contractors, timber, merchants, transporters, and drugs/arms traffickers who have become the main beneficiaries of the war economy. The third class consists of professionals, such as doctors, teachers, and engineers. This category also includes educated elites like journalists, students, nongovernmental organization employees, and both active and retired members of the military. This group also includes members of the bureaucracy, individuals who oppose the status quo, and activists who aspire for social change. Fourth, the "common people" typically consist of farmers, sharecroppers, landless peasants, artisans, workers in the transport sector, and unemployed youth. They have no civil or political rights and are dissatisfied with the existing hierarchy. A fifth category (not referenced by the World Bank report cited above) includes migrants *en route* to the Karachi and Gulf region, who, like the professionals and common people, are dissatisfied with the existing order.

According to a survey conducted by the Community Appraisal and Motivation Program (CAMP) in 2008, the FATA is economically the most backward area of Pakistan. Some 60% of its population lives low below the national poverty range, and per capita income in the area is as little as half of the national per capita income. Per capita, public development expenditure is one-third of the national average. Only 17.42% of the population of the Tribal Areas is estimated to be literate, of which less than 3% are female.

As was the case after the Soviet invasion of Afghanistan in the 1980s, after 9/11, the FATA came to the limelight once again. The Musharraf regime announced that it had received a U.S. $16.5 million development package alongside military operation assistance, which would be focused in FATA. The United States pledged $750 million in aid for the development of infrastructure and human resources.

The social structure of tribal society consists of clans (or *Khels*), sub-clans, and an extended family network. Although these clans have different names, they tend to be somewhat similar and cohesive in character, due to the nature of inter-clan kinship. The family's structure and dynamic is possibly the most complex feature of tribal society. The maintenance of their property and inter-family relationships is characterized by love and hate. Each family is headed by a patriarch who is well respected; his decisions are obeyed by the entire family. Underpinning all of this is a deep sense of family honor. *Maliks* and *Longi* holders head each of the sub-clans. The *Maliks* are a hereditary line, although sometimes the Political Agent is granted this title with the approval of the Governor. The title of the *Longi* holder is a lower rank and is granted by the Political Agent. Both *Malik* and *Longi* holders are responsible for maintaining peace within their respective areas. They also communicate information about their regions to the Political Administration. This becomes even more important when a state of conflict arises. Because of their duties to the political administration, the government pays them in allowances and subsidies.

The communication network in the FATA consists of roads, telephone infrastructure, and post offices. In total, 4427.30 km of roads connect the network, of which 2499.70 km are classified as "High Type" and 1927.60 km are "Low Type." Six telegraph offices and 46 telephone exchange locations continue to operate in the FATA. Of the education facilities and infrastructure present in the FATA, there are a total of 2,567 primary schools, 278 middle schools, 201 high schools, as well as nine colleges offering both Intermediate and Advanced Degree levels in the tribal areas. Recently, the University of the Tribal Areas was established, which consists of six departments. Although its main office is located at *Derra Adam Khel*, management intends to expand the institution by establishing a sub-campus in each tribal agency.

Within the health sector, there are 41 hospitals, 190 dispensaries, five Rural Health Units (HRC), 16 Maternal and Pediatric Health Centres (MCHC), six T.B. Clinics, 167 Basic Health Units (BHUs), five Leprosy Centres, and three Sub-Health Centres. Private Doctors also practice in their health clinics and provide services to the people of the tribal area.

Pakistan Viewed as a "Frontline State" in the War Against Communism

In 1979, two significant regional geo-political events changed the strategic landscape of the region overnight: the Islamic Revolution in Iran and the Soviet invasion of Afghanistan. In the wake of these events, Washington lost its regional surrogate in the region. Thus, the balance of power tilted in favor of the Soviet Union. Pakistan's Federally Administered Tribal Areas cannot be disentangled from the strategic perspective of its broader national foreign policy's objectives. Once Pakistan was viewed as a "front line state" first in the War against Communism and then later in the War on Terror, Pakistan's Afghan policy, by extension, amplified FATA's importance as a pivotal region.

For this reason, it is not only vital to examine this region but to understand it as an integral part of Pakistan's policymakers' strategic behavior. The stability, or rather, the instability of the FATA, plays a considerable role in the context of geo-political patterns rippling throughout the region. In other words, the strategic importance of Federally Administered Tribal Areas is strongly linked to the ever-changing geo-political dynamics of the region.

Zia's Guerrilla Jehad and ISI

Historically, the physical constants—terrain and climate—remain the dominant concern for any invader of Afghanistan. When Alexander the Great penetrated Afghanistan from the west between 331 and 326 B.C., he faced the very same strategic problem which confronted the Soviet army in the 1980s. Despite the advances of modern technology, fighting remains an occupation during the spring and summer: between October and April, snow blocks almost all means of communication except major roads. Before the development of blue-war navigation technology, the areas represented the junction of overland trade routes linking South, East, and West Asia and beyond to the Mediterranean and Europe. Along these routes came Greek armies and art, Indian Buddhism, Mongolian conquest; it also implicitly fused Arabian Islam with Turkic military formations and Persian administrative techniques. In truth, all of these dimensions have helped shape the heritage of the region.

Afghanistan's terrain consists of both highlands and low lands. Although some tribesmen live in the high mountains, others prefer to raise their crops and tend to their sheep in the lush valleys. In either case, the highlands are suitable both for peaceful pastoral activities and for the acts of war, such as ambush and raids. The tribal warriors can live off the land, even if conditions are such that their families cannot accompany them. Traditionally, they take to the hills during the war season and live in their villages in the "off-war" cold season. Few other countries offer such ideal terrain opportunities for guerrilla warfare than Afghanistan. Perhaps, this is the reason why the region is referred to as "Afghanistan, Graveyard of Empires."

It would be impossible to understand the jihadi infrastructure of the militant terrorists at either the local or the international level without considering the nexus between both the religious identity and political history of Pakistan. Likewise, the creation of the Taliban in Afghanistan cannot be properly understood without looking at the intentions behind Pakistani policymakers' decisions. What measures have been undertaken in support of the Taliban on the grounds of establishing "strategic depth" via the presence of proxy influences there?

General Zia ul Haq, in a coup known as Operation Fair Play, ousted and arrested an elected leader. To ward off any potential threat of his return, he was charged with murder and hanged in April 1979. Unlike the earlier generation of Pakistani military dictators who aligned with the country's Islamic political party, *Jamaat-i-Islami* sought to transform and Islamize Pakistan's future trajectory. General Zia sought and received the endorsement of Maualana Maududi, who enthusiastically praised the new regime.

The growth of Islamic Madrassa contributed heavily to the expansion of institutional Islam. By 1988, their numbers increased from 900 to 8,000 official religious schools and some 25,000 unregistered ones; many of them were clustered along the Pakistan-Afghanistan frontier and funded by wealthy patrons from Saudi Arabia and other Gulf states. Zia also made the diplomas obtained through these madrasas equal to degrees obtained from secular universities. Thus, the influence of the Madrasa showed a directly proportional increase throughout the country. Also, the social status of the army rose when Zia (in much the same pattern as the Ayub regime) started granting retiring army officers state land expanding the program. He even gave favored officers prime pieces of property in Pakistan's growing urban areas. By 1999, the armed forces collectively owned the largest share of urban real estate in Pakistan. Troops were also required to join communal prayers on the grounds of promoting moral and religious conduct as well as "maintaining satisfactory military performance."

Ishtiaq Ahmed notes that the army's Inter-Services Intelligence (ISI) was originally the brainchild of Major General R. Cawthome, an Australian who was serving as deputy chief of staff in the Pakistan army. After its founding in 1948, the Directorate of the ISI (under the Ayub regime) grew in size and gained international recognition throughout the Afghan jihad. The war against the Soviet Union in Afghanistan led to a major expansion of its resources through the distribution of American and Saudi arms and aid as it has had a significant role not only in managing the guerrilla war [jihad] in Afghanistan but also in Kashmir as well as in internal Pakistani politics.

Unlike the earlier generation of Pakistan's military dictators, Zia was an Islamist. He openly aligned himself with the country's Islamic political party, *Jamat-i-Islami*. He also solicited and received significant endorsements from the party leader, Mawlana Syid Abu A'ala Mawdudi. Zia transformed Pakistan and altered the course of its future more than anyone since the leadership of Jinnah. One dimension of this transformation is evident in the enormous growth of Islamic schools, or *madrassas*, which multiplied from 900 officially registered institutions in 1971 to 8,000 in 1988. These figures do *not* include an estimated 25,000 unregistered schools also teaching. Many of them are clustered along the Pakistan-Afghanistan frontier and funded by wealthy patrons from Saudi Arabia and other Gulf states.

General Zia paid special attention to ISI-appointed General Akhtar Abdur Rehman as its new director. His subordinate, Brigadier Mohammad Yousaf, who served as the ISI's Afghan Bureau Chief from 1983 to 1987, provides an insider account of ISI's war and the role of its director in it from a Pakistani perspective in two books. The first is titled, *The Bear Trap: Afghanistan's Untold Story* co-authored with Mark Adkin and the second, *Silent Soldier: The Man behind the Afghan Jehad, General Akjhtar Abdur Rahman Shaheed*. Under Zia's direction, the military expanded in size and strength. He also developed a partnership with both the Saudi General Intelligence Department and the United States Central Intelligence Agency. According to one account, the ISI staff increased from 2,000 in 1978 to 40,000 in 1988 with a billion-dollar budget.

One legacy of Zia's long rule was that successive governments in Pakistan were heavily subject to military influence. This would prove to be problematic for the ISI, who was pushed to continue to support hardline Islamist *mujahideen* in the civil war in Afghanistan. Along this trajectory, securing "strategic depth" necessitated installing a pliant regime in Afghanistan. Islamabad perceived this to be a critical foreign policy tool for its regional interests because of Pakistan's rivalry with India (especially over India's occupation of Kashmir) and politicians who were on the Pakistani payroll. Although much of the ISI's energies were directed at keeping Zia in power, a significant proportion of resources were allocated to waging jihad. Yousaf remarked that ISI was and still is probably the most powerful and influential organization in the country, Akhtar, the object of either envy or fear among his fellow officers.

The United States helped Pakistan establish the Special Services Group (SSG). Tracing the timeline of the SSG, Ahmed defers to Lieutenant Colonel Ghulam Jilani Khan's account of the SSG's history, evolution, composition, and tasks undertaken by the group: *Tarikh key Ayeney Mein (The SSG in the Mirror of History)*, 2004. In this composition, the author relies upon interviews with people who served in the SSG. An elite group backed by U.S. military support became fully operational in 1956. Its headquarters were located in Chitral, and another facility was based at Attack Fort. The U.S. hoped that both could be used against the Soviet Union.

By the early 1980s, the call to arms for the guerrilla *jihad* (holy war) had reached all corners of the Islamic world, motivating Muslims both young and old to travel to Pakistan to fight along this contested border region and support Afghanistan against the USSR. The religious dimension of this call was strategically emphasized. The *Islamic Jihad* was used as a means to muster the maximum possible resistance while enhancing the intensity and credibility of the guerrilla jihad.

Stephen P. Cohen argues that "American contact exposed Pakistan's military to the concept of 'guerrilla warfare, and people's war'… [when in fact] the American objective was primarily to *suppress* such a war." Conversely, Pakistan undertook detailed studies of the concept of guerrilla jihad and employed it as both a second line of defense and as a strategic weapon. It proved to be a slow but sure (and relatively inexpensive) strategy that quickly overshadowed traditional means of warfare. Pakistan's close connection to China was strengthened by their doctrine's apparent relevance to Kashmir, particularly its frugality. Cohen observed that "Maoist military doctrine was particularly attractive to many Pakistani officers." In explaining the Pakistani stance, he listed a number of requisites for guerrilla war such as: "a worthy cause; and difficult terrain; a determined warlike people (the Pakistanis); a sympathetic local population (the Kashmiris); the availability of weapons and equipment; and a high degree of leadership and discipline existed."

Further, Cohen argues that "Pakistan employed some of these tactics and strategies in the 1965 war against India," in the hopes that the Kashmiris would fight fiercely against the Indian rule.

> "Their first significant implementation was in East Pakistan, when civil war broke out in 1970–71... Irregular forces were raised among non-Bengalis and Bengalis who were pro-Pakistan (primarily militant religious groups). The result of their brutal tactics was the further alienation of [the] Bengalis. Pakistani veterans of that conflict pointed out, however, that they were subject to acts of extreme cruelty, including the torture and execution of prisoners by Bengali guerrilla forces." ~Stephen P. Cohen

Earlier in strategic literature highlighting the "utility" of nuclear weapons in their "non-use," Bernard Brodie used the phrase, "weird byways," to describe thinking that had taken "strange twists and turns" about what the dimension of, "nuclear weapons would mean in war and therefore in the basic affairs of mankind."

Carrying this terminology forward in this study, the phrase *strategic byways* is employed here regarding the discursive approach of strategic thinking and management of the nuclear policy. A particular focus is placed upon the policy produced by General Zia-ul Haq and his successors, who, generally under the shadow of political Islam was inspired by an *Islamic* approach, which blended strategy and military doctrine. Consequently, from the prolonged experience of the Afghan War, came the doctrine of Islamic guerrilla jihad as an inexpensive "strategic weapon" at the lower level of force and also as an adjunct to the rise of nuclear capabilities in Kashmir. They backed this by their unconditional belief in "existential deterrence" against India in the 1987 and 1990 crises. Superbly trained and supported *Mujahideen* were deployed in massive special operations in Afghanistan between 1980 and 1989 to defeat the Soviet Union's superpower. On the topic of the Soviet Union's intervention in Afghanistan, Simes postulates:

> "... In the view of 'Soviet expansionism elsewhere, the United States had little choice but to fight the invasion of Afghanistan once it occurred. The Reagan Administration's decision to 'outsource' responsibility for arming and organizing the resistance to Pakistan's intelligence service and Saudi-funded foreign Mujahideen was insufficiently thought out. Although no one could reasonably have been expected to predict that the same groups would attack New York approximately twenty years later. In the wake of the Iranian Revolution, stronger reservations were appropriate. This example alone shows how easily Muslim extremists could turn against the United States... It was also no secret that some of the Mujahidin commanders in Afghanistan were, even during the 1980s, already talking about establishing an Islamic caliphate and about the United States being next on the receiving end of their righteous zeal.... A lack of sober evaluation explains why, when the United States had an opportunity to try to put the Islamist genie back into the bottle, we [Americans] failed to take it." ~Simes

In hindsight, the derivative strategic significance of Pakistan offered an opportunity to its policymakers to keep "its nuclear program going" covertly, to the point of an eventual acquisition of the nuclear capability, "that angered the Americans" who by then "could do nothing." Haqqani adds that "Pakistan['s] involvement in

Afghanistan was not just the inadvertent consequence of America's proxy war against the Soviet Union."

Cohen argued that General Zia-ul-Haq's "major contribution was the revival and legitimization of irregular or covert jihad launched on two fronts: the major covert war in Afghanistan, blessed by a wide range of states, including America, China, and many Islamic countries; and the limited support provided to Sikh separatists after 1984." However, the venture in the Indian Punjab "diminished as the Indians re-established control over the state of Punjab."
Cohen pointed out:

> "Pakistan's next attempt at what has acquired the euphemistic name 'special operations' was the massive 1980–1989 U.S.-Pakistan effort to dislodge the Soviet installed regime in Kabul and force the departure of Soviet forces—or at least to make them pay a high price for occupying Afghanistan... This was very successful in purely military terms and emboldened the Pakistan army... officers were deeply involved in supporting the Afghan mujahideen, providing them with logistics and training, and serving as the prime conduit for American, Chinese, and other weapons." ~Stephen P. Cohen

General Zia-ul-Haq's rule contributed to Pakistan's strategic byways, "in three respects: his emphasis on Islam, his stress on irregular war or low-intensity conflict, and his acceleration of the nuclear programme." The following explanation of the elements that General Zia contributed to Pakistan's *strategic byways* will help enrich readers' understanding of Pakistan's strategic byways themselves and the intelligence services' strategic shortsightedness of setting the country down these "weird ways" with far-reaching security implications for the country.

A non-proliferation analyst, Michel Reiss, also pointed out that containing and rolling back Soviet expansion in the region now took precedence over concerns about Islamabad's pursuit of nuclear weapons. He argues that the United States would support Pakistan, who, in turn, would then funnel military and logistical assistance to the Afghan resistance to counter Soviet influence. Reiss extrapolated that the major assumptions underlying the logic of the U.S. administration continuing to pursue non-proliferation was to dissuade Islamabad from acquiring nuclear weapons. Conversely, Pakistan's desire to obtain nuclear weapons was driven primarily by its perception of military insecurity vis-à-vis India's suspected possession of nuclear technology. Pakistan hoped that by developing its nuclear system that this insecurity would be alleviated.

However, in 1983, a U.S. State Department report concluded on unambiguous evidence that Pakistan was actively pursuing a nuclear weapons development program and it also highlighted Islamabad's clandestine procurement of nuclear technology and materials from private western firms and its significant progress in key areas of weapons manufacturing with assistance from China. In early 1984, Dr. A.Q. Khan announced that the Kahuta plant had succeeded in producing enriched uranium. President Zia subsequently confirmed this development publicly but emphasized that only low-enriched, non-weapon-grade material had been produced. Notwithstanding official Pakistani denials, these revelations prompted President Ronald Reagan to write a letter to Zia seeking assurances from him that Islamabad would not enrich uranium beyond five percent. In response, Zia reassured Reagan that Pakistan would observe the 5% limit.

However, in 1985, Senator Larry Pressler introduced legislation that required the president to certify annually to Congress that Pakistan did not possess a nuclear explosive device. If Islamabad was to step closer to acquiring weapons of mass destruction, then the proposed United States Assistance Program was to be reduced significantly. Reiss noted that unlike previous legislation in the non-proliferation area, the Pressler Amendment singled out Pakistan, and did not allow the president to waive its application in the interest of U.S. national security. Even so, later, it became clear that Pakistan had gone well beyond the 5% enrichment level of uranium, yet this invoked no change in U.S.-Pakistan relations at all. In fact, in 1986, Congress approved a second assistance package of $4.02 billion.

Indeed, as Chakma noted, from 1985 to 1989, both President Ronald Reagan and George H.W. Bush certified every year that Pakistan did not possess a nuclear explosive device in order to facilitate military and economic aid to Islamabad. They provided the certificate to avoid the imposition of a sanction under the Pressler Amendment, knowing that Americans were far too obsessed with driving out the Soviet Union to waste time on trying to stop Pakistan from acquiring nuclear capabilities. Ultimately, the U.S. prioritized its proxy war in Afghanistan and its contest with the USSR over its issue against nuclear proliferation in Pakistan. This was a blessing for Pakistan, who had been covertly advancing its nuclear program for quite some time. On top of this, the Soviet intervention in Afghanistan consequently raised security alarms in Pakistan from the western side of its border. For this reason, Pakistan ardently sought "stronger security guarantees from Washington but with the absence of such a commitment from the U.S. hardened Islamabad resolve to depend on its own resources for its security and hence the development of national strategic capability became necessary to deter external aggression."

Milton Bearden, who served as CIA station chief in Pakistan from 1986 to 1989, in his excellent essay, *"Afghanistan, Graveyard of Empires"* writes:

> "There were genuine volunteers on missions of humanitarian value, there were adventure seekers looking for paths to glory, and there were psychopaths... As the war dragged on, a number of Arab states discreetly emptied their prisons of home-grown troublemakers and sent them off to the jihad with the fervent hope that they might not return... Over the ten years of war... as many as 25,000 Arabs may have passed through Pakistan and Afghanistan... The idea that the Afghans somehow needed fighters from outside their

culture was deeply flawed and ignored basic historical and cultural facts... The Arabs who did travel to Afghanistan from Peshawar were generally considered nuisances by mujahideen commanders... some of whom viewed them as only slightly less bothersome than the Soviets... As fundraisers, however, the Arabs from the Persian Gulf played a positive, often critical role in the background of the war... During some months in 1987 and 1988, Arab fundraisers in both Pakistan and their home countries raised as much as $425 million for their largely humanitarian and construction project... Among the more prominent of these Arab fundraisers was one Osama bin Laden, the son of a Saudi billionaire... Active in Afghanistan since the early 1980s, having previously worked in the Persian Gulf to recruit Arabs for the jihad, bin Laden focused his early energies on construction projects, building orphanages and homes for widows as well as roads and bunkers systems in eastern Afghanistan.... [Osama] and a few of his Saudi followers saw some combat in 1987, while associated with Islamic Unity Party of Abdul Rasul Sayaf, an Egyptian-trained Afghan member of the Muslim Brotherhood who later in the jihad embraced Saudi Wahhabism." ~Milton Bearden

In his account of the Afghan war, Bearden's insights are extensive:

"At the crucial battle of Zazi and Ali Khel, Sayaf and his Saudis [Osama and company] acquitted themselves well by stopping a Soviet and DRA advance that could have resulted in large scale destruction of mujahideen supply dumps and staging areas in the province of Paktia... More than two dozen Saudis died in those engagements... [Thus, the so-called] military legend of Osama bin Laden was born. At this point in the war, there came growing criticism by Western humanitarian organizations of the harsh fundamentalism of the Saudi Wahhabis and Deobandis, whose influence in the refugee camps in Pakistan, now bursting with about three million Afghans, was pervasive. It was in these squalid camps that a generation of young Afghan males would be born into and raised in the strictest fundamentalism of the Deobandi Madrassas (Islamic Schools) [where] the seeds of the Taliban were sown... Both the [elements] Islamic ideology and the Afghan nationalism lend credence to their war fighting strategy [that] eventually mounted tremendous pressure on the Soviet forces.... Two events in the late summer of 1986 changed the course of the war. [First] on August 20 a lucky shot by the Mujahideen sent a 107 mm rocket into a DRA supply dump on the outskirts of Kabul, setting off [a chain of] secondary explosions that destroyed tens of thousands of tons of ordnance, lighting up the skies of the Afghan capital by night and smoldering during the day. [Second] a month later, on September 25, a team led by a resistance commander with the unlikely name of Ghaffar ("The forgiver," one of the 99 names of Allah) brought down three M1–24 helicopters in the first Stinger ambush of the war... The effect of these events on the mujahideen was electric, and within days the setbacks for the Soviet forces were snowballing, with one or two aircraft per day falling from the skies at the end of the Stringers' telltale white plumes." ~Milton Bearden

Following this incident, Afghanistan was referenced as a "bleeding wound" in Mikhail S. Gorbachev's (1986) *Vladivostok Speech*. Two years later, the signing of the Geneva Accords in April of 1988 "decided to withdraw Soviet troops from Afghanistan and was looking for a face-saving solution that would create a coalition government in Kabul to avoid chaos and prevent Pakistani-supported Muslim extremists from taking over the country." Simes observes:

> "The feasibility of a coalition government [was] substantiated by the fact that even after the withdrawal of Soviet troops, the Najibullah regime managed to control Kabul for over three years ... with a modicum of U.S. support, a coalition government in Afghanistan could have been created that would probably have prevented the Taliban's rise to power, with consequences for Al-Qaeda's ability to operate in Afghanistan with impunity." ~Simes

Further, the Afghan Mujahideen assault on Jalalabad promoted by ISI's head General Hamid Gul proved to be a failure. Jack Matlock, the then-U.S. ambassador to the USSR, wrote that "the U.S. attitude [toward Afghanistan] was driven more by politics in Washington than by the situation in Afghanistan." It was clear that if Soviet troops could not defeat the Afghan resistance, then the Soviet-backed regime "could hardly do so whether or not it received additional military supplies from Moscow." After the Red Army's exit from Afghanistan in February 1989, the U.S. dumped both the Afghan Mujahideen and Pakistan. Bearden articulates the exit of the United States from the region:

> "Though there were heroic efforts by relief agencies to provide humanitarian aid, the senior officials of President George H.W. Bush's administration did not look back to that former war zone, their energies instead consumed by the stunning denouement of the Cold War... In the turn away from Afghanistan, the United States would dismiss even its staunch ally, Pakistan... Though the Soviets left Afghanistan in 1989, it was not until April 1992 that the mujahideen finally took out Najibullah from the UN office and killed him mercilessly and declared what passed for victory. But the situation on the ground was far from passed for victory, as the then U.S.-based Pakistani scholar, the late Eqbal Ahmed, wrote, 'a potentially engulfing civil war had actually begun in Afghanistan when an Interim Islamic Council was put together in Peshawar, and given the mandate to enforce a complex alternative to the collapsed UN plan for peace. Thereupon, the Peshawar based leaders expeditiously decided to return to Kabul.'" ~Milton Bearden

Prior to his passing, in 1998, Eqbal Ahmed described the tense scene of the Afghani during the transition of power in Afghanistan after the West pulled out. The context was anything but peaceful:

> "The opposing forces in Kabul were already locked in armed conflict throughout the city... [It's] embattled airport was unsafe and unfit for landing. The journey of resistance leaders caravan from Peshawar to Kabul was both geographically and politically hazardous... The caravan arrived in Kabul to the welcome of a thousand-gun salute. On arrival, Professor Mujaddedi, a moderate, septuagenarian religious leader and head of the Interim Islamic Council, was sworn in as Afghanistan's new President ... officials of the outgoing government including Prime Minister Fazal Haq Khaliqyar, and vice

Premier Waheed Saroobi were among the first to congratulate the new President... Outside, within yards of the foreign office, a gun battle broke out between Mujahideen forces of Ahmad Shah Masood and Gul Baddin Hekmatyar." ~Eqbal Ahmed

Alongside the depictions of Bearden and Ahmed, John K. Cooley observes that "the holy alliance of the American and Afghan Mujahideen's courtesy of Pakistan against the so-called Soviets' evil empire 'ended in a series of distinctly unholy wars and epidemics of violence.'"

"Old adversaries had become allies while the Islamic resistance was at war over the spoils of power... I cannot recall a more ironic transfer of power in the history-armed liberation... Pakistan's role in helping to put together an alternative to civil war entails one ... liability: Afghan sensitivity to foreign interference has deep roots [as] the government in Kabul was perceived as being made in Islamabad." ~Eqbal Ahmed

Feeding on the violent legacy of political Islam of the Soviet-Afghan War, the centrifugal forces (namely, warlords, ethnicity, tribalism, and Islamic fundamentalism) surfaced with renewed vigor and fresh strategies hoping to bring peace in Afghanistan. Instead, however, Afghanistan became a "market of violence." According to Bearden, "Old hatreds and ethnic realities once again drove events, and without the unifying presence of foreign armies on Afghan soil... The civil war resumed with horrendous brutality until the population was ready for any path to peace, and soon one presented itself."

Haqqani observed that the Afghan "market of violence" essentially paved the way for the Taliban to rise to power in 1994 with the blessing of Pakistan. Al Qaeda's financing of the Taliban's medieval-style rule in Afghanistan offered to isolate jihadi elements existing across the Islamic world the chance to connect. They claimed to offer an opportunity to "re-organize," thus setting their future dangerous on course "in the dark alleys of globalization."

A Pakistani independent English newspaper, *The Daily Times*, noted that "within the parameters set by Washington itself, [Pakistan] pursued different regional agendas ranging from the Afghan front to Indian-held Kashmir." Experts believe that "the Taliban, and their friends in Al-Qaeda, were also used by the Pakistani military to provide facilities and expertise for [the] training [of] Pakistani, Kashmiri, Arab and Afghan terrorists steeped in the jihadist ideology, who were then infiltrated across the Line of Control in the Indian-administered part of Jammu and Kashmir; they created mayhem in the Kashmir Valley."

The Pakistani ISI coached the mujahideen in a purely tactical and utilitarian-military perspective of the war. This approach became an integral part of the psyche of Pakistani intelligence agencies and, "[the] military, which considered politics antithetical to government or policy." As Rubin points out, "[Pakistani] generals had never accepted order from political leader, [to whom] they conceded no legitimate role in security issues, let alone war."

The ISIs became a powerful arm of the General Zia state during the Afghan Jihad when its Director General was promoted from Brigadier to Major General. From this role, Zia organized multi-billion-dollar arms and funds transactions with both the USA and Saudi Arabia. On the eve of the 1988 general elections, he also helped organize a coalition of nine religo-political parties, including the Islamic Democratic Alliance (*Islami Jamhoori Ittihad*). It was an obvious attempt to contain the resurgent Pakistan People's Party (PPP) from sweeping the election and coming into power.

This strategy backfired in that Pakistani media attributed destabilization to be the fault of the ISI. Conspiracies began to circulate that the ISI had a role in toppling the Benazir Bhutto government. One of the most infamous of the strategies they employed included *Operation Midnight Jackal*. The ISI, under General Asad Durrani, did, in fact, help bring Nawaz Sharif to power in 1990, courtesy of Mehran Gate. Under General Javed Ashraf Qazi, he was nudged out of office in 1993. In 1999, two pro-ISI generals—Mohammad Aziz, GCS, and Mahmood Ahmed, Corps Commander Rawalpindi—staged a coup against Nawaz Sharif. The former was an ex-ISI man and the latter a future Director General (DG). Following the coup, they installed General Pervez Musharraf into office, along with a selection of handpicked new cabinet members. Musharraf then promoted General Ashfaq Kayani to Director General of the ISI and later Army Chief; this was an unprecedented act. It also served as the final push needed to complete the merger of the ISI with the GHQ. Henceforth, it became the right of the army chief to nominate their own candidate to fulfill such a sensitive role.

After General Ahmad Shuja Pasha (DG-ISI, 2009–2012) was nominated by General Kayani, he was soon promoted by him to the rank of Lieutenant General and given an extension in tenure. To be clear, civilians have tried and failed to seize control or reform the ISI. For example, although Benazir Bhutto replaced General Hameed Gul with General (Rtd.) Kallu Khan, his role in the ISI, was limited to that of a rank and file member, which ultimately rendered him ineffective. Similarly, Nawaz Sharif sent the DG-ISI's General Asad Durrani back to GHQ, appointed General Javed Nasir as DG-ISI over the head of COAS General Asif Nawaz, but Mr. Sharif did not stay in office long enough to effect lasting institutional change.

When Nawaz Sharif returned to power in 1999, he appointed General Musharraf as the Army Chief and General Ziauddin Butt as Director General of ISI. However, Sharif made General Bhutto ineffective by packing the ISI with persons loyal to Sharif (not to Bhutto). When Asif Zardar set up the PPP government in 2008, he tried to seize control of the internal political wing of the ISI by assuming its command and control within the interior ministry, but the GHQ and ISI manipulated media and opposition in order to thwart this move. Under General Pasha, the ISI became monolithic and had a hand in both domestic and international affairs. The ISI affected internal policy, formulated foreign policy, disobeyed declarations, embarrassed, and even destabilized the Zardari government. It was not until the Prime Minister, Yousaf Raza Gillani, bitterly decried this "state within a state" that this issue was declared publicly.

According to Rubine, "the ISI claimed that its strategy during the Soviet occupation was solely to inflict maximum military damage on the Soviet forces in Afghanistan." Likewise, Brigadier Mohammed Yousaf also acknowledges that the Director General of ISI, General Akhtar, "was conscious [of the fact that] that if political activity were initiated before the capture of Kabul, it would so weaken the Jihad that a military victory might prove unattainable." Perhaps this apolitical understanding of the war and "the ethical model" that was supposedly at the heart of the actions of the Mujahideen [guerrilla] jihad and their Pakistani ISI peers present a paradox. At the threshold of military victory, a high cost was imposed. Contesting parties that would have organically risen were prohibited. In other words, no alternative politico-administrative structures were allowed to exist in parallel to Dr. Najibullah's government in Kabul. Oliver Roy countered that the guerrilla jihad knew no political space such as that of the state:

> "The symbolic space [of Umma], that one traces in an ascending direction, toward conquest, or in a descending one, from the hijra [with] no borders ... only an instrumental vision of state [dawla], the provisional incarnation of the Muslim nation (milla); in reality, it exists only in crises and is not institutionalized. Modern guerrilla warfare should take place within a geographic space defined in terms of military strategy, with ethnic questions becoming secondary."
>
> ~Oliver Roy

N. I. Klonis believed that this style of warfare was a red flag for other criminal activity:

> "Guerrilla warfare is never an end in itself. When this appears to be happening, it is an indication that guerrillas have degenerated into banditry or other forms of ordinary criminal activity.... The tactics and philosophy of the guerrillas are immutable, and any commander who attempts to change them does so at his [own] peril. It is one of the paradoxes of the guerrilla that the most flexible form of warfare is in fact governed by the strictest of rules." ~N. I. Klonis

Given the withdrawal of Soviet forces from Afghanistan, the Mujahideen and their architect ISI and the religo-political parties and generally other religious elements in Pakistani state and society began to assert passionately, not always with much reflection, the defeat of Communist ideology by Islamists and the victory of Mujahideen. Whereas the "U.S. officials of that period acknowledge that the United States made a mistake in continuing to support the largely ISI-driven Pakistan policy on Afghanistan." Richard Armitage, Assistant Secretary of Defense for International Security Affairs at the time, acknowledged, "We drifted too long in 1989 and failed to understand the independent role that the ISI was playing." Simes affirms the notion:

> "Though history rarely gives second chances, the United States did have another opportunity to blunt Islamic extremism in Afghanistan in the 1990s... While few still take seriously Francis Fukuuyama's claim that history ended with the U.S-led Western victory in the Cold War, there is no doubt that the absence of the apocalyptic Soviet challenge gave America considerably greater freedom of choice in defining its foreign policy priorities... One would have thought that the World Trade Centre bombing in 1993, the simultaneous attack on U.S. embassies in Africa in 1998 and the strike on the USS Cole in 2000, among other incidents, would have alerted policymakers that a new major challenge to American interests and American lives was in the making. [However] instead of combating this threat, the United States focused on 'wars of choice' and haphazard attempts at 'nation-building.'" ~Simes

Pakistan's Quest for "Strategic Depth"

The Soviet Union collapsed from the inside and folded like a house of cards. Rubin elaborates:

> "Afghanistan lost the strategic position it had previously enjoyed as a buffer state, first between the Russian and British empires and then between the Soviets and United States-led block.... A buffer state, of course, is consistent with closed frontiers, and for the past century, several of Afghanistan's frontiers, especially the northern one, were effectively closed... The isolation imposed on the country by Amir Abdul Rahman (1880–1901) gradually eased, but almost all the country's population remained isolated and relatively immobile... [This] constituted a break with much of the region's history." ~Rubin

> "For millennia before the development of blue-water navigation technologies ... Today's Afghanistan was at the crossroads of overland trade routes linking South, East, and West Asia and beyond to the Mediterranean and Europe... These routes brought Greek armies and art, Indian Buddhism, Mongol conquest, and Arab Islam together with its Turkic military formations and Persian administration, all of which helped shape the country's heritage... The combined effect of the jihad and the dissolution of the Soviet Union have restored Afghanistan's previous status as a country with open borders crossed by trade routes and subject to the conflicting ambitions of regional powers." ~Rubin

> "[As Afghanistan's closest neighbor], Pakistan saw the jihad in Afghanistan as a way to reverse its relations with the country and provide itself with a security border to the west and north, thereby giving it 'strategic depth' in its confrontation with India. Hence successive Pakistani governments, regardless of ideology, supported only Islamic rather

than nationalist groups in Afghanistan, as the former opposed nationalist claims against a fellow Muslim state or at least did not raise them so loudly. But Pakistan's deep involvement in the jihad also helped incorporate many Pashtuns more firmly into its key military and civilian elites." ~Rubin

Zia's long rule left a legacy of extensive military influence in politics. In many ways, it condemned all successive Pakistani administrations to this influence. Zia created a momentum that pushed administrations to continue "to support hard-line Islamist mujahideen in the ensuing civil war." "Strategic depth" was seen as something which could be attained by installing a pliant regime in Afghanistan. Islamabad perceived this to be indispensable for its regional interests, such as attending to its rivalry with India. Ayoob noted that "this need became particularly acute in the 1990s, as war over Kashmir appeared to be a distinct possibility with the Pakistan-supported insurgency escalating in the Kashmir Valley." Rubin elaborates on the security and economic implications of Zia's legacy:

"The opening of Central Asia after the disintegration of the Soviet Union added a new dimension to the concept of 'strategic depth.' Historical memories of cultural, and economic links among Central Asia, Afghanistan, and the Muslims of the Indian subcontinent [in mind] some in Pakistan saw trade and pipeline routes through Afghanistan to Central Asia as a key to Pakistan's future security [because] these would add yet greater strategic depth. Until over two years after the fall of Najibullah, support for Gulbuddin Hikmatyar's Hizb-I Islami remained the main means through which Pakistan pursued the goal of installing a Pashtun-dominated client regime in Kabul. In mid-1994, however, the government of Prime Minister Benazir Bhurtto shifted support to the Taliban, and 'originally the goal seems to have been limited to clearing the road from Quetta to Qandahar and the Qandahar-Herat highway of tribal militias who had regularly extorted tolls from traders and terrorized travelers.' After ascending to power, 'the Taliban developed their own ambitions, however, and Pakistan eventually threw the full weight of its support behind them as the future government of Afghanistan. Pakistan Foreign Minister Gohar Ayub Khan signaled a new level of public support in May 1997 when he flew to Mazar-i-Sharif with a large delegation immediately after the Taliban's initial, short-lived capture of the city, recognized the Taliban government, and announced that all others should follow suit, as the civil war was now over. Pakistan was supported in this policy by Saudi Arabia and the United Arab Emirates... [who continued] to fund much of Pakistan's policy in Afghanistan through both official and unofficial channels. [For example] some Saudi companies and individuals also have interests in the various pipeline proposals under consideration." ~Rubin

To Pakistani strategists, Evans asserted, "Afghanistan mattered because the impression in Kashmir was that Mujahideen had defeated the massed forces of the Soviet Union." Therefore, the impression of the defeat of communism boosted and emboldened the Islamists both in-and-outside the establishment in Pakistan state and society, and belief in a victory over the Godless ideology had also vindicated the success of mard-e-momin's *jihad* for obtaining "strategic depth in Afghanistan." Mirza Aslam Beg had argued even during Zia ul-Haq's lifetime that "Pakistan need[ed] to show its spine" to the United States. From this perspective, he argued that "Pakistan's nuclear capability was its greatest strategic asset." It was under his stewardship that "the ISI assembled a coalition-Islamic Jamhoori Ittehad (IJI) of Islamist and pro-military parties to serve as the military's proxy" on the political plane in the country. Christina Lamb noted, "they funded the IJI and ran a dirty tricks campaign (in the 1988 national election) on its behalf." According to Haqqani:

> "The Jamaat-e-Islami's position [during the early 1990s] usually followed closely the line taken by General Beg in public and the ISI in intra-government discussions… That, notwithstanding the size of its representation in parliament, it had the right to define policies of the Sharif's government, because the IJI's electoral victory was a mandate for the Islamist worldview." ~Haqqani

> "[It] publicly disagreed with Sharif on a number of issues, notably the war to liberate Kuwait from Iraqi occupation. Ironically, the Islamists' support for Iraq against the United States was in harmony with the public stand of the army chief, General Mirza Aslam Beg, and with Pakistani public opinion, which showed overwhelming support for Saddam Hussain." ~Haqqani

The former U.S. Ambassador in Pakistan, Dinnis Kux, recorded that "on January 28, 1991, General Beg told an audience of Pakistani military officers that the Gulf War was part of the Zionist strategy." Haqqani also noted that,

> "Beg spoke of the need for 'strategic defiance' by medium-sized powers such as Iraq, Iran, and Pakistan, with the help of China, against the dictates of the United States… Such defiance [in Beg's view] would protect the sovereignty of smaller nations. The argument was later expanded by Professor Khurshid Ahmad in an article in Jamaat-e-Islami's monthly journal, Tarjuman-al-Quran (interpretation of the Quran)." ~Haqqani

Haqqani further noted:

> "Pakistan's support for insurgents in Indian-controlled Kashmir spiked during Bhutto's second term. Jamaat-e-Islami and other organizations were now openly recruiting volunteers for jihad in Kashmir… Pakistani media regularly reported on the 'martyrdom' of Pakistanis fighting in Kashmir even though the government continued to claim that the freedom struggle there was being waged by Kashmiris." ~Haqqani

> "The 1990s Pakistan pursued an interventionist policy in Afghanistan to advance a kind of long shopping list: to counter Afghan claim on Pakistan's Pashtun-majority area, to gain access to the oil and gas resources of Central Asia via Afghan territory, to undermine Iran's influence in Southwest and Central Asia, to gain strategic depth against India, and

to recruit Afghan religious extremists as well as Taliban-trained Kashmiri and Pakistani militants for the insurgency in Kashmir." ~Hasan Askari-Rizvi

Parallel to Pakistan's untiring efforts toward the attainment of the nuclear deterrent, and coping with nuclear non-proliferation problems over the years, Maleeha Lodhi comments upon General Zia's strategy and legacy:

> "'Engagement in the long Afghan war' won him international applause and legitimacy in a way, but exposed the country to multidimensional after-shocks: the proliferation of weapons and narcotics, as well as state patronage of orthodox and increasingly militant religious organizations whose fervor to promote the Jihad, was not limited to expelling the Russians from Afghanistan." ~Maleeha Lodhi

According to Lodhi:

> "The culture of violence that subsequently pulverized the country and strained the national fabric was spawned by the Zia years... The use of the public assets to set up networks of venal dependency between politicians and state institutions not only fostered a pervasive system of patronage and corruption but also drained scarce public resources... The Zia years were an extraordinary missed economic opportunity, just when generous levels of Western aid were forthcoming for a country regarded as a key Cold War ally, remittances from overseas Pakistani were also peaking... However, the $25 million in remittances was not translated into investment in productive sectors. A uniquely fortuitous situation was thus frittered away by a regime whose fiscal irresponsibility left unprecedented budget and trade deficits... Faced with this legacy and the end of Pakistan's Cold War importance, Zia's civilian successors working in an uncharted democracy only compounded the financial woes by borrowing their way out of the situation... Crushing internal and external debt was created, which remained among Pakistan's most pressing economic problems." ~Maleeha Lodhi

According to a prominent Pakistani journalist, Ahmed Rashid:

> "... With the active encouragement of the CIA and Pakistan's ISI, who wanted to turn the Afghan jihad into a global war waged by all Muslim states against the Soviet Union, some 35,000 Muslim radicals from 40 Islamic countries joined Afghanistan's fight between 1982 and 1992... Tens of thousands more came to study in Pakistani madrasahs. Eventually, more than 100,000 foreign Muslim radicals were directly influenced by the Afghan jihad... The camps in Pakistan and Afghanistan where they trained became virtual universities for promoting pan-Islamic radicalism in Algeria, Egypt, Yenmen, Sudan, Jordan, the Philippines, and Bangladesh... Americans woke up to the danger only in 1993, when Afghan-trained Arab militants blew up the World Trade Center in New York, killing six people and injuring 1,000. The bombers believed that just as Afghanistan had defeated one superpower—the Soviet Union—they would defeat a second... One of the main recruiters of Arab militants for the Afghan jihad was bin Laden. As the richest and highest-ranking Saudi to participate in the struggle, he was heavily patronized by the ISI and Saudi intelligence... bin Laden left Afghanistan in 1990 but returned in May 1996. Soon he turned on his former patrons and issued his first 'Declaration of Jihad' against the Saudi

royal family and the Americans, whom he accused of occupying his homeland... After the August 1998 bombing of U.S. embassies in Kenya and Tanzania, and that the United States accused bin Laden of financing terrorist camps in Somalia, Egypt, Sudan, Yemen, Egypt, and Afghanistan... A few days later, America fired cruise missiles at bin Laden's camps in eastern Afghanistan, killing nearly 20 militants but leaving his network unharmed... The Saudi terrorist has been helpful to the Kashmiris, and the JUI would protest if Islamabad was seen to do Washington's bidding-capturing and extraditing—that it demanded."
~Ahmed Rashid

Khaled Ahmed highlights a point of concern:

"Elements within the Pakistani military establishment... nursed an expansionist scheme behind the pan-Islamic war of Taliban and the Jihadi organizations mustered by the ISI."
~Khaled Ahmed

Haqqani also notes the influence of Islam:

"Pakistan's national security policy grew several-fold during the period of jihad against the Soviet Union. He further wrote 'the much-enlarged ISI... Its covert operations capability enhanced ten-fold,' which 'became a greater factor in Pakistan's domestic and foreign policies'... Pakistan's military and security services were deeply influenced by their close ties to the Islamist groups. Islamists staunchly adopted the Pakistani state's national security agenda and, in return, increasing numbers of officers accepted the Islamist view of a more religious state ... The frontiers of Pakistan, it was said, would not stop at the Durand Line but go beyond Amudarya into Central Asia."
~Haqqani

Refocusing Attention on the Nuclear Flashpoint

The perennial Indo-Pakistan dispute over Kashmir has defied resolution for over half a century. "The onus of bringing India to account on the basis of 1948 UN Security Council resolutions was on Pakistan.... It [Pakistan] kept reminding itself that its sound legal position had to be hinged to international support... After the end of the Cold War, this objective expanded. Specifically, they sought "to draw international attentions [towards] human right[s] violations by Indian troops in Kashmir..."

"Leaders were pushed by the military strategists into thinking that by, 'highlighting the Kashmir issue through all sorts of means,' [they] could refocus international attention of the big powers to 'impose' some sort of resolution on India because of the [potential] nuclear holocaust.' Strategically, Haider pointed out, 'Pakistan's Kashmir policy can be described as a compellence strategy pegged to the diplomacy of violence.' An inseparable component of this 'strategy has been the attractive concept of nuclear weapons providing a shield to Pakistan's involvement in the low-intensity conflict in Kashmir.' According to Pattanik, 'this factor percolated to strategic thinking only after Pakistan publicly stated its nuclear capability in the late 1980s and the 'approach' remained in hold at the forefront of policy even up until now.'"

The Role of Nuclear Weapons

As Siddiqa-Agha points out, Pakistan's desire to possess nuclear weapons was fueled by its contest with India:

> "One of the recurring themes in the recent South Asian military crisis has been the threatened use of nuclear weapons by leaders in India and Pakistan, following the practices of Soviet and the U.S. leader during the Cold War... The tactics predate the 1998 nuclear test; now, it is widely believed that Pakistani leaders resorted to nuclear threat during the military crisis in 1987 and 1990 as a way of signaling their determination to forestall potential Indian attacks or invasions."

~Siddiqa-Agha

In this context, Pakistan's military and intelligence agency (ISI) gained a tremendous amount of confidence. They perceived the Afghan guerrilla to have been highly successful. They believed it to be a "campaign [launched] purely in military terms [by] supporting the Afghan Muhajideen, providing them with logistics and training, and serving as the prime conduit for American, Chinese, and others' weapons to them against a superpower."

Burki noted that due to "the success of the jihad in Afghanistan in the 1980s and after the demonstration that an inspired group of reasonably trained warriors could defeat even a superpower, it was tempting for Pakistani strategists, especially with nuclear weapons magnifying the risk of conflict, to allow the same tactics ... to be used in Kashmir... [They] were tempted to use Islamic zeal as one way of putting pressure on India over Kashmir."

Two factors were crucial in shaping this temptation. First, Pakistani policy elites drew heavily upon situational factors and anecdotal experiences of their Afghan policy. With scant reflection, they assumed "that a Taliban-controlled Afghanistan will be an ally and give its army strategic depth in its ongoing conflict with India." Secondly, the allure of acquiring nuclear weapons overshadowed their study of sound nuclear deterrence and compellence strategy. The acquisition of nuclear capability in the late 1980s emboldened Pakistani policymakers to believe in the efficacy of "existential deterrence... without postulating how nuclear war could be managed and how deterrence could be extended across a range of conventional and nuclear scenarios."

The High-Risks Kargil Gamble

In the wake of Pakistan's *tit-for-tat* nuclear tests, most people reported in a survey that they felt "South Asia had become a more dangerous place." This is not surprising given that Pakistan has fought three major wars against India, in 1947–1948, 1965, and 1971, as well as two large scale border skirmishes, as in the relatively brief Rann of Kutch incident (1965) and a mini-war on Siachen Glacier (1984). Pakistan has also been engaged in two more recent crises with India in 1987 and 1990, mainly over the unresolved Kashmir dispute. Alongside this turmoil, the region has been plagued by intermittent upsurges of covert warfare, frequent border skirmishes, and guerrilla attacks. There is merit to this "gloomy assessment." Haider's words indicate no end in sight: "India's [persistent] refusal to accept that there is a dispute over Kashmir and honor its earlier commitment to hold a plebiscite under United Nations Security Council resolution, Pakistan chose to exploit and sustain the insurgency."

Three months before the Kargil operation, Nazir Kamal, a Pakistani security analyst, wrote, "Most fundamentalist and non-fundamentalists hardliners looked upon nuclear weapons as providing the country with a security cover for initiating government-backed operations to assist the militancy in Kashmir." By then, Pakistan seemed "to have decided to use the nuclear overhang to pursue a more aggressive military strategy." Haider argued that it did this "by allowing the Islamist groups to step up violence… sending troops out of uniform along with Islamist militant fighter[s] and resorting to limited probes across the Line of Control." In the wake of undisguised weapons testing and "overt nuclear capability," he continued to say, "Pakistan's military strategists embarked apparently, as evident by subsequent unfolding events, on a 'secret plan' to over-milk its nuclear deterrence."

As is often the case with the policy-making process, strategizing nuclear deterrence at times is like "over-milking a fat cow; you see the milk coming out, you press more and the milk bubbles and flows, and just as the bucket is full, the cow with its tail whips the bucket, and all is spilled." This is the epitome of what happened in Pakistan. So to speak, when it "launched a militarily brilliant but politically reckless" operation by going covertly into the Kargil Heights, on the Indian side of the border, all of the milk spilled.

Pakistan attempted to use an aggressive form of nuclear deterrence to safeguard its Kashmir policy. In doing so, it expected to refocus the "world's attention on nuclear flash point" in its "favor" and place pressure on India via third parties for "the eventual resolution of the issue." Historically, the events in the Kargil were an extension of the larger Kashmir conflict. According to afar Iqbal Cheema, "a small number of senior officials in the Pakistan army planned the Kargil operation as a reaction to the Indian Army's forward military policy which culminated in the occupation of the Siachin glacier in 1984." Brigadier (Rtd.) Qadir stated that the "knowledge of the plan was ... confined to four people: General Pervez Musharraf, Lt-Gen. Mahmud Ahmed, then Lt. Gen. Mohammad Aziz and the then Major General, Javed Hassan." The plan was kept so secret that even, "Pakistan air and naval chiefs and other corps commanders [were] not taken in confidence before launching the operation." Just the planners of the operation surmised, "Islamabad's nuclear capability would deter an Indian conventional attack while Pakistan pursued its foreign policy objectives in Kashmir."

An influential Pakistani military analyst argued that the Pakistani authorities decided to seize this opportunity to occupy the heights across the LOC because "Lieutenant-General M. L. Chibber, former Commander-in-Chief of India's Northern Command, had, in 1984, violated the Simla Agreement 'by occupying' parts of the Siachen Glacier." Consequently, "Pakistan paid back India in the same coin in May 1999."

> "Cheema contended the Pakistan's military planners worked on the premise that occupation of un-held areas in Kargil would enable them to choke Indian defenses in Leh and Siachin... Other concerns behind the move, in Cheem's view, ranging from the operational ... alleviating Indian military pressure on Pakistani line of communications in the Neelam Valley to the strategic, such as reviving the insurgency in Indian-held Kashmir, coloured Pakistan's decision-making prior to and during the Kargil conflict."
> ~Levoy and Ganguli

Pakistani military analysts described the Kargil operation as "indeed a brilliant tactical move." However, Hoyt counters that it "was launched at an extremely inauspicious time from a strategic perspective." From the latter vantage point, it was a sheer "strategic failure, as it ran against what Pakistan's political leadership, about three months earlier, had committed themselves." The operation did anything but reinforce the "Lahore summit with the Indian prime minister, namely a journey of peace and security." The Kargil debacle scuttled that nascent hope.

Narrating the episode, Qadir noted that in early May 1999, the Indian army informed their leadership about the intruders' penetration. He argued that initially, "[the] Indian army made numerous unsuccessful forays into the region and suffered heavy losses." However, their losses "eventually precipitated in a determined Indian retaliation quite unexpectedly to the Pakistani planners of the operation." Ramana and Mian argued that "to dislodge the intruders the Indian Army both literally and figuratively [they had] to fight an uphill battle, taking heavy casualties in the process." Qadir explained that "the Indians decided to escalate the war vertically, by using air power. [They] decided to bring in their 400-odd 'Bofors guns.'" On 28 May, two MIGs were shot down by Pakistan; the following day, Pakistan shot down two helicopters. "It was for the first time since the 1971 war that led to the independence of East Pakistan and the creation of Bangladesh, that India used its air force to launch an attack." However, "in response, Pakistan put its air force on 'red alert,' scrambled its own fighters and tested air raid sirens in its capital city, Islamabad."

As the tension mounted, Pakistan's Foreign Secretary, Shamshad Ahmed, warned India that Islamabad could use "any weapon to defend the country's territorial integrity." One should note when considering the situation that "this is significantly different from a commitment to use nuclear weapons only if the destruction of the state is imminent." Reportedly, "estimates of the total number of casualties sustained by both sides vary from 1,200 to 2,000."

When India retaliated conventionally, it bore its might on its intended target. The Kargil Heights began to fall, one after another, while Pakistan "stood diplomatically isolated." A "deeply worried" Prime Minister Nawaz Sharif flew to China and then to Washington on July 4, 1999, seeking a way out of the crisis. Bruce Reidel, Special Assistant to President William J. Clinton, writes that he was present when "Clinton asked Nawaz Sharif if he knew how advanced the threat of nuclear war really was [and did he] know [if] his military was preparing their nuclear-tipped missiles." Cohen mentions that the Pakistani Prime Minister Nawaz Sharif, "on the President's [Clinton's] advice, asked his general to retreat from Kargil."

According to Cohen, "the army was infuriated at what they regarded as a betrayal by an uninformed civilian, especially since they claimed that Nawaz had been briefed fully on the operation." In either case, the information was out. "He had, but probably did not fully understand the implications of what he was being told by the generals." Equally the generals, Hussain argued, were unaware of the ensuing implications of the Kargil miscalculation and, "to counter internal unrest, Prime Minister Sharif attempted to shift the blame for the Kargil operation on [to the] Army Chief of Staff, General Pervez Musharraf."

Reports suggested, "that nuclear weapons were kept ready on the Indian side." Some even insinuated that India had "activated all its three types of nuclear delivery vehicles and kept them at what is known as 'Readiness State 3'—meaning that some nuclear bombs would be ready to be mated with their delivery vehicle at short notice." Analysts believe that "these temporary deployments [may well] become regular practice, driven by the belief attributed to Indian policy makers [that] Pakistan's willingness to exploit its nuclear weaponry for even the most mundane ends might require India to consider developing at least a small set of rapid-response capabilities."

Importantly, as Haqqani observes, "ignoring the likely international reaction and the predictable domestic consequences of the operation contributed significantly to the effects of the Kargil operation on the security of Pakistan." At the height of the two-month war and the ensuing nuclear crisis, both the civilian and military managers of Pakistan's security amidst disarray were clueless: where did the security of the state actually lie? It was under the dictates of these uncertain, dangerous and tense moments within the Kargil crisis that General Musharraf flew to China for a consultation: "on his return from China on June 2, 1999, he told the meeting of the federal cabinet that 'China had advised him to call back the Mujahideen from Kargil.'" In the cabinet meeting (at which General Musharraf was present), he requested that Nawaz Sharif step up to his role in saving the prestige of the Pakistani army.

Similarly, Foreign Minister Sartaj Aziz, during his one-day state visit to China, was "counselled that Pakistan should avoid confrontation and find a diplomatic solution to the crisis." When he reached New Delhi on June 12, "the Indian leadership gave him a cold shoulder." Meanwhile, international newspapers published stories about Pakistan's Kargil operation on its front page on June 14, "rallying the international community behind India and isolating Pakistan at the international level."

Couched in the words of R. K. Betts, the "wisdom" of this brilliant tactical operation was presumably rested on "the implausibility" that India "would dare take a chance on testing it." In other words, it was not on the wisdom of "making the threat good." In launching the tactically brilliant Kargil move, Pakistan's policymakers did not ponder the consequences that might follow. This became evident as the Kargil crisis exposed confusion between Prime Minister Nawaz Sharif and the military on the one hand and the retreat from Kargil on the other.

India did not intervene across the Line of Control. Rather, the BJP government launched a major military offensive against the Pakistani intruders, signaling its intention to escalate the fighting through a massive building of troops along the LOC and international border. According to Ahmed, "both sides also resorted to coercive nuclear diplomacy, issuing implicit and explicit nuclear threats. According to one estimate, "during the Kargil war, Indian and Pakistani officials and ministers delivered indirect and direct nuclear threats no fewer than 13 times." Outside observers perhaps could not recognize what inside observers had gone through in real-time. Insiders experienced the intense effects of the crisis, awaiting potentially horrendous consequences.

International pressure and India's determined retaliation, along with its astute diplomacy, drove "the infiltrators from their icy eyries" whereas New Delhi also refused to "accept outside involvement" in the Kashmir dispute, although "the West has so far been happy to oblige." Yet, Blank argued, "the prospect of nuclear exchange makes Kashmir too dangerous to ignore."

According to Bett, in the overtly nuclearized context, this "incautious tactical approach of Pakistan presumed that India, perhaps less motivated to risk war, would behave rationally in the face of the uncertain probability of disaster." Thus, Islamabad, while pursuing its policy objectives, thought that it would "deter" India from testing its resolve in "the gamble of confrontation." On the wings of these miscalculations, Pakistani policymakers oversimplified a complex situation. Inseparable from the "overall strategic environment, the international reaction, the economic environment, the country's financial ability to sustain an operation of this nature, especially if it had escalated into a war and diplomatic relations in their totality were some of the factors that should have [been] considered." Policymakers had no clear idea and understanding of "mutual nuclear deterrence… a mere extension of the principles of self-regulation based on self-interest to a situation involving two parties each depending on the self-interest of the other to avoid undesirable costly behavior," and the dynamics of deterrence.

Pakistan, after overtly demonstrating its nuclear capability, Paul argued, attempted a "high-risk" gamble by, "mixing nuclear deterrence, compellence and conventional strategy in going up to Kargil Heights in 1999." It was a provocative and risky path that even major powers with nuclear capability would have avoided treading. Pakistani strategists perhaps did not realize the fact "that deterrence is always a two-way relationship with risks to both sides." Rather, as earlier stated, they had simply developed a faith in the "basic and mutual deterrent effects of one country's capability to drop a nuclear weapon on another."

It was in this simple belief that Pakistan's political and military strategists relied expansively on "crude deterrence" for security cover in the action of their perception for conventional operations. India retaliated against Pakistan in Kargil and limited its action to that sector. In other words, Pakistani policymakers misunderstood the limitations of nuclear deterrence in the face of limited conventional response. Moreover, they expected the nascent nuclear umbrella of their country to do too much. However, fears of the bitter Kargil conflict getting out of control prompted the international community, especially the timely diplomatic efforts of Washington D.C., and Pakistan's withdrawal of forces in the wake of Washington's July 4, 2001 statement facilitated the defusing of the crisis.

Kargil's Fall-Out

The "Kargil mini-war" demonstrated that becoming a nuclear power does not necessarily herald the coming of an automatic "political and strategic wisdom." Pakistani policymakers did not understand the difficulty of extending the function of their nuclear capability from deterrence to compellence. By mounting a serious provocation on its enemy, Pakistan brought "the blame of conflict onto itself." The potential Indian response was such that an overly aggressive policy raised too many risks. Kargil demonstrated the limits of even a little "nuclear blackmail" in the context of nuclear balance, however "existential" and "uncertain." Indeed, the existence of such a nuclear balance of terror made conventional warfare so much riskier, whereas resorting to it became even more dangerous.

Moreover, as Kargil demonstrated, Pakistani policymakers perhaps focused only on *compelling* action from India. With no experience in nuclear strategy, they failed to draw proper lessons from the East-West history of deterrence, that is, "in deterrence strategy, one seeks to reinforce enemy's apparent preference not to resort to military force" and that "assuming a rational behavior, one deters the enemy by reinforcing the benefits of peace relative to war and by highlighting the cost that would be involved in war."

Regardless of fulfilling the essential "requirements" and other demands of "nuclear deterrence" strategy that states adopt to deter enemies, Pakistani policymakers exercised the discursive approach of strategic byways that led them "to grave risk-taking in saber-rattling crises." In the words of Turner, "this hypnosis exercised by the weapons of mass destruction, by making military strategy too dependent on one set of tools ... deprived the nation of flexibility." In this case, Pakistan was no exception to his warning, that "with a rigid military strategy, no policies can be formulated and no objectives can be achieved, [and, that] it is one thing to negotiate through strength; it is quite another to negotiate on the basis of a power which breeds self-destruction."

The Kargil debacle landed Pakistan's security system in a position where it was required to handle back-to-back crises. This vicious spiral compounded Pakistan's existing and panoptic crises as both Pakistani and Indian scholars, Eqbal Ahmed and Ashley J. Tellis, have pointed out. Tellis explained that "although strategic, economic, political and societal obstacles exist and each has its specific cause, in their totality they [crises] indicate Pakistan's failure to resolve its internal and external security problems without resorting to military rule."

This is not to say that the crises would not have occurred without this blunder. According to Stanely Hoffman, "crises, however, are twilight regions between peace and war. Indeed, the nuclear revolution encourages 'the substitution of crises for war.'" The historical context and processes, that is, Pakistan's Afghan policy situational factors and experience in the war, plus the overt nuclearization in 1998, were at the heart of Pakistani policymakers' thinking in configuring and deciding about how the nuclear strategy would run its initial course on the "weird byways."

It was due to the fear and threat that the Kargil crisis could escalate and bring nuclear weapons into play that Pakistani policymakers turned against Zia and his successors' complex elementary-composite approach and thinking, encapsulated in the concept of strategic byways. In particular, covert guerrilla jihad against a nuclear-armed enemy turned out to be a sheer miscalculation which President General Musharraf has repeatedly referred to as a "strategic miscalculation."

Samina Ahmed argued that "Pakistan's failure to sustain its military operation in Kargil and its unconditional military withdrawal had resulted in an unprecedented question of the notion of nuclear deterrence within and without parliament." Carranza argued that "the Kargil war was the first major Indo-Pakistani armed conflict in an environment of declared nuclear weapons status and a test of the hypothesis that the nuclear tests favor Pakistan because nuclear weapons are the 'great equalizer' in international relations." Strategically, the Kargil war significantly changed the strategic interactions between the two nuclear-armed South Asian rivals and their mutual calculus of deterrence.

Changing Mutual Calculus of Deterrence

The Kargil incident altered the way India and Pakistan behaved within their rivalry. Now, a mutual calculus of deterrence was at play. Carranza highlights the following elements that unfolded throughout the Kargil Heights as well as the strategic interactions that shaped it:

(1) Pakistan tried to capitalize upon its newly declared nuclear weapons status. Pakistan gambled that it could militarily support the Muslim militants' insurgency in the Kargil peaks *without* an Indian response.
(2) Pakistan clearly overestimated the deterrent effect of its nuclear might. India was *not* deterred from launching a successful counter-offensive on its side of the LOC despite the threats made by Pakistani that it would use its nuclear weaponry. In hindsight, while India won the Kargil war both on military and diplomatic fronts, it could have won the war much faster (and with much fewer casualties) by attacking the intruders' supply line in Pakistan-controlled Kashmir. However, India was deterred from using this method, and from expanding the war into Pakistani territory, for two reasons: (a) fear of provoking a full war that could escalate to the nuclear level, and (b) fear of destroying the goodwill of foreign powers, such as the United States and China, who have traditionally been an ally of Pakistan.

The Kargil conflict reflected a discursive ambiguity in Pakistani policymaking. Their approach was based upon a rigid polarization of strategic objectives: either total peace or total war, self-destruction, or deterrence. This paradigm contradicted the basic thinking required to honor the basic principles of nuclear deterrence, namely self-interest *and* self-regulation. After the coming of nuclear weapons to Pakistan, or rather to South Asia, its strategists were faced with a new task: "find ways to permit greater freedom of maneuver by providing more alternative objectives." According to Turner and Challener, this was because "nothing would limit them, that is, but their own range of thinking and an unwillingness to alter [their] thought processes." Although nuclear weapons helped explain Pakistan's decision to start the Kargil conflict, the outcomes of the war show that the "great equalizer" argument cut both ways.

Shortly after the Lakeshore Summit, Sharif played a controversial role in the Kargil conflict. Malik noted that Sharif refused to openly acknowledge "Pakistan's role in the offensive in the face of the negative global reaction." This was in large part because he wanted to present India as the aggressor of the conflict and obtain the sympathy of the international community. It was a vain attempt. According to Cohen, even afterward, "Pakistan's army [and] the service chiefs declined to accord full honors to the Indian prime minister, failing to turn up to greet him at the border crossing where he entered Pakistan." The Kargil venture "in a powerful way exposed the serious differences between the army and prime minister" as the revelation of ongoing secret parleys between emissaries of Sharif and India's Vajpayee. During this period of heightened tensions, this was gravely resented by the army, who feared the surrender of traditional Pakistani interests to India much more strongly.

September 11 and the Changed International Context

The unprecedented terrorists' attacks on the United States on September 11, 2001, dramatically reoriented American policy interests in South Asia. Before the attack, the George W. Bush administration appeared to have all but relegated Pakistan as a rogue state because of the coup staged against its own democratically-elected government, its support for the Taliban regime, and alleged insurgency groups wreaking havoc in Indian-controlled Kashmir. In lieu of the changed context, Pakistan's strategic significance became reminiscent of its earlier importance following the Soviet invasion of Afghanistan. Thus, the Bush administration turned *volte-face* in its dealing with Pakistan.

Pakistan as a "Frontline State" in the War Against Terror

In Vandenburg's view, a political realist, just as the attack on Pearl Harbor ended isolationism in the United States, so did the 9/11 terrorist attacks bring President Bush and his administration's isolationist tendencies to a full stop. The Bush administration was grasping for a more pro-active, unifying national policy. It also increasingly blamed President Clinton's administration for failing to take effective action against Osama bin Laden and terrorism after the first bombings of the World Trade Center and the terrorists' attack on Khobar Towers in Saudi Arabia. Likewise, it faulted their conduct following incidents targeting the U.S. embassies in Kenya and Tanzania. All the negative consequences of these events were attributed to the former administration's inefficient foreign policy. Thus, the Bush administration's initial isolationism gave way to an aggressive unilateralism.

When the U.S. targeted Afghanistan as the focal point of action, it dramatically changed the regional and strategic context with deep ramifications. In the conduct of "inter-state and intrastate relations," violence committed by non-state actors or sub-national groups which had been, until that point, considered as a necessary politico-military tool in the struggle for self-determination, could now be easily dubbed and rejected as terrorism. In recent history, Washington has launched six major military operations since the fall of the Berlin Wall: in Panama, Somalia, Kosovo, Afghanistan and twice in Iraq. This changed discourse and logic have had far-reaching implications for Pakistan's internal and external security. The country, "on the eve of September 11, 2001, looked like a state that had lost its way, with a 38 billion dollar external-debt stagnant economy, a military government, and political and social institutions in disarray." More than three decades of war in Afghanistan pitted America and Pakistan into a "Deadly Embrace." The two countries maintain mutually misunderstood deceptive relations.

Moreover, the event vindicated what Paul Kennedy, Robert Chase, and Emily Hill argued that Pakistan had emerged one of the "nine pivotal States" as a key to a global counterterrorism strategy that could not only determine the fate of its region but also affect international stability and security. The creation of the Friends of Democratic Pakistan aid consortium and the U.S. Congressional Kerry-Lugar Act, with its support for non-military expenditures, were enticing policy steps to Pakistan being too important to fail and the growing importance of FATA to Western security interests led to a series of policy briefs and initiatives such as the FATA Sustainable Development Plan 2007–2015.

The *Tehrik-e-Taliban* movement emerged not abruptly, but as the Taliban regime tenure in Afghanistan and (non-regime) insurgent durability gradually consolidated Taliban movement in the FATA region and eventually in settled adjacent districts. The question—will the war on terror and the prevailing anti-U.S. sentiment translate into more seats for the religious, political parties in the general elections in Pakistan in 2008 and 2013—remained at the top of the campaigns.

The Taliban movement was, in fact, built and deliberately employed by the Pakistani intelligence agencies (especially the ISI) over the years; it was groomed as a subversive guerrilla force in the war against Soviet forces in Afghanistan as well as against the Indian occupation of Kashmir. These radical policy tactics played with fire, and the result was irreversible. When this began in the late 1970s, the Pakistani tribal structure was subverted. This accelerated dramatically after the withdrawal of Soviet forces from Afghanistan in February 1989.

The *Operation Enduring Freedom* in Afghanistan in October 2001 spurred an influx of *Taliban* and *Al-Qaeda* militants into the FATA. Riedel acknowledges that Pakistan has been wracked by terror and militancy from one end of the country to the other, mass casualty attacks occur almost daily, and many Pakistani believe that the United States has its share in creating this monster. To some extent, they are right. Riedel argues that America had been a fickle friend, sometimes working as Pakistan's closest ally and collaborating on secret programs, while at other times moving to isolate and impose sanctions against it. For good as well as bad reasons, successive U.S. Presidents from both parties have pursued narrow, short-term interests in Pakistan that have contributed to its radicalization, thereby creating a more fertile ground for global jihad. Riedel also claims that Pakistan is equally fickle to deal with, especially for outsiders, such as U.S. Presidents seeking to grasp its policymakers' deceptive behavior and motives.

Pakistan is much more than a U.S. counterterrorism policy issue. Pakistan is now the fifth-largest populist country in the world, and with its rapid growth rate of population, it will soon be the world's sixth-largest Muslim country, and one with a growing nuclear arsenal at that. Today, that arsenal includes tactical nuclear weapons, chain-linked to strategic competition with its rival India, who is also nuclear-armed. Although the region is at a crossroads, certain elements cannot be disputed: Pakistan is situated in such a way that its foreign policies and those of its neighbors are characterized more by looking back to antiquated forms of *venial geopolitics* (which looks at the "two-block scenario" between the United States and India versus China and Pakistan) rather than by leaning forward toward progressive geo-economics. Among other impediments to progress, economic development depends upon policymakers to sincerely redress grandfathered notions of geo-political strategy throughout the region.

CHAPTER FOUR

The Socioeconomic Profile of the Federally Administered Tribal Areas

DR. NOREEN NASEER

Department of Political Science, University of Peshawar

Introduction

This chapter addresses and highlights the socioeconomic situation of Federally Administered Tribal Areas (FATA) from 2001–2014. Socioeconomic indicators of the FATA refer to the provision of basic facilities, all of which rank lower than those of the settled areas. These indicators evaluate access to vital amenities such as access to clean water, sanitation, health, education, employment opportunities, and the like. The majority of FATA's population resides in rural areas. Traditionally, they maintain an agrarian economy, although they possess many under-utilized natural resources as well. There are a few medium- and small-scale industrial enterprises, and these provide a limited selection of jobs to FATA's residents. Most of the workers are unskilled, thus hindering commercial and industrial expansion. Due to state apathy, conflict, and FATA's *special* constitutional status, the region has experienced limited social and economic development. In the following sections, the present socioeconomic situation of the FATA is discussed in detail, highlighting the conditions prevailing in these areas.

Education Facilities in the FATA

The FATA's literacy rate is at 17.42%, and within the female demographic, this statistic drops to just 3%. There are a total of 3,697 primary schools, 391 middle

Table 4.1. School, College, and University Statistics (for both Girls and Boys)

Primary Schools	3,697
Middle Schools	391
High Schools	255
Higher Secondary Schools	14
Colleges	33
Universities	1
Schools blown up by militants (unofficial count)	500

schools, 255 high schools, and 14 primary elementary schools teaching the girls and boys of the FATA. Within higher education, there are 33 interdisciplinary colleges and one recently established university for the whole FATA. On average, per every one to three teachers in each class, there are more than 65 students (in school and college). From primary to secondary level, children's enrollment in the schools is only 40%, and the dropout rates are high at the primary level (Bureau of Statistics, 2014). Still, this official data is dubious. Some reports claim that many school buildings are either used for running businesses or converted into *Hujras*, meaning that many "teachers" collect their salaries without even conducting classes. Recently, militancy in the FATA has also negatively affected primary schools. The Taliban in FATA have either taken over school buildings for their activities or blown them up. According to unofficial data, militants have decimated almost 500 schools (Mohmand, 2012: 6).

In addition to the threat of militancy, poverty is the major factor that drives both boys and girls to discontinue their education. Additionally, there are an insufficient number of schools and a lack of trained teaching staff to teach those who are able to continue. For girls, social factors such as early marriage, cultural taboos, and tribal enmities are the main causes in discontinuation of their education. Boys who drop out typically do so to pursue other professions to earn for their families rather than pursuing education. Similarly, there are no schools or teachers for handicapped children in the FATA (Civil Secretariat, FATA, 2005: 5–6).

Health Facilities in the FATA

Healthwise, the FATA also lags far behind other regions within Pakistan. There is only one basic health unit for every 50 square kilometers, and at each, they attempt to serve an overwhelming number of patients, including Afghan refugees and nationals residing on the other side of Durand Line. In every agency, there are two or three hospitals at the *Tehsil* level and no private hospitals. There are a total of 32 hospitals, 428 dispensaries, eight rural health centers, and 159 basic health centers in the FATA. Infectious diseases such as Hepatitis and Typhoid are rampant, with the risk of widespread HIV infection. Drug addiction is also another serious health hazard; however, there are no rehabilitation centers for such patients (Bureau of Statistics, 2014).

While unregistered, private doctors and practitioners provide services throughout the region; they operate with scarce laboratories, facilities, or medicine. Poor quality and spurious drugs are available to the general public, with no government oversight or regulation. Unregistered medical practitioners, naturally, are mostly dependent on these unregulated medicines. Further, the conservative culture and tribal restrictions on the freedoms of women prevent them from consulting male doctors. For this reason (among others), modern healthcare practices such as giving birth in a proper hospital and neonatal care are inaccessible. The result is an alarmingly high infant mortality rate. According to the Bureau of Statistics Planning and Development Government of Khyber Pakhtunkhwa and FATA, this is much higher than the settled region of Pakistan; 87 babies die out of every 1,000 births. Likewise, maternal mortality is also elevated; 600 deaths are reported in 100,000 deliveries (Bureau of Statistics, 2009: iv).

Access to Clean Water and Sanitation

The basic facilities, such as access to clean drinking water and sanitation, also depict a depressing picture. About 56% of the population has access to clean drinking water; however, less than 3% of houses have individual access to this water. Sanitation and hygiene facilities are also scarce; only 10% of the population has access to adequate sanitation in the form of toilets, sewerage, drainage, and solid waste disposal. According to official reports of the Governor Media cell, 37% of houses in the FATA have separate latrines, while 56% do not have this facility (Governor Secretariat, 1998: 3).

Housing and Living Conditions

Almost 97% of the FATA population is living in poor housing, and 60% of these houses are made of mud or built of unbaked bricks with wood and *mazri* palm. Of this 60%, those that are brick houses and have wood or (*mazri*) palm/bamboo (*dargay*) roofing account for 36%. Only 62% of homes have electricity for lighting and cooking (load shedding is eighteen hours per day). This means that 92% of FATA's population relies on oil lamps for lighting and wood for cooking. There is no access to natural gas, and according to the Bureau of Statistic Planning

Table 4.2. Access to Basic Facilities

Budget Allocation	Education 20%	Health 20%	Road Building 30%	Agriculture 2½%
Health	Hospitals (32)	Dispensaries (428)	Rural Health Centers (8)	Basic Health Centers (159)
Housing	Poor Living (97%)	Mud Houses (60%)	Brick and Mazri Houses (37%)	Brick and Cement Houses (3%)
Electricity & Natural Gas	Access to Electricity (62%)	Load Shedding 18 hrs. per day	Access to Natural Gas (2%)	Reliance on Wood (92%)
Clean Water & Sanitation	Access to Water (56%)	Access to Clean Water (3%)	Access to Proper Sanitation (10%)	Lack of Sanitary (90%)

and Development Government of Khyber Pakhtunkhwa and FATA, only 2% have access to natural gas. The situation of road provision is somewhat better; the FATA possesses 0.17 km of roads, slightly more than the 0.13 km existing in the settled part of Khyber Pakhtunkhwa. According to official data, 30% of the budget is allocated to road construction, 20% to education, 9% to health, and a meager 2½% to agriculture (Governor Secretariat, 1998: 3).

Economic Conditions of the FATA

The FATA presents a bleak economic profile; although it makes up 2.40% of Pakistan's population, it contributes a mere 1.5% to the state's GDP. Of this meager contribution, the majority is earned either through remittances or small-scale commerce (Bureau of Statistics, 2014: 37). Traditionally, it depends upon agriculture. The FATA's industrial sector is limited, poorly accompanied by a weak service sector that fails to provide its people with even basic amenities. There are two distinct sources for the stagnancy in economic growth. The first is the perennial state of both internal conflict and international warfare. The second source is the unjust and unrepresentative nature of the administrative system itself. Ultimately, the primary responsibility of an administration is to provide stability to all regions it serves; for the FATA, it has failed on numerous grounds. For example, FATA's economy is entirely undocumented. This is due to a combination of the hidden nature of the informal economy and overt apathy on the part of the state, such as the FATA's exclusion from annual government surveys.

Table 4.3. Land Used for Agriculture in the FATA

Reported Area	2.72 million hectares
Cultivated Area	0.22 million hectares
Uncultivated Area	2.50 million hectares
Net Sown Area	0.16 million hectares
Total Cropped Area	0.20 million hectares
Irrigated Area	0.08 million hectares
Forest Area	0.05 million hectares
Not Available for Cultivation	2.28 million hectares

Agriculture in FATA. The main source of livelihood in the FATA is subsistence agriculture, such as farming, ranching, and livestock rearing. The majority of the farmers are small-scale landholders, practicing subsistence level of farming. There is also the problem of under-utilized land, thus resulting in poor productivity. According to official data, FATA is composed of about 2.72 million hectares. Out of this, 0.22 million hectares are cultivated, while 2.28 is not possible to cultivate due to inaccessibility. The terrain is difficult and mountainous, exposed to extreme climates, and impossible to irrigate. In total, 2.50 million hectares of FATA's territory is uncultivated land. About .04 million hectares have been sown more than once, even though it proved to be less fertile. Another portion of land is considered "cultivable waste," and this amounts to .016 million hectares (Civil Secretariat FATA, 2005: 6). The land, which is entirely barren, rugged, and mountainous, renders it less conducive to traditional agriculture and more conducive to growing illicit crops such as poppy. In such areas, where earning a living is already difficult, growing poppy is an extremely attractive venture. It requires fewer land holdings and needs little maintenance (Agricultural University, Peshawar, 2012/2013).

Although different crops, fruits, and vegetables are cultivated in the FATA, three main crops such as wheat, rice, and certain varieties of wheat and grains can be cultivated in nearly every agency. Due to inferior farming methods, terrain inaccessibility, expensive fertilizers, and costly planting seeds, food is a source of insecurity in the FATA. The following tables illustrate details about the production of different grains as well as consumption levels concerning the food deficit (Bureau of Statistics, 2014: i).

Table 4.4. Wheat

Wheat Net Production	60.6 metric tons
Consumption	409.7 metric tons
Surplus/Deficit	-86%

Table 4.5. Rice

Production	14.2 metric tons
Consumption	25.7 metric tons
Surplus/Deficit	-59%

Table 4.6. Grains. Source: Bureau of Statistics, FATA.

Cereals Production	74.8 metric tons
Consumption	435.5 metric tons
Surplus/Deficit	-82.8%

Table 4.7. Livestock in FATA. Source: Bureau of Statistics, FATA.

Cattle	1 million
Goats	2.2 million
Sheep	1.4 million
Buffalos	.1 million

The World Food Program also declared the FATA a high food insecure area in Pakistan due to poor agriculture, the apathy of the government, the underutilization of land, and fewer landholdings. Although farming is the primary source of income and employment for the residents of FATA, it is still insufficient to fulfill the socioeconomic demands of the FATA. Because almost all basic food grains are imported to the tribal areas and taxed through *Rahadari* (passage taxes) from other parts of Pakistan, this makes it much more expensive than in the settled area markets (World Food Program, 2012: 2–29). Presently, the ongoing conflict has also affected farming in the FATA. Due to military operations and the Taliban, tribal members have migrated, or those living in different agencies cannot cultivate their lands (Tribal People, 2013).

Livestock and poultry are other important sources of income in the FATA. There are many problems faced by the farmers and their livestock not only in terms of feed shortages, and lack of proper shelter to animals in winter, but also in basic veterinary services. A mere 25 veterinary hospitals and about 200 veterinary centers exist within the entire FATA region. Malnourished livestock is far more prone to different kinds of diseases (Civil Secretariat FATA, 2005: 8). After 2007, it became impossible to record and collect accurate data on the situation due to the war on terror and the displacement that followed. However, given the available data of livestock, we can infer that if the needs of people living in the FATA were unfulfilled then, they certainly are not now.

Tribal Women in FATA's Economy

Tribal women in the FATA perform 60% of the agriculture labor; they help in sowing, harvesting, woodcutting, and making dairy products at homes through traditional methods. The majority of the women cultivate kitchen gardens, grow vegetables and fruits to sustain huge families and, in some cases, even sell it to nearby houses. Almost every woman raises livestock, poultry (cow, goat, lamb, hens, and turkeys). In the absence of veterinary facilities, they also treat livestock with traditional cures. For them, their livestock, poultry, and the dairy products they produce are a lifeline. Milk, butter, and ghee are not only used for family consumption but also sold in the nearby markets. Typically, these products are put on the market through family and tribal connections. Every tribe owns a mountain and trees; therefore, there is no restriction on honey extraction or woodcutting. For honey extraction, they go together in groups, search for honeycombs, and hunt down the bees without damaging either the tree or the comb; the honey is then divided amongst the group. Alongside this work, others are involved in sewing clothes and running beauty parlors at home with the limited resources available. Many make handicrafts and jewelry specific to their tribal region.

In some cases, these same artisans repair household utensils and other homewares. Collectively, the community helps grow and clean rice, wheat, curate the orchards, pick fruit, make homemade jams, and jellies all sold locally. However, due to conflicts and militancy in tribal areas, forced displacement became more and more frequent, disrupting this cycle. The Taliban imposed restrictions on women's movement, which deeply affected those engaged in agricultural and other activities. Ultimately, this pushed tribal people further into poverty (Tribal Women, 2013/2014). Because women play such a crucial role in the fulfillment of all of these activities, restricting them is detrimental to the healthy functioning of daily life for the entire community.

Industries in FATA. Different reports and surveys classify two types of industries in the FATA. One of them is mineral excavation and furnishing for rural living and cottage needs. The other is the processing, assembling of rural living enterprises. A few loom units and "cottage industries" have been operating since 1947 to the mid-1970s; however, following the provision of electricity to the tribal belt at this time, a new diverse array of the industry was born in the region. It was bolstered by investments made by the socialist government of Zulfiqar Ali Bhutto. At the time, he invested in industrial projects such as marble, edible oil, ghee, cigarettes, woolen mills, leather tanneries, match production, and glass making. These quasi-governmental projects provided jobs to 1,400 people in the FATA (see Table 4.8). However, these projects were dismantled due to a combination of flagging government financial support. Later, the projects were privatized by

Table 4.8. Industrial Units Established in the FATA. Source: Bureau of Statistics, FATA.

Industry	Established	Closed	Investment	Employees
Oil Refining	Bajaur (1988)	Oct. 1993	14.3 m Rs.	159
Mohmand Glass	Mohmand (1977)	July 1979	2.87 m Rs	50
Bara Cigarette Factory	Khyber (1976)	Oct. 1986	9.98 m Rs	105
Bara Ghee Mill	Khyber (1978)	Oct. 1978	17.2 m Rs.	273
Mullagori Marble Factory	Khyber (1980)	Sept. 1986	9.27 m Rs.	147
Kurram Food Products	Kurram (1977)	Jan. 1983	5.83 m Rs.	41
Tochi Village Match Factory	N. Waziristan (1975)	Aug. 1984	12.6 m Rs.	221
Tochi Woollen Mill	N. Waziristan (1978)	Aug. 1985	12.6 m Rs.	84
Loom Unit	N. Waziristan (1982)	Jan. 1885	2.97 m Rs.	30
S. Waziristan Tanneries	S. Waziristan (1978)	May 1982	11.1 m Rs.	93
S. Waziristan Footwear/ Leather Goods	S. Waziristan (1982)	May 1985	10.3 m Rs.	202

inadequate organizations that mismanaged these businesses until they ran dry (Bureau of Statistics, 2014: 34).

Presently, there is a total of 1,815 industries in the FATA (see Table 4.9). Of these, 1,198 are small-scale industrial units, 583 are medium-scale enterprises, and just 27 units qualify as large-scale enterprises. These industrial and manufacturing units include sporting goods, flourmills, ice factories, stone processing, brickmaking, marble processing, textile weaving, furniture factories, and firearm outlets. Of these industrial units, 1,332 are manufacturing units, 283 are processing, and 22 are involved in assembling, while 178 units cater to other services. Approximately 49.1% of the raw materials needed to support these industries are imported from the settled areas of Khyber Pakhtunkhwa, Afghanistan, and China (FATA Development Authority, 2010: 25–150).

Approximately 10,000 skilled and semi-skilled laborers work in these units. In these industries, 80.3% of the labor is unskilled and untrained; the remaining 19.7% of skilled and semi-skilled workers are mainly engaged in weapon and furniture workshops. Unskilled laborers between the ages of 16–65 working in these units are paid approximately Rs. 2000 to 5000. The

Table 4.9. Industrial Statistics in FATA (2010). Source: FATA Development Authority & CAMP.

FR Peshawar	2
FR Kohat	599 (mostly arms and cigarettes)
FR Tank	12
FR D.I.Khan	67
FR Bannu	18
FR Lakki Marwat	7
Bajaur Agency	90
Khyber Agency	537 (mostly arms and cigarettes)
Kurram Agency	50
Orakzai Agency	170
Mohmand Agency	228 (mostly marble)
North Waziristan	26
South Waziristan	9

majority of these units (those with better quality are of assembling nature) have no access to advanced technological gadgets. Thus, they must work with limited tools that cannot truly match finer quality goods (FATA Development Authority, 2010: 25–150).

There are several government banks such as the National Bank, Agriculture Development Bank, and Habib Bank operating in tribal areas, but none of these are willing to extend credit to either the industrial or service sector. Moreover, their reluctance on other matters has worsened due to policies by the State Bank of Pakistan. Genuine fear of financial risk is another central dissuasion. Banks refuse loans to tribal people because security mechanisms protecting these areas are severely lacking, principally because there are no police and no courts to recover the loans. Loans and credits are extended to only those tribal people who are either property holders in settled areas or who work a government job (State Bank, 2013). For this reason, 94.3% of the industrial units are self-financed. Usually, this money is borrowed from family and friends and without any government or bank assistance (FATA Development Authority, 2010: 25–150). There is a Tribal Chamber of Commerce and Industries to aid tribal areas in development, industry, and commercial activities in the FATA. However, this body exists only "in ceremony" and most proactively deals with trade and transit trade activities with Afghanistan.

At present, the FATA is devoid of legal protections and regulations. This means that there are no real laws that formally define the process of establishing a business, acquiring property rights, making contracts, acquiring a credit/guarantee, mortgage mechanisms or insurance systems, or employing and protecting workers. Lack of a coherent legal net and general insecurity drives away large firms or investors from FATA, which might otherwise have had an interest in investing in the region. Conducting business is limited by uncontrollable variables (power shortages, for example) and a hefty dose of avoidable misfortunes such as mismanagement and insufficient supervision. The prevailing deficit of law and order compounds these issues. A workable industrial sector is, at the moment, absent. In short, this system must see extensive reforms before it can ever hope to cater to the employment needs of its people.

Natural and Mineral Resources of FATA. There is an abundance of tapped and untapped minerals present in the FATA and provides a source of livelihood to tribal people. According to Pakistan's Mineral Department, geological surveys indicate that as much as 85% of the tribal area contains immense prospects for mineral wealth. (At one point, there was also the FATA Department of Minerals established by the Pakistan government, but now, it is non-functional). The minerals referenced by these surveys (see Table 4.10) include metallic and non-metallic matter, energy minerals, precious stones, and different rocks of industrial use (FATA Development Authority, 2010).

Despite this potential, the actual quantity of extracted minerals is low (see Table 4.11). The Bureau of Statistics Planning and Development Department Government of KP documented the minerals extracted over a two-year interval (2006–2008). It should be noted that post-2008, any extraction that might have occurred went unrecorded by any official program or project due to security reasons (Bureau of Statistics, 2009: 118–120). For this reason, 2006–2008 is the most current data available.

Table 4.10. Minerals in FATA. Source: FATA Development Authority.

FR Peshawar	Bentonite and Limestone
FR D.I.Khan	Gypsum, Marl and Cement grade Limestone
FR Kohat	Coal and Limestone
FR Tank	Bentonite
Bajaur Agency	Marble, Manganese, Chromite, and Emerald
Kurram Agency	Soapstone, Coal, Marble, Magnetite, Barite, Iron Ore, and Lead
Khyber Agency	Marble, Barite, Graphite, Soapstone, and Limestone
Mohmand	Marble, Chromite, Silica sand, dolomite, Manganese, Quartz, Feldspar, and Emerald
Orakzai Agency	Coal and Iron Ore
N. Waziristan	Copper, Manganese, Chromite, Magnetite, Coal, and Granite
S. Waziristan	Copper, Chromite, Marble, and Granite

Table 4.11. Minerals Extracted from FATA (2006–2008). Source: FATA Development Authority.

Marble	818,987 tons
Chromite	66,381 tons
Lime Stone	1,461,859 tons
Soap Stone	16,600 tons
Coal	26,6490 tons
Manganese	90 tons
Quartz	34,935 tons
Serpentine	3,405 tons
Barite	10 tons
Mica	450 tons
Scrap	1,760 tons
Fluorite	892 tons

Most of these natural resources are not utilized and extracted properly by the government, although there are some local efforts on behalf of tribal people to explore it. Approximately 1,000 people are involved in the mining sector, and of them, most are either semi-skilled tribal people or workers from other areas of Pakistan. Mineral extraction as an industry is hindered by a deficit of field experts, tribal feuds over property, the absence of infrastructure, limited access to credit, an inadequate legal and regulatory system, and a constant state of insecurity (Interview with a Mohmand Agency resident, 2012/2013).

Forests and rivers are also an essential part of the rural economy of FATA's mountainous region. Forests account for about .05 million hectares of the FATA region. Wood provides fuel, fodder, and timber to the tribal people. Along with fulfilling a part of their daily routine requirements, these forests also create jobs in the form of logging and supporting industries (as in transportation carts production), sawmills and furniture factories. Some people in the FATA collect and sell wild plants and weeds for the herbal medicines, and in this way, it serves as a source of income for the poor tribal people (Civil Secretariat FATA, 2005: 9–10).

Services Sector in FATA. Approximately 18% of the tribal population provides different private and public services in the FATA. These include general stores, medicine stores, sports goods shops, hunting arms shops, cloth shops, vehicle mechanic workshops, vegetable/fruit kiosks, barber shops/beauty parlors, rest houses, and small hotels/restaurants. In addition to these small private shops and hotels, many people are engaged in various public services. Public employment opportunities might include working with the *tehsils*, the health sector, veterinary clinics, or the public-school system. Tribal members have also been known to serve in the paramilitary forces as well (FATA Development Authority &

CAMP, 2010: 25–150). Although both private and public sector enterprises in the FATA suffered deeply due to conflicts, terrorism, counterterrorism initiatives, and military operations, the private sector lacked the securities and "safety nets" that came with government work. For this reason, many tribal people who were formerly involved in private sector services had to migrate to the settled areas because their shops were shut down. Throughout the region, music and CD stores, barbershops and beauty parlors, hotels, private schools, private clinics, and other enterprises were closed (Interviews at Kurram and Bajaur Agencies, 2013).

Trade and Commerce in FATA. Pakistan and Afghanistan bilateral trade is worth 2.3 billion dollars, and 34% of Afghan transit commodities pass through the FATA (Abbasi, 2011: 3). According to different reports and surveys, trade is another critical source of income of the tribesmen (Civil Secretariat FATA, 2005: 8–50). Thus, tribesmen involved in trade activities are wholesale and retail trade in consumer goods and "durables," clearance and freight services, warehousing, used vehicle spare parts, and vehicles. However, most of this information is neither documented nor recorded. Approximately 50,000 large and small retail shops buy and sell their goods through a combination of formal, informal, and transit trade.

Economic Migrants of FATA. Many tribal people (four out of ten males) are either working in urban locations of Pakistan or the Middle East in a labor capacity (Civil Secretariat FATA, 2005: 10–11). Approximately 1.8 million tribal laborers are serving in settled cities of Pakistan and foreign countries (Bureau of Immigration and Overseas Employment, 2012: 7–9). A select few highly educated and skilled tribal people have permanently settled down in the settled areas of Pakistan with their families. Most likely, they maintain the domicile within that agency for other fringe benefits (Interview with Tribal students, 2012–2013).

Funds and Grants Allocated to FATA

Prior to 2001, the FATA's development funds were meager and insufficient relative to the population's and the area's needs. Assessing the government's official reports, the tribal areas from 1947 to 2001 reveal that the Annual Developmental Program (ADP) has received extremely weak financial supports (Rs. 1 billion). Although the tribal areas contributed 1.5% to the GDP from remittances and other services to the national economy, resources were too scarce to reach the ADP (Ministry of Finance, 1980s–1990s). This changed after 2002, with the help of foreign donors. At this point, the Pakistani government started allocating Public Sector Developmental Project (PSDP) funds for other settled parts and tribal areas too. ADP allocations of FATA gradually increased to Rs. 9 billion (Ministry of Finance, 2015).

In 2006, the United States pledged $150 million annually for 5 years to aid development in the FATA (Congressional Research Report, 2011: 10). According to the USAID report, out of this grant, in 2007–2008, $43 million was spent on building infrastructure for the FATA Secretariat. This grant provided money for the construction of a space where FATA's local development agencies could access administrative and management training programs (Congressional Research Report, 2011: 6–7). Under the Livelihoods Program, $300 million was allocated to youth vocational training and scholarship programs. The education sector received $15.4 million for training teachers, managing, and furnishing schools. The health sector received $16.7 million. Rather than building well-equipped hospitals and units, this sum was dedicated to training health officers and supporting existing facilities (Congressional Research Report, 2011: 6–7).

Out of USAID funds, Rs. 6,700.97 was allocated to the FATA Development Authority, and the money spent was Rs. 6,431.93 million (see Table 4.12). Over the last 7 years, these development funds have contributed to infrastructural projects in the FATA, such as building roads and small dams as well as providing youth vocational training (FATA Development Authority, 2015). Additionally, five dams were constructed with these grants and funds: Sheen Kach Dam FR Tank, Moto Shah Dam Mohmand, Zoo Dam Khyber, Dargai Pal Dam S. Waziristan, and Dandy Dam N. Waziristan. Also, 226 km of roads were built via the construction of the Tank-Makeen and Kaur-Wana Highway in South Waziristan along with the Bannu-Miransha-Ghulam Khan Road which connects North and South Waziristan. Additionally, grant money provided vocational training to 33,434 young tribal men and women.

For the agricultural and industrial sectors, the only legitimate reports and surveys are carried out on an independent project basis (as opposed to regular data collection by the government, for example). Sixty-five villages are provided with solar energy for tube wells as well as funds for exploration and resource estimation

Table 4.12. FDA Funds Allocated to the Development of the FATA

Years	Allocation	Releases	Expenditures
2007–2008	Rs. 698.8 m	Rs. 698.8 m	Rs. 698.8 m
2008–2009	Rs. 660.08 m	Rs. 660.08 m	Rs. 659.61 m
2009–2010	Rs. 660.8 m	Rs. 660.8 m	Rs. 659.6 m
2010–2011	Rs. 873.8 m	Rs. 873.8 m	Rs. 873.78 m
2011–2012	Rs. 968.48 m	Rs. 968.48 m	Rs. 870.62 m
2012–2013	Rs. 1181 m	Rs. 1181 m	Rs. 1181 m
2013–2014	1658 m	1658 m	1488.51 m
Total	6700.97 m	6700.97 m	6431.93 m

of coal in FR D.I. (FATA Development Authority, 2014: 7–52). In their 2014–2015 budget, the Ministry of State and Region (SAFRON) also demanded an additional Rs. 15 billion in grant funding for the development of the tribal areas, stating that special attention was needed for these impoverished areas (Ministry of States & Frontier Region, 2015: 1). However, the FATA Reforms Commission's interim report stated that $75 billion would be needed to successfully develop and mainstream the FATA region (Qureshi, 2015: 43). Below is a consolidated table indicating the development funds allocated to FATA. Per the need of the region, these are largely deemed as insufficient for the region's development and progress.

The total amount pledged and released in the last 10 years is more than $750 million, and the amount spent officially is $439 million, hence, questioning the credibility of the government's efficiency in the development of the FATA. Various newspapers have reported on the embezzlement of FATA's developmental funds by the FATA Secretariat and political agents stationed throughout the different agencies. In some sectors, funds were lavishly spent without any fruitful results and lacked sustainability (Bureau Report, 2013: 4). It is observed that the misappropriation of the funds and with insufficient budget allocations, the FATA is lagging in socioeconomic development as compared to the rest of the country.

Conclusion

Moving forward, policymakers must address the desperation in the FATA with the seriousness that its socioeconomic statistics reveal. Approximately 66% of FATA's population is living below the poverty line; its annual growth rate of 2.19% is mostly earned either through remittances or informal commerce (FATA Civil Secretariat, 2006: 12–24). Further, traditional agriculture is insufficient to feed or sustain its population and is only moderately supplemented by a limited industrial sector. Altogether, the lack of service provisions has resulted in an entire demographic that lives without basic facilities. This is worsened by an unjust and unrepresentative administrative system, as well as seemingly endless internal conflicts and international wars. While the FATA's economic growth has indeed stagnated due to these obstacles, this makes it all the more important to mainstream and re-orientate FATA's economy. If Pakistan is to bring the tribal areas up to the level of Pakistan's settled districts, then rigorous economic reforms to agriculture, manufacturing, and trade policies are needed. This can only be accomplished through a concerted effort. However, with due diligence, the impoverished Pashtun border regions can be economically developed in a way that simultaneously increases security, and amplifies its value as a strategic location.

Bibliography

Abbasi, R. N. (2011). *Afghanistan-Pakistan Transit Trade Agreement 2010*. Peshawar: Pakistan Custom.
Bureau of Emigration & Overseas Employment, Pakistan. (2012). *Export of Man Power 2010–11*. Peshawar.
Bureau Report. (2013). "FIA Given Go-Ahead to Investigate FATA Secretariat Corruption Case." *The Express Tribune*.
Bureau of Statistics, FATA Cell. (2014). *Important Agency/FR-Wise Socio-Economic Indicators of FATA 2013*. Peshawar.
Bureau of Statistics NWFP (Khyber Pakhtunkhwa) and FATA. (2009). *Important Agency/F.R.-Wise Socio-Economic Indicators of FATA 2008*. Peshawar.
Civil Secretariat FATA. (2005). *FATA Sustainable Development Plan 2007–2015*. Peshawar.
Congressional Research Service Report. (2011). *U.S. Foreign Assistance to Pakistan*. Washington D.C.
FATA Development Authority. (2009). *Major Geological Features of FATA*. http://www.fatada.gov.pk/geological.php, accessed on 20 March 2010.
FATA Development Authority. (2015). *FATA DA Development Funds 2007–14*. FATA DA Peshawar.
FATA Development Authority & CAMP. (2010). *Survey Enumeration of Industries, Labor Force and Identifying Constrain in FATA*. Peshawar.
Governor Secretariat FATA. (1998). *Focus on FATA*. Peshawar.
Interview conducted at the Agriculture University Peshawar in 2012–2013.
Interview conducted with tribal people from Kurram and North Waziristan in 2013.
Interview conducted with tribal women from different agencies between 2013 and 2014.
Interview conducted with State Bank officials at Peshawar in 2013.
Interviews conducted with tribal people of the Mohmand Agency (owners of marble industry) at Shabqadar in 2012–2013.
Interviews conducted with tribal people from Kurram and Bajaur in 2013.
Interviews conducted with tribal students at Peshawar University in 2012–2013.
Khan, M. M. (2014). "50 pc Fata Officials Corrupt, says PA." *The News International*.
Ministry of Finance. (1990). *Pakistan Annual Budgets 1980s–90s*. Islamabad.
Ministry of Finance. (2015). *Pakistan Annual Budget 2015*. Islamabad.
Mohmand, M. (2012). "Education Under Siege: FATA Schools in Dire Straits." *The Express Tribune*.
Qureshi, E. A. (2015). *Interim Report FATA. Reforms Commission*. Peshawar: Governors' Secretariat.
Shaheed Bhutto Foundation. (2011). *Annual Report 2009–10 FATA Figures*. Islamabad.
Shinwari. N. (2008). *Understanding FATA: Attitudes Towards Governance, Religion & Society in Pakistan's Federally Administered Tribal Areas*. Peshawar: CAMP.

CHAPTER FIVE

Religion and Politics in FATA

DR. FAZAL WAHID
Research Scholar, Department of International Relations,
University of Peshawar

Introducing the FATA

The Federally Administered Tribal Areas (FATA) is a region located toward the northwest of Pakistan. It borders the province of Khyber Pakhtunkhwa (KP), formerly known as the North West Frontier Province (NWFP). The FATA consists of seven agencies, namely Mohmand, Khyber, Kurram, North Waziristan, South Waziristan, Bajaur, and Orakzai Agencies. Its territory includes the Frontier Regions of Peshawar, Kohat, Bannu, Lakki Marwat, Dera Ismail Khan and Tank.

Pakistan's border with Afghanistan in the FATA region stretches 1,360 km and is home to the main tribes of Mohmand, Afridi, Shinwari, Turi, Bangash, Wazir, Mehsud, Dawar and Aurakzai. Other tribes also inhabit the Bajaur Agency. Surrounded by rugged mountains with heights ranging from 8,000 to 15,000 feet, subject to harsh winters and scorching heat in the summers, the FATA terrain is inhospitable and inaccessible. Further, the region is devoid of all but a handful of roads and other infrastructural facilities. During the colonial period, British transit was bounded by these roads; they covered a spread of over 27,220 square kilometers. FATA is ruled by centuries-old customs called *Riwaj*, with *Malaks* or tribal elders, who serve as the sources of political and military influence and authority over their tribes. The tribes primarily follow the Islamic religion, but the role of the *Mullah* is limited to mosques. According to Article

247 of the Constitution of Pakistan, the region is governed by the Federal Government, which is represented by *Political Agents* (PA). These Political Agents control the area through levies and a local police force called *Khasadars*.

Pakistan's border with Afghanistan cuts across diverse tribes of the region, dividing people with deep ethnic and social bonds. A provision in the Durand Line Agreement of 1893 that bifurcated India [now Pakistan] from Afghanistan, commonly known as "Easement Rights," permitted cross-border social and commercial interaction for the tribes in the last days of the British Empire. The practice continues to date. Although tribal people are ferocious fighters, they are also considered to be incredibly loyal to their country, Pakistan.

Afghanistan and the Issue of the "Free State of Pukhtoonistan"

Afghanistan was the sole country that voted against the entry of Pakistan into the United Nations in 1948. Kabul was against the referendum held in NWFP (now KP) in 1947 on the grounds that the policy allowing the Pukhtoons to choose between living southeast of the Durand Line and the western bank of River Indus or, to join either India or Pakistan, was wrong. The Government of Afghanistan demanded that a third choice be presented: that the Pukhtoons could join Afghanistan. The nationalist forces in NWFP were supporting the Indian National Congress, the dominant political party of the united India that mainly strove for the cause of Hindus at that time. Thus, they boycotted the referendum to support Kabul's demand. As a result, the Pukhtoons of the area overwhelmingly cast their votes in favor of joining Pakistan. Due to Afghanistan's resentment against the state of Pakistan, Afghan decided to chime in at the United Nations referendum in 1948.

During the 1950s, Afghanistan continued to interfere in the tribal belt. Once certain Afridis in the Khyber Agency announced the coming of the "free state of Pukhtoonistan," this was even broadcasted by the All India Radio station. Afghanistan was the first and only state who recognized the free state of Pukhtoonistan. Soon, the revolt lost its momentum, and the issue of the "free state of Pukhtoonistan" evaporated.

After Pakistan joined the Western-sponsored alliances of the Baghdad Pact and South East Asian Treaty Organization (SEATO) in the mid-1950s, it politically leaned toward the West. Later, SEATO was renamed the Central Treaty Organization, CENTO, after the departure of Iraq. Meanwhile, the Afghan government was under the premiership of Muhammad Daoud. Prime Minister Muhammad Daoud was a staunch nationalist, and he tried to use his ultra-nationalism against the state of Pakistan. Although the ruling elite in Kabul walked a fine line trying to balance the Soviet Union with the United States, Daoud's bias toward the Soviet Union was highly visible. General Taqat recalled memories of the 1950s and 1960s when Kabul had enlisted various tribal leaders in the Khyber and Waziristan Agencies. Kabul authorities paid these leaders handsome sums. In exchange, they would be used as the vanguards of the future State of Pukhtoonistan. General Taqat also revealed that a handful of Afridi Maleks from the Zakha Khel and Kuki Khel tribes were actively advocating for the cause of Pukhtoonistan at the behest of Kabul.

In 1959, Afghanistan's special envoy to the United Nations tabled a resolution in the U.N. General Assembly by demanding that the establishment of the free state of Pukhtoonistan would be carved out of the Pukhtoons living between southeast of Durand Line up to the River Indus, including the Pukhtoons living in Baluchistan. The resolution met defeat in the Assembly, and also led to the deterioration of bilateral relations between Kabul and Karachi.

In 1973, Muhammad Daoud carried out a *coup d'état* against King Zahir Shah, and Afghanistan's monarchy was replaced with a Republic. Daoud had been helped in his bid for power by the Soviets, and his move was not welcomed by the Afghan community. To divert the attention of his countrymen from his unconstitutional acts, Daoud made an ambitious move in Afghan foreign relations and, once again, raised the issue of Pukhtoonistan. The Soviet Union's interference in Afghanistan in the mid-1970s (and its eventual invasion in 1979) provided a golden opportunity for Islamabad to "settle the score" with Kabul.

The Soviet Invasion of Afghanistan

After the Soviet invasion of Afghanistan in the late 1970s, the Red Army reached up to the Durand Line. Because tribesmen on both sides of the Durand Line maintained deep-rooted social and cultural bonds, they readily supported the Afghan Resistance Force (*Mujahideen*) in their struggle against the Soviet forces. Tribal people welcomed Afghan Refugees (*Muhajireen*) into their lands. The Afghan Resistance Force also received political, moral and diplomatic support from the Government of Pakistan. For the second time since 1947, the people of FATA supported a cause belonging to the State of Pakistan. The first time that the tribesmen from FATA had participated and supported Pakistan's objectives was in the Kashmir War of Independence in 1948 in response to the call of Quaid-e-Azam Muhammad Ali Jinnah.

At the onset of the 1980s, the West became more strongly cognizant of the events in Afghanistan and started supporting the Afghan *Mujahideen's* struggle against the invading Soviet forces. Soon, the CIA made a deal with the Pakistani military establishment and aided the construction of a pipeline between Pakistan and Afghanistan, which would pass through the FATA region. Later, the United States provided arms and equipment to Pakistan, which would be transported to Afghan resistance groups by the Pakistani authorities. Although FATA served as a conduit for the Afghan *Mujahideen's* struggle against the Soviet Union, there remained relative peace and stability in the region throughout this period.

Schools of Thought in the FATA

People in the FATA are mainly followers of the Barelvi school of thought, which favors a soft image of the religion and opts for peaceful coexistence in society. They derive their strength from the famous four Sufi orders (Chishtia, Suherwardia, Naqshbandia, and Qadria). These orders are inspired by the philosophical thoughts of the fourth Pious Caliph of Islam, Hazrat Ali (R.A.W).

In the Khyber tribal agency (district) of erstwhile FATA, Sheikh Gul Sahib had a large following in Afridi, Shinwari, and Malagori tribes of the agency. In the Mohmand and Bajuar agencies, Sarkano Mullah Sahib had a large following in the area. Similarly, the people of North and South Waziristan agencies were inspired by the philosophical thoughts of the disciples of Pir Bayazeed Roshan. In contrast to the five tribal agencies, there was a sectarian divide on Shia Sunni lines in the tribal agencies of Kurram and Aurakzai. Even so, this divide on sectarian lines never led to sectarian violence during the first 40 years of Pakistan's independence. If we analyze the political and religious history of the FATA region from 1947 through the late 1970s, there was a general tone of religious harmony and sectarian peace in the region. Conversely, on the political front, there were disturbances in the Khyber and Mohmand agencies, at the behest of Afghanistan. Still, on the whole, peace, tranquility, and relative harmony existed in the FATA region until the arrival of the Soviet Union into Afghanistan in 1979.

The arrival of the Soviet Union into Afghanistan was a nightmare for the West in general, and for the United States in particular. The United States wanted to set up stiff resistance against the Soviet Union in Afghanistan to keep her from potentially crossing the Durand Line and reaching the warm waters of the Persian Gulf. Encouraged by both Pakistan and the U.S., the guerrilla struggle against the Soviet Union was well supported. Pakistan, the pro-Western countries of the Arab world, and the United States began to give a religious coloration to the Afghan resistance movement. Now, liberation fighters were painted as the Holy Warriors. Seemingly overnight, these *Mujahideen* leaders became one with the blue-eyed West. This marriage of convenience between Islam and Christianity was intended to forestall the "godless Soviet Union." A network of religious seminaries sprung up throughout these five tribal agencies. Religious seminaries were also established in the province of Khyber Pakhtunkhwa (then NWFP), Balochistan, and Southern Punjab. These religious seminaries introduced and encouraged a new school of thought, the Wahabi/Salafi school of thought, overtly at the behest of Saudi Arabia.

Shortly before the Soviet invasion of Afghanistan (1979), the Iranian Islamic Revolution toppled the former administration. The influential clerics who led the revolt quickly established a new order. The leaders of the Iranian Revolution raised the slogan of "Neither East nor West, Islam is the best." Although the clerics were projecting that the Revolution in Iran had Islamic origins, many turned a blind eye to both the Shia nature and Soviet support of the Iranian Revolution. As Shiaism became entrenched in Iran, the Soviet Union carved a foothold in Afghanistan.

Meanwhile, the United States, Saudi Arabia, and Pakistan began to collectively support the Wahabi/Salafi school of thought, which was now proliferating in Khyber, Mohmand, Bajar, South Waziristan, and North Waziristan. They also encouraged a Sunni sect in the Kurram and Aurakzai agencies. In this way, the Wahabi/Salafi school of thought would galvanize the U.S. *jihadi* efforts in Afghanistan, while a Saudi-sponsored Sunni sect would cater to the rising threat of Shiaism in the Kurram and Aurakzai agencies. Since Islamabad was facing a geo-political threat not only from Afghanistan in the northwest but also from India in the east, it readily welcomed the U.S. and Saudi influence in the FATA region in return for the flow of economic and military aid to Pakistan. Gradually, what was once a geo-political and geo-strategic issue that was unfolding in the FATA region became a fully-fledged religious war; in which, the FATA would burn in these violent flames for the foreseeable time to come. The militaristic and nationalistic rhetoric of Afghanistan was blunted by the concept of Islamic Ummah. Likewise, "Indian blackmailing" was neutralized by Pakistan as it became a frontline state for the U.S. in their Cold War with the Soviet Union. Over time, religion became an instrument of state policy in the FATA in particular. Gradually, this spread throughout the entire country vis-à-vis the presence of a purely geo-political threat.

Super Power Politics in the FATA

After the U.S. attacked Afghanistan, they began pushing *Taliban* and *Al-Qaeda* fighters toward Southern Afghanistan (Tora Bora). They later drove them toward the Pak-Afghan border area (FATA), although some strategists criticized this military strategy. Their concern was that, if they were to "hammer without an anvil" in terms of driving the fleeing militants southward, then they would flush out through Pakistan. This would then have dire consequences for the situation of law and order in the country. Pakistan would not only be required to safeguard its northwestern border with Afghanistan but also be required to chase these militants through the length and breadth of the country. Ultimately, this would tax the security forces of Pakistan to the extent that they would be unable to live up to the expectations of the U.S.-led NATO forces in the region. The scourge of terrorism would not be eliminated; rather, the disease would spread to the entire region. In this context, the then-U.S. Secretary of Defense Robert Gates tells the story from his perspective:

> "I wrote that the core goals and priorities, Obama had decided were valid. However, we had to narrow the mission and better communicate what you were trying to do. We could not realistically expect to eliminate the Taliban; they were now a part of the political fabric of Afghanistan. But we could realistically work to reverse their political momentum, deny them the ability to hold or control major population centers and pressure them along the Pakistani border. We ought to be able to reduce their level of activity and violence to that which existed in 2004 or thereabouts. I recommended focusing our military forces in the south and east and charging our allies with holding the North and West. Our military efforts should be intended to stabilize the situation in Afghanistan and buy time to expand and train the Afghan security forces, who, despite their many deficiencies were courageous fighters; many of them were prepared to die—and had died—fighting the Taliban. We should 'quietly' shelve trying to develop a strong, effective central government in Afghanistan. What we needed, I wrote, was some central government capacity in a few key institutions—defense, interior, finance, education, and rural development. We should help broker some kind of 'national unity' government or other means to give the Karzai government at least a modicum of legitimacy in the eyes of the Afghan people. We also had to get a handle on corruption. 'Our kids must not die so that corrupt Afghan officials can line their pockets.'" ~Robert Gates

Robert Gates goes on to state that,

> "All this would give us a mission that the [both] public and the politicians could easily understand: '*Deny* them [the *Taliban*] drive and control, *facilitate* them to get reintegrated, *build* Afghan Government's capability selectively, *grow* Afghanistan's security forces, *transfer* security duties, and finally *defeat* Al Qaeda.'"

Conflagration in the FATA

In her book, *The Wrong Enemy, America in Afghanistan 2001–2014*, Carlotta Gall elaborates:

> "A few days after 9/11, Musharraf invited several political analysts to a meeting, among them the retired Lieutenant General Talat Masood, who was an influential liberal voice

well known in diplomatic circles, on talk shows, and at conferences. Musharraf asked them for advice on what the government should do. Masood told the general that he should cease support for the Taliban and all militant groups, including the Pakistani ones that operated in Kashmir.

'My suggestion to him was you should fully stop providing support to the Taliban and Jihadi forces in Pakistan, that is to say, that the government, the state, must follow the policy, fully stopping support,' Masood told me. Musharraf argued that supporting the Taliban should end but reiterated that the government would not stop its support for the freedom fighters operating in Kashmir. Both the groups could be 'compartmentalized,' he said. Masood had warned Musharraf that it would not be possible to shut one operation down while keeping the other open. Still, Musharraf insisted that he could do it.

'As a matter of policy, he did not want the Taliban to be controlled,' Masood told me. 'But this invasion took place; the Taliban were pushed into Pakistan, along with Al Qaeda. And as there was no anvil, and there was only a hammer, and the border was porous .... They filtered all over the place in Pakistan, wherever they found it more convenient to carry on their activities and to feel safe.'

'... And Pakistan did not really understand the implications of having the Taliban based in Pakistan, and that in turn gave rise to their own Talibanization.'

Masood was not the only person to warn Musharraf in the months after 9/11, but the general was set on keeping at least some militant groups alive. His decision was to have dangerous repercussions for Pakistan and the wider region."

~Carlotta Gall

Lieutenant General (retired) Shahid Aziz has also criticized this U.S. strategy of invading from the north without establishing any coordinated effort from Southern Afghanistan. In his book (*Ye Khamoshi Kahan Tak*), he narrated a similar story: while the U.S. was devising its strategy and attacking the *Taliban* and *Al-Qaeda* forces in conjunction with the Northern Alliance, the U.S. was committing a serious blunder. He says that he was apprehensive of this U.S. strategy to flush out *Taliban* and *Al-Qaeda* fighters from Afghanistan into the FATA region, and it would not be possible for Pakistan to provide a barrier at the Durand Line. First, the porous nature of the Afghan-Pakistani border rendered the tribal belt situated along this frontier impossible to protect. Secondly, infrastructural development was so lacking that it could not accommodate large scale troop movements from Pakistani Cantonments to the border region. Thirdly, the Pakistani Armed Forces have a limited capacity to carry out even low-intensity conflict operations in any region, let alone a high-intensity operation in a region as inhospitable as the FATA.

War Report: Week Ten

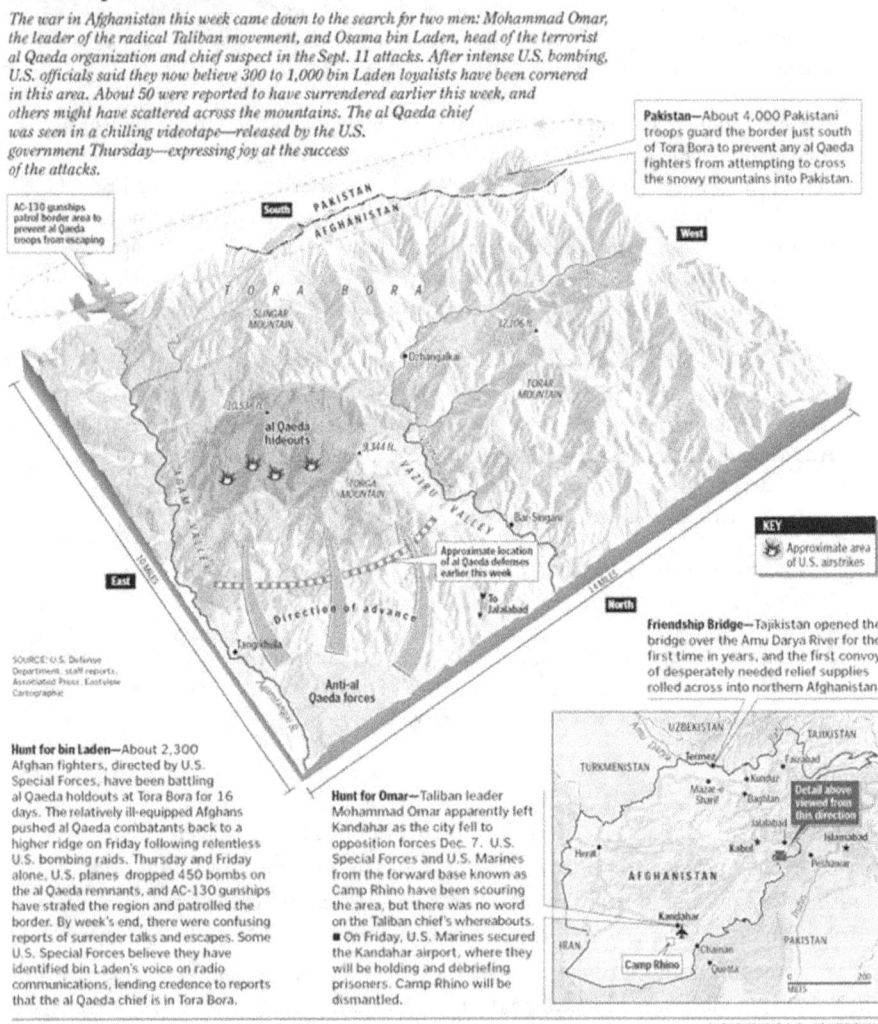

Figure 5.1: War Report: Week Ten. *Source*: Gene Thorp/The Washington Post

FATA Becomes the Hub of *Al-Qaeda* Activities

The multi-millionaire Arab Sheikh, Osama bin Laden, had been deprived of his nationality by the Saudi Government in the early 1990s. He then decided to live in Sudan; from there, he carried out his terrorist activities against the U.S. and its allies across the world. After the U.S. attacked his bases in Sudan, Osama bin Laden decided to make Afghanistan his permanent abode, and he landed in the war-torn Afghanistan, which was being ruled by the warlords after the Soviet withdrawal somewhere around 1993–1994. Soon afterward, the *Taliban* emerged on the political horizon of Afghanistan. By the end of 1996, the *Taliban* had captured Kabul. The convenient alliance between the powerful *Taliban* and the wealthy and ideologue Osama bin Laden deepened. The *Al-Qaeda* network used Afghanistan as a launchpad for terrorist activities across the globe.

The September 11 attacks on the U.S. changed the entire paradigm of world politics. The U.S. delivered an ultimatum to the *Taliban* government: handover Osama bin Laden to the U.S. for his alleged responsibility in carrying out the terrorist activity against the U.S. or face the consequences. The *Taliban's* refusal to do so invited the U.S. attack in October 2001. After the fall of the *Taliban* government, both the *Taliban* and the *Al-Qaeda* fighters took refuge in Tora Bora. U.S. bombers rained down on the caved complex of Tora Bora for weeks. As a result, the *Al-Qaeda* fighters fled toward FATA, to the adjoining tribal belt of Pakistan just across the Durand Line. Because FATA is notoriously underdeveloped and lacks proper governmental influence, it was convenient for these fighters to settle in Waziristan. They established themselves in Afghanistan, braced for long guerrilla warfare against the invading forces. With their money, they bought the loyalties of their hosts; some of them were even able to marry tribal girls. Already linked by ideological affiliations, they were viewed as more than holy warriors; through marriage, they soon shared kinship as well. Elevated from "foreign guests" to "family," they then proceeded to exploit the FATA, relying heavily upon the Waziristan Agency as a hub for their terrorist activities.

After the Pakistani Army moved to the FATA in 2003, these *Al-Qaeda* fighters, along with their tribal brethren, put up stiff resistance to the Pakistani security forces. In the first phase of the operation, their security forces suffered heavy casualties due to the non-orientation of the region and lack of local sympathy in Waziristan. In 2007, Pakistan's security forces operation against *Lal Masjid* and *Jami'a-e Hafsa* in Islamabad led to the creation of the *Tehreek-e Taliban* Pakistan (TTP). Soon, the *Al-Qaeda* and TTP were hand-in-hand in a Holy War waged against the U.S.-led NATO forces and Pakistan's security forces.

The porous border between Afghanistan and Pakistan facilitated the to-and-fro movement of these fighters. Afghanistan was used as a transit route for the passage of these international terrorists. Later, it was surmised that among these persons were the masterminds behind terrorist activities, which were carried out in Great Britain and other parts of Europe by *Al-Qaeda*.

Governance System of the FATA Collapsed

The Federally Administered Tribal Areas of Pakistan had a peculiar political-administrative structure under the Constitution. The area was directly governed by the President through his representative in the concerned province, as in the Governor. The Governor ruled the different agencies through Political Agents (PA). The Political Agents were the first pillar of the political administration system of FATA. The tribal leader, as in the *Malek* was the second pillar of political set up in the FATA, through which the PA conducted the day-to-day business of the agency. The third pillar of the set up was the religious leader or the *Mullah*. Although the *Mullah* enjoyed considerable clout amongst the tribal people, this role was restricted to the mosques.

After the conflagration in FATA after 9/11, the *Mullah*, one of the pillars of authority in the Tribal Areas' political set up, now had weapons and money, and thus the means of mobilizing fighting men. They had been provided with these resources by Pakistani and their allied intelligence agencies. The government would often bypass two other pillars of authority, i.e., the tribal elder (*Malek*) and the Political Agent (PA), by going directly to the religious leaders (*Mullah*). Almost overnight, the *Mullahs* had been elevated to a primary leadership role in FATA, early in Waziristan, in the most significant war in the region in living memory. Pakistani and their allied intelligence agencies quickly discovered that the networks of *madaris* run by *mullahs* were a ready-made pool of zealous soldiers training to fight for Islam. The Islam of *madaris* was of a rough and ready kind. This interpretation of Islam demanded absolute obedience as well as a willingness to sacrifice one's life and property without a moment's hesitation. In short, it was informal or tribal Islam. The tribal instinct for revenge (against the state of Pakistan) was now joined with a zeal for Islam as they threw themselves into *jihad* (religious war) in Afghanistan. The *Mullahs*, who once looked to the tribal elders for support, were now seen as the guardians of Islam and dominated the political agenda of FATA. This newly emerged society began to upset the delicate balance between the three pillars of authority in FATA.

As a result of the U.S. operations in Afghanistan (anti-clockwise military strategy to flush out the *Al Qaeda* and the *Taliban* fighters), the militants retreated to Tora Bora and subsequently to the FATA region of Pakistan. The Pakistan Army was not prepared to cope with the situation, and the atmosphere of the FATA was demanding an immediate response. As mentioned earlier, the United States' strategic error to effectively apply the hammer and anvil strategy in Afghanistan caused Pakistan to rush its armed forces toward FATA in 2003. This was the first time in the history of Pakistan that the Pakistani Army moved into the FATA region. At the same time, the U.S. had already decided to shift its operations to Iraq, leaving the chaos in Afghanistan to its own fate. The Pakistan Army's inexperience with the low-intensity conflict to which it was confronted with now in the FATA cost it dearly. Since the Government of Pakistan had not provided proper budgetary supports to the FATA regions, there was an acute dearth of communication infrastructure in the area. Before the armed forces could establish themselves on the rugged and porous border between the two countries, these fleeing militants had already dispersed throughout the entirety of FATA, as well as to the other distant cities of Pakistan. The Taliban's cause and the *Al-Qaeda* fighters' wealth soon found a soft corner in the tribal areas of Pakistan.

Meanwhile, the U.S. had diverted its attention from Afghanistan to Iraq; it was at this critical juncture that the regional powers reactivated their dormant role of interference in Afghanistan. As a result, fighting against the U.S. and NATO forces increased in Afghanistan. At that time, Pakistan's affairs were almost entirely controlled by the whimsical decisions of its military ruler, and Pakistan was blamed by the U.S. for this increased wave of resistance against NATO forces in Afghanistan. There was also a massive campaign against the fleeing *Taliban* and *Al-Qaeda* fighters in Pakistan launched by the Law Enforcement Agencies (LEAs). Hundreds of Arab fighters were captured and handed over to the U.S. authorities. Moreover, dozens of Taliban leaders were also rounded up by the LEAs of Pakistan and were detained for years. In the FATA, this act by the Government of Pakistan created sympathizers to the cause of the *Taliban* and the *Al-Qaeda*, who construed the State of Pakistan as a stooge of the U.S.

As per the views of several political and academic analysts in both Afghanistan and Pakistan, Pakistan played the same role in FATA as the U.S. did in Afghanistan. The result was the same. As resistance to the U.S.-led NATO forces in Afghanistan stiffened, the same happened in FATA. The Pakistan Army also faced stiff resistance from tribal people who considered the security forces of Pakistan as invaders in FATA. A nefarious propaganda campaign was launched against the State of Pakistan, which fueled the fire; thus, the conflagration in the FATA increased.

War of Independence in Afghanistan and Religious Coloration

On March 25, 2000, United States President William J. Clinton addressed the Pakistani nation while he was on a brief visit to Pakistan. During his speech, which lasted for fourteen minutes and which was telecasted by Pakistan Television, the U.S. President stated,

"This era does not pay the people who ... redefine ... borders with bloodshed.... Pakistan may achieve great things in this new world ... but there are real obstacles... Political instability, economic stagnation, and ... in this region are holding Pakistan back from achieving its full potential in the global economy..."

President Clinton's sermon played a crucial role in a significant comeback of an international theory that had been badly damaged by E. H. Carr in his critique of liberal utopianism in the late 1930s. In short, President Clinton warned that the world has to face reality in the post-Cold War world in which war (*Jihad* in Pakistan's case) has to be shunned as a policy option.

Peter Chamberlin interviewed a CIA agent and then wrote: "The U.S. Jihadism had transformed Afghans into freedom fighters .... Then we had secretive American government figures, like Charlie Wilson and Zbigniew Brzezinski ... who would travel to the secret camps in Pakistan ... asking them, 'Is God on your side?'"

Peter Chamberlin also interviewed Zbigniew Brzezinski: "The day that the Soviets officially crossed the border, I wrote to President Carter, 'We now have the opportunity of giving to the USSR its Vietnam War.' Indeed, for almost 10 years, Moscow had to fight a war that was not supported by the government. This conflict was responsible for bringing about the dejection and, ultimately, the collapse of the Soviet empire. When asked a question about the moral implications of fostering war in Muslim countries, Brzezinski replied, "What is most important to the history of the world? The Taliban or the collapse of the Soviet Empire? Some stirred-up Muslims, or the liberation of Central Europe and the end of the Cold War?"

The references above underline the glaring lesson of the *realpolitik* that marked the U.S. policy toward the region that is home to Afghanistan and Pakistan. When President Bush allied with Pervez Musharraf and his military after 9/11, he did so at the expense of state institutions and democratic processes. Amongst the people of Pakistan (who felt suffocated by Musharraf), he fostered extreme resentment. Although he did so unconsciously, President Bush was heavily responsible for creating immense hatred against the U.S. Army and America itself. This dramatic turn in the U.S. policy came about in less than 2 years.

FATA and Afghanistan

After the Soviet invasion of Afghanistan in the late 1970s, the Red Army reached up to the Durand Line. As tribesmen on both sides of the Durand Line shared deeply-rooted social and cultural bonds, they readily supported the Afghan Resistance Force (*Mujahideen*) in their resistance struggle against the Soviet forces. These tribal people warmly welcomed the Afghan Refugees (*Muhajireen*) into their lands. The Afghan Resistance Force was also provided with political, moral, and diplomatic support by the Government of Pakistan. It was the second time since 1947 that the people of FATA supported a cause that was owned by the State of Pakistan. Before that, the tribesmen from FATA had participated in the Kashmir War of Independence in 1948 at the call of Quaid-e-Azam Muhammad Ali Jinnah.

In the early 1980s, the U.S. and the West took cognizance of the events in Afghanistan and started supporting the Afghan *Mujahideen's* struggle against the Soviet invading forces. Soon, the CIA made its liaison with the Pakistani military establishment. Consequently, an aid pipeline was established between Pakistan and Afghanistan that went through FATA. The U.S. would provide arms and equipment to Pakistan that would be further transported to various Afghan resistance groups by the Pakistani authorities. Thus, although FATA served as a conduit for the Afghan *Mujahideen's* struggle against the Soviet Union, there remained relative peace and stability in the region throughout this period.

The U.S. Espousal of Political Islam and Religious Extremism in FATA and Afghanistan

A prominent Afghan journalist agreed, on the condition of anonymity, to reveal highly sensitive insights on the U.S. policy on ISIS and Afghanistan. This is what he had to say:

> "Immediately after the Iraq war, Al-Qaeda and the Iraqi resistance forces led by Abu Mas'ab al Zarqavi joined their hands, and the latter agreed to carry out his activities under the command of Al-Qaeda. The joining of hands between Al-Qaeda's deputy chief, Aiman Al-Zawahiri, and Masa'b al Zarqavi renewed the war efforts of Iraqi resistance forces. Because both organizations (Al-Qaeda and Zarqavi's organization) were composed of Sunni fighters, readily welcomed both ISIS and Al-Qaeda. This was the case in FATA as well. Al-Qaeda leadership issued a Fatwa (a religious sanction) which supported the ISIS struggle in Iraq and Syria. The U.S. was in [a] hurry to launch ISIS forces in Afghanistan as well, and Pakistan was demanded to cooperate in this regard. As per the U.S. designs, the FATA region would be used for raising, training, and equipping the ISIS fighters (keeping in view the specific nature of FATA's constitutional status and its proximity to Afghanistan), but Pakistan squarely refused. This refusal became a question of prestige for the U.S. policymakers, and the subsequent wave of terror in the cities of Pakistan, particularly in Khyber Pakhtunkhwa, was the practical manifestation of this U.S. indignation." ~Anonymous Afghan journalist

CHAPTER SIX

From Jihad to Salam in Pursuit of Political Change: A Perspective Based on Qur'ānic Sources

DR. MUQTEDAR KHAN
Professor, University of Delaware, USA

DR. TAHIR SHAD
Associate Professor, Washington College, USA

Introduction

يَاأَيُّهَا الَّذِينَ آمَنُوا إِذَا ضَرَبْتُمْ فِي سَبِيلِ اللَّهِ فَتَبَيَّنُوا وَلَا تَقُولُوا لِمَنْ أَلْقَى إِلَيْكُمُ السَّلَامَ لَسْتَ مُؤْمِنًا

"O You who believe, when you go forth to fight for the sake of Allah, investigate, and do not tell anyone who offers you peace, You are not a believer." (Quran 4:94)

In the past few years, the Muslim Middle East has experienced a political roller coaster that gave the region a brief taste of democracy, during the Arab Spring 2011 to 2013, and then restored authoritarianism with an added dose of uncertainty, chaos, and a steady erosion of the state as a viable political entity.

While 2011 promised comprehensive change and democratization, through a wave of revolutions, usually described as the Arab Spring,[1] recent developments not only reversed the gains of 2011 but have brought more war, more oppression, and violence to the region. Muslims have experienced and witnessed how change could be brought through peaceful means, as in Tunisia and Egypt, and they also witnessed how violence and civil war can destroy states and unleash demons of sectarianism and terrorism as in Syria, Yemen, and Iraq.

In 2011, some commentators had argued that the emerging trend of political protests, as witnessed so spectacularly by the protests in Tahrir Square, Cairo, would make violent extremist groups such as Al-Qaeda extinct. However, history has proven them wrong with the emergence of the Islamic State in Iraq and Syria.[2] The Jihadi group has not only proven to be crueler and more extreme than even Al-Qaeda, but it had also stepped up in terms of activities. Whereas Al-Qaeda merely attacked, the Islamic State captured and tried to hold territory and had gone so far as to declare an Islamic Caliphate. It is the failure of peaceful efforts to bring about a political transformation in Syria that has led to the Syrian Civil War and the subsequent rise of the Islamic State. Even though the Islamic State is on the run, and its demise seems imminent at the time of this writing, the conditions in the region are not experiencing any repair. This essay, while inspired by these events is, however, not about the region's geo-politics. It reflects more on the theology of the use of force for political change in Islamic sources. It is about *Jihad* and *Salam* while seeking political change.[3]

The most pressing problem of the contemporary Islamic world is how to bring about fundamental political, social, and economic changes while continuing to maintain peace. The Muslim world cannot be allowed to degenerate into religious intolerance, and it cannot exist under secular tyranny. People in most Muslim societies today are deprived of their basic rights, have little freedom of religion, and scarce opportunities for economic development. Many resources are being wasted in wars, civil wars, and weapons accumulation. The states in most Muslim countries seem to have a *raison d'etre* independent of the people's interests. Except in oil-rich Gulf states where consent is bought through welfare and economic concessions, the rest of the Muslim states, particularly in Asia and Africa, have very little to offer to their people. Some states like Syria and Egypt have even become the cause of great misery for their people. Given these pathetic conditions, one has to recognize the absolute necessity for systemic change in the Muslim world.[4]

While most of the problems in the Muslim and Arab world appear to be political and religious (as people demand democracy and more freedom for religion in the public sphere), one cannot escape the reality of economic underdevelopment in the Muslim world. Those states that seem to have a comparatively stable political atmosphere, such as Saudi Arabia, demonstrate that economic development, providing for their people higher incomes and standards of living, is more important than regime type.[5] Alternatively, each country from the Arab Spring faced economic decline prior to its revolution, failing to provide adequately for their citizenry and pushing them even more vehemently toward an uprising against those in power.

The Muslim world has yet to recover from the post-colonial moral crisis that they all have experienced.[6] The colonial domination precipitated a gradual but systematic erosion of the institutions of Muslim civil society. The decline of traditional institutions of justice, social welfare, education, and social affiliations has left a huge moral vacuum. The end of the colonial era did not give Muslim societies any respite from the culture and value invasion of the West. Indeed, the new regimes often led by ultra-nationalists (like Ataturk of Turkey and Naser of Egypt) sought to rapidly transform and even westernize the societies they inherited. They never gave themselves the opportunity to collect themselves and resuscitate the moral fabric of their societies, which were ravaged by foreign domination. Once free from the foreigners, these leaders rushed to emulate their former oppressors. Thus after fighting foreign colonialism, the already debilitated Muslim society had to fight another war of independence, this time against internal colonialism in pursuit of authentic identity and society.[7] This second wave of anti-colonial upsurge has come primarily through the resurgence of Islam, which in many ways is an effort to resuscitate and revive the *authentic* moral fabric of Muslim societies.[8]

Authoritarian regimes in the Muslim Middle East have caused widespread poverty, unemployment, and human rights violations, which have made the political status quo unviable.[9] That change is imperative in the Middle East, and both political and economical is an incontrovertible reality. The issue that scholars, Muslim intellectuals, community leaders, political movements and parties, and opinion-makers must deliberate is whether this change can be precipitated peacefully or if it will have to be brought about violently. Before we can reflect on any concrete issues regarding the impulse for change and the form this change will take, we must examine the idea of peace and nonviolence itself. What is the intrinsic, inherent, and moral value of peace and nonviolence? Are they to be valued in themselves to such an extent that the fear of violence and instability (*fitna*), division and discord, in the process of change compel us to indefinitely defer change? Traditional Muslim scholars have tended to privilege order from fear of discord (*fitna*) to such an extent that they were willing to tolerate institutionalized tyranny and injustices. Should we, in the name of peace, continue that same old tradition or can we advocate for change but also find ways to do so peacefully. But more importantly, can we find in our divine sources pathways to change through peaceful means?

The key challenges that newly-democratized regimes in Egypt and Tunisia faced after the Arab Spring was the daunting task of bringing social equality and economic development to their population. Social equality is an economic reality, not a political strategy or policy. In both Egypt and Tunisia, the Islamic governments sought to make symbolic gains without genuine material transformation and eventually failed. The Arab Spring was driven by economic despair and a search for dignity, not political participation. Democracy was a means to realize those goals, but ultimately, it was about economic well-being. Political gains without economic gains are not a solution, and this situation was unsustainable, leading to counter-revolutions[10] and recurring violence.[11]

The Muslim world is perennially beset with political struggles accompanied by violent conflict. At one level, the Muslim world is still locked in an ideological, political, and sometimes violent struggle with states which are non-Muslim. At another level, Muslim states are involved in conflicts against each other. These are internal conflicts between Muslim states, which have led to foreign and civil wars. Even democracies like Pakistan face both peaceful and violent challenges from within while being engrossed in conflicts without.

Then there is the conflict between state and society as in Syria and Iraq. This type of conflict has attracted the most attention as it pits the Islamists against usually non-democratic but secular and sometimes pro-Western regimes. These conflicts inspire great fear in the West because most analysts in the West assume all potential Islamist states, if the Islamists succeed, will be like Iran, virulently anti-West, and anti-Israel. Finally, we have the civil conflict between the secularists and the Islamists.[12] The state is inevitably involved in this struggle as it is often pressed into the service of one or the other party as in Turkey, Pakistan, and Algeria. All these struggles have resulted in much violence raising questions such as *can Muslims resolve their differences peacefully?* Do they have a tradition for tolerance and peaceful resolution of the conflict? Can we find some philosophical foundations for peaceful resolution of the conflict in Muslim mores whose revival may help introduce regimes that can facilitate peaceful conflict resolution and peaceful socio-political change? Search for answers to these questions will entail an analysis of Islamic sources for injunctions on peace and cognition of barriers to peaceful processes. I shall limit my arguments to the Quran; for today, the Quran alone remains an uncontested source of moral authority in almost all sections of the Muslim world.

Preference for peace and nonviolence as preferable to destabilizing changes leads to the privileging of the status quo. If authoritarian regimes and ruling coalitions are reluctant to relinquish power, as they often are, even in the face of popular opposition like in Syria, then advocacy of peace, stability, and nonviolence becomes a defense of status quo even in the absence of legitimacy. Decades of stagnant politics with no development, no progress, and no political reforms as in Egypt under the rule of Hosni Mubarak and in Libya under Muammar Gaddafi, can engender deep resentment and create tipping points that can unleash revolutionary violence and sustained conflict as in present-day Syria and Iraq. However, the need for change should not be taken as a license to resort to egregious violence that destroys the social fabric, historical monuments, and any hope of reconciliation between different segments of the society.

Alternatively, if peace and nonviolence are to be deemed as instrumental values, then there must be other recognizable values whose intrinsic worth is perceived as more than that of peace itself. It is only when such values are identified that peace can be risked in pursuit of these values, which are perceived as more precious than peace. Some Muslim thinkers and activists consider the pursuit of justice or the establishment of an Islamic order as definitely values that must be fought for. This view is the reason why we see the proliferation of armed non-state actors across the Muslim world, indulging in violence, and justifying their actions as the pursuit of justice and Islamic order. We, on the other hand, contend that justice, equality, and freedom are values more valuable than peace. We are not willing to give up our freedom or allow ourselves to be oppressed or be treated unjustly without a fight. Can we demand that people give up their rights, their freedoms and accept injustices in the interest of maintaining flawed orders?

Certainly not! But we can appeal to the suffering and the marginalized to give "peaceful change" a chance. We can at least defend instrumental peace if not peace as an inherent value worth achieving above everything else. Particularly with respect to a region where change is necessary, the engineering of peaceful, gradual, and systematic change will preclude violent and revolutionary transformations. We believe we can develop a discourse based on Qur'ānic principles of peace to advance the cause of peace both between nations and within nations.[13]

Jihad and Salam for Change

وَقَاتِلُوا فِي سَبِيلِ اللَّهِ الَّذِينَ يُقَاتِلُونَكُمْ وَلَا تَعْتَدُوا إِنَّ اللَّهَ لَا يُحِبُّ الْمُعْتَدِينَ

> *"And fight in the path of Allah those who fight you, but violate not his limits. Truly, Allah likes not those who transgressors."* (Quran 2:190)

The Quran advances a very sophisticated view of peace (Al-Salam).[14] In many verses, peace is presented as a final reward for a virtuous life (Quran 5:16). It also describes *dar al-Islam*, the house of Islam, as the abode of peace (Quran 10:25). The Quran teaches Muslims to greet each other every time they meet by wishing peace for each other (Quran 6:54). However, the Quran does not shy away from the use of force to deter and end persecution and religious intolerance. The strongest statement on the use of force against oppression is in the second chapter of the Quran al-Baqarah (verse 191):

> *"And kill them wherever you find them, and expel them out of the places from where they expelled you, for persecution is worse than slaughter."*

This verse in the Quran clearly precludes a complete prohibition of the use of force by Muslims. The verse is important because, despite the enormous importance that the Quran attaches to peace and harmony, it is categorical in its assertion that persecution is worse than killing. There is nothing allegorical in this verse; it is clear: *"persecution is worse than killing"* (Quran 2:217). The Quran also states: *"And fight them until persecution is no more"* (Quran 8:39). The Qur'ānic preference for the struggle against persecution and its promise to reward those who struggle in the path of Allah (4:74) means that the only way violence can be eliminated from the Muslim world is by eliminating injustices and persecution. However, the Quran also demands that violence cease as soon as persecution ceases, and thus it seeks to balance the absence of conflict with an absence of injustice. At the risk of sounding circular, one is back at square one, in order for there to be peace, there must be change, but can this change be peaceful? Can this change happen without causing persecution? Perhaps we can minimize areas where violence is legitimized by the Quran.

In Surah Baqarah, the Quran says: *"And fight them until persecution is terminated, and religion is for Allah. But if they stop, then let there be no hostility except against the wrong-doers"* (Quran 2:193). This verse is an ethical standard for it limits retaliation against all except those who are directly responsible for wrongdoing and also suggests that persecution could mean religious.

From Jihad to Salam in Pursuit of Political Change: Persecution. Meaning that when the practice of religion is prohibited, it is a condition that can be deemed as persecution, and therefore fighting this persecution is desired. The standard set by this verse has implications for conflicts among Muslim states and between Muslim states and Islamic groups. Where citizens are allowed to practice their faith freely, as in Saudi Arabia, Pakistan, and Iran, violence cannot be an option. The Quran sets another profound ethical standard in Surah al-Anfal:

> *"Tell those who disbelieve that if they cease (from persecution of believers) that which is past will be forgiven them."* (Quran 8:38)

This commandment further reduces the scope for violent response against persecution by granting amnesty to those who desist from indulging in persecution. One of the reasons why tyrannical regimes persist in the Muslim world is due to their fear of retaliation. Regimes are resisting change and democratization for fear of being prosecuted for past crimes by new regimes. A promise of general amnesty for past deeds by potential challengers could create an atmosphere where existing regimes may permit gradual change.

In a philosophical sense, we may not be able to eliminate the revolutionary option for precipitating change, but there is enough probative content in the Quran to limit the use of force to only egregious cases of religious domination and repression. Force thus can only be used to preserve freedom of religion. The Quran also makes a strong case for forgiveness and peace as soon as hostilities are ceased. It also does not permit the use of force against those who do not use force.

The Quran on Peace

The significance and desirability of peace are manifest in the message of the Quran. It treats peace as the desired way as well as a value or reward for righteousness. In the fifth chapter of Surah al-Maidah, the Quran states that "God guides all those who seek his pleasure to ways of peace and security" (Quran 5:18). The same verse draws a profound parallel between the ways of peace and the movement from darkness to light, onto the straight path. There can be no doubt that this verse of Surah al-Maidah is positing the transition from *Jahiliyyah* to Islam, from darkness to enlightenment, from being misguided onto the *siratul mustaqeem* (straight path) as a way to peace!

> "Whereby Allah guides whoever seeks His good pleasure unto paths of peace. He brings them out of darkness unto light by his will, and guides them unto the straight path." (Quran 5:16)

In the verse cited at the beginning of this paper, the Quran describes Islam as the abode of peace (10:25). Indeed, the word "Islam," which means submission, is a derivative of the word *salaam*, which means peace. Muslims greet each other by wishing/praying for peace for each other—Assalamu ʿAlaykum (may peace be upon you). This is not based on tradition or convention. It is a practice based on the injunctions of the Quran. The Quran states that the greeting of those who are righteous and have been admitted to the heavens is "Peace!" (Quran 14:23). It is quite amazing the degree to which Muslims have lost their self-awareness about being Muslim and its significance. If they only become more self-conscious about their faith and the elements of their faith that they practice, as a matter of fact, it would help bring more social harmony and peace to the Muslim world.

Peace as an important goal is not limited to relations within the Muslim community. It is desired with the "others" too. The Quran prohibits Muslims from initiating aggression or causing *fitna* (chaos, violence, instability, rioting) and encourages them to make peace with their enemies if they incline toward peace.

> "Do not wrong humanity in their goods, and do no evil or mischief on earth." (Quran 26:183)

> "Fight in the way of Allah against those who fight against you, but do not initiate hostilities. Indeed, Allah does not love aggressors." (Quran 2:190)

> "If they withdraw from you and stop fighting you and (instead) send you peace, then Allah does not permit you (to war against them)." (Quran 4:90)

> "But if the enemy incline towards peace, you too should incline towards peace, and trust in God: for He is One that hears and knows (all things)." (Quran 8:61)

This verse (8:61) has direct contemporary relevance. One of the biggest hurdles to peace today is insecurity stemming from distrust of potential partners in peace. Parties are demanding guarantees of peace and imposing preconditions for peace, which in themselves have become barriers to peace. However, the Quran addresses these insecurities and advises Muslims to go ahead and make peace if the enemy shows even the slightest inclination and to do so with trust and faith in Allah, who knows and hears everything. Clearly, Allah supports those who make peace, and they need not let uncertainties preclude the realization of peace.

Two Pillars of Islamic Peace

In this section, we identify two verses from the Quran that, in our opinion, can serve as the scaffolding for a new discourse on peace. Indeed, these two verses capture the fundamental relationship between Islamic teachings and peace. We believe if they are emphasized and repeatedly widely by Muslim preachers and teachers, the very idea of Islam as an empire that conquers and spreads, can be superseded by the vision that Islam is a civilization that seeks to bring peace to humanity and Islamic values and ethos are directing the believers toward submission to the divine rather than exhorting them toward domination over others. The Islamist and politicized conceptions of Islam are about global domination and hence the glorification of empires and conquerors in Muslim historiography. But Islam itself means submission, the mystical side of Islam, Sufism, seeks *fana'a*, annihilation not an assertion of the self.[15]

Islamic mystical understanding lays great store by the names of God. In the work of Ibn Arabi, we can see the best articulation of this view that the entire creation is nothing but the manifestation—*tajalli*—of the various attributes and essence of Allah.[16] In that tradition,

مَن قَتَلَ نَفْسًا بِغَيْرِ نَفْسٍ أَوْ فَسَادٍ فِي الْأَرْضِ فَكَأَنَّمَا قَتَلَ النَّاسَ جَمِيعًا

understanding the name Allah as *Al-Salam* (Quran 59:23) becomes the key to the development of an understanding of peace itself. Al-Salam means peace. Thus, peace itself is a divine essence and a divine attribute. Therefore, for those who believe peace can come only from the source of peace, Al-Salam. Bringing peace in this world requires us to make peace with Al-Salam, to submit to Al-Salam, and through this submission to Al-Salam, we first internalize peace. Through our now divinely guided actions, politics, we manifest peace to create a peaceful world.

"*He who has killed an innocent soul is as if he has killed all of humanity.*" (Quran 5:32)

The first verse is the thirty-second verse of Surah *Maidah*, which has been so widely used in the West, particularly after the terrorist attacks on September 11, 2001, in the United States. The verse was revealed in the context of the Quran's narration of the story of the sons of Adam, Cain and Abel, and the murder of Abel by Cain. The verse suggests that the killing of an innocent person is like killing all of humanity because, in Cain's case, it was the first murder ever and therefore as the one who taught humanity to kill he has a share in every killing that occurs since and hence the killing of one innocent is like killing all of humanity. This verse also states that the saving of one soul is also akin to saving all of humanity.

Apart from the context of its revelation, in the past two decades, this verse has taken on great significance for the Muslim discourse on peace and against terrorism. The meaning that is now drawn from this verse is that the Quran specifically forbids the taking of human life, except in pursuit of justice, as punishment for murder and terrorism (*fisad fi alard*). Not only does the Quran forbid the killing of innocent people, but it treats this act so egregiously as to equate the killing of one innocent person with that of universal genocide. The point is that the Quran teaches Muslims to value human life very deeply and this verse is now becoming the go-to verse

يَاأَيُّهَا الَّذِينَ آمَنُوا ادْخُلُوا فِي السِّلْمِ كَافَّةً

for scholars of Islam to assert the fundamental peaceful nature of Islam.[17]

"O you who believe, enter peace without reservation" (Quran 2:208). While Quran 5:32 has gained significance in the contemporary discourse as a pillar of the Islamic conception of nonviolence and peace, verse 208 from Surah *Baqrah* is very clear in its meaning. "O you who believe, enter the state of peace without any reservation." Sometimes commentators mistranslate this verse to state "enter Islam" without reservations or completely, but the verse is clear in stating that the believer should enter *fi al-silm*, *peace*. As one considers this verse on the pure merit of its text, without the interpretive corruption from commentators who may or may not have ideological axes to grind, it is clear that the verse is commanding believers to enter into a state of peace; the state can be either mystical (*maqam al-silm*) or political (*dar al-silm*). This verse is the statement of the Quran, which equates belief with a complete commitment to peace.[18]

Conclusion

To conclude, the Quran forbids Muslims from initiating or perpetuating violence except in self-defense and to fight persecution. Persecution is a complex term, and the meaning of the term often is contingent on contemporary realities. But broadly, one may consider it as a condition where people are deprived of the freedom to practice their beliefs and wherein their property, their land, and their lives are always in jeopardy. The Quran is a strong advocate of peace but permits Muslims to fight to protect their faith, their freedom, and their lands and property.

In the interest of peace, and to avoid the inevitable persecution and misery that comes along with violence, Muslim scholars and intellectuals can argue that violence is made the last resort and demand of all agents of change that they pursue all avenues of peaceful change before they resort to revolutionary tactics. This brief discussion of the Quran is indicative of the value of peace for Muslims both within the community and outside. However, the mere presence of divine injunctions for peace is not a guarantee of peace. The task of translating these Qur'ānic principles into concrete reality remains one of the biggest challenges for Muslim scholars and Muslim intellectuals.

Journal of Islamic & Religious Studies, July–December 2017

This work is licensed under a Creative Commons Attribution 4.0 International License.

Notes

1 Tariq Ramadan, *The Arab Awakening: Islam and the New Middle East* (London: Oxford University Press, 2012).
2 M. A. Muqtedar Khan, "View of the Arab Spring Through a French Window." *Huffington Post*, October 21, 2011. http://www.huffingtonpost.com/muqtedar-khan/view-of-the-arab-spring-t_b_1023068.html
3 For a systematic study of *Jihad*, see Asma Afsaruddin, *Striving in the Path of God: Jihad and Martyrdom in Islamic Thought* (London: Oxford University Press, 2013). Also see M. A Muqtedar Khan, *Jihad for Jerusalem: Identity and Strategy in International Relations* (New York: Greenwood Publishing Group, 2004).
4 See John L. Esposito, and M. A. Muqtedar Khan, "Religion and Politics in the Middle East," in Deborah Gerner (Ed.), *Understanding the Contemporary Middle East* (Boulder and London: Lynne Rienner Publishers, 2000).
5 See also Rodney Wilson, *Economic Development in the Middle East* (New York: Routledge, 2012).
6 T. Mitchell, *Colonizing Egypt* (Los Angeles: University of California Press, 1991).
7 Muqtedar Khan. "Constructing Identity in 'Glocal' Politics." *American Journal of Islamic Social Sciences* 15, no. 3 (1998): 81–106.
8 See Peter Mansfield and Nicholas Pelham, *A History of the Middle East* (London: Penguin Books, 2013). M. Kabir Hassan, and Mervyn K. Lewis. "1. Islam, The Economy and Economic Life." *Handbook on Islam and Economic Life* (2014): 1.
9 M. A. Muqtedar Khan, *Debating Moderate Islam: The Geopolitics of Islam and the West* (Salt Lake City: University of Utah Press, 2007).

10 Muqtedar Khan, "Islam, Democracy and Islamism After the Counterrevolution in Egypt." *Middle East Policy*, 21, no. 1 (2014): 75–86.
11 Magdi Amin, et al. *After the Spring: Economic Transitions in the Arab World*. (Oxford: Oxford University Press, 2012). Malik, Adeel, and Bassem Awadallah. "The Economics of the Arab Spring." *World Development* 45 (2013): 296–313.
12 M. A. Muqtedar Khan, "The Political Philosophy of Islamic Resurgence," *Cultural Dynamics*, 13, no. 2, (Summer 2001), pp. 211–229. Also see M.A. Muqtedar Khan, "The Islamic States," in *Routledge Encyclopedia of Political Science* (2004).
13 M. A. Muqtedar Khan, "Islam as an Ethical Tradition of International Relations," *Islam and Christian-Muslim Relations*, 8, no. 2 (Summer 1997): 177–192.
14 Maulana Waheeduddin Khan, *Islam and Peace* (New Delhi: Goodword Books, 2013).
15 C. Chittick, *Sufism: A Short Introduction* (London: Oneworld, *Creative imagination in the Sufism of Ibn'Arabi*. Vol. 91. Publications Limited, 2000).
16 Henry Corbin. Routledge, 2013.
17 See commentary on this verse by Muqtedar Khan. https://www.youtube.com/watch?v=6T-dONBaJS3A&t=4s
18 Ibid.

CHAPTER SEVEN

Indigenous Economics and the Role of Women in Economic Development of Federally Administered Tribal Areas

DR. ZAINAB AZMAT
Assistant Professor, Institute of Management Sciences, Peshawar

Introduction

Geographic, political, social, and economic underdevelopment of the FATA has sown chaos in the state of affairs of the area. The ongoing conflicts and decade-long operations against terrorist and extremist factions in FATA have broken down the negligible amount of progress seen in the FATA. This instability has had a disastrous impact, not just at the local level, but on the national and international level as well.

Mainstreaming the FATA within Pakistan's national development scheme bears certain risks, and understandably this is met with some concern. In the wake of temporarily displaced peoples, the pressure on public resource provision increases. Host-communities strain to offer education and health services, and livelihood means are scarce. Even so, the spillover effects of terrorism are far more costly. Given that the extreme collateral cost of terrorism in this region and the whole of Pakistan continues to take a toll, here is an urgent need to solve the FATA's security issues. When the needs of displaced persons go unmet, they either continue where they land or return to their respective agencies desperate. This makes them far more vulnerable to recruitment by extremist groups.

Indigenous economics is not a novel concept, by any means. It has and is being practiced in different communities across the globe. Even so, its recognition as a potential form of a sustainable economic model is presently lacking. To date, no serious initiative has explored the immense potential of indigenous economics. This limited scale is surprising, given the high global demand for environment-friendly development practices. For those who are capitalizing on indigenous economic models, we see the most significant evidence of success at the community level. More and more countries are tapping into the potential of their indigenous economies to achieve their development goals.

While Pakistan's policy projections for 2025 do include brief segments discussing this concept, these discussions are limited to the theoretical level. No practical initiatives have taken shape. Indigenous economics, as a formal concept, is only offhandedly mentioned in scattered paragraphs of various policy documents. A consolidated section about indigenous economics, as well as its role in the future developmental scheme of Pakistan, is still missing.

There is great potential in indigenous economics. Specifically, women's roles within this system should be promoted from the top-down and bottom-up. In other words, it should be supported both by administrative policy and encouraged at the grassroots level of the community. Most likely, the key factors in this endeavor will depend upon the quality of holistic awareness, formal recognition, updated research, implementation support, active stakeholders, and proper application of indigenous knowledge. Above all, participatory methods of the community will be critical to achieving success in the future.

In this, a hybrid economic model is ideal. Such a model would cater to indigenous economic practices while seeking to increase the role of women within these activities—the goal of this being to optimize revenue generation in a way that is both sustainable and inclusive.

Already, women of the FATA are heavily involved in indigenous economic activities. However, they are also subjected to additional societal limitations not imposed upon their male peers. This, in turn, limits their capacity to contribute back to society. Supporting the agricultural economy with regional practices in mind could increase opportunities for women in the community while boosting household income.

The Federally Administered Tribal Areas (FATA)

The Federally Administered Tribal Areas (FATA) is a semi-autonomous region in northwest Pakistan. To the east and south, it borders the provinces of Khyber Pakhtunkhwa (KP) and Balochistan. To the west and north, it is closest to Afghanistan's provinces of Nangarhar, Paktia, Khost, Kunar, and Paktika. FATA consists of seven Tribal Agencies (equivalent to "districts" in the rest of Pakistan) and six

Frontier Regions (FRs). The territory is almost exclusively inhabited by Pashtun tribes. Like districts, agencies are governed by the Federal Government of Pakistan. However, they are regulated by a special constitutional arrangement. The administrative head of each tribal agency is the Political Agent (PA), who is appointed by the Governor of Khyber Pakhtunkhwa province (Bureau of Statistics, 2015).

Erum Ayaz (2012: 19) states in her work that "since the Soviet Invasion of Afghanistan in 1979, the border region of Pakistan and Afghanistan is the epicenter of turmoil and instability." Over the last three and half decades, the Federally Administered Tribal Areas have been the most insular and isolated regions of Pakistan. The conflict wrought devastation in the region. It collapsed the system of governance, infrastructure, and most poignantly, shredded the already fragile vestiges of the economy that could have provided foundations for peace in the region (Ayaz, 2012).

The FATA has consistently been one of the poorest regions in Pakistan, and its situation has worsened due to ongoing crises. The FATA lags behind the rest of Pakistan across a wide range of social and economic indicators (Bureau of Statistics, 2015). The conflict has internally displaced much of the FATA's population to temporary camps, typically based in the settled areas. Instability has thoroughly shattered the fragile market of legitimate economic activity. The net result being the unstable sociopolitical environment that we see today. Jonathan Hand (2003) defines the *war economy* as one where all economic activities, legal or illegal, are carried out in wartime or conflict time. He further divides the war economy into three distinct sub-groupings: combat, shadow, and coping economies. Respectively, these economies enable different groups to wage war or conflict, profit, or cope or survive (Hand, 2003). In FATA's case, these economies are intertwined and overlapping.

It is not only the negative nature of the war economy in FATA, but the overall economic cost of terrorism is a disturbing fact. The most serious consequence of the ongoing War on Terror and conflict in FATA is the multiple layers of costs that it has incurred on the tribal community specifically and the country in general. As Arshad Ali (2010) mentions in his research paper, the immediate costs of terrorist acts are loss of human lives, destruction of property and infrastructure, and curtailment of short-term economic activity. Terrorism creates a context of uncertainty, reduced confidence, and elevated risk. This has led to lower rates of investment and lower economic growth. Pakistan has not only lost precious lives and infrastructure; according to official estimates, it has also suffered financial losses of about $35–40 billion as of 2001–2002. These figures encompass only the quantitative effects of the War on Terror. After years of living in the shadow of military operations carried out by security forces in the North West Frontier Province (NWFP), the Federally Administered Tribal Areas (FATA) bordering on Afghanistan have suffered an impact greater than numbers can fully express.

The direct losses due to war are compounded by the displacement of some three million-plus people from their homes. Both the War on Terror and the rehabilitation of these internally displaced persons (IDPs) consumed the bulk of the government's financial resources. This widened the fiscal deficit and halted economic growth (Ali, 2010)

Profile of FATA's Development Statistics

The following illustrates a brief profile of the FATA's basic socioeconomic indicators according to government data sources. Amongst the most informational of these was the FATA Development Indicators Household Survey (FDIHS) 2013–2014.

Education: In education, the overall literacy rate in FATA is 33.3%, which is far less than the national average of 58% (2013–2014). Similarly, the adult literacy rate in FATA is only 28.4% relative to the national average of 57%. There is a marked gender gap in literacy: the male adult literacy rate in FATA is 45%, while the female rate is just 7.8%. The Gross Enrollment Rate (GER) at the primary level (age 6–10 years) is 77.4% for FATA overall; in the rest of Pakistan, this is 91% (Bureau of Statistics, 2015).

Health: Health indicators paint a similar picture to education. The proportion of births attended by skilled health personnel is 29.5% in FATA, which is far below the national average of 86%. The maternal mortality ratio (MMR) for the FATA is 395 per 100,000 as compared to 275 per 100,000 for KP. The total fertility rate for the FATA is 5, whereas it is 3.8 in Pakistan. Additionally, the share of fully immunized children under 12–23 months in FATA is just 33.9%, while the corresponding figure for Pakistan is 76% (Bureau of Statistics, 2015).

Employment: Turning to employment, the "crude activity" rate for FATA at 24.2% is lower than that of Pakistan (32.3%); the "refined activity" rate (35.2%) is also lower than the national average (45.5%). As mentioned, there is an extreme gender gap: the official labor force participation for men in FATA is recorded at 38.6% as compared to 5.9% of women. The construction sector accounts for the largest share (36.2%) of workers in FATA as a whole (Bureau of Statistics, 2015).

Foreign Remittances: Family members working abroad (or simply outside FATA) are an important source of remittances. Unemployment rates (age 15–64 years) in FATA are higher than the rest of Pakistan (7.1% among adults in FATA to 5.6% national average); unemployment among FATA youth is particularly high at 11.8% (national average 10.3%). This age group is the main resource pool for militant recruitment (Bureau of Statistics, 2015).

Indeed, these development statistics of the FATA paint a grim picture. The findings produced by the FDIHS reflect the realities of the ongoing conflicts in

FATA. The region continues to lack any formal economic activities. If the FATA region were to become stable, then genuine security in Pakistan would not only be possible but sustainable as well.

In order to guarantee peace and sustainable development in the FATA, there is no other option than to strengthen the economic ventures and economy of FATA. Erum Ayaz (2012: 19), in her research, states that "alongside other approaches, economic development holds the most promise with regard to bringing stability to the troubled FATA region." The need of the hour is to understand the economic realities of the region, which will provide for a more effective approach. Winning peace along the Pakistan-Afghanistan frontier will depend upon Pakistan's ability to transform the FATA from a "war economy" into a "peace economy." Only then, will FATA see long-term serenity and security (Ayaz, 2012).

Population Demographics and the Youth Bulge

The population growth rate, as well as the large youth bulge prevalent in Pakistan, is both key elements to be aware of. The dramatic increase in the population of the "active youth" group bracket can be harnessed either positively or negatively. This demographic can become a positive transformational force if opportunities are accessible to them. However, if deprived and desperate, this same group could become more vulnerable to extremist tendencies and terrorist recruitment.

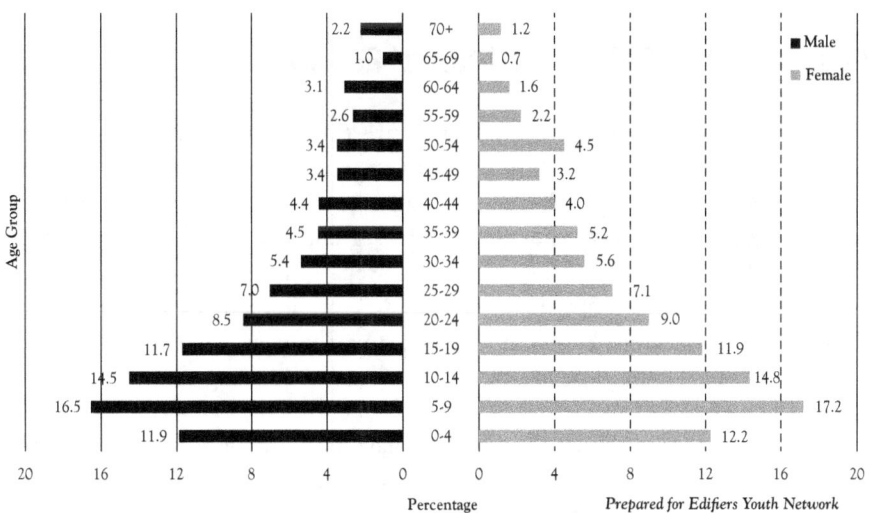

Figure 7.1: Percentage of population by age group and gender (FATA, 2007).

The World Bank Group, in its 2013 Country Partnership Strategy (CPS) for Pakistan, reported that the country's economic growth and development are challenged by six critical elements. There is a scarcity of financial resources, which makes the region heavily dependent on external financing. Further, slow progress on the Millennium Developmental Goals (MDGs) is slowed even further by ever-increasing population growth rates. Here, we see a situation where the need is growing (especially in urban zones), but limited resources and infrastructure are available to match this demand. Accelerating urbanization has led to the large-scale energy crisis and water scarcity that we are witnessing today. Recurring natural disasters and deteriorating law and order are detrimental to the state of security. Collectively, all of these elements are holding back development in Pakistan.

Still, there is promise too. On a more optimistic note, there has been a recent and promising democratic political transition. This is bolstered by a wealth of natural resources and an increasing population of working-age young men and women. These are critical opportunities for Pakistan that can contribute to the economic revival and growth in the country (Bank, 2013). The main "takeaway" from the WBG's CPS is the possibility to empower working-age youth demographics, most importantly young women. Empowering the economic capacities of both genders is not a globally novel idea by any means; simply, it is something that has yet to be achieved in the FATA region. It would be a crucial turning point for the fate of rural as well as urban communities. Due to a combination of insecurity and status quo, essentially 50% of the populace has been economically inactive. Investing in women would yield positive results from both an empowerment stance, and for the national GDP and the political-economic stability of the nation as well.

Restoring the FATA's Traditional Economy

The Federally Administered Tribal Areas are the most left out and economically off pace in the mainstream economy of Pakistan. The constant conflicts over the last three and half decades alongside the War on Terror have devastated infrastructure, displaced the populace of the region, and mainly transformed the economy of the area. Before the region was swept with war and conflict, FATA's economy was based on subsistence agriculture and nomadic pastoralism. Much the opposite, the current "economy of war" primarily engages in the illegal import and export of narcotics and weapons as well as kidnapping and trafficking of goods and people.

Although counterterrorism initiatives have become more effective in combating FATA-based insurgency groups, the situation remains dire. The region is something of a safe haven for terrorist and extremist groups, namely the *Tehreek-e Taliban Pakistan* (TTP). Lawlessness is one reason for this; another is desperation.

Amongst the many issues embedded in the region, widespread desperation makes the population more open to extremist tendencies of the TTP. To address this, an effective development strategy aiming to rehabilitate the FATA region will be essential. Because peace and development go hand-in-hand, this rehabilitation cannot happen until there is stability in the region. In order to bring lasting peace to FATA, there is no healthy alternative to economic development.

At this point in the discussion, it is essential to acknowledge that FATA is a "geographical belt," more comparable to a buffer zone. The FATA is a tribal region in the northwest of Pakistan, lying between the provinces of Khyber Pakhtunkhwa (to the north and east), Baluchistan (to the south), and the neighboring country of Afghanistan (to the west). The territory is almost exclusively inhabited by Pashtun tribes. The FATA consists of seven Tribal Agencies and six Frontier Regions (FADA Development Authority, 2007–2014). Although the Pashtun tribes residing in FATA bear some commonalities, there are prominent ethnic and cultural differences as well. Developing one model and expecting it to fit all of the different agencies and tribes would be an impractical approach for the economic development of the region.

Nevertheless, the fact that locals are still familiar with the agricultural and nomadic pastoral practices that used to dominate FATA's economy is valuable. This knowledge provides a foothold for positive economic growth. If available practices are supported, these could bring the region closer to legitimate economic activity and further from illicit trade. The people of FATA are well acquainted with these economies and have local knowledge about the subsistence economy based on these two existing fields. Existing practices must be nourished. Likewise, any hybrid economic model that is developed must accommodate both the indigenous economy of FATA people (excluding the war economy factors) and the current employable generation of Pakistan.

Economic development has all but stalled in the FATA, and lack of education is amongst the most prominent reasons why. There have been no employment opportunities for the locals, no industries circulating wealth back into the community, nor in any form of skilled labor. Without the extension of the Constitution and law in FATA, the public has been deprived of even their basic rights and facilities. The FATA has been left out of all mainstream economic development initiatives at work in the rest of the country.

The Implications of Economic Devastation in the FATA

Failing to develop this economy properly has come with consequences. Deprivation was one of the major reasons behind the high proportions of people enlisting to extremist groups. For terrorist recruitment, the FATA region is a stronghold. People in the FATA, especially male youth, had no employment opportunities or the chance of a better life. This was at the core of the rhetoric that terrorists used to recruit youth into their organization. Youngsters were promised attractive sums of money as well as unlimited power and control. This worsened the entire social, economic, and political situation in FATA. Young recruits saw enlisting in extremist groups as a means of obtaining a better life for themselves.

In a context such as this, there is a dire need to formulate a firm strategy—a plan that can not only counter terrorism—but also help stop youth from resorting to radicalization and relapsing into the clutches of terrorist organizations. For nearly a decade and counting, people have been suffering from displacement from their homes, and end up living in camps. There, they end up facing integration problems with the host communities in settled-area districts. By this point, the people of FATA are already in a vulnerable situation, both psychologically and physically. Collectively, these factors paint a dreadful picture of the future if it is not dealt with vigilantly and prudently.

Indigenous Economics

An Integrated Approach to Sustainable Development

Development must be thought of in a holistic and sustainable way. Sustainable development has three main dimensions: (a) economic, (b) social, and (c) environmental. These elements both determine and reflect the condition of the economy as well as that of equality, and ecology, respectively. Some authors also add a fourth dimension or "pillar" consisting of cultural institutions or governance. For the FATA to develop in a sustainable, strategic direction, then any form of intervention should seek to encompass all of these dimensions in an integrated manner. In this context, indigenous economics can play a pivotal role in the economic development of the FATA region. However, this will only be possible if its potential role is adequately recognized and tapped into sensitively.

The Basics of Indigenous Economics

It is difficult to define "indigenous economics." While we can quickly point to many examples and practices, each of them subsists according to context-specific dimensions. Therefore, an interpretation or definition in one part of the world might not be applicable in another. Indigenous economics is based on insights and solutions localized to a particular culture or society. Unique decision-making systems regarding education, farming, food preparation, and natural and other resource management are all examples of "indigenous economics" (Act for Libraries, 2017).

Because their economies tend to be traditional, indigenous economics varies from nation to nation according to the communities which make up these groups. In other words, this involves activities of original inhabitants with their respective nations as they strive to survive and to interact within their parts of the world. This form of economics can include a myriad of activities such as farming processes, traditional means of providing health and human services, food preparation, and even micro-businesses. In some form, each of these relates the individual with their regional and national interests. These elements also articulate valuable knowledge embedded within the cultural concerns of the nation.

Supporting indigenous economies promotes sustainable development from the bottom up by uniting diverse communities from distant geographical settings. Sustainable development can only be attained by integrating economic, environmental, and social development considerations. Using the knowledge that has been passed down through generations, they efficiently utilize natural resources for economic and survival purposes. In turn, this also strengthens the social fiber of their communities. Hence, indigenous economics seems to be a nexus of the three pillars of sustainable development.

International Success Stories: Indigenous Economics in Action

A diverse array of indigenous economies has been active for centuries in communities all over the globe. Although there is no standardized procedure or operational structure that unifies these economies, they share key elements that set them apart from the traditional canon of economics. Even so, they are unique enough that several valid concerns as to how to design policies with indigenous economic practices are in mind. If each economy is unique, should they be approached in the same manner? While some might even harbor reservations as to the extent to which such economies can contribute to their respective communities, success stories abroad provide ample hope for the tribal people in Pakistan as well.

There are several success stories where indigenous economies, after receiving support from their respective governments, implicitly strengthened their nations in return. Developing communities improve the general economic well-being of the entire country. Currently, the Australian Government's initiatives are at the forefront of indigenous economic initiatives. Other global examples include indigenous economic approaches of Native Americans, Inuit communities, the indigenous communities of Northern Ecuadorian Amazon, and the economic model of Uma-Economy in Lawanda, Sumba (Eastern Indonesia), and others. Below is a collection of insights from various specialists on the matter based in diverse regions of the globe.

Socio-Cultural Knowledge as a Pillar of Indigenous Economics. Jacqueline Vel (1994) conducted six-year-long observational research in Lawanda Sumba,

(Eastern Indonesia) to understand the nature of indigenous economics and development work in the region. Her research analyzes the Uma-economy:

> "... In the first part [of my work], I make a stand against mono-disciplinary micro-economic analysis that explains farmers' economic behavior in terms of optimizing resource use in farm production under given market conditions. Micro-economies are part of life within a specific social space. Within this space, men and women, rich and poor, old aged and young lead their daily life, think about the past and the future and try to find ways to improve what they consider unsatisfactory. Their economy, their politics, their social and religious life are intertwined. Studying the micro-economy, I tried to grasp this colorful complexity. A first exercise in this effort for agricultural economists, trained in the neoclassical school of their profession like me, is to question the implicit assumptions of neoclassical economics, and critically assess the applicability of its methods." (Vel, 1994)

The "Uma Economy" provides a detailed analysis of indigenous economic practices, featuring transactions both with and without money. Most importantly, her work analyzes agricultural economics with respect to local knowledge as well as the cultural and social values of the community involved.

Blending Environmental and Mixed Economy Objectives. Similarly, Holt, Bilsborrow, and Oña (2014) in their research titled, "Demography, Household Economics, and Land and Resource Use of Five Indigenous Populations in the Northern Ecuadorian Amazon," mentions that:

> "... [I]t is critical to take culture into account when trying to understand how people use land and resources. Even with a sample of only eight communities representing five different ethnic groups, we observe important inter-cultural variations that fly in the face of common assumptions that indigenous Amazonian populations are essentially homogeneous. One of the quintessential characteristics of indigenous peoples is their reliance on the natural environment, an assertion that finds confirmation in our research, but to varying extents. Another similarity of all the groups studied is that none is a purely subsistence economy—all communities are involved in the market to some degree and purchase things such as clothing and food. However, within these mixed economies lies a diverse range of degrees of market integration." (Holt, Bilsborrow, and Oña, 2014)

This work highlights two other vital aspects that characterize indigenous economies: cultural dependence upon the environment and natural resource allocation. Here, it is essential to remember that indigenous economies depend on the local indigenous knowledge that is shared by the community involved. Culture itself is a form of the regional or local knowledge and practices passed on from generation-to-generation in any specific community. Therefore, culture tends to be of the utmost importance to indigenous economies. They rely heavily on their immediate natural environment for community resources. It also shows that indigenous economies do not have to be purely subsistence-based, but instead, they can be mixed economies (or *hybrid economies* as we shall soon discuss).

Understanding Customary Management Responsibilities: Sustainable Natural Resource Allocation and Hybrid Economies. The Australian Government has made great efforts to build an inclusive development model that integrates its rural indigenous communities. In addition to making significant investments in various indigenous economic practices, they have actively made policy-level interventions to ensure that these indigenous economies flourish. One of the most successful labor market strategies for indigenous economic involvement was put into action in the remote regions of the country. This initiative promoted jobs with roles that fulfilled both cultural obligations for "caring for country" *and* employment in natural resource management programs. The term "caring for country" describes indigenous people's customary management responsibilities. They strive to take care of their land, their ocean, and to use their resources sustainably.

Altman (2005, 2007) developed the concept of the *hybrid economy* to articulate the way both the customary and the mainstream market can be brought together. Through government-supported natural resource management programs, *hybrid economies* can create a mutually beneficial economic arrangement.

The Role of Warruwi Women in Developmental Programs. Research findings confirmed that Warruwi women are key advocates for community development and generating employment opportunities in their community. Because women are strongly concerned for their children and families (both in the present and in the future), there is a genuinely untapped potential for indigenous women to drive development programs in their communities (Fleming, Petheram, and Stacey, 2014). Studies have shown that women tend to use their earnings to improve the quality of life for their respective families, which is also a top priority and also community development. A similar model could very well benefit the tribal people of Pakistan's FATA. Empowering women in itself could bring the region much closer to reaching sustainable peace and stability. To apply these lessons in the FATA, in-depth research and responsive interventions are imperative.

The Future of International Indigenous Economics

If we want indigenous economic development to meet wide-ranging and durable success, then legislators and policymakers must fuse these traditional customary roles and community responsibilities with contemporary employment opportunities. They will need to increase job opportunities using available endemic resources, both human and natural. Studies on indigenous entrepreneurship in small business settings across the globe have also highlighted the "need to reconcile tradition with innovation and the need to understand how indigenous world-view[s] and values impact upon enterprises" (Fleming, Petheram, and Stacey, 2014).

New Zealand, the United States, and Canada have all reported that indigenous entrepreneurship rates increased and that these positive changes directly correlate to reforms made in government policy. These new policies encourage self-directed advancement and try to accommodate non-economic motivations (as in cultural and social motives) for engaging with the formal economy.

Review

After reviewing the international practices of indigenous economics in diverse communities across the globe, we can infer three principles. First and foremost, the value of natural resources and, likewise, the health of the environment is inter-dependent. The community's economic activity depends upon the environment as much as the environment, in terms of resource depletion, is at the mercy of economics. This concept is the nexus of all successful indigenous economic models. In lieu of contemporary environmental concerns (such as the preservation of available natural resources and climate change), indigenous economic practices present both a valuable and viable solution. Economically developing underprivileged communities *without* incurring grave costs or disturbing the social and environmental system of that community would be a great achievement. Secondly, culture and indigenous knowledge are assets and should be considered as such. These elements can and should play a vital role in the growth of the indigenous economy within any community. Indigenous economics ensure that the social responsibilities of communities align with economic roles. In this manner, the community can perform their role while indulging in economic activities as well. Third, there is a key lesson to be learned regarding the role of women in the success rate of indigenous economic models. It was observed that women tend to utilize indigenous economic models both for their community development and the revenue for the betterment of their families. Here, one major point of concern related to revenue and finance management needs to be clarified; that is, the financial management needs to be with the women involved in the indigenous economic activities and not the community elders, who are usually men.

Another important lesson learned is the need to distinguish and clarify indigenous economics as an independent model of economics. It is distinct from both the subsistence economy and neoclassical economic models. Indigenous economic models do not necessarily restrict any given community to choose subsistence economic practices over more industrial, capitalistic initiatives. It fosters mixed or *hybrid economies*. It is better to establish the existing economic practices of the community, but those very practices need to be further formalized and polished.

The 2025 Vision drafted by Pakistan references indigenous economics several times. It suggests investing in these communities for the benefit of both the tribal peoples and the country as a whole. However, it is important to point out that all of these brief mentions are discrete and meekly scattered throughout the document. There is no singular, consolidated statement, policy, or recommendation which simultaneously covers all of the bases needed for a comprehensive response strategy.

Investment in Indigenous Economics in the FATA

The idea of investment in the indigenous economic development of the FATA is based on three main assumptions. The first of which is that the Government of Pakistan cannot afford the time and financial resources required for establishing basic infrastructure, skilled human resources, and industries required for the economic development of FATA. Secondly, shifting global trends placed economic development in the limelight. Increased attention to drastic climate changes and environmental protection prioritizes investment in indigenous practices, which might prove to be far more sustainable in the long run. Third, the population statistics of FATA shows that the percentage of female youth (52%) presents a situation where half of the region's populace has not been educated or trained in any new technical skills since their displacement from FATA. Once they return to their villages and communities, this group of the FATA population needs to be invested in if they are to contribute to the economic development of their communities positively.

Active community involvement in a productive economic activity serves as a positive autonomous defense mechanism. This helps both the community and the nation weather extremely stressful and conflict situations. Furthermore, it also curbs illegal economic activities. The result is a continuance of peaceful coexistence. As such, it can serve a key role in peaceful solutions in the rehabilitation of the FATA and its affected regions.

Encouraging women within indigenous economies simultaneously addresses two pressing issues: mobility and displacement. Concerning mobility, the economic empowerment of the women of FATA, as well as the general economic development of FATA, is limited because of longstanding restrictions on freedom of movement. Women have long been involved in agricultural activities and livestock management, and this is a great asset for the region, but because of this, their contributions have not been optimized. Although women in FATA have been earning petty cash by selling eggs, dairy products, and livestock, all of this occurs on an informal level, with no proper records, organization, or support. This key inhibiting factor pertaining to the integration of women in formal economic ventures is one based upon cultural restrictions. Because they are rarely allowed to move or travel, external markets are inaccessible for them. Instead, they trade goods within their village communities. How best to navigate this situation from a policy standpoint can only be addressed after ascertaining and analyzing the local norms and methods of buying and selling practiced by the women of FATA. One item to note is that men of the family are often relied upon for market linkages, particularly for household-based business activities known as "cottage enterprises." Much of the policies that would confront women's participation in their indigenous communities are hindered by the fact that their communities are displaced. One silver lining to this tragic situation is that this population has been introduced to public and private facilities of the settled area districts. This also shows them the value of money in terms of increasing one's quality of life. Even if many of these amenities are currently out of reach for much of the population, it provides a vision, a goal.

Moving Forward

The key to achieving development in the FATA cannot stop after acknowledging that indigenous economics is indeed a distinct model. Rather, this information is only valuable if it becomes catalytic for responsive political action. Ideally, this would involve blending initiatives aiming to enhance and actualize the implicit potential of FATA's indigenous economy.

Policy Context. Policymakers must consolidate this information in one document, similar to successful policy initiatives employed in other regions. In this regard, the Australian Government has set the standard in terms of defining a clear future strategy. How they intend to expand indigenous economic practices and integrate their indigenous demographic is straightforward and precise. The same could be attempted in the rural and indigenous communities of Pakistan.

As attention turns to the economic development of the tribal regions, women should not be forgotten in these initiatives. Women must be allowed to fulfill active roles in developing and finalizing the policy instruments related to the indigenous economy in Pakistan. A key feature of these plans should explicitly seek to involve illiterate women as well. Doing so would spell economic empowerment in the form of revenue generation, and their contribution would also improve Pakistan's GDP.

Future policies must integrate a detailed implementation plan for researching indigenous economic models for the FATA and efficient implementation at all levels of bureaucracy and community. A key challenge faced by policymakers and governments is to determine or devise methods and approaches that ensure active participation of women as agents of social change, peace processes, and, most importantly of economic activities. By involving women in public socioeconomic spheres, it is likely that better living conditions for their respective families will follow.

Research and Explorative Studies. Indigenous economics tends to lack one specific definition because of its flexible nature and diverse practice, as it can be easily customized to the indigenous practices of the community for which it is being developed. For this reason, there is a great need for further research in this field of study. Concern for subsistence economies, environmentally-friendly economic initiatives, and efficient natural resource use can be fused into a single economic model. This model becomes a hybrid of neoclassical economic theories and indigenous economic practices.

This will result in more relevant indigenous economic models for the different tribal communities of the FATA. It will also help answer the key issue of ensuring that women are not only the contributing force in such economic activities but also the ones receiving the earnings of these initiatives. The hypothesis that women use their earnings for the food, health, education, and better living of their families has been researched in other contexts but can be explored in light of its contribution to the overall sustainable development of the FATA as well.

Encouraging the Role of Women. The role of women in the leadership of indigenous agricultural and pastoral economy of the FATA must be encouraged. Whenever indigenous women are involved in economic activities or revenue generation, it has almost always been observed that they use their earnings for investment in the family and children. They strive to improve the lifestyle of their families and greatly invest in positive activities such as improved education, health, and food for their family members. Fleming et al. found that "Warruwi women were key advocates for community development and generating employment. Because women tend to be very strongly concerned for [the well-being of] their children and families, there is a real, untapped potential for indigenous women to drive development programs in their communities" (Fleming, Petheram, and Stacey, 2014).

Indigenous Entrepreneurship and Market Linkages. The first initiative should encourage entrepreneurship and build mainstream market linkages for indigenous enterprises. Appropriate policies should encourage self-directed advancements. Ideally, these would also foster non-economic motivations such as cultural and social responsibility. New Zealand, the United States, and Canada are already working along similar lines of thought.

Participatory Approaches for Indigenous Economic Development. The most valuable part of indigenous economics and its usefulness to the future of global economic development is the fact that it preserves indigenous cultures, knowledge assets, and practices of the community. Jacqueline Vel, in her work, "The Uma-Economy," states that it would be impossible to understand local knowledge and practices better than locals themselves. Policymakers, researchers, development practitioners, and donors must recognize the intrinsic value of local men and women of the community. The success of indigenous economic initiatives will depend upon local leaders. Participatory approaches will also be an indispensable dimension for future initiatives in FATA. Thus, all relevant stakeholders need to work together in synergy to ensure the success of indigenous economics in the FATA.

There is a dire need for updated development initiatives that accommodate the shifting nature of politics, climate change, and social paradigms. Collectively, we need to be more open about researching and developing more customized economic models in congruence with customized social change and peace models. Policy and programmatic initiatives must seek to create integrated approaches. In sum, a holistic approach should not only address different (yet interrelated) aspects of living within indigenous communities but also be able to connect the FATA to national and international spheres.

Bibliography

Act for Libraries. (2017). *The Difference Between Global Economics and Indigenous Economics*. Retrieved April 20, 2017, from http://www.actforlibraries.org/the-difference-between-global-economics-and-indigenous-economics/

Ali, A. (2010). Economic Cost of Terrorism: A Case Study of Pakistan. *Strategic Studies*, 30(1–2): 157–170.

Altman, J. (2005). 'Economic Futures on Aboriginal Land in Remote and Very Remote Australia: Hybrid Economies and Joint Ventures.' In D. Austin-Broos and G. Macdonald (Eds.), *Aborigines, Culture and Economy: The Past, Present, and Future of Rural and Remote Indigenous Lives* (pp. 121–134). Sydney, Australia: University of Sydney Press.

Altman, J. (2007). Alleviating Poverty in Remote Indigenous Australia: The Role of the Hybrid Economy. *Development Bulletin (Canberra)*, 72(March): 47–51.

Ayaz, E. (July 2012). Peace and Development in FATA through Economic Transformation. *TIGAH, A Journal of Peace and Development*, 2(23).

Bank, W. (2013). *FATA Consultation Report World Bank Group (WBG) Country Partnership Strategy (CPS) 2015–19*. Islamabad, Pakistan: World Bank Group.

Bureau of Statistics. (2015). *FATA Development Indicators Household Survey*. Peshawar, KP: Bureau of Statistics, Planning & Development Department FATA Secretariat.

FATA Development Authority. (2007–2014). *About FATA*. Retrieved April 20, 2017, from http://fatada.gov.pk/about-us/about-fata/

Fleming, A., Petheram, E., and Stacey, N. (2014). Australian Indigenous Women. *Emerald Insight*, 27.

Hand, J. G. (2003). From War Economy to Peace Economy? In J. G. Hand, *From War Economy to Peace Economy?* (p. 7). London: SOAS, University of London.

Holt, F. L., Bilsborrow, R. E., and Oña, A. I. (2014). *Demography, Household Economics, and Land and Resource Use of Five Indigenous Populations in the Northern Ecuadorian Amazon* . Chapel Hill, NC: Carolina Population Center.

Vel, J. (1994). *The Uma-Economy: Indigenous Economics and Development Work in Lawanda, Sumba (Eastern Indonesia)*. Grafisch bedrijf Ponsen & Looijen b.v. Wageningen.

CHAPTER EIGHT

Women Empowerment Through Livestock Management: A Strategy for Achieving the Sustainable Development Goals

(A Case Study of Mohmand Agency of Federally Administered Tribal Areas)

DR. SHAISTA NAZ
Lecturer, Rural Development Department,
The University of Agriculture, Peshawar

NOOR PAIO KHAN
Professor, Institute of Development Studies,
The University of Agriculture, Peshawar

Introduction

In Pakistan, there is a need to determine women's empowerment by geographical, social, cultural, ethnic, professional, and political hierarchies (Sustainable Development Policy Institute, 2008). Also, the Millennium Development Goals (MDGs) targets for women's empowerment did not meet its goals and objectives in the country. The Sustainable Development Goals (SDGs) had already been formulated and accepted, so it needs attention from the researchers and development specialists to address the issue on a priority basis for achieving the targets of SDGs by 2030.

The SDGs supportable advancement objectives attempt to change the course of the 21st century, tending to key difficulties, such as destitution, imbalance, and brutality against women. Women are the prime concern of SDGs, as many are explicitly distinguishing women's fairness, and it is a major aspect of the agreement. Objective 5 of the SDGs is known as the remained solitary gender empowerment objective since it is committed to accomplishing these goals. Women have a privilege of uniformity in all regions. It must be implanted crosswise over legitimate frameworks, maintained in both laws and legitimate works, including proactive measures, for example, amounts. Since all zones of life identify with gender orientation balance, endeavors must be made to cut the underlying foundations of gender segregation wherever they show up. Women make significant commitments each day from conveying a wage to her family unit as a utilized breadwinner, to gaining employment as a business visionary, to dealing with her family and senior citizens. Be that as it may, a lady rancher, for example, may not have the capacity to make her harvests flourish like a man can since she does not have similar access to seeds, credit, innovation, and expansion administrations (World Bank Indicators, 2013).

Destitution can be dangerous, and segregation leaves women vulnerable. In a financial downturn, poor women are less inclined to have investment funds and capacities to compensate for losses. Poor young women are more than twice as likely to wed in their adolescence as rich individuals. They then face conceivably life-threatening dangers from other family matters. Women have a privilege to equivalent access to all roads to end neediness, from social security well-being nets to utilization of the most recent innovations, and understanding that right will be critical to accomplishing the SDGs development agenda.

Empowerment is believed to be the road to women's equality, rights, and fulfillment, while the instrumental view regarding women's empowerment is the means to a better family, economy, society, and nation. Empowerment is fundamental to the achievement of the 2030 development agenda of the Sustainable Development Goals. According to a scooping study of the Gender Equality Programme (Aurat Foundation, 2013), women's empowerment includes access to material resources such as land, livestock, money, credit, and income, availability of decent employment opportunities that involve good working conditions, access to power through representation in political and decision-making bodies, the freedom to make choices in life, enjoyment of basic rights granted in the constitution and international agreements, equal access to quality education and health facilities, mobility to be able to access various facilities, and control over one's body, sexuality, and reproductive choices.

Livestock plays a significant role in the rural economy of Pakistan with its multiple roles in providing traction power, manure, domestic energy, cash, raw materials, and protein-rich food. In the country, 85% traction power for cultivation and transportation has been derived from livestock. Similarly, farmyard manure is used to improve soil fertility, which leads to higher agricultural yield, and it also serves as a cheaper source of domestic energy. Cash profits are mainly derived in rural areas from livestock, which is further used for the social and economic needs of households. Nutritional requirements are also fulfilled from livestock by the consumption of milk and various other dairy products. Livestock not only provides raw materials to industries but also generates export earnings from various livestock products, which accounted for Rs. 12 billion in 2013 (Menhas et al., 2014).

Women are extensively involved in livestock rearing all over the world but are mostly poor livestock keepers. According to the State of Food and Agriculture (2011 and 2012), 70% of the world's poor is comprised of women, and the majority of them are involved in livestock keeping. It is estimated that worldwide, around two-thirds of poor people (600 million) are comprised of poor livestock keepers, and most of them are rural women. These poor livestock keepers mainly derived their livelihoods from livestock income. In this connection, Kristjanson et al. (2010) describe livestock as an asset that not only women can easily own, but it also has the potential to narrow down the gender asset gap within the households. Livestock is used as a tool for narrowing down the gender asset gap and equality promotion in rural areas of developing countries, because of the abundant evidence in different parts of the world that women play a significant role in livestock production and management (Tipilda and Kristjanson, 2009).

Pakistan ranks low in other measures of gender equality and women empowerment. In 2011, the country ranked 133 among 135 countries in the Global Gender Gap Index, while in 2012, it was ranked 55th out of 86 countries in the Social Institutions and Gender Index (OECD, 2012). In 2013, the Global Gender Report by the World Economic Forum Pakistan ranked 135 among 136 countries. Similarly, in 2016, Pakistan ranked 143 among 144 countries. Rural differences are particularly important and can explain the reasons for high poverty and income inequality (World Bank Indicators, 2013). Rural women also work more hours; however, their participation in the labor force in Pakistan is largely under-reported, especially for women who take part in agricultural activities (The State of Food and Agriculture, 2013).

In Pakistan, women are predominantly involved in the agricultural activity of livestock farming. It has been found that women are mainly involved in the dairy sector as compared to other agricultural activities, and two-thirds of all the individuals participating in wage-related livestock work are women (Nazli et al., 2012; Pakistan Bureau of Statistics, 2012). According to the International Fund for Agricultural Development, rural women allocate 6.5 hours/day to various livestock management activities in the country (Niamir-Fuller, 1994). Regardless of women's predominant role in livestock management, they remain marginalized (Azhar-Hewitt, 1999). Köhler-Rollefson (2012) calls these women the "Invisible Guardians" as they are primary caretakers of livestock but are not fully rewarded for this. It is through the livestock management activities that women in rural Pakistan are closely connected to the dairy sector. Of the total produced milk in the country, 80% of the milk products are derived from rural areas on small farms with an average of two to five animals per household, where livestock management activities are primarily done by rural women (Pakistan Dairy Development Company, 2006). An average of 30% to 40% of household income is derived from the livestock reared on these small farms (Zia, Mahmood, and Ali, 2011).

The promotion of gender equality is challenging in countries where culturally and traditionally, women remain oppressed and discriminated in almost every sphere of life. Even if women empowerment policies are supported politically, their implementations remain a question mark in such contexts of deeply embedded gender stereotypes. Federally Administered Tribal Areas of Pakistan (FATA) is a good example of such a situation. Tribal women are one of the severely overloaded, differentiated, and disregarded groups of Pakistani society. The worse conditions of tribal women are due to the region's social, educational, political, and legal arrangements. Their economic status is no better than their social, political, and educational status. Women of FATA have only a 12% literacy rate, which is perhaps the lowest in the world (Planning and Development Department of FATA, 2014). Tribal women are predominantly involved in livestock rearing because it is a source of livelihood, social protection, and income that can be used for supporting their families (FAO, 2013). Thus, livestock management is the only agricultural activity that can promote gender equity in tribal areas. Due to the logic mentioned above, the present research focuses on designing a strategy for women's empowerment through livestock management in the Mohmand Agency of FATA with the following specific objectives.

Objectives

1) To assess the contribution of livestock to rural livelihoods in the Mohmand Agency.
2) To analyze the role of women in rural livelihoods by managing livestock.
3) To design a strategy for achieving the sustainable development goals of women's empowerment.

Research Methodology

This research was conducted in 2016 in the Mohmand Agency of the Federally Administered Tribal Areas of Pakistan by designing cross-sectional survey research. A multi-stage sampling technique was used for sample selection. At the first stage, one tehsil, each from Lower Mohmand (i.e., Pandiyali) and Upper Mohmand (i.e., Halimzai), was randomly chosen. In the second stage, three sub-tribes were also randomly selected from each tehsil: (1) Isa Khel, Bar Burhan Khel, and Kuz Burhan Khel, (2) from tehsil Pandiyali and Kachi Khel, (3) Hamza Khel and Kuz Kadi Khel from tehsil Haimzai. At the final stage, households were randomly chosen for data collection, and data were collected from 323 women in the selected households through a pre-tested questionnaire. The following statistical tools were used to study the significance of women's empowerment through livestock rearing.

Contribution of Livestock to Rural Livelihoods

Livestock's contribution to the livelihoods of the sampled households was assessed in terms of five dimensions by following the research study of Biradar et al. (2013) and was quantified, as discussed below. Figure 8.1 represents the theoretical framework of livestock's contribution to rural livelihoods in the study area.

- *Income Provision*: The percentage and average contribution of livestock income to the total household income was computed.
- *Food Provision*: Livestock contribution to sample households was also assessed in terms of food provision. The food items from livestock included milk and milk products (i.e., yogurt, butter, and butter oil). The average quantity of milk and milk products available for household consumption was estimated in the study area.
- *Fuel Provision*: Percentage of the sampled households using dung cakes as fuel was computed.
- *Employment Generation*: Number of hours engaged in livestock rearing per day was collected for household labor. Then, the annual working hours for household labor was computed. Total hours spent in a year was divided by 8 hours to convert them into man-days. A total number of man-days contributed by each category of household labor was expressed as mean values.
- *Security for Uncertainties*: Percentage of the number of households having used livestock to face the uncertainties in the past 2 years was collected and presented.

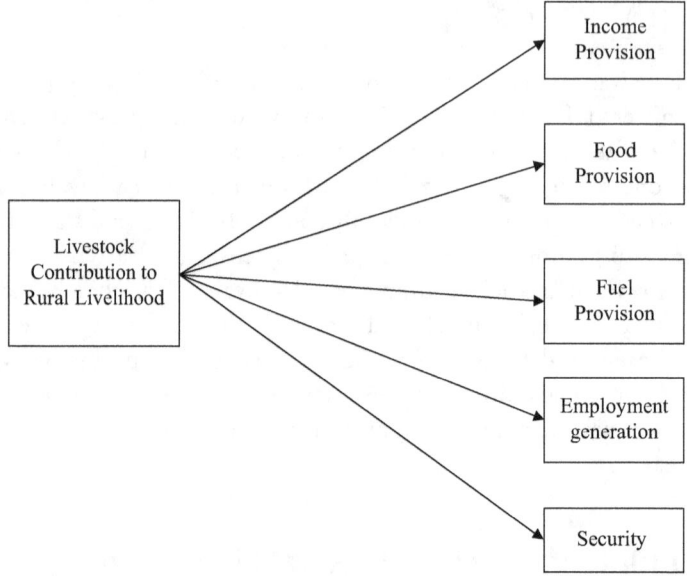

Figure 8.1: Theoretical Framework of Livestock's Contribution to Rural Livelihoods.

Women's Role in Rural Livelihoods by Managing Livestock

To estimate the women's role in rural livelihoods by managing livestock, a Chi-square test and simple linear regression analysis were carried out.

The Chi-Square Test: The test is mostly used for checking the significant association between the variables. The general formula of the Chi-square test is given as follows.

$$\chi^2 = \sum_{i=1}^{k} \frac{(O_i - E_i)^2}{E_i}$$

Where:

χ^2 = Chi-square test
O_i = observed frequencies
E_i = Expected frequencies

In this research study, the Chi-square test was used to test the association between the following variables as used by Ahmad (2014).

i. Rural women's time allocation to livestock management activities and the income earned from livestock.

ii. Rural women's time allocation to livestock management activities and the quantity of milk available for household consumption.
iii. Rural women's time allocation to livestock management activities and the fuel provision for household requirements.

Simple Linear Regression Analysis: A simple linear regression model was used to find out women's contribution to rural livelihoods through livestock management. Regression analysis is used to test the relation between the following variables as used by Ahmad (2014).

i. Rural women's time allocation to livestock management activities and the income earned from livestock.
ii. Rural women's time allocation to livestock management activities and the quantity of milk available for household consumption.
iii. Rural women's time allocation to livestock management activities and the fuel provision for household requirements.

For this, three sets of simple linear regressions were constructed as follows:

$$WTLM = \beta_0 + \beta_1 LI + e_i \qquad 2.1$$

Where:

WTLM = Women's time allocation to livestock management activities (hours/day)
LI = Livestock Income (Rs./day)
β_s = Constant
e_i = Error term

$$WTLM = \beta_0 + \beta_1 QMH + e_i \qquad 2.2.$$

Where:

WTLM = Women's time allocation to livestock management activities (hours/day)
QMH = Quantity of milk available for household consumption (Liters/day)
β_0 = Constant
e_i = Error term

$$WTLM = \beta_0 + \beta_1 FA + e_i \qquad 2.3.$$

Where:

WTLM = Women's time allocation to livestock management activities (hours/day)

FA = Fuel (dung cakes) availability for household requirements (categorical Yes=1, No=0)
β_0 = Constant
e_i = Error term

Results and Discussion

Contribution of Livestock to Rural Livelihoods

Livestock rearing is profitable in terms of its direct and indirect benefits. The direct benefits obtained from the livestock rearing in the study area included the provision of income, food, fuel, employment, and security to meet uncertainties, which are discussed next.

Income Provision: Table 1 shows that a considerable part of the rural households' total income is derived from livestock rearing in the study area. The sources of livestock income included milk, milk products, farmyard manure, and fuel (dung cakes). On average, a total of Rs. 75, 961.81/- per annum per household has been received from the different livestock sources in the study area. It shows that livestock is reared for income generation and, thus, poverty reduction in the study area. The result is in line with Menhas et al. (2014), who found that livestock is reared for income generation and thus poverty reduction. In tehsil Halimzai, the average annual livestock earning (Rs. 98, 748/-) was found to be higher as compared to tehsil Pandyali (Rs. 53176/-). The possible reason was that in tehsil Halimzai, milk and milk products were mostly sold out as compared to tehsil Pandyali. Livestock was found to be the second major source of livelihood, with a 19% share to the total household income in the study area.

Food Provision: The livestock products like milk, yogurt, butter, and butter oil serve as protein-rich food. On average, 3.60 liters/day milk was available in the study area for home consumption, as presented in Table 8.1. The average quantity of milk products such as yogurt (13.215 Kg/week), butter (0.329 Kg/week), and butter oil (0.181Kg/week) were also available for household consumption in the study area. The results revealed that a substantial quantity of milk and milk products were made available for household consumption. The provision of these dairy products not only provides a protein-rich diet for household members, which improves their health status but also lowers the household budget.

Fuel Provision: Livestock also provides fuel in the shape of dung cakes. Rural women collect dung and make dung cakes, thus providing fuel for cooking to their households in the study area. The use of dung cake is an important form of an energy source that rural households depend on for domestic cooking. Dung cakes serve as a cheaper source of energy for cooking in the study area. For a rural household to feed well and have high nutritional status, they need to cook their food very well by using fuel derived from livestock. Dung collection and the making of dung cakes were the prime responsibilities of women in the study area. Table 8.1 shows that a great majority (70%) of the total sample households used dung cakes as a source of energy for cooking in the study area.

Employment Generation: Data in Table 8.1 indicate that livestock generated annual employment of 207.59 man-days for women and 29.66 man-days for adult men in the study area. The results are in line with Biradar et al. (2013), who found that livestock is generating more annual employment than men in India. Livestock rearing is a labor-intensive activity, and it requires daily care and regular performance of certain related activities. In addition to this, women were extensively involved in carrying out all the livestock management activities by giving

Table 8.1. Contribution of Livestock to Rural Livelihood in the Study Area

Type of Contribution		Halimzai	Pandyali	Overall Area
Income provision	The ranking order of livestock as a source of income to total household income	2nd	2nd	2nd
	Average annual income from livestock (Rs.)	98748	53176	75962
	Percent of total household income earned from livestock	19	19	19
Food provision	Average quantity of milk for household consumption (Liter/day)	3.16	4.05	3.60
	Average quantity of yogurt for household consumption (Kg/week)	9.95	16.47	13.22
	Average quantity of butter for household consumption (Kg/week)	0.157	0.502	0.32
	Average quantity of butter oil for household consumption (Kg/week)	0.0682	0.294	0.18
Fuel provision	Percent of households using dung cake as a source of fuel	67	73	70
Employment generation	Man-days/year by women	211.7	204.13	207.59
	Man-days/year by men	9.67	49.67	29.66
Security for uncertainties	Percentage of households used livestock as an asset to meet uncertainties	20	15	17.5

more time on a daily basis; thus, the annual employment generation of women is much higher than men in the study area.

Security Provision: Table 8.1 shows that 17.5% of households used livestock for meeting uncertainties in the study area. In tehsil Halimzai, more households (20%) used livestock as an asset to meet uncertainties as compared to tehsil Pandyali (15%). Formal sources of credit did not prevail in the study area, and in sudden need for the money, households might have felt it easier to rely on the sale of livestock. On social occasions like marriage and funerals, livestock is also sold to meet cash needs and butchered for food. Thus, livestock served as an important asset to meet social and economic uncertainties in the study area.

Women's Role in Rural Livelihoods by Managing Livestock

Rural women play an essential role in rural livelihoods by managing livestock. Tables 8.2 and 8.3 outline the role of rural women in managing livestock. The results of the Chi-square test show that a significant association existed between women's time allocation to livestock management activities and the total income earned from livestock by the sample households in the study area (Table 8.2). The result is in line with Ahmad (2014), who found a significant association between women's level of participation in livestock management activities and the income earned by households from livestock in district Punjab. This implies that in the study area, households mostly depend on livestock to earn their income, and women's time allocation to livestock management activities are significantly related to the household's part of the income earned from livestock.

Table 8.2. Empirical Results of the Chi-Square Test Showing Women's Role in Rural Livelihoods by Managing Livestock

Variables	Pearson Chi-Square Value	df	Asymp. Sig. (2-sided)
Rural women's time allocation to livestock management activities and the income earned from livestock	31.631	4	0.000
Rural women's time allocation to livestock management activities and the quantity of milk available for household consumption	12.106	4	0.017
Rural women's time allocation to livestock management activities and fuel (dung cakes) availability for household requirements	120.202	2	0.000

Table 8.3. Empirical Results of the Simple Linear Regression Analysis Showing Women's Role in Rural Livelihoods by Managing Livestock

Regression Models	Constant	Coefficients	Std-Error	t-ratio	p-value
Model-1: Women's time allocation to livestock management activities (Dependent variable) and livestock income (independent variable)	3.718	.003	.000	8.056	.000
Model-2: Women's time allocation to livestock management activities (Dependent variable) and quantity of milk available for household consumption (independent variable)	4.513	-.027	.051	-.538	.591
Model-3: Women's time allocation to livestock management activities (Dependent variable) and fuel provision for household energy use	2.972	1.943	.122	15.981	.000

Table 8.3 also shows that women's time allocation to livestock management activities is positively and significantly related to the income earned from livestock in the study area. The findings are supported by Ahmad (2014). It reveals that women allocated time to livestock management activities and thus earning income in the study area. It is also found by Chayal, Dkaka, and Suwika (2010) that, in rural areas within the household, more benefits are derived from women's income than men. They spend considerable time in feeding animals, milking of animals, shed cleaning, fodder cutting, preparation of milk products, and thus providing milk, farmyard manure and sometimes dung cakes for sale in the study area. Therefore, women's time allocation to livestock management activities had a significant impact on the livelihoods of the sample households in the shape of income provision. This is also supported by the results that out of the total household income, a large percentage of income has been derived from the livestock. Results of the Chi-square test (Table 8.2) also denote that a significant association exists between the rural women's time allocation and the provision of milk for household consumption in the study area. The result conforms with that of Ahmad (2014), who also reported a significant association between women's

level of participation in livestock management activities and the amount of milk available for home consumption in Punjab. This determines the important role of rural women in the provision of nutritious food to their families by managing livestock. Hence, the considerable time allocation of rural women to the livestock management activities made it easier to access and provide high-valued protein food for the sample households.

Furthermore, the livestock products contribute to improving the health and nutritional status of the local population by providing much protein-rich food like milk, meat, yogurt, butter, butter oil, milk-based hot and cold drinks, such as tea and buttermilk with its various uses in daily routines. Therefore, livestock sources explicitly contribute to the richness of diets and reduce various dietary deficiencies. Despite women's significant role in the provision of livestock income, milk, and milk products for household consumption, women also collect dung and make dung cakes, which provides fuel for cooking to their households in the study area. The use of dung cake is an essential form of an energy source that rural households depend on for domestic cooking. Dung cakes serve as a cheaper source of energy for cooking in the study area. For a rural household to eat well and have high nutritional status, they need to cook their food very well by using fuel derived from livestock. Dung collection and the making of dung cakes were the prime responsibilities of women in the study area. Table 8.2 shows that 70% of the total sample households used dung cakes as a source of energy, mostly for cooking bread and such. This finding conforms with that of Ahmad (2014) and Biradar et al. (2013). It implies that rural women allocated considerable time to livestock management activities and positively contributed to the livelihoods of their households in the study area.

The results of the simple linear regression in Table 8.3 depict that women's time allocation to livestock management activities is negatively and insignificantly related to the quantity of milk provision for household consumption in the study area. The negative relation is because when women's time allocation to livestock management activities increases the provision of milk for household consumption, it is not increasing because the milk is sold out to earn cash.

Conclusion and Recommendations

This study found that livestock was the second primary source of earnings in the study area and supported rural livelihoods by the provision of income, food, fuel, employment, social and economic security during bad times. Livestock provides an average quantity of 3.60 liters/day milk, 13.22 Kg/week yogurt, 0.32 Kg/week butter, and 0.81 Kg/week butter oil for household consumption. It generates annual employment of 207.59 man-days for women and 29.66 man-days for adult men. A total of 17.5% of the households used livestock for mitigating uncertainties at the household level. The Chi-square results confirmed that women's time allocation to livestock management is significantly associated with income, food, and fuel provisions. The econometric model results also revealed that women's time allocation to livestock activities is positively related to the income and fuel provision, while it is negatively related to the quantity of milk available for household consumption. It is concluded that women were extensively involved in livestock management and significantly contributed to rural livelihoods.

The study also concludes that livestock contributes economically and socially to the livelihoods of the women. Thus, it can be used as a strategy for achieving the women's empowerment targets of sustainable development goals. The full integration of gender equality goals into livestock development policies can effectively increase livestock production for food security, income generation, protection, and enhancement of public health. Substitution of the words "men and women" related to livestock management can highlight the concept that gender differences matter and must be accounted for. More gender-focused research is also suggested for an in-depth analysis of the subject matter.

Bibliography

Ahmad, T. I. (2014). *The Role of Rural Women in Livestock Management: Socioeconomic Evidences from Diverse Geographical Location of Punjab (Pakistan).* Geography Uinversit_e Toulose le Mirail-Toulouse II, 2013.

Aurat Foundation. (2013). *Gender Equality Programme: Women's Empowerment in Pakistan.* A scoping study funded by USAID.

Azhar-Hewitt, F. (1999). Women of the High Pastures and the Global Economy: Reflections on the Impacts of Modernization in the Hushe Valley of the Karakorum, Northern Pakistan. *Mountain Research and Development, 19*(2), 141–151.

Biradar, N., Desai, M., Manjunath, L., and Doddamani, M. T. (2013). Assessing Contribution of Livestock to the Livelihood of Farmers of Western Maharashtra. *Journal of Human Ecology, 41*(2), 107–112.

Chayal, K., Dkaka, B. L., and Suwika. R. L. (2010). Analysis of Role Performed by Women in Agriculture. *Journal of Human Social Sciences, 5*(2010), 68–72.

Köhler-Rollefson, I. (2012). *Invisible Guardians: Women Manage Livestock Diversity.* Rome: FAO Animal Production and Health Paper No. 174.

Kristjanson, P., Bayer, A. W., Johnson, N. A., Tipilda, J. N., Baltenweck, I., Grace, D., and MacMillan, S. (2010). *Livestock and Women's Livelihoods: A Review of the Recent Evidence.* Discussion Paper No. 20. Livestock Research for Rural Development.

Menhas, R., Yaqoob, M., Akhtar., S., and Jabeen, N. (2014). Gender Empowerment Through Livestock Care and Management: A Case Study of District Jhang. *Innovare Journal of Social Sciences, 1*(2), 35–37.

Nazli, H., Haider, S., Hausladen, S., Tariq, A., Shafiq, H., and Shahzad, S. (2012). *Pakistan Rural Household Panel Survey 2012 (Round 1)—Household Characteristics*. Retrieved January 27, 2017, from http://www.ifpri.org/publication/pakistan-ruralhousehold-panel-survey-2012-round-1

Niamir-Fuller, M. (1994). *Women Livestock Managers in the Third World: A Focus on Technical Knowledge*. Rome: International Fund for Agricultural Development.

Organisation for Economic Co-operation and Development. (2012). *Gender Index Pakistan*. Retrieved April 4, 2013, from http://genderindex.org/

Pakistan Bureau of Statistics. (2012). *Pakistan Labor Force Survey 2010–2011*. Retrieved January, 2017, from http://www.pbs.gov.pk/sites/default/files/Labour%20Force/ publications/lfs2010_11/results.pdf

Pakistan Dairy Development Company. (2006). *The White Revolution White Paper on Pakistan's Dairy Sector*. Islamabad: Pakistan Dairy Development Company.

Planning and Development Department of FATA. (2014). *FATA in Figures*. Bureau of Statistics, FATA Cell.

State of Food and Agriculture, The. (2011). *The Women in Agriculture: Closing the Gender Gap for Development*. Rome. Available at http://www.fao.org/docrep/013/i2050e/i2050e00.html.

State of Food and Agriculture, The. (2012). *The Role of Women in Agriculture*. ESA Working Paper No. 11–02.

State of Food and Agriculture, The. (2012). *Invisible Guardians: Women Manage Livestock Diversity*. Rome: FAO Animal Production and Health Paper No. 174.

State of Food and Agriculture, The. (2013). *Asia's Women in Agriculture, Environment and Rural Production—Pakistan*. Retrieved January 26, 2017, from http://www.fao.org/sd/wpdirect/wpre0111.htm

Sustainable Development Policy Institute. (2008). *Pakistan: Country Gender Profile*. Retrieved January, 2017, from http://www.jica.go.jp/pakistan/english/office/others/pdf/ CGP_01.pdf

Tipilda, A., and Kristjanson, P. (2009). *Women and Livestock Development: A Review of the Literature*. ILRI Innovations Work Discussion Paper 01–09. Nairobi, ILRI.

World Bank Indicators. (2013). *Pakistan Statistics*. Retrieved June 21, 2013, from http://www.ruralpovertyportal.org/country/statistics/tags/pakistan

Zia, U. E., Mahmood, T., and Ali, M. (2011). *Dairy Development in Pakistan*. Retrieved June 20, 2013, from http://www.fao.org/docrep/014/al750e/al750e00.pdf

CHAPTER NINE

Exposure to Violence, Human Capital, and Market Development: The Case of FATA

DR. MUHAMMAD NASIR
Pakistan Institute of Development Economics (PIDE), Islamabad

Introduction

The Federally Administered Tribal Areas (FATA), a region that borders with Afghanistan, has historically remained underdeveloped due to backwardness, lack of education and health facilities, lawlessness, and poverty. Consequently, it has a small share (1.5%) in the total GDP of Pakistan. Also, the region has been a victim of violence in the post-9/11 era. The United States' invasion of Afghanistan in 2001 resulted in the collapse of the Taliban regime, and they tried to find safe sanctuaries in this rugged and difficult terrain on this (Pakistan's) side of the border. This led to the launch of military operations by the Pakistani Government against the militants in the North Waziristan Agency, which was subsequently extended to other agencies in the region. What followed was a decade of extreme violence witnessed by the people of FATA. There were more than 27,000 fatalities during the period 2006–2016 (South Asian Terrorism Portal, 2016). This violence was the direct result of terrorist attacks and the counter-insurgency actions by the government. Various military operations were conducted in the region to wipe out militants. A detailed analysis of the effectiveness of counter-insurgency efforts, including peace accords, military operations, and the National Action Plan (NAP), is provided by Rehman et al. (2017). According to their findings, only the National Action Plan, along with Operation Zarb-e-Azb, was successful in reducing violence.

The FATA is now in a transitioning period from conflict to the post-conflict situation. The government is determined for the economic development and financial stability of the region. It is seeking ways to deal with challenges faced by the post-military operations in FATA and explore opportunities for economic growth in this tribal belt. Exposure to the decade-long violence, however, has had significant detrimental effects on the residents of this part of the country. Nonetheless, the focus has been on estimating the direct and tangible costs of conflict, such as economic, military, and environmental. Subsequently, the discussions and policies are also directed toward dealing with these challenges.

What is missing from the debate on the effect of terrorism is the indirect cost of exposure to violence that can have long-term welfare effects. This can take at least two forms: (i) impact of violence on children's health, which in turn can affect future human capital, and (ii) impact on adults' risk preference and social behavior through the channel of psychological health. Children's health is important because the literature on child development has shown that exposure to shocks (such as violence or floods) early in life deteriorates children's human capital, which is a link to their educational and labor market performance in the future. The importance of early-life conditions in shaping the adult outcomes has been substantiated by a growing body of literature (Almond and Currie, 2011; Barker, 1992; Cunha and Heckman, 2007). On the other hand, exposure to violence may make people more risk-averse, which can affect their investment decisions. Violence may also affect social cohesion by reducing between-group cooperation (Nasir et al., 2016). The first situation can adversely affect the supply of a strong labor force, whereas the second situation can hinder market development. Together, these situations can affect future economic growth and development of the region. Without taking these impacts into account, the effectiveness of any long-term policy for the welfare of the region will remain in doubt.

This chapter explores the first situation. More specifically, the study examines the impact of exposure to violence on children's (aged 1–6 years) height-for-age-Z score (HAZ). Impacts of both prenatal and postnatal exposures are examined. This is done by combining the data on children's health from the FATA Development Indicators Household Survey (FDIHS 2015) with the total monthly number of fatalities at the agency level. Using the sibling fixed-effect strategy, the results reveal that exposure to violence, both *in-utero* and during *childhood*, significantly affect children's health. An increase in violence reduces a child's height-for-age-Z score, on average, by 0.19 standard deviation. The results are robust to different specifications and show considerable heterogeneity across the children's gender and household's region of residence.

Violence and Child Health in FATA

Pakistan has observed various waves of violence throughout her history. The communal riots in 1947, the political violence in Karachi, the ethnic and sectarian violence in different parts of the country reflect the spatial and temporal violence that Pakistan has been a victim from the time it came into being (Alavi, 1988; Cohen, 2004; Grare, 2013; Nasr, 2002). Nonetheless, the government was somehow able to restrict the spread and intensity of these violent episodes.

The most dreadful outburst of violence, however, has been witnessed at the beginning of the new millennium owing to the rise of Islamic militancy. As a consequence of the 9/11 attacks, the United States, along with her allies, invaded Afghanistan to hunt down Osama bin Laden—the al-Qaeda leader. This U.S. invasion was effective in collapsing the Taliban's regime in Afghanistan. The militants found safe hideouts in the rough terrains along the Pakistan–Afghanistan border and started attacking the coalition forces in Afghanistan (Yusuf, 2014). This forced Pakistan to launch a military operation in the Waziristan Agency in 2004.[1] The military operation, along with drone attacks, led to the formation of the Tahreek-e-Taliban Pakistan (TTP) in 2006. The TTP declared war against the Pakistani Government. The insurgencies and counter-insurgencies resulted in collateral damage, which worsened the situation, and violence started to spread to other parts of the FATA region. Subsequently, the entire country was affected. More than 60,000 Pakistanis died, and the country incurred a cost of $118 billion in this War on Terror (Pakistan Economic Survey, 2014–15). The spatial and temporal variations in violence in the FATA region are shown in Figure 9.1 and Figure 9.2.

Next is a discussion on the situation of children's health in FATA. Among the various measures of child health, child height adjusted for age and gender is commonly considered an appropriate indicator of a child's long-run nutritional status because the height exhibits the stock of past outcomes and is found to be associated with adult height, cognitive ability, productivity, and earnings (Strauss and Thomas, 2008). For this purpose, a Z-score for each child's height-for-age is computed. The Z-score for a child is calculated as the difference between that child's height and the mean height of the same-aged international reference population. This difference is then divided by the standard deviation of the reference population. According to this criterion, a stunted child will be the one whose height-for-age-Z-score is below -2. For a severely stunted child, this score will be below -3. Therefore, stunted and severely stunted children have a high probability of being on a different growth trajectory for the rest of their lives (Thomas et al., 1996).

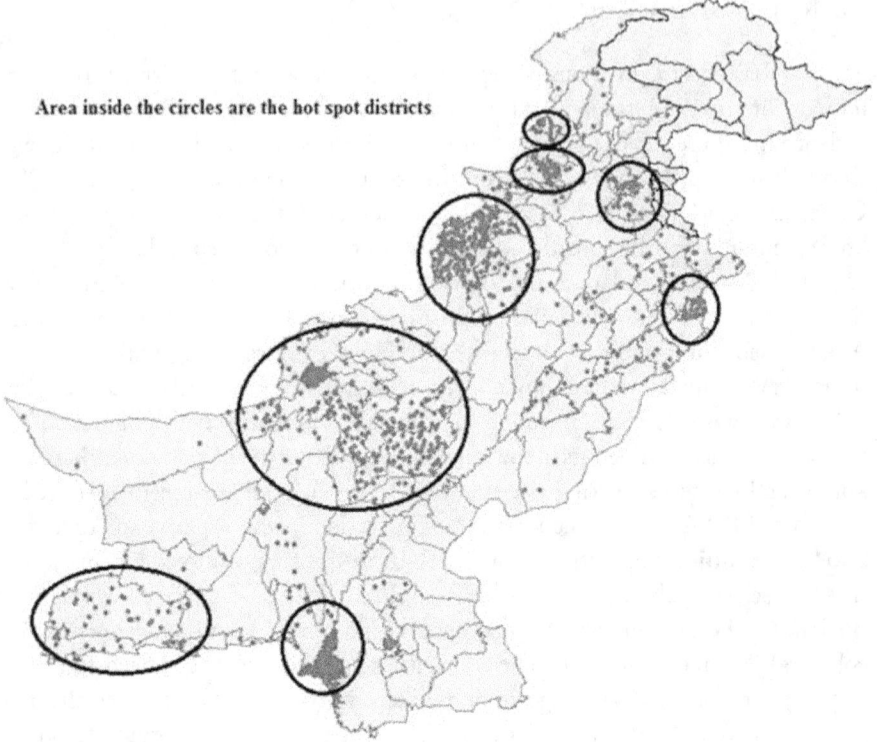

Figure 9.1: Terrorist incidents 2001–2006.

Table 9.1 shows a comparison of various child health indicators between FATA and Khyber Pakhtunkhwa (KP). This province is not only close to FATA but also shares common cultures and linguistic values. It is evident from the table that children in FATA perform worse compared to those in KP in all indicators. Most importantly, almost 50% of children in FATA are stunted, which is a worrisome situation for future human capital.

Literature Review

Various studies have examined the link between violent conflicts that individuals experience in their early years of life and various outcomes in the latter part of their life, such as labor market returns, health, and education. One strand of literature propagates that exposure to war during early years of life adversely affects an individual's height, educational level, and outcomes of the labor market (Chamarbagwala and Moran, 2011; Galdo, 2013; Grimard and Laszlo, 2014;

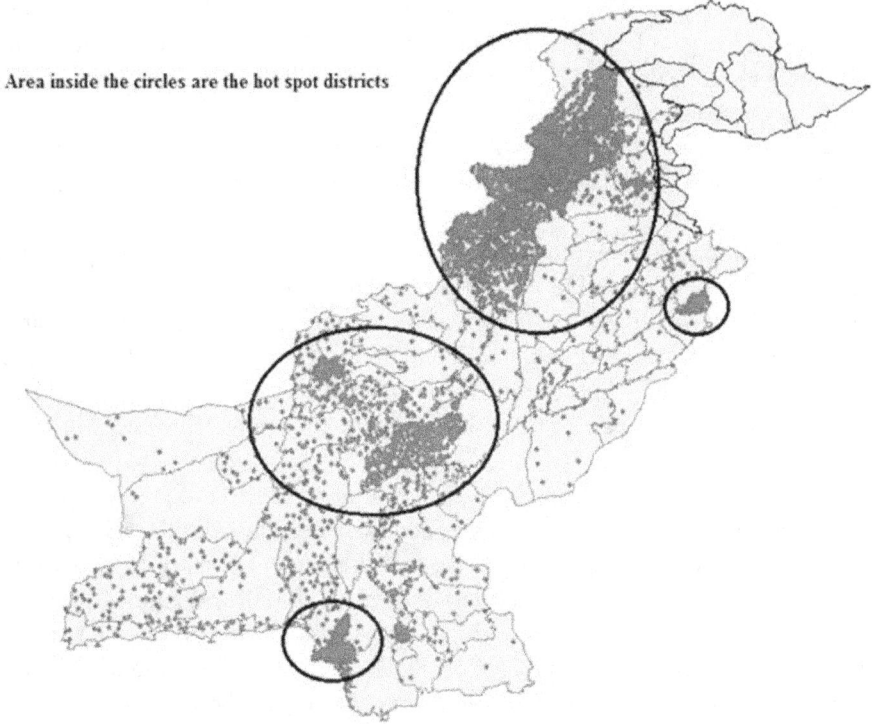

Figure 9.2: Terrorist incidents 2007–2012.

Table 9.1. Comparison of Health Indicators in FATA and KP

Indicator	FATA	KP
Wasted Prevalence (%)	14.7	12
Underweight Prevalence (%)	29.3	26.1
Stunted Prevalence (%)	48.6	41.9
Diarrhea in the last 30 days (%)	12	7

Note: Data sources include the FATA Development Indicators Household Survey (FDIHS 2015) and Pakistan Demographic Health Survey (PDHS 2013). KP is the abbreviation for Khyber Pakhtunkhwa.

Leon, 2012). Conversely, Sharkey et al. (2012) enquired into the impact the exposure to homicides has on the quality of education and attitude of children in Chicago. Their study concluded that the test scores and attention of children were adversely affected. Similarly, the link between vulnerability to armed conflict and test performances of children in Colombia was investigated by Rodriguez and

Sanchez (2013). It was deduced that the exposure reduced the standardized test performance of children between the ages of 11–18 by 0.86 standard deviations. As far as child health is concerned, many studies investigated the prenatal vulnerability to violence such as Camacho (2008), Valente (2011), Mansour and Rees (2012), and Brown (2015). These studies reached a similar conclusion in that the exposure to violence leads to a higher incidence of miscarriages or stillbirths and lower birth weight.

The relationship between vulnerability to violence during the early years and height-for-age-Z-scores (HAZ) has also been explored by numerous studies. Such studies have utilized cross-sectional and over time, changes in vulnerabilities to war for young children, and found an association between the height of children and violence. Specifically, the vulnerability to war decreases the HAZ of a child by approximately 0.2 to 1.0 standard deviation (Akresh et al., 2012; Minoiu and Shemyakina, 2012).

Nevertheless, these studies have analyzed the total effect of pre- and postnatal vulnerability to violence as no distinction has been made with regards to the conflict exposure in-utero and initial years of life. However, recently, two studies have attempted to cover this gap. First, Akresh et al. (2014) examined the effect of a conflict between Eritrea and Ethiopia by utilizing GPS information to determine the distance between areas of conflict and computed exposure to the war of children via village surveys in both nations. Moreover, the study differentiated the effect of in-utero and vulnerability to violence during the early years of life on HAZ. It was deduced that HAZ was reduced among the children in both nations.

Furthermore, the addition of GPS data showed that the adverse effect of violence vulnerability increased by 35%–65% in comparison to the vague regional estimation of vulnerability. Second, Duque (2014) disentangled the in-utero and early years of vulnerability to violent combat in Colombia. It was concluded that the vulnerabilities adversely affected cognitive capabilities, HAZ, and children's socio-emotional outcomes. Her study was distinct from prior studies in that the effect of civil wars was investigated in the prior studies, while Colombia experienced a modest degree of violence as compared to other nations at war. Moreover, the prior studies have been conducted for less-developed African nations that suffer from poor nutritional values even when the atrocities were absent and hence resulted in a considerable impact of violence. In contrast, Duque (2014) examined a developing country. Nevertheless, no such study has been conducted that investigates the effect of violence and terrorism on the health of children in the FATA region of Pakistan.

Potential Channels

One of the challenges faced by the literature on violence and child health is that of finding empirical support for various potential channels through which violence can affect child development. This is because of the data constraints. Nonetheless, several potential mechanisms have been identified in the literature. The first group of mechanisms consists of supply-side effects. Violence can diminish the quality and quantity of resources in a community. For example, conflict can destroy infrastructure such as hospitals as well as frighten away skilled doctors affecting both the quantity and quality of the health services in the community.

Similarly, violent conflict may force the government to divert resources from development expenditures such as education and healthcare toward the non-developmental military expenditures to ensure security in the country or community. Also, private investors will be reluctant to invest in a violent environment, which can disrupt the economy and hence reduce the household income. The fall in household income will not only reduce the demand for healthcare services but can also disturb the household's ability to provide nutritional supplements for the children. All these can have disastrous consequences for child development (Akbulut-Yuksel, 2009; Minoiu and Shemyakina, 2012).

Another brand of channels includes biological and psychological pathways through which child health is affected by violence. According to Barker (1992), the Fetal Origin Hypothesis (FOH) suggests that future health can be affected by changes in the prenatal environment. Specifically, nutritional deprivation and chronic maternal stress during pregnancy can have severe consequences for fetal and newborn health (Denckel-Schetter, 2011; Gluckman and Hanson, 2005). For instance, exposure to stressful shocks such as violence can lead to the release of stress hormones like a corticotropin-releasing hormone (CRH), adrenocorticotropic hormone (ACTH), and cortisol causing reduced gestational age and low birth weight (Hobel and Culhane, 2003). Also, these excess stress hormones can affect brain development (and, therefore, the I.Q. level of the child) as well as increase the probability of chronic health conditions at a younger age. Several studies have shown that the release of stress hormones and nutritional deprivation during different stages (i.e., trimesters) of pregnancy can adversely affect birth weight, cognitive ability, and child height (Gluckman and Hanson, 2005; Stein and Lumey, 2000; Victora et al., 2010).

Parental quality is another important mechanism through which child health may get affected in a violent environment. Violent conflicts can affect the family environment because of the effect on parents' mental health. This, in turn, can cause lower attention and lesser time allocation for childcare. According to the attachment theory in psychology, there is a positive association between strong mother-child attachment and child development (Schore, 2001). Some studies also highlight a positive relationship between violence and parent's mental health (Sharkey et al., 2012). Hence, mental stress, resulting from exposure to violence, may disturb parent-children interactions and subsequently affect child development. Parents may also take measures to prevent children from going outside to play in the streets. This could also distress children's mental and physical growth.

Last but not the least, displacement of people, theft of assets, destruction of various crops, and exposure to disease and unsafe drinking water are some of the other potential mechanisms that can affect child health (see, for example, Akresh et al., 2011; Akresh et al., 2012; Akresh et al., 2014). Unfortunately, the data that we use in this study do not have information on the variables that can help us explore these mechanisms empirically. However, it was important to highlight these channels through which exposure to violence can deteriorate children's health, and one or more of these channels could be at play in this FATA region.

Data and Methodology

Data and Variables

In this sub-section, we discuss the data along with the sources and the construction of variables. Violence is quantified by using the total number of fatalities in each month across all the agencies. The data on violence is obtained from the Global Terrorism Database [GTD] (2013) of the National Consortium for the Study of Terrorism and Responses to Terrorism (START). According to the GTD, "a terrorist attack which fulfills the following three criterions: (i) The incident must be intentional, (ii) The incident must entail some level of violence or threat of violence, and (iii) The perpetrators of the incidents must be sub-national actors. In addition, at least two of the following three criteria must be present for an incident to be included in the GTD: (i) The act must be aimed at attaining a political, economic, religious or social goal, (ii) There must be evidence of an intention to coerce, intimidate or convey some other message to a larger audience (or audiences) than the immediate victims, and (iii) The action must be outside the context of legitimate warfare activities."

We construct two primary variables for exposure to violence: *in-utero* exposure and *childhood* exposure. The *in-utero* exposure is formed by counting the number of fatalities in the nine months before birth (i.e., during pregnancy period). The variable for *childhood* exposure is constructed using the total number of fatalities in every month since the month of birth. The *in-utero* exposure is further divided into three trimesters, each consisting of three months.

Data on the children's health and other control variables are obtained from the FATA Development Household Indicators Survey (FDIHS, 2015). The FDIHS surveyed a total of 4,070 households across all agencies of FATA (except North Waziristan for security reasons) and Frontier Regions. Of these households, 482 were surveyed from urban regions, whereas 3,588 were interviewed from rural areas. Child health is measured using a height-for-age-Z score (HAZ). Since data on this variable is not available from the North Waziristan Agency, our sample covers only six (out of seven) agencies in FATA. However, since these agencies are not very different from each other, these results from our analysis may also be generalizable for the North Waziristan Agency. In total, our sample consists of 2,506 children, age 1–6 years. In addition to HAZ, we also control for child age and gender. Age is measured using the number of months. The gender variable takes the value of 1 and 0 otherwise. Moreover, mother's education (i.e., years of school), marital status (1= married; 0 otherwise), mother's age (in years), household size (number of people sharing a kitchen), and place of residence (1=urban; 0=rural) were also controlled for. Furthermore, years of birth and region of residence fixed effects were also used in the analysis.

The descriptive statistics are provided in Table 9.2. These statistics reveal that the average HAZ for children in FATA is -1.50, suggesting that these children, on average, are below the 1.50 standard deviation compared to the cohorts that were not exposed to violence. The table further shows that 55% of children in the sample are males, and the average age of the children is 44 months. Moreover, the mother's average age is 31 years, and they are mostly illiterate with no formal education. Almost all the women in the sample are married, which should not be surprising given the culture in FATA. The table reveals that 17% of households belong to the urban region. The average household size in the sample is eight.

Table 9.2. Descriptive Statistics

Variable	Observations	Mean	Std. Deviation
HAZ	2506	-1.496	1.742
In-Utero Violence	2506	188.3	174.5
Childhood Violence	2506	573.1	535.9
Gender of Child	2506	0.556	0.496
Age of Child	2506	44.22	19.88
Mother's Age	2506	31.45	10.62
Education	2506	0.221	1.602
Marital Status	2506	0.992	0.084
Household Size	2506	8.687	3.254
Region	2506	0.169	0.374

Econometric Methodology

As discussed in the section on mechanisms, exposure to violence at different trimesters can have differential effects. Hence, I disaggregated the exposure to violence in three trimesters as well as exposure during childhood. Since the dependent variable (HAZ) is continuous, simple OLS methodology can be applied here. However, an important concern for the identification of the pure effect of violence is that the results could be driven by time-invariant unobservable mother characteristics (such as genetics). The estimates would be biased in case these characteristics are correlated with conflict intensity. In order to take account of this worry, I use the sibling fixed-effects strategy for estimation. This considerably improves the identification strategy and is the favored specification in this study.

Hence, the causal effect of prenatal and childhood exposure to violence on children's health is estimated using the following sibling fixed specification:

$$HAZ_{ijtm} = \alpha + \phi_1 Vio_{trim1_t} + \phi_2 Vio_{trim2_t} + \phi_3 Vio_{trim3_t} + \phi_4 Vio_{childhood_t} + \eta_m + \theta_{YOB} + \beta X_{itm} + u_{ijtm} \qquad (1)$$

Here, HAZ_{ijtmk} is an indicator for the health of child i born in agency j in time t to mother m; $Vio_{trim1_{kt}}$ and $Vio_{childhood_{kt}}$ shows the exposure to violence in the first trimester and childhood in the agency of mother's residence, k, for the specified period; η_m are the sibling/mother fixed-effects; θ_{YOB} are the year of birth fixed-effects; X_{itm} is vector of the time-varying child, mother, and household characteristics.

Results and Discussion

Impact on HAZ

This section examines the impact of terrorism on height-for-age-Z-score (HAZ). The results are provided in Table 9.3. Model 1 provides the findings for both prenatal exposure (*in-utero* exposure) and postnatal (exposure during childhood). The results suggest that there is no significant impact of *in-utero* exposure on HAZ. While the sign of childhood exposure is negative, the coefficient is statistically insignificant. However, as we discussed in earlier sections, the timing of exposure to a shock also plays an important role and can have differential effects. It is possible that aggregation is veiling important differential effects of the trimesters. Subsequently, I divided the exposure during pregnancy into three trimesters, and the results are presented in Model 2. Although the signs for second and third trimesters are negative, their coefficients are imprecisely estimated.

Table 9.3. Impact of Violence on HAZ

Variables	Model 1	Model 2	Model 3	Model 4
One year before conception				0.001
				(0.001)
In-utero violence	0.001			
	(0.000)			
Violence in First Trimester		0.000	0.001	0.000
		(0.002)	(0.002)	(0.002)
Violence in Second Trimester		-0.000	-0.001**	-0.001*
		(0.001)	(0.000)	(0.000)
Violence in Third Trimester		-0.001	-0.002	-0.001
		(0.001)	(0.001)	(0.001)
Violence in Childhood	-0.000	-0.001	-0.001**	-0.001**
	(0.000)	(0.001)	(0.000)	(0.000)
Constant	2.626	2.748*	5.684**	5.270*
	(2.925)	(1.116)	(1.818)	(1.929)
Observations	2,462	2,311	1,596	1,596
R-squared	0.367	0.380	0.229	0.234
YOB FE	YES	YES	YES	YES
Agency FE	YES	YES	NO	NO
Sibling FE	NO	NO	YES	YES
Mothers			689	689
Effect			0.19	0.19

Note: Robust standard errors are in parentheses. *** p < 0.01, ** p < 0.05, * p < 0.1. YOB FE=Year of Birth Fixed Effects; Agency FE=Agency Fixed Effects; Sibling FE=Sibling Fixed Effects

The insignificant results in the first two models compel one to consider the role of unobserved heterogeneity across different households. It is, therefore, important to control for this time-invariant unobserved characteristic to get a clear identification. For this purpose, the sibling fixed-effect model is used, and the results are provided in Model 3. Interestingly, the coefficient for violence exposure in the second trimester becomes significant. It suggests that an increase in fatalities by one unit decrease the HAZ by 0.001 standard deviation (SD). Since the average increase in the number of fatalities between 2006 (pre-escalation period) and 2013 (the violent period) is 189, the average number of fatalities in each trimester is 45. Hence, an increase in the average level of violence reduces the HAZ by 0.045 SD. This reduction could be attributed to the release of stress hormones during pregnancy, as well as due to nutritional deprivation. Which one of these mechanisms are at play or the dominant one cannot be explored with the data that is available, and this is also one of the limitations of the FDIHS.

Interestingly, the coefficient for childhood exposure also becomes significant. The coefficient value suggests that HAZ decreases by 0.001 SD due to the increase in fatalities by unit. An increase in the average level of terrorism between pre-violence and violence periods decreases the HAZ by 0.189 SD. This could possibly be due to the nutritional deficit caused by the fall in income resulting from living in a violent environment. To reach a concrete mechanism, however, one would need data on household income before and after the surge in terrorism, which is, unfortunately, not available.

Combining the effect of both prenatal and childhood exposure indicates a total reduction of 0.19 SD in HAZ. The value is consistent with the ones found in the literature. Various studies on the effect of violence on HAZ documented a fall in the range of 0.2–1.0 SD (Akresh et al., 2012; Minoiu and Shemyakina, 2012). The findings in Table 9.3 confirm the adverse impacts that exposure to terrorism has on children in the FATA region. These impacts are not usually directly observable and are therefore found missing from policy debates and discussions. Nonetheless, these effects can have long-term welfare effects because children's human capital is found to be associated with labor market outcomes in adulthood.

Falsification Test

It is imperative to run a falsification test to confirm the validity of the identification strategy. It is quite possible that the results obtained in Model 3 are compelled by the trend in terrorism in the region. In order to deal with this concern, I included the violence level one year before conception in the model. If our concern is valid, the coefficient of the variable should be significant. The results for this specification are provided in Model 4 of Table 9.3. The coefficient is insignificant, suggesting that these effects are not caused by any prior trend in the violence in FATA. This validates our identification strategy.

Robustness of Results

One might ask whether the coefficients for the second trimester and childhood exposure become significant only when the sibling fixed effects are used in the analysis. This could raise the doubt that these findings are not the outcome of the use of the sibling fixed effect but the sibling sample. If this is indeed the case, then we would wrongly associate our findings to the use of this identification strategy. Moreover, if we get a similar result by applying OLS on the sibling sample, then our results will not be generalizable to the entire sample, which also include nonsibling children. This causes doubt on the robustness of our results.

Table 9.4. Impact of Violence on HAZ: Robustness

Variables	Model 1	Model 2
Violence in First Trimester	0.001	0.005**
	(0.002)	(0.002)
Violence in Second Trimester	-0.001**	0.002**
	(0.000)	(0.001)
Violence in Third Trimester	-0.002	0.003***
	(0.001)	(0.000)
Violence in Childhood	-0.001**	0.001***
	(0.000)	(0.000)
Constant	5.684**	3.295*
	(1.818)	(1.189)
Observations	1,596	1,596
R-squared	0.229	0.387
Mothers	689	
YOB FE	YES	YES
Agency FE	NO	NO
Sibling FE Effect	YES	YES

Note: Robust standard errors are in parentheses. *** $p < 0.01$, ** $p < 0.05$, * $p < 0.1$. YOB FE=Year of Birth Fixed Effects; Agency FE=Agency Fixed Effects; Sibling FE=Sibling Fixed Effects

In order to check the robustness, therefore, I used the sibling sample without using sibling fixed effects. The results are provided in Table 9.4. If the concern mentioned above is true, the results of Model 2 should be similar to those of Model 1 (obtained from Model 3 of Table 9.3). As we can see, the results of the sibling sample (without sibling fixed effects) are not similar to that of Model 1. Hence, we can conclude that the findings in Model 3 (Table 9.3) are not driven by the sibling sample. This also confirms the robustness of the results.

Heterogeneous Effects

We now examine the heterogeneity of results across two dimensions—gender and region of residence. The results are provided in Table 9.5. For gender, we observe the effect for a female child only during childhood. On the other hand, the male child is affected only because of prenatal exposure. These outcomes highlight two points: (i) the male fetus is more vulnerable than the female fetus which is in line with the literature; (ii) when there is a fall in household income, and availability of resources is limited, the intra-household resource allocation may go against

Table 9.5. Impact of Violence on HAZ: Heterogeneous Effects

Variables	Gender		Region	
	Female	Male	Rural	Urban
Violence in First Trimester	-0.001	0.000	0.001	-0.003
	(0.001)	(0.004)	(0.002)	(0.002)
Violence in Second Trimester	-0.002	-0.001*	-0.002**	0.000
	(0.001)	(0.001)	(0.001)	(0.000)
Violence in Third Trimester	-0.002	-0.002	-0.001	0.002
	(0.002)	(0.001)	(0.001)	(0.001)
Violence in Childhood	-0.001*	-0.001	-0.001*	0.004*
	(0.001)	(0.000)	(0.000)	(0.000)
Constant	-1.975	4.034*	2.911**	1.487
	(1.344)	(1.506)	(1.003)	(0.927)
Observations	702	894	1,326	270
R-squared	0.232	0.247	0.250	0.453
Mothers	487	561	567	122
YOB FE	YES	YES	YES	YES
Agency FE	NO	NO	NO	NO
Sibling FE Effect	YES	YES	YES	YES

Note: Robust standard errors are in parentheses. *** $p < 0.01$, ** $p < 0.05$, * $p < 0.1$. YOB FE=Year of Birth Fixed Effects; Agency FE=Agency Fixed Effects; Sibling FE=Sibling Fixed Effects

the female child thereby providing suggestive evidence of gender discrimination. I would, however, emphasize the fact that this is just suggestive evidence and will require extensive data on decision-making and household resource allocation to confirm it as tangible evidence.

With regard to the region of residence, we observe that the impact is coming from the rural region, and the children in rural areas are more vulnerable. This should not be surprising since the residents in rural areas have a lower standard of living in terms of access to health, education, and income opportunities. This result could also be the outcome of the fact that the sample is taken mainly from rural areas, as discussed previously.

Conclusion

The policy discussions regarding the economic development in the post-conflict FATA are mostly focused on the tangible costs of insurgency in the region. An essential missing aspect is the children's health affected by exposure to terrorism in the past decade or so. This is important because children's health is an essential component of our future human capital, which is then associated with social and economic outcomes in adulthood. It is, therefore, important to examine how the children in FATA have been affected by this decade-long violence in the region.

The findings of this study suggest that exposure to violence in the second trimester as well as during childhood have substantial negative effects on children's health—measured by the HAZ. On average, the HAZ is reduced by approximately 0.2 SD. Moreover, the results are robust to different specifications and sample selection. We also find evidence of effect heterogeneity across gender and region of residence.

Due to a lack of data, it was not possible to examine the impact of violence on behavior, which is another important aspect. However, the literature suggests that living in a violent environment can increase the probability of risk aversion and reduce social cohesion due to decreased between-group cooperation. Combining the results of this study for children's health with the literature on behavior, one can conclude that this situation will halt the market development in the region, which can become an obstacle for economic development. Hence, these two aspects should be on the priority list in our policy discussions.

Note

1 Agency is geographically equivalent to a district in the settled areas. The seven agencies in FATA are Khyber, Bajaur, Orakzai, Mohmand, Kurram, South Waziristan, and North Waziristan.

Bibliography

Akbulut-Yuksel, M. (2009). *Children of the war: The long-run effects of large scale physical destruction and warfare on children*. Institute for the Study of Labor Discussion Paper No. 4407.

Akresh, R., Caruso, G. D., & Thirumurthy, H. (2014). *GPS data, war exposure, and child health*. Presented at the NEUDC, BU.

Akresh, R., Lucchetti, L., & Thirumurthy, H. (2012). Wars and child health: Evidence from the Eritrean-Ethiopian conflict. *Journal of Development Economics, 99*(2012), 330–340.

Akresh, R., Verwimp, P., & Bundervoet, T. (2011). Civil war, crop failure, and child stunting in Rwanda. *Economic Development and Cultural Change, 59*(4), 777–810.

Alavi, H. (1988). Pakistan and Islam: Ethnicity and ideology. In F. Halliday and H. Alavi (Eds.), *State and Ideology in the Middle East and Pakistan* (pp. 64–111). New York: Monthly Review Press.

Almond, D., & Currie, J. (2011). *Handbook of Labor Economics. Vol. 4B, Chapter Human Capital Development before Age 5, 1315–1486*. Amsterdam: Elsevier.

Barker, D. J. P. (1992). The fetal and infant origins of adult disease. *British Medical Journal, 304*(6827), 638–639.

Brown, R. (2015). *The Mexican drug war and early life health: The impact of violent crime on birth outcomes.* Working Paper.

Camacho, A. (2008). Stress and birth weight: Evidence from terrorist attacks. *American Economic Review: Papers and Proceedings, 98*(2), 511–515.

Chamarbagwala, R., & Moran, H. E. (2011). The human capital consequences of Civil War: Evidence from Guatemala. *Journal of Development Economics, 94*(1), 41–61.

Cohen, S. (2004). *The idea of Pakistan.* Washington, DC: Brookings Institution.

Cunha, F., & Heckman, J. J. (2007). The technology of skill formation. *American Economic Review, 97*(2), 31–47.

Denckel-Schetter, C. (2011). Psychological science on pregnancy: Stress processes, biopsychosocial models, and emerging research issues. *Annual Review of Psychology, 62,* 531–558. doi: 10.1146/annurev.psych.031809.130727

Duque, V. (2014). *Early life conditions, parental investments, and child development: Evidence from violent conflict.* Presented at the NEUDC, BU.

Galdo, J. (2013). The long-run labor-market consequences of Civil War: Evidence from the shining path in Peru. *Economic Development and Cultural Change, 61*(4), 789–823.

Global Terrorism Database. (2013). *National Consortium for the Study of Terrorism and Responses to Terrorism* (START) [Data File]. Technical report.

Gluckman, P. D., & Hanson, M. A. (2005). *The fetal matrix: Evolution, development, and disease.* Cambridge: Cambridge University Press.

Grare, F. (2013). *Balochistan: The state versus the nation.* Washington, DC: Carnegie Endowment for International Peace.

Grimard, F., & Laszlo, S. (2014). Long-term effects of civil conflict on women's health outcomes in Peru. *World Development, 54*(2014), 139–155.

Hobel, C., & Culhane, J. (2003). Role of psychosocial and nutritional stress on poor pregnancy outcome. *Journal of Nutrition, 133*(5), 1709S–1717S.

Leon, G. (2012). Civil conflict and human capital accumulation: The long term effects of political violence in Peru. *Journal of Human Resources, 47*(4), 991–1022.

Mansour, H., & Rees, D. (2012). Armed conflict and birth weight: Evidence from the al-Aqsa Intifada. *Journal of Development Economics, 99*(1), 190–199.

Minoiu, C., & Shemyakina, O. (2012). *Armed conflict, household victimization, and child health in Cota d'Ivoire.* Working paper.

Nasir, M., Rockmore, M., & Tan, C. M. (2016). *It's no spring break in Cancun: The effects of exposure to violence on risk preferences, pro-social behavior, and mental health in Mexico.* Working paper.

Nasr, S. V. R. (2002). Islam, the state and rise of sectarian militancy in Pakistan. In C. Jaffrelot (Ed.), *Pakistan: Nationalism without A Nation.* London: Zed Books Ltd.

Pakistan Economic Survey. (2014–15). Ministry of Finance, Government of Pakistan.

Rehman, F. U., Nasir, M., & Shahbaz, M. (2017). What have we learned? Assessing the effectiveness of counterterrorism strategies in Pakistan. *Economic Modelling, 64,* 487–495.

Schore, A. (2001). Effects of a secure attachment relationship on right brain development, affect regulation and infant mental health. *Infant Mental Health Journal, 22,* 7–66.

Sharkey, P. T., Tirado-Strayer, N., Papachristos, A. V., & Raver, C. C. (2012). The effect of local violence on children's attention and impulse control. *American Journal of Public Health, 102*(12), 2287–2293.

Stein, A. D., & Lumey, L. H. (2000). The relationship between maternal and offspring birth weights after maternal prenatal famine exposure: The Dutch famine birth cohort study. *Human Biology, 72*(4), 641–654.

Strauss, J., & Thomas, D. (2008). Health over the life course. In Paul Schultz and John Strauss (Eds.), *Handbook of Development Economics*, vol. 4 (pp. 3375–3474). Amsterdam: North-Holland.

Thomas, D., Lavy, V., & Strauss, J. (1996). Public policy and anthropometric outcomes in the Cote D'Ivoire. *Journal of Public Economics, 61*(2), 155–192.

Valente, C. (2011). *Children of the revolution: Fetal and child health amidst violent civil conflict.* Sheffield Economics Research Papers Series 2011018.

Victora, C. G., de Onis, M., Hallal, P. C., Blössner, M., & Shrimpton. R. 2010. Worldwide timing of growth faltering: Revisiting implications for interventions. *Pediatrics, 125*(3), 473–480.

Yusuf, M. (2014). *Pakistan's counterterrorism challenge.* Washington, DC: Georgetown University Press.

CHAPTER TEN

Education and Socioeconomic Development of FATA: Challenges and Opportunities

DR. SAJID ALI

Associate Professor, Institute for Educational Development
Aga Khan University, Karachi

Introduction

This chapter is written in an exploratory mode to determine the possible role that education can play in the development of FATA. The exploration is timely as FATA moves to a new trajectory within the socio-political space of Pakistan. The chapter does not merely take an empirical look at the possibilities that education offers for economic development; it also delves into the theoretical connections between education and socioeconomic development, particularly citing modernization and human capital theory, recognizing human development theory. In this chapter, I explore whether education can contribute to the socioeconomic development of FATA and, if so, what contribution can it make and what value people of FATA place on education. I then examine the current education status of FATA and suggest the improvements that are needed in the education system so that it can fully contribute to socioeconomic development of the region. It is the contention of this chapter that if systemic conditions are not improved, and the quality of education provided is not enhanced, the expectations from education to improve the conditions of people of FATA may be dashed. However, with quality education provisions and due diligence to other critical developmental dimensions, the FATA could become one of the most prosperous regions of Pakistan.

Can Education Contribute to the Socioeconomic Development of FATA?

To respond to this question thoroughly, we need to look at the connections between education and socioeconomic development in at least two ways—theoretically and empirically. Theoretically, the link between education and socioeconomic development connects with the modernization theory and the theory of human capital. The Modernization Theory, in its classic sense, relies upon the work of social thinkers like Marx, Weber, and Durkheim, and later, social scientists of the 20th century such as Sociologist Talcott Parsons and Economist W. W. Rostow (Webster, 1984). Essentially, the modernization theory argues that societies evolve from traditional to modern through various stages of development. This change from traditional to modern is symbolized by a change in family structure, mode of economic activity, political organization, and religious preferences. Most modernization theorists have kept the Western nations as ideals and have drawn development lessons from there to be applied to the so-called Third World or—as is now the more fashionable term—"Developing Countries." The modernization theory places central importance on the economic conditions that carry the majority of the responsibility for growth and development, and that subsequently triggers changes in other domains of social life. However, the most important change that precedes any movement toward modernization is the change in people's attitudes. Generally, people express dissatisfaction with the current state of affairs and desire for betterment and feel ready to make an effort toward that goal. The Economic Take-off Theory by W. W. Rostow explicitly outlines the stages of economic growth and the conditions visible in each of those stages. He labels these stages as (1) traditional society, (2) preconditions for take-off, (3) take-off, (4) drive to maturity, and (5) age of high mass consumption (Rostow, 2004). For the sake of this chapter, we refer to this theory as a reference. We believe that this is critiqued and may not be applicable in all situations. Nevertheless, it is important that it remains inspirational for many societies.

The other theory that informs the discussion of the socioeconomic development of any society is the theory of human capital. The Theory of Human Capital focuses on socioeconomic development within society. This theory suggests that, just as financial capital is necessary for fiscal growth, human capital is also essential for development. As such, growth does not just come through the investment of financial capital in industry, trade, and economic services, but also through the refined human capabilities that effectively and efficiently put these financial resources to use. Thus, investment in the education and lifelong learning of a nation should not merely be seen as a service that a nation-state provides to its citizens but is an investment that results in long-term economic growth for the whole nation.

U.S. Economists Theodore Schultz (1961) and Gary Becker (1964) are credited with promoting this theory, which gained significant credibility during the 1960s and 1970s (Woodhall, 1997: 219). The Human Capital Theory was further worked out by Mahboobul Haq and Amartya Sen. They argued that not only do we need to focus on the economic development of the citizens but also their development as human beings. What a person earns is important, but this is not enough to make him/her a fully participating citizen free of poverty and difficult conditions. A holistic understanding of human development considers that individuals should have a good quality of life, free of social, political, and economic pressures (Haq, 1998; Sen, 1999). The Human Development Theory is complementary to the Human Capital Theory. The human development theory thus furthers the human capital theory by bringing in a holistic development perspective beyond only economic growth.

Thus the two theories—human capital and modernization—in combination argue that socioeconomic growth is not simply the growth in the economy but is part of a complex process of modernization whereby social, economic, political, and religious are all intertwined and sometimes work in different directions. Moreover, education can contribute to this modernization process through building human capability that is essentially needed to spearhead the socioeconomic growth and overall development.

Let us now turn to empirical considerations, i.e., whether education contributes to the socioeconomic growth in reality or not. Psacharopoulos (1973 and 1981, cited in Woodhall, 1997: 220–221) has demonstrated, based on the data of 44 countries, that education has a high rate of return, both at the private and social level, for all the countries that were studied, particularly at the primary level and for countries that are less developed. For Asia, Woodhall calculated a private rate of return of 32% at primary, 17% at secondary, and 19% at higher education levels. The social rate of return for primary, secondary, and higher education was calculated to be 16%, 12%, and 11%, respectively. Woodhall (1997) argues that research on human capital has shown that "education affects attitudes, motivation, and other personal characteristics, as well as providing knowledge and skills" (222), which together increase the productivity of educated human resources for the person and society at large.

Ashton and Sung (1997) analyzed the contrasting role that education played in the economic growth of the United Kingdom and Singapore. While the U.K. had a very loose link of education with the economy in the earlier stages due to its unique social, economic and political environment, Singapore had a very explicit connection between education and economy from the outset. The government of Singapore deliberately linked its education development to industrial and economic priorities. The authors identified distinctive periods of economic development in Singapore and showed how education and workplace training was designed to serve their economic vision. Even in the U.K., when the economy needed highly skilled, knowledgeable workers, the link between education and economy was direct. The Singaporean case demonstrates that education contributes directly to the socioeconomic growth of a country. It also shows that education and the economy are embedded within particular social and political fabric. Without the alignment of all of these aspects, education alone cannot guarantee economic success.

Coming to the Pakistani context, the connection between education and economic development is checkered, to say the least. The country has a history of developing grand 5-year plans and national visionary documents but has produced very little in terms of actual achievements. The literacy rate has shown an upward trend, but at a very slow pace. Unlike Singapore, the vision of the Pakistani Government, as stated in the policy documents and as practiced in actual work, appears quite different. There is much rhetoric about providing free access to quality education, but in reality, education itself has become divisive and class-based. Instead of being used for socioeconomic development, it has become an instrument of solidifying social and economic division (Alif Ailaan and SAHE, 2016; Rahman, 2004). The PSLM 2013–2014 shows that enrollment to private schools increases as you go higher in terms of income quintiles, indicating a preference for private schooling for richer people. And as you go down the income quintile, the enrollment of richer children in government schools decreases (Pakistan Federal Bureau of Statistics, 2014). The report by Alif Ailaan and SAHE (2016) poignantly titled their research as *"Who Gets the Good Jobs? Educational Experiences That Result in Economic and Social Mobility"* to highlight the income inequalities based on schooling and the type of education one receives. Although education does indeed contribute to the economic well-being of people in Pakistan, the returns depend highly on the quality of education one receives.

In the Pakistani context, are there any positive empirical examples where education has contributed to socioeconomic development? One example worth pondering is from the region, Gilgit Baltistan (GB). Gilgit Baltistan shares many features with FATA because it, too, is a federal administration with a problematic constitutional status, harsh geography, and a high degree of religious tensions. Looking at the development of GB over the past 20 years, we see a gradual upward shift. The *Aga Khan Rural Support Programme* (AKRSP) played a catalytic role in the rural and economic development of the region, but it placed a strong emphasis on educational development. Benz (2013) shows that while the net enrollment ra   from 42% to 66% during 1998 and 2005–2006, this increased from 51% to 83% for Gilgit-Baltistan, a growth of 32% (see Table 10.1 below).

Not only is Gilgit Baltistan showing great progress in its enrollment, but it has also shown qualitative improvements in the quality of life of the people of

Table 10.1. Primary Net Enrollment Rate of Pakistan. Source: Benz (2013).

Primary Net Enrollment Rate	1998	2005–2006	Difference
Pakistan	42%	66%	24%
Punjab	44%	68%	24%
Sindh	41%	67%	26%
Khyber Pakhtunkhwa	39%	66%	27%
Balochistan	36%	40%	04%
Azad Jammu and Kashmir	45%	57%	12%
Gilgit Baltistan	51%	83%	32%

GB. As per the Annual Status of Education Report (ASER), the GB students are amongst the highest achievers on the ASER test (ASER, 2015). The GB seems to be at a very important juncture due to the China-Pakistan Economic Corridor (CPEC) project. Given its now highly educated population, GB can fully exploit the economic opportunities that are being offered by this project. Time will tell whether this becomes a truly comparable example or not, but even at present, it has useful lessons that apply to the FATA as well.

In sum, the global, international, and even initial examples show that education can contribute to the socioeconomic development of FATA. However, education must work alongside other social, political, and cultural dimensions to bear the full fruit of its benefit. It is also clear that different quality of education results in different life opportunities.

What Can Education Contribute to the Socioeconomic Development of FATA?

Although education shows promising prospects for the socioeconomic development of FATA, it cannot do it on its own. It is dependent upon the available economic opportunities, the political will of the government, governance structure, and availability of basic services to the population. In general, education is one part of the overall system, and will only be able to deliver positive results if the system functions efficiently and equitably. In addition to these factors, FATA uniquely needs a peaceful environment within which the system can function. The military operations in FATA have brought peace and stability in the tribal areas but at the heavy cost of lives lost, infrastructural damage, and population displacement. Despite this destruction, there is a strong desire by political and military leadership as well as by its people to move toward stability and development. The Centre for FATA Studies at the Peshawar University has shown, through a series of conferences and publications, the sociopolitical currents that are shaping not only the past but future of FATA. Within these currents, there is a massive opportunity for economic growth. This is an opportune time for the people of FATA, which should be seized in order to uplift the region; of course, education plays a fundamental role in this development ambition.

Undoubtedly, the people of FATA place a high priority on education. A survey carried out by the Community Appraisal and Motivation Program (CAMP) provides some useful insights about the priorities of the people of FATA. The survey traces the change in people's attitudes between the years 2008–2011. The following lines elaborate on the peculiar findings of the survey showing FATA's priorities concerning education.

If we look at Tables 10.2 and 10.3, it is quite visible that education is a high priority for parents of FATA, particularly for family's male children. If we read further in the tables, one can argue that parents are more concerned about the security of their female children than their male children; however, in terms of employment, their expectations of male child's employment are higher than females. Due to these differing expectations, there is a higher priority for male children's education compared with females. Nevertheless, parents want an education for their children.

Table 10.2. Want for a Male Child by FATA Parents. Source: Shinwari (2012), CAMP Survey.

Wants	2008 (%)	2011 (%)
Education	70	62
Security	9	8
Employment	21	19
Marriage	0.3	3
Religious Education	N/A	6

Table 10.3. Want for a Female Child by FATA Parents. Source: Shinwari (2012), CAMP Survey.

Wants	2008 (%)	2011 (%)
Education	37	27
Security	53	14
Employment	2	3
Marriage	8	15
Religious Education	0.2	23
Purdah	0.1	14

Table 10.4. Services That Government Should Provide to Residents of FATA. Source: Shinwari (2012), CAMP Survey.

Services	2008 (%)	2011 (%)
Security	37	45
Justice	73	21
Policing	11	7
Education / Schooling	65	45
Health / Hospital	52	40
Water and Sanitation	42	26
Roads	36	23
Tackling Terrorism	48	28
Food Supply	28	4
Electricity Supply	49	45
Employment	N/A	41

This priority for education is also reflected in the parental demand for other public services that they require from the government. In Table 10.4, educational services are clearly prioritized by the people of FATA over the years. There may be some fluctuations in how strongly they want it depending on various external factors, but it is certainly among the top services that the people of FATA expect from the government.

The survey considers a lack of education to be one of the biggest problems that people of FATA face. This section can safely conclude that people of FATA have a high demand for education, and they consider it amongst a top priority for their children. It is also fair to say that they link educational attainment with employability. Their expectations of education for their male children are higher when compared with their female peers, which attest to prevalent cultural values which see males as "breadwinners." Nevertheless, education is amongst the top services that people of FATA consider essential for their future development.

Current Education Status of FATA

It is also important for us to take note of the existing educational situation in FATA to pragmatically work out the starting points from where the future attainment can be measured. If we look at the basic education data from the FATA Education Secretariat, this is predominantly composed of government schools with very few private schools and *Deeni Madaris* (see Table 10.5). Consequently,

Table 10.5. FATA Education Statistics. Source: FATA Education Secretariat, Annual School Census 2013–2014.

	Schools	Teachers	Enrollment
Government	5,686	19,720[a]	600,967
Private	369	4,707	154,067
Deeni Madaris	409	1,963	83,442

Table 10.6. "In and Out" of School Children in FATA. Source: ASER, various years.

			% Children In Different Types of Schools			% Out-of-School		
				Non-State Provider				
Year	Age Group	Govt.	Private	Madrasah	Other	Never Enrolled	Drop-Out	Total
2015	6–16	60.4	15.1	3.7	0.3	16.1	4.4	100
	Total	79.5				20.5		100
2014	6–16	51.1	25.9	2.2	0.4	15.5	4.9	100
	Total	79.6				20.4		100
2013	6–16	58	17.9	2.3	0.5	16.6	4.8	100
	Total	78.6				21.4		100
2012	6–16	55.9	17.5	1.3	0.1	21.5	3.8	100
	Total	74.8				25.3		100

the number of teachers and enrolled students in the government sector is higher compared with the private sector and *madaris*.

The survey by ASER shows a much more nuanced picture of FATA education statistics for both inside schools and out of school children. Table 10.6 shows that, despite significant numbers of children who are out of school, the yearly trend is positive as it shows a gradual decline in those numbers over the years.

If we compare the FATA with other provinces and regions of Pakistan, the picture is dismal. Alif Ailaan issued rankings and considered FATA almost at the bottom in 2014 and 2015 with a slight improvement in 2016 (see Table 10.7).

What is even more interesting is the ranking of the various agencies and frontier regions that form the FATA. The following table (Table 10.8) presents comparative scores for enrollment, achievement, and gender parity. This table shows the disparities amongst FATA's regions. Any attempt to improve education in FATA should develop a different strategy that takes note of these differences.

Being in the school and having high enrollments and being high on district ranking is all good, but the fundamental determinant of any education system is the learning achievement of its students. In this regard, the survey

Table 10.7. Provincial and National Education Scores of FATA. Source: Alif Ailan (2016); there are a total of eight regions, so the 8th rank is at the bottom.

Year	Educational Score	Achievement Score	Attainment Score	Rank
2014	47.3	31.83	48.0	8
2015	55.52	67.63	46.7	8
2016	54.05	62.1	50.8	7

Table 10.8. Educational Index-District Ranking. Source: Alif Ailaan (2016).

	Educational Index-District Ranking			
Rank	District	Enrollment Score	Achievement Score	Gender Parity Score
1	Bajaur Agency	65.69	61.1	68.08
2	Mohmand Agency	65.69	51.8	65.76
3	FR Peshawar	74.15	21.63	70.52
4	FR Bannu	50.08	21.50	86.40
5	Orakzai Agency	72.76	57.97	54.64
6	FR Tank	71.71	6.23	69.65
7	Khyber Agency	72.36	39.47	44.55
8	FR Lakki Marwat	44.72	21.1	71.99
9	FR DI Khan	32.52	19.33	60.99
The agencies below are not ranked due to insufficient data				
–	North Waristan Agency	–	–	91.20
–	South Waristan Agency	–	–	62.88
–	Kurram Agency	–	–	73.36
–	FR Kohat	–	–	33.85

by ASER reveals interesting statistics showing the achievement of primary children in the subject of English, the local language, and Mathematics (see Tables 10.9–10.11).

The overall learning results are not very encouraging across subjects, and they oscillate between years. It should also be noted that the achievement scores of private school children are relatively higher than those of government schools. However, even on an absolute scale, both public and private schools' results are not satisfactory. Please note that the majority of the schools in FATA are government, and therefore, the majority of the students do not attain suitable learning targets. This observation suggests that not only is getting children into schools important, but the provision of quality education is also essential.

Table 10.9. Learning Levels of FATA's Students (English). Source: ASER (2016).

	Learning Levels (English)					
	Government			Private		
Year	Can Read At Least Small Letter	Can Read At Least Words	Can Read At Least Sentence	Can Read At Least Small Letter	Can Read At Least Words	Can Read At Least Sentence
2015	38	54	45	62	76	57
2014	52	49	42	68	74	55
2013	39	47	20	67	70	54
2012	43	51	40	70	76	73

Table 10.10. Learning Levels of FATA's Students (Urdu/Pashto). Source: ASER (2016).

	Learning Levels—Urdu/Pashto					
	Government			Private		
Year	Can Read the Alphabet	Can Read Sentences	Can Read Stories	Can Read the Alphabet	Can Read Sentences	Can Read Stories
2015	74	41	52	87	58	57
2014	86	39	42	93	56	54
2013	72	31	24	92	54	49
2012	74	38	38	93	55	64

Table 10.11. Learning Levels of FATA's Students (Arithmetic). Source: ASER (2016).

	Learning Levels—Arithmetic					
	Government			Private		
Year	Can Recognize Numbers	Can do Subtraction	Can do Division	Can Recognize Numbers	Can do Subtraction	Can do Division
2015	46	48	52	65	74	60
2014	55	43	43	71	68	63
2013	44	41	32	66	61	54
2012	46	40	35	69	61	59

What Improvements Are Needed in the Education System to Contribute to the Socioeconomic Development of FATA?

Thus, far, this chapter has tried to show that education plays a critical role in the socioeconomic development of any country. Strong theoretical arguments are championed by the Theory of Modernization and Human Capital as well as bolstered by the Human Capability Theory. These theoretical arguments are further supported by empirical evidence across nations to show that years of schooling directly affect the productivity of citizens. The research carried out in Pakistan also shows that educational attainment is an important determinant of later success. However, a recent research study carried out by Alif Ailaan and SAHE (2016) complicates this assertion by demonstrating that the chances of getting good jobs by graduates depend heavily on the quality of education and type of schooling one receives.

We then considered the priorities of the people of FATA through a survey carried out by CAMP, where they overwhelmingly desired education for their children and considered it amongst the top services that the government should provide. In order to see the existing status of education, we looked at various statistics by the governmental and nongovernmental sources. However, in terms of overall system performance, FATA is ranked at the bottom of various Pakistani regions. The ASER survey, which shows the achievement scores of primary students, also shows that although the performance of private school students is better than government, the overall attainment is quite low. It also shows that approximately 20% of children are still out of school and need to be enrolled.

Based on these understandings, the following steps are proposed to improve the education system of FATA. We already know that the quality of schooling one receives determines the life opportunities for children. Hence, not only do we need children in school, but we also need to provide quality education to them. The students who achieve better can work diligently for the overall upliftment of FATA in terms of social and economic prospects.

1. *Educational Provisions Need To Be Improved*: There are 5,686 government schools and another 369 private schools in FATA, but they fail to enroll all children. There are still approximately 20.5% of children who are out of school. In order to get these children into school, new schools need to be constructed, particularly for girls who are culturally restricted to go long distances. Increasing the number of schools also means recruiting additional

teachers and the provision of other linked resources. The children who have missed the chance to learn how to read and write need to be engaged in some kind of literacy program to improve their functional literacy.

2. *Facilities For Basic Education Should Be Improved*: A conducive learning environment attracts children to school. Unfortunately, many of our educational facilities are not well kept, which repels students. The drop-out rate of 4.4%, as noted by ASER (Table 10.6), is caused by, amongst other elements, the dismal condition of the educational facilities at school. In extreme weather conditions, the learning environment needs to be made more hospitable and inviting for children.

3. *Teachers' Pedagogical Improvement*: The teacher-student ratio in government and private schools is similar (Table 10.5), in fact, slightly higher for private schools. However, the achievement of children in English, Urdu/Pashto, and Mathematics (Tables 10.9–10.11) was better in private schools than the government schools. Research, conducted both internationally and nationally, shows that teachers' pedagogical practices make a huge difference in children's learning (Ali and Rizvi, 2007; Barrett et al., 2007; Lampert, 2003; Webb, 2005). It is also important to note that a low-quality education may not take students far enough (Alif Ailaan and SAHE, 2016). Hence, it is critically important that students in FATA should be able to access good quality education. This will only be possible if children are taught by skillful teachers, who are properly qualified, well paid, and rewarded for better outcomes. The system of recruitment of such teachers and their continuous professional development is essential for this.

4. *Curriculum Aligned to the Local Needs:* Since the passing of the 18th Constitutional Amendment, the making of the curriculum was delegated to the provinces. The Khyber Pakhtunkhwa (KP) Government is taking practical steps to lead curriculum development at the provincial level and include local priorities and languages in the curriculum. To truly take advantage of this opportunity, FATA's Education Department should involve teachers and curriculum and textbook specialists to devise curriculum as per local needs. It is important to note that teachers' capacity to achieve curricular objectives is the most significant resource in the classroom, more important than the textbook itself. Thus, effective teachers and localized curriculum is the need of time for FATA. It is also essential that the curriculum in public and private schools remain consistent to avoid inequities generated and sustained throughout the education system.

5. *Education to Be Linked to Employment Opportunities in the Region*: Table 10.2 shows that, along with education, parents of FATA want

employment opportunities for their children, particularly for male students. This expectation needs to be seriously tackled. Secondary and post-secondary programs in FATA should focus on developing both technical and professional skills amongst its students. Although traditional vocational training is important, skills desirable in the 21st century need to be inculcated at the school level, which include leadership, teamwork, critical thinking, and problem-solving, among others. Such an education will have an explicit connection with the job market and is desirable both by parents and the education system.

Conclusion

This chapter sought to respond to several questions pertaining to education and socioeconomic development in FATA. I tried to explore whether education, in general, is linked with socioeconomic development and, if so, what contributions can education make toward the socioeconomic development of FATA. It was found that education does have a strong link with development in general, at both the theoretical and empirical levels. The recent research by Alif Ailaan and SAHE also confirms this assertion. They also add that higher quality education provided by high-end private or government schools make significant contributions toward job opportunities for students once they graduate. Thus, although education can create opportunities, it can also become a source of division, particularly when educational provisions are not equitable, which is the current case in Pakistan.

I then looked at the current education status of FATA, and what expectations people of FATA hold toward education. Although the education status in terms of provision and attainment is quite low, the people of FATA are very keen on obtaining a quality education. As the chapter comes to a close, suggestions are made with the proviso that increasing the *quality* of education would make the most significant contributions toward FATA's socioeconomic development. Recommendations are made to explain what improvements need to be made in the existing education system in various educational domains to improve the quality of education in FATA. A brief example shared in the chapter of GB provides us hope that education could be the key factor for FATA's future. This area is at a historical crossroads where it is experiencing political shifts that bring in high hopes for the future. Making the right kinds of interventions in the provision and quality of education in FATA will help this region reap the benefits of changing political and economic conditions around it.

Bibliography

ASER-Pakistan 2014. (2015). *Annual Status of Education Report 2012*. Lahore: South Asian Forum for Educational Development.

ASER-Pakistan 2015. (2016). *Annual Status of Education Report 2012*. Lahore: South Asian Forum for Educational Development.

Ali, S., and Rizvi, M. (Eds.). (2007). *Quality in Education: Teaching and Leadership in Challenging Times*. Proceedings of the International Conference. Karachi: Aga Khan University, Institute for Educational Development.

Alif Ailaan, and SAHE. (2016). *Who Gets the Good Jobs? Educational Experiences that Result in Economic and Social Mobility*. Islamabad: Alif Ailaan.

Alif Ailaan, and SDPI. (2016). *Alif Ailaan Pakistan District Education Rankings 2016*. Islamabad: Alif Ailaan.

Ashton, D. N., and Sung, J. (1997). Education, Skill Formation, and Economic Development: The Singaporean Approach. In A. H. Halsey, H. Lauder, P. Brown, and A. S. Wells (Eds.), *Education: Culture, Economy, and Society* (pp. 207–218). Oxford: Oxford University Press.

Barrett, A., Ali, S., Clegg, J., Hinostroza, J. E., Lowe, J., Nikel, J., and Yu, G. (2007). *Initiatives to Improve the Quality of Teaching and Learning: A Review of Recent Literature*. Bristol: A Research Programme Consortium on Implementing Education Quality in Low Income Countries (EdQual).

Becker, G. (1964). *Human Capital*. New York: Columbia University Press.

Benz, A. (2013). Education and Development in the Karakorum: Educational Expansion and its Impacts in Gilgit-Baltistan, Pakistan. *Erdkunde*, 67(2), 123–136.

Education Management Information System (EMIS). (2014). *FATA Statistical Profile of Deeni Madaris 2013–14*. Directorate of Education FATA.

Education Management Information System (EMIS). (2014a). *Annual Statistical Report 2013–14 of Government Educational Institutions*. Directorate of Education FATA.

Education Management Information System (EMIS). (2014b). *Statistical Report 2013–14 of Private Institutes in FATA*. Directorate of Education FATA.

Haq, M. (1998). *Education for Human Development in South Asia*. Karachi: Oxford University Press.

Lampert, M. (2003). *Teaching the Whole Class: Teaching Problems and the Problems of Teaching*. London: Yale University Press.

Pakistan Federal Bureau of Statistics. (2014). *Pakistan Social and Living Measurement Survey (2013–14) - PSLM 2013–14*. Islamabad: Government of Pakistan, Statistics Division.

Rahman, T. (2004). *Denizens of Alien Worlds: A Study of Education, Inequality and Polarization in Pakistan*. Karachi: Oxford University Press.

Rostow, W. W. (2004). The Five Stages of Growth. In M. A. Seligson and J. T. Passe-Smith (Eds.), *Development and Underdevelopment*. New Dehli: Viva Books.

Schultz, T. W. (1961). Investment in Human Capital. *The American Economic Review*, 51(1), 1–17.

Sen, A. (1999). *Development as Freedom*. Oxford: Oxford University Press.

Shinwari, N. A. (2012). *Understanding FATA: Attitudes Towards Governance, Religion & Society in Pakistan's Federally Administered Tribal Areas* (Vol. V). Islamabad: Community Appraisal & Motivation Programme (CAMP).

Webb, R. (2005). Leading Teaching and Learning in the Primary School. *Educational Management Administration & Leadership*, 33(1), 69–91.

Webster, A. (1984). *Introduction to the Sociology of Development*. London: Macmillan.

Woodhall, M. (1997). Education, Skill Formation, and Economic Development: The Singaporean Approach. In A. H. Halsey, H. Lauder, P. Brown, and A. S. Wells (Eds.), *Education: Culture, Economy, and Society* (pp. 219–223). Oxford: Oxford University Press.

CHAPTER ELEVEN

Economic Development in the FATA and Impediments to Progress

AMINA KHAN
Senior Research Fellow, Institute of Strategic Studies, Islamabad

Introduction

Since times immemorial, the areas that now constitute the Federally Administered Tribal Areas (FATA) of Pakistan have been a region of great strategic, economic and political importance. For this, the FATA has captured the attention of the region as well as the international community at large. Located next to Pakistan's Khyber Pakhtunkhwa province on one side and straddling along the Pak-Afghan border in the west, FATA is home to a predominantly Pashtun population of around 3.18 million people.[1] The FATA covers an area of 27,220 sq. km, and consists of seven administrative areas which are referred to as *Agencies* (Bajaur, Mohmand, Khyber, Orakzai, Kurram, North and South Waziristan), as well as six smaller settled districts known as Frontier Regions (FRs) (Bannu, Dera Ismail Khan, Kohat, Lakki Marwat, Peshawar and Tank).

The FATA is a direct legacy of the British Empire in that the laws that continue to govern the state's dealings with FATA are vestiges of those enacted by the British Raj in 1901. Even after the creation of Pakistan in 1947 (and subsequent departure of the British), FATA continues to operate under a reminiscent social, economic, political, and legal system of administration. Except for a few minor amendments, Islamabad exercises much of the outdated British model of administration. They have even retained the Frontier Crimes Regulation (FCR). Despite nearly 70 years of Pakistani independence, the people of the FATA are still subjected to outdated laws. Ultimately, this excludes them from any hope of involvement in democratic processes, fundamental human rights, or economic opportunities, which they would otherwise have increased access to if they were integrated with the rest of Pakistan.

Under Article 1 of the Constitution of the Islamic Republic of Pakistan, the FATA is designated as a "special area" and is included among the territories of the country.[2] The Constitution stipulates that the President of Pakistan is the chief executive for FATA, and hence directly responsible for the tribal areas. As is evident from its name—the Federally Administered Tribal Areas—FATA exists under the direct administration of the Federal Government, which is also responsible for the region's finances and resources.[3] Despite the FATA's "special" status in the Constitution, it is amongst Pakistan's most neglected, underdeveloped, and impoverished regions. The region has witnessed unprecedented turmoil and instability. Today, only 17% of the overall population is literate.[4] The FATA has the highest poverty rate, where three out of every four persons (73.7%) are impoverished, and almost 60% of the population live below the poverty line.[5]

Although the FATA is rich in natural resources and possesses a wealth of untapped resources, economic development has failed to take place. With limited means for economic activity and alternatives to earn a living, a large part of the population is dependent on subsistence agriculture, livestock rearing, or the transport sector.[6] However, there is a considerable gap between current productivity outputs and the region's *potential* agriculture output. Only 7% of the total geographic area of FATA is cultivated, with another 1% recorded as fallow, accounting for roughly half of all potentially cultivable land.[7] Almost 50% of the labor force is employed in unskilled jobs, due to limited skilled job opportunities.[8]

Although the FATA is situated along a vital transit route for trade, it has not been able to reap the economic benefits from its strategic position. With limited livelihood options, many have resorted to illicit trade mainly with Afghanistan through smuggling (of consumer goods, arms, drugs, timber, marble, minerals, gems, etcetera).[9]

Historically, FATA's development has been under-funded, slow, and ineffective. One exception was a brief period of institutional stability, which happened under the political leadership of Zulfiqar Ali Bhutto (1971–1977) of the Pakistan People's Party (PPP). In this, they not only successfully extended the Federal Government's authority to the FATA through the 1973 Constitution but also established the FATA Development Corporation (FATADC).[10] Bhutto played an instrumental role by focusing on development and economic reforms. He initiated the construction of schools, colleges, hospitals, industrial units, and road networks. Since then, development in the FATA, if at all, has been carried out in an unsuccessful compartmentalized manner. Namely, this has entailed hyper-focusing on specific segments within FATA's society while ignoring larger segments of the population. Despite numerous pledges of development and integration, the FATA has consistently been treated as an issue of secondary importance. While FATA's existing structure of governance has often been blamed for the lack of development in FATA, the fact is that FATA's lack of development is chiefly due to neglect and lack of interest on the part of all successive governments. For development to take place, the FATA's current political and administrative structure does not necessarily need to be replaced; rather, it can be modified and developed into a solid and effective system. Neglect, combined with a lack of political will and legislative support, has left the region politically, economically, and socially weak. The tragedy of FATA has been that, despite numerous promises of reform and development, the area remains mostly neglected by those in power. By failing to integrate FATA into mainstream Pakistan, the state is responsible for the current unrest and lawless nature of the area that has made it a perfect breeding ground for extremist elements.

Half-Hearted Reforms

Projects implemented have never directly benefited the local population. This has resulted in the economic empowerment and social uplift of certain sections, chiefly benefiting the local elites, while the larger section of the society continues to live in poverty. Even those projects that have been implemented failed to achieve the much-needed impact on the ground, while others have not been sustained. It is certainly no surprise that the "development indicators" for the FATA lag far behind those of the rest of Pakistan.[11]

FATA's current state of affairs is undermined by both internal and external factors. Poor planning and skewed development priorities coupled with outdated administrative arrangements amplify the destabilizing effects of regional conflicts (such as those in neighboring in Afghanistan). As a result, FATA's condition is defined by rampant poverty and dismally low literacy rates. Inability and reluctance on the part of Islamabad to acknowledge FATA as a significant and integral part of Pakistan that needs to be integrated have resulted in FATA falling into the hands of terrorist groups such as the *Tehreek-e Taliban* Pakistan (TTP). The TTP sought refuge in the FATA because there was little or no state authority to curb their activities. To a large extent, poverty has made the masses in FATA vulnerable to illicit means and extremist tendencies. The TTP capitalized on the prevailing circumstances of poverty, illiteracy, state neglect, and institutional isolation in the FATA, and used widespread desperation to their advantage. As the TTP gained support from the masses, they established parallel government institutions. Traditionally, transit trade with Afghanistan has been (and continues to be) a major source of employment for masses living on the Pak-Afghan border. Since few laws providing for the regulation of economic activity have been extended to the tribal areas, the economy operates on an informal basis and is undocumented (Ali, 2003). However, in the absence of viable means for economic activity and alternatives to earn a living, the masses have resorted to illicit trade, mainly with Afghanistan through smuggling of consumer goods, arms, drugs, etcetera.

In the recent past, many have resorted to extremist ideologies by joining militant groups. As mentioned, one of the most prominent of these is the TTP. They preyed upon the desperation of the masses by providing them with much-needed economic benefits and incentives. Apart from giving hefty salaries to foot soldiers, the TTP also captured emerald and coal mines and re-distributed the seized land.[12] In return, the masses welcomed them with open arms.[13] Over the past decade, security has been a major impediment to FATA's development. However, with growing regional challenges, security can no longer be allowed to paralyze the future of the FATA nor its development. Militant groups need to be denied safe havens. For this to be possible, integrating FATA with mainstream Pakistan is an essential requisite. Development in the FATA can only take place once the status of FATA is determined and changed from a "special area"—"tribal" to an integral part of Pakistan. Only then can the area come into the national mainstream and be politically, economically, socially, and judicially at par with the rest of Pakistan.

While the battle against the TTP is an ongoing struggle (as is the continuing military operations), infrastructural development must be emphasized despite these challenges. Already, communications networks and electronic media are present and accessible in most areas of FATA. Thus, development (such as building schools, roads, and hospitals) needs to be achieved in a phased manner by focusing initially on those more stable regions that have been cleared by the military's ongoing operations. Integration is the only viable option for the future of FATA.

The FATA's Economic Potential

There is much debate about the FATA's potential in terms of natural resources, and the exact quantity of minerals found in FATA. According to official sources, FATA is rich in natural resources and has enormous reserves of minerals (marble, granite, copper, and gold), oil, and natural gas.[14,15] Optimizing these industries could certainly enhance the FATA's economic activity, but this is not to say that mineral extraction has not already been tapped into. For example, there is significant marble mining potential in all the seven agencies, with an annual potential of more than two million tons of marble.[16] The most productive output comes from the Mohmand, Bajaur, and Khyber Agencies, where more than 7,000 million tons of good quality marble have been excavated.

Similarly, the demand for soapstone, which is mined in the Mohmand Agency, has significantly increased because it is used both locally and exported to Europe.[17] In North Waziristan, an estimated reserve of 35 million tons of copper has been identified, with confirmed reserves of 8 million tons.[18,19] While small-scale coal mining is already taking place in various parts of the FATA, significant deposits of high-quality, and untouched coal have also been discovered in North Waziristan, Kurram, Orakzai as well as in Kohat.[20]

It has also been revealed via the geological, seismic surveys carried out in certain parts of FATA that an estimated 20 trillion cubic feet of gas may be explored.[21] According to figures from the Directorate, between the years 2001–2002 and 2005–2006, the overall volume of mineral production has increased from 0.55 to 2.40 million tons, leading to a rise in royalty revenues from 8.8 million rupees to 61.5 million.

Another area with growth potential is the presence of precious and semi-precious gemstones in the FATA. While studies have identified the occurrence/presence of emerald, tourmaline, garnet, and quartz, these reserves have not been properly identified or explored. Hence, despite the potential, the gemstone sector in FATA has not reached its true potential as an industry.[22,23]

Although industries do exist in the FATA, industrial activity has been limited to small, self-financed units, typically operating without government oversight. Currently, 1,082 industrial units are unregulated by the government. These units are operating in the private sector (predominantly stone processing, textile weaving, firearms manufacture, and cooking oil). However, due to poor infrastructure, and the dearth of skilled labor, these industries have not been able to generate significant economic activity. Thus, the FATA remains at a comparative disadvantage compared to the industrial output in the rest of the country.[24]

Impediments to Progress

Although the FATA has immense economic potential, surrounding circumstances continue to prevent the growth and progress of the area as well as its people. While the battle against the TTP is an ongoing struggle (as are continuing military operations), infrastructural development must be emphasized. In FATA's case, this means that integration with mainstream Pakistan is all the more imperative. In this regard, the recently announced FATA reforms package by the government is highly appreciated and a much-needed step in the right direction. If implemented in its true spirit, not only will the FATA merge successfully with the Khyber Pakhtunkhwa province, but the future trajectory of FATA will change for the better. For this, the government has approved an allocation of Rs110 billion for the FATA.[25] The FATA reforms have proposed that a 10-year comprehensive development plan be formulated. Ideally, the plan should envisage large scale infrastructure and irrigation projects, as well as establish industrial zones and mineral development initiatives.[26]

Additionally, the Accelerated Development Strategy (ADS) of FATA was created to assist the FATA Secretariat with development and investments. Keeping in mind FATA's unique state of affairs and the complex power structures at play, the ADS program provides a comprehensive development strategy and investment plan. For the next 10 years, it will not only highlight investment needs but also the modes of investment that would best suit FATA. It is a program tailored specifically for the FATA. The ADS program also delves into the implementation mechanisms by spelling out the specific requirements for conducting institutional development and capacity-building demands.

The Way Forward

It is imperative that key reforms be implemented in the Tribal Areas as soon as possible. In this regard, the newly announced FATA reform package is highly welcomed and a much-needed step in the right direction. Given security concerns prevalent in the FATA, one cannot expect sustainable development to be implemented throughout FATA in one go, hence phased reform is the need of the hour, and focus should be laid on relatively stable areas first.

The FATA is possibly going through the most critical point in its history—the ultimate test for FATA is social and economic development. However, this cannot be achieved unless and until its status in the Constitution is determined. The essential prerequisite for any change in the FATA begins with a change in the status of FATA from a "special area" to an integral part of Pakistan, in FATA's case, through its merger with the province of Khyber Pakhtunkhwa. By becoming a part of the mainstream, issues that have been challenging the area for decades (such as poverty, illiteracy, militancy) will be given greater priority. Through its merger, the FATA will not only be dependent on the government, but it will attract much-needed private enterprises and investments which has been lacking in FATA due to the security situation as well as FATA's location.

Agriculture, for instance, is a pillar of the tribal economy. Two-thirds of the population relies on agriculture and its sub-sectors. However, agricultural performance in the FATA has withered over the years due to several challenges and constraints.[27] Therefore, the government should focus on developing the agriculture sector. For example, better access to water can be developed by upgrading irrigation systems already in place. Similarly, livestock rearing, another essential part of FATA's household economy, also possesses significant growth potential.

Likewise, fish farming, although practiced mainly at the household level, and mostly on wasteland and marginal lands, is an important sub-sector. Fish farming has seen immense success in the Kurram and Khyber Agencies. While fish hatcheries do exist, because fish farming is mainly done on private farms, were the government to invest in this promising sector, this industry has a huge potential for growth.

The private sector should be encouraged to invest in the social and economic development of the FATA. Private enterprises and investments in infrastructure, education, health, and small-scale industry should be both encouraged and supported. Financial aid from the "West" can also play a decisive role in helping develop the FATA into a stable and peaceful area. Investing in FATA's natural resources, such as coal, is one area that will attract private investments and could also be encouraged. Although industrializing this region is no easy task, it is not only possible but quite achievable. In this regard, the government should encourage the U.S. to establish the much talked about reconstruction opportunity zones in the tribal areas and also allocate resources for socioeconomic uplift from grassroots movements.

Conclusion

With a booming population, limited capital resources, and innumerable domestic and external challenges, one must be aware of the constraints that a developing country like Pakistan faces when dealing with a complex area like the FATA. In itself, the region presents undoubtedly a complicated issue. Even so, it is the sole responsibility of the state to consolidate its territory and look after its people. This is something that Pakistan has not done. Half-hearted policies have not worked; they have ignited resentment. Mismanagement has warranted the doubt that lingers in the minds of the masses against the state. If it wants to become a consolidated state, Pakistan needs to grow out of its dependence on colonial structures of governance and mindset and adopt a holistic and pragmatic approach. The Federally Administered Tribal Areas cannot be isolated anymore, nor can its people be neglected as they have been in the past. Bringing reforms and development to the FATA lie within the ambit and purview of the government and decision-makers of the country. Hence, pledges made by the current government for changing the status of FATA and bringing reforms and development to FATA must be seen through and implemented in letter and spirit. If the reform process is inconsistent or is abandoned midway, as has been the case in the past, it could lead to the complete breakdown of the FATA. It is sincerely hoped that these promises of reform are followed through rather than buried beneath issues deemed 'more immediate and significant' as has been the norm with the FATA.

Notes

1. Irimia, R., & Gottschling, M. (2016). Taxonomic Revision of Rochefortia Sw. (Ehretiaceae, Boraginales). *Biodiversity Data Journal 4*: E7720. https://doi.org/10.3897/BDJ.4.e7720, doi:10.3897/bdj.4.e7720.figure2f.
2. "The Constitution of Pakistan," accessed May 15, 2019, http://www.pakistani.org/pakistan/constitution/
3. The Constitution of Pakistan, Part XII: Chapter 3, Tribal Areas (Articles 246–247). Article 145 of the 1973 Constitution of Pakistan authorizes Governor NWFP to take charge of the area as an Agent to the President of Pakistan.
4. FATA Sustainable Development Plan 2007–2015, Peshawar: Civil Secretariat FATA Peshawar.
5. Raza Ahmad. (2011). Towards State-Building in FATA. *Social Science and Policy Bulletin 2*, no. 4. https://lums.edu.pk/sites/default/files/research-publication/sspb-vol2-no4-spring2011.pdf
6. Hasaan Khawar. (2017). Bringing prosperity to FATA, *Express Tribune*, April 5, 2017.
7. FATA Sustainable Development Plan 2007–2015, Civil Secretariat FATA Peshawar. http://urban.unhabitat.org.pk/Portals/0/Portal_Contents/FATA/Landi%20Kotal/FATA%20Sustainable%20Dev%20Plan%202007-2015.pdf
8. Hasaan Khawar. (2017). Bringing prosperity to FATA, *Express Tribune*, April 5. Ibid.
9. Amina Khan. (2014). FATA: Voice of the Unheard–Path-Dependency and Why History Matters. *Strategic Studies Journal*, http://issi.org.pk/wp-content/uploads/2014/06/1315805584_65172321.pdf
10. See Note 7.
11. Isambard Wilkinson Ashfaq Yusufzai in Mingora, "Taliban Jihad against West Funded by Emeralds from Pakistan," *The Telegraph*, April 04, 2009, accessed May 15, 2019, http://www.telegraph.co.uk/news/worldnews/asia/pakistan/5106526/Taliban-jihad-against-West-funded-by-emeralds-from-Pakistan.html
12. Mona Sheikh. (2016). *Guardians of GOD, Inside the Religious Mind of the Pakistani Taliban*. New Delhi: Oxford University Press.
13. Azhar Khan. (2013). *Sustainable Utilization of Natural Resources of the Khyber Pakhtunkhwa and FATA*. Mineral Wing, Ministry of Petroleum and Natural Resources, http://nceg.uop.edu.pk/GeologicalBulletin/Vol-Special-2013/Abstract15.pdf
14. "FATA, FR Regions Abundant in Oil, Gas, Says Report," *The Express Tribune*, December 26, 2012, accessed May 15, 2019, https://tribune.com.pk/story/484440/new-hope-springs-fata-fr-regions-abundant-in-oil-gas-says-report/
15. Razi Syed. (2016). Marble Mining, Excavation Activities Better in FATA, Mohmand Agency. *Daily Times*, September 16.
16. Ibid.
17. "Fata Has Vast Gas Reserves, Suggest Surveys," December 22, 2016.

18 "North Waziristan Is Rich in Unexploited Mineral Wealth," *The News*, March 14, 2014.
19 Ibid; FATA Sustainable Development Plan 2007–2015, Peshawar: Civil Secretariat FATA Peshawar.
20 Ibid; "Fata Has Vast Gas Reserves, Suggest Surveys," December 22, 2016.
21 Fata.gov, https://fata.gov.pk/Global-fac.php?iId=389&fid=53&pId=341&mId=199
22 Ibid; FATA Sustainable Development Plan 2007–2015, Peshawar: Civil Secretariat FATA Peshawar.
23 Ibid.
24 Syed Irfan. (2017). "Cabinet Approves Steps for Fata's Merger with Khyber Pakhtunkhwa," March 3.
25 "FATA Reforms Approved by Federal Cabinet," *The Nation*, March 2, 2017.
26 Agriculture Policy for FATA, Policy Period [of] Ten Years (2014–2024), October 14, 2014, Retrieved from https://fata.gov.pk/cp/uploads/downloads/14147536475453480a016a4.pdf
27 Ibid.

Bibliography

Ahmad, Raza. (2011). Towards State-Building in FATA. *Social Science and Policy Bulletin* 2, no. 4. https://lums.edu.pk/sites/default/files/research-publication/sspb-vol2-no4-spring2011.pdf.
Ashfaq Yusufzai in Mingora, and Isambard Wilkinson. (2009, April 4). Taliban Jihad against West Funded by Emeralds from Pakistan. *The Telegraph*, accessed May 15, 2019. http://www.telegraph.co.uk/news/worldnews/asia/pakistan/5106526/Taliban-jihad-against-West-funded-by-emeralds-from-Pakistan.html .
"Fata Has Vast Gas Reserves, Suggest Surveys." December 22, 2016.
"FATA Reforms Approved by Federal Cabinet." *The Nation*, March 2, 2017.
FATA Secretariat and the Food and Agriculture Organization of the United Nations. (2014). *Agriculture Policy for FATA, Policy Period Ten Years (2014–2024)*. October 14. https://fata.gov.pk/cp/uploads/downloads/14147536475453480a016a4.pdf.
FATA Sustainable Development Plan 2007–2015. Peshawar: Civil Secretariat FATA Peshawar. http://urban.unhabitat.org.pk/Portals/0/Portal_Contents/FATA/LandiKotal/FATA Sustainable Dev Plan 2007-2015.pdf
Figure 2f From: Irimia, R. and Gottschling, M. (2016). Taxonomic Revision of *Rochefortia Sw.* (Ehretiaceae, Boraginales). *Biodiversity Data Journal* 4: E7720. https://doi.org/10.3897/BDJ.4.e7720; doi:10.3897/bdj.4.e7720.figure2f.
Irfan, Syed. (2017). "Cabinet Approves Steps for Fata's Merger with Khyber Pakhtunkhwa." March 3.
Khan, Amina. (2014). FATA: Voice of the Unheard—Path-Dependency and Why History Matters. *Strategic Studies Journal*. http://issi.org.pk/wp-content/uploads/2014/06/1315805584_65172321.pdf .
Khan, Azhar. (2013). *Sustainable Utilization of Natural Resources of the Khyber Pakhtunkhwa and FATA*. Mineral Wing, Ministry of Petroleum and Natural Resources. http://nceg.uop.edu.pk/GeologicalBulletin/Vol-Special-2013/Abstract15.pdf .
"North Waziristan Is Rich in Unexploited Mineral Wealth." *The News*, March 14, 2014.
Sheikh, Mona. (2016). *Guardians of GOD, Inside the Religious Mind of the Pakistani Taliban*. New Delhi: Oxford University Press.

Syed, Razi. (2016). Marble Mining, Excavation Activities Better in FATA, Mohmand Agency. *Daily Times*, September 16.

"The Constitution of Pakistan," accessed May 15, 2019. http://www.pakistani.org/pakistan/constitution/.

Tribune.com.pk. (2012, December 26). FATA, FR Regions Abundant in Oil, Gas, Says Report. *The Express Tribune*, accessed May 15, 2019, https://tribune.com.pk/story/484440/new-hope-springs-fata-fr-regions-abundant-in-oil-gas-says-report/.

*Food and Agriculture Organization of the United Nations

CHAPTER TWELVE

Assessing the Potential for Food Self-Sufficiency on Fragmented Farms in FATA

DR. SHAHNAZ AKHTAR
Institute of Development Studies (IDS),
University of Agriculture, Peshawar

SHER AYAZ
Government Degree College, Mir Ali,
North Waziristan Tribal District

DR. MUHAMMAD SABIR AFRIDI
NUST Business School, National University of Sciences and Technology, Islamabad, Pakistan

Introduction

The Federally Administrative Tribal Areas (FATA) stretches over a mountainous area of 27,220 km^2 and is mainly hilly and mountainous with about 7–8% of isolated pockets of arable land. It has an extreme climate where the temperature ranges from 40°C to freezing zero in winter with infrequent rainfall of 1,300 mm per year (Government of Pakistan, 2014–2018). The 1998 census reported the total population of FATA as 3.176 million. However, current projections indicate that the population grew to about 4.674 million in 2015–2016 (FATA Development Indicators Household Survey (FDIHS) 2013–14). The population density is 172 persons per km^2 (varying from 26 persons per km^2 to 624 persons per km2 in the F.R. Dera Ismail Khan and Bajaur Agencies, respectively). More than 97%

of the population lives in rural areas; the remaining 2.7% of the population has settled in urban areas (Government of Pakistan, 2014–2018).

The postural economy of FATA mainly depends on subsistent agriculture for a livelihood since manufacturing and trading offer limited opportunities for its growing population. Livestock and farming serve as both assets and sources of income for almost 90% of households. They rear livestock to fulfill their meat and dairy needs. On average, FATA's per capita income is about $663, whereas the national level sits at about $1,200. Although FATA's per capita income is higher than that of Khyber Pakhtunkhwa (KP), both areas fall far short of the national average of $1,560 (Government of Pakistan, 2016). In recent years, income inequality has increased to as much as 60% of the population; this demographic lives below the national poverty line of $12 per month (FATA Sustainable Development Plan, 2007–2015). Agricultural dependence seems to be no more than a default option for FATA people quarantined in adverse geography and low underdeveloped resource base. Hence, maintaining food security and food self-sufficiency is a fundamental reason for depending on agriculture. The absence of either may further deprive FATA that already lags on all indicators from the rest of the KP province and the country.

A blend of the importance for food self-sufficiency, optimized land utilization, and the existing law and order situation motivates assessing the production abilities of small, dispersed parcels of land in the FATA area. This study uses survey data uniquely to address similar issues present in three villages of the North Waziristan Agency. These issues can conveniently (in terms of conducting the study) be generalized to the rest of the FATA region due to their similar geo-economic conditions. This study enjoys exclusive pride for being first of its kind in the empirical analyses from the most backward no-go areas of Pakistan that are not only inaccessible to the mainstream scholars to acquire real field data, especially during a period when the North Waziristan remained confined for the general public. With food security and land use issues being in the core of the daily struggle for these residents, the main goal of this study was to identify factors affecting maize yield in the study area.

The following section presents a literature survey distinguishing *Food Security* and *Self-Sufficiency*. This is followed by reviews related to the subject matter. Section 3 delineates details about the survey methodology, such as the variables, their parameters, and the strategies used to analyze the data. This section also includes descriptive statistics and econometric models used in the analysis. Moving forward, the next section presents an estimation of the econometric models and discussion of these findings. Section 5 concludes the paper by providing policy recommendations.

Literature Review

The terms *Food Security* and *Food Self-Sufficiency* are used as synonyms generally; however, subject matter specialists differentiate between these two terms interchangeably. Food security depends on three essential elements: availability, access, and utilization. *Food Availability* is the overall food supply obtained domestically or by imports. *Access* refers to the household's purchasing power to acquire food, and *utilization* is the way food is transformed into energy, affecting human beings' activities and health. It gains further importance, especially for regions having scarce arable lands, adverse topography, and underdeveloped means of alternative livelihood. Increasing food security from local production has remained a challenge for such regions where demand for food is on the rise and large-scale, mechanized agriculture is impractical (Roussin et al., 2015).

On the other hand, *Food Self-Sufficiency* is a component of food security referring to the share of effective demand that is fulfilled by domestic production (Staatz, 1991) and is measured by the self-sufficiency ratio (SSR; as in the share of domestic production in total domestic use, net of stock changes). In other words, this means that as a function of output per unit of input (all other variables held constant), food self-sufficiency is within reach as about "one-half a hectare of farmland is needed to produce food for a person per year with the existing state of technologies" (B.C. Ministry of Agriculture and Lands 2006).

A self-sustaining region can fulfill its needs from the local production rather than relying on imports (Minot and Pelijor, 2010). It declares local production as the ultimate supply, while food security allows imports and food aid to be incorporated in total stock.

The literature on food self-sufficiency has regionally identified various factors that affect yield: parcel size and fragmentation, mechanization and seed technology, irrigation, input-output markets, fertilizer, and pesticide usage. Although this diverse set of factors are all at play, this study's core objective is to assess the effects of parcel fragmentation on yields in FATA. The following review orbits mainly around the land use issues, such as parcel size and fragmentation.

Landholding is assumed to be a single parcel without any accessibility issues. Studies conducted by Berry and Cline (1979), Ellis (1989), Ram et al., (1999), and Van Dijk (2003) differentiate between *Land Parcel* and *Landholding*. 'Landholding' identifies an ownership unit. In contrast, the 'Land Parcel' is a unit operated by a single farmer. The scholarly discussion on the inverse relationship between parcel size and its productivity was started by Schultz (1964), and has been sustained by many researchers.

Land fragmentation is the situation of operating on more than one disjoining, scattered plot. This phenomenon is widely considered *unfavorable* for agricultural productivity due to inefficient resource allocation and dis-economies of scale, increased costs of transportation, increased number of disputes, general inconvenience, and wasted time. Particularly, in South Asia, land consolidation programs exist mainly to reverse hurdles for farmers seeking to increase their per unit output, decreasing per every unit of land fragmented.

Empirical research studying the consequence of fragmentation on farm productivity does not seem to be in agreement with Schultz's (1964) thesis of inverse relation, which provides a unique opportunity of availing a variety of soil, crop rotation at different ecological zones, activity intermix by managing labor shortages and failure risks on multiple plots. Moreover, most studies analyzed the impact of the land's 'holding size' rather than the 'parcel size,' although there is often a positive correlation with parcel size (Nguyen et al., 1996). Therefore, the impacts of land parcel fragmentation should be analyzed, particularly in the South Asian region, where fragmentation is steadily underway (Niroula and Thapa, 2005).

The research during the last century was focused mainly on input use efficiency and productivity. While differentiating high productivity from high efficiency, empirical research rarely addresses land-use issues like land conversion, fragmentation, or the effects of investment programs on land productivity and profitability (Clay, Guizlo, and Wallace, 1994; Niroula and Thapa, 2005). Niroula and Thapa (2005) also assessed the effects of land fragmentation on resource use efficiency and farmers' income, concluding that small plots were more productive and efficient than large farms in South Asia where the farm size is gradually on the decline. In the pioneering work studying the relationship between fragmentation and land productivity in Ghana, Blarel et al. (1992) appraised whether fragmentation was inefficient and non-productive. Rejecting the null hypothesis, they found that fragmentation was caused by inefficiencies in land size, labor, credit, and food markets.

Jha, Nagarajan, and Prasanna (2005) measured these effects on productivity in India using a panel dataset from landholding households. They measured the degree of technical efficiency and related it to the degree of land fragmentation. Their findings showed that the technical efficiency of farm production *was* significantly related to farm size yield and that this yield was affected by the degree of fragmentation, significantly and adversely. In other words, the higher the fragmentation, the lower the productivity.

Conversely, Patrik, and Andersson (2006) examined the scope for a fragmented land consolidation program and found weak but positive correlations between fragmentation and productivity. According to them, this was caused by excessive use of fertilizers and labor on small farms. Thus, they advocated for the non-consolidation of fragmented plots. Rahman and Rahman (2008) came up with a more realistic two-layer analysis technique, finding that this relationship was positive in technologically-advanced regions, whereas the typical inverse relationship still exists in backward areas.

Monchuk, Deininger, and Nagarajan (2010) addressed the prospects and problems of land consolidation in India. They were guided by the question: Does land fragmentation reduce efficiency? According to them, "while certain measures of land fragmentation show its adverse effects on production, in economic terms, these impacts were somewhat small." Their work also explored a second research question: Will further efforts to reduce fragmentation produce a net societal gain? To this end, they concluded that "the accounts of land consolidation programs in India appeared to be costly in terms of time and hindered by a number of adverse sections and agent/agency problems." Although conceptually benefiting, it was recommended to assess the cost of consolidation programs in future studies.

Austin and colleagues (2012) calculated the effect of land fragmentation on arable crop productivity using Cobb-Douglas (CD) and the Generalized Linear Model (GLM) in Abia State, Nigeria. The range of land fragmentation was quantified by the *Januszewski Index*. It found a negative correlation between land fragmentation and agricultural productivity. In contrast, 'labor' was seen as the single most important factor for increasing crop yields. Cooperative farming was considered an enabling factor in improving farm productivity by adopting new technologies.

Sauer, Davidova, and Gorton (2012) criticized the notion that "economics of fragmentation presumes a homogeneous technology to measure the effects of fragmentation." Rather, they emphasized that, because the units of analysis are small, then it is even more crucial to account for heterogeneity amongst 'poor households' as a unit. Using the *Latent Class Frontier Method* and estimating allocation efficiency changes, their results show different levels of efficiency, and the proxies for land fragmentation and market integration have also shown different signs over these classes.

Identifying pathways for improving household food self-sufficiency (FSS), Karki et al. (2015) explored many factors such as land fragmentation, challenging landscape, short labor availability, and low technical knowledge in the case of Nepal. Their statistical model proved a correlation between *agronomic strategies* and the adoption of improved crop cultivars after realizing the ineffectiveness of changes in plot size through a series of development schemes. The study-highlighted methods focusing on agricultural intensification to improve crop yields and effectively transfer technology to increase the adoption of these methods, alternatively.

The effects of land fragmentation in a land distribution scheme in Sri Lanka reviewed by Wickramaarachchi and Weerahewa (2016) found that the size of land parcels paired with positive and significant effects. In contrast, the greater the number of plots and the wider their distance produced a significant, but negative effect on productivity. Therefore, they proposed to increase the parcel size and to decrease fragmentation in Sri Lanka, to improve land productivity of the land distribution policies.

Abubakari et al. (2016) explored the feasibility of land consolidation within the local tenure by comparing the conditions highlighted in the literature. Their study revealed similarities such as the state of land fragmentation, topographic and soil conditions, and differences with respect to the local conditions. However, conditions such as the existence of a land bank, technical expertise, and infrastructure, and supportive legal frameworks were partially met. The remaining conditions, such as the willingness to take part in the study, as well as the ready availability of a land information database system and favorable land ownership structure, were non-existent. The circumstances of these unmet conditions are deeply embedded in customs and traditions that hardly yield to change. Since these conditions are fundamental for land consolidation, their absence negates the feasibility of land consolidation under the current tenure system of the study areas.

It will be worth saying that all studies do not strictly agree to these verdicts, in terms of the time frame and on regional variations. There have been endeavors, with varying methodologies and results, quantifying the impacts of land fragmentation on crop yields, production efficiencies, and on the causes of fragmentation, as well (Blarel et al., 1992; Clay et al., 1994; Niroula and Thapa, 2005, 2007).

In the wake of the events, an empirical investigation was conducted on small-sized, dispersed, and fragmented farms in the North Waziristan Agency to observe the farmers' persuasion and progression in crop productivity by managing multiple risks confronted to them.

Data Sources

This study is based on a set of primary data. The data was collected from three villages—Mussaki, Hassukhel, and Tappi—all in North Waziristan. It is important to mention that the data was collected between 2013 and 2014; this was precisely when the law and order situation in this region had been adverse due to roads that were blocked for normal traffic and commuting. In the absence of any agriculture extension workers, senior villagers helped in selecting 50 farmers on a random basis, from each village. The selected farmers were informed about the objectives of the study and investigations. The data were collected through field survey interviews and a structured questionnaire (see Annexure I). The data were collected via completed questioners, and then the questioner's data were transferred to the computer. Statistical Package for Social Sciences (SPSS) was used to analyze the data. The descriptive statistics for all variables of the study are shown below in Table 12.1.

Table 12.1. Descriptive Statistics of Output and Input Used in the Study Area

	Yield (40 kg per acre)	Farm Size (in acres)	Seed (kgs. per acre)	Irrigation (no. of times)	Farm Segments	Fertilizer (kgs. per acre)	Tractor Hours
Mean	23.05	3.36	29.49	3.71	3.57	28.36	2.73
Median	23.00	3.00	30.00	4.00	3.00	28.00	3.00
Std. Deviation	1.647	1.341	1.034	0.894	1.43	0.788	0.672
Minimum	19	1	27	2	1	26	2
Maximum	27	7	33	6	8	30	4

Wheat, maize, fodders, vegetables, fruits, especially citrus, are the main agriculture products in FATA. The data collection was initiated at the plantation time of the maize crop, while some autumn vegetables and fodder for animals were also being planted for local use. Other than crops, many livestock types have also been highly effective in addressing household demand for food. The average and median yield values are about 23 mounds (i.e., 1200 kg) per acre in the study villages. The yield value per acre ranges between 19 and 27 kg., which represents a mixed effect of both local and hybrid seeds (that was experimented on almost 30% of the selected farms).

Research Methodology

The main objective of this study was to empirically examine the effect of pouch farming on per acre yield of consumable crops, ultimately, to generalize the outcome toward food self-sufficiency in FATA. Concurrently, this study also aimed to determine the effects of factors like the new seed on farms yield. A survey-based approach was adopted following a convenient method of data collection in all villages. A multiple regression model was employed (Equation 1) to find the effects of the factors, such as land parcel size, parcel fragments, seed variety and quantity, irrigation, fertilizer, and tractor hours on maize yield. We used SPSS software for data management and analysis.

$$Yield = \alpha 0 + \alpha 1\ FSize + \alpha 2\ FFragmen + \alpha 3\ SVariaties + \alpha 4\ SQuantity + \alpha 5\ Irregation + \alpha 6\ Fertilizer + \alpha 7\ TractorHr \tag{1}$$

Where, *Yield* is producing 40 kg per acre,
FSize is farm size in acres;

FFrqagmen is an abbreviation representing 1 for 0 fragmentation and 0 otherwise;
Svariaties is an abbreviation for seed varieties (i.e., 1 for new variety and 0 otherwise);
SQuantitiy is seed quantity in kg per acre;
Irrigation is the number of watering times;
Fertilizer in kg. per acre; *and*
TractorHr usage in hours, respectively.

The Estimations and Discussion

The results of the linear regression model (Equation 1) are reported in Table 12.2 and Table 12.3. Table 12.2 illustrates what is called an "Analysis of Variance" for the overall model. In general, the model performed well, explaining around 80% of the total variation and the F-statistics (76.48). In statistical terms, this is highly significant.

Table 12.2. ANOVA and Model Fit Information

	Sum of Square	Mean Statistics	F-Statistics
Regression	319.43	45.63	76.48**
Residual	84.72	0.59	
Total	404.15		
R^2 =0.79		Adjusted R^2 = 0.78	
Number of Observations = 150			

** Statistically significant at 1%.

Table 12.3. Regression Results

Variables	Coefficients	Standard Errors	t-values
Farm Size in Acres	0.158**	(0.054)	2.914
Segmentations (Dummy)	-1.123**	(.380)	-2.957
Seed Variety	1.231**	(0.172)	7.174
Seed Quantity	0.155*	(0.064)	2.419
Irrigations	0.685*	(0.092)	7.420
Fertilizer (per acre)	0.310*	(0.095)	3.252
Tractor Hours	0.222	(0.124)	1.783
(Constant)	6.484*	(3.007)	2.157

Note: (1) Dependent variable is Yield (40 kg per acre)
(2) Coefficients with * and ** are statistically significant at 5% and 1%, respectively.

Table 12.3 presents the coefficient values of the explanatory variables of Equation (1). All explanatory variables were found to be statistically significant except for 'tractor hours.' Irrigation has been the most significant factor in enhancing maize yield per acre, followed by fertilizer and seed variety. The coefficients indicate that the yield increased by 0.68, 0.231, and 0.15 mounds for every additional unit of irrigation, fertilizer, and seed variety.

The most interesting result shown in Table 12.3 relates to the relationship between yield per acre and land segmentation. The coefficient of parcel segmentation clearly shows that maize yield per acre decreases for every additional segment relative to the single-parcel farms. The farmers, on average, get 1.23 mounds per acre lower yield from segmented farms compared to a consolidated parcel of land.

Discussion

Maize yield per acre recorded in the area was much lower than the national and provincial average yield. The results vividly reveal that lack of irrigation water is the foremost limiting factor for productivity per acre, given the current state of technology. Although 50% of the farms in the study area were being irrigated by private wells, the remaining depended upon spurious rainfall in natural inundations or suffered from a failed crop, which was then mainly used as pasture. In the study area, the maize crop was being irrigated two to six times, depending on the supply from commercial tube-wells or infrequent rain. Consequently, the nonexistence of irrigation mechanisms and minimal rainfall (as low as 1300 mm/year) were among the farmers' echoing grievances.

The use of the hybrid seed increased production significantly, yielding 1.23 additional kg per acre for its users. Other factors positively affecting maize crops were parcel size (of the cultivated land) and whether the farmer had access to fertilizer. Both resulted in conformity with practice and theoretical underpinnings. The unimpressive effect of tractor hours is justified by small farm size; this was then dispersed further into three to four segments.

Although the study's major objective was *not* to evaluate cost-effectiveness, however, traditionally, the cost components were seeds, tractor hours, irrigation, fertilizer, labor, and transportation, respectively. The average per-acre cost to produce 30 mounds of produce was about Rs. 20,201. Total revenue per acre as estimated Rs. 36120, and the total profit per acre has been Rs. 15,919, approximately. The majority of the farmers in the study were sowing a local variety hybrid seed, which was not only unaffordable but also lacked sowing instructions regarding planting time and other success-building methods.

The supply of chemical fertilizers, pesticides, and the like have been restricted for a long time due to the adverse security circumstances. Thus, the fertilizer application was as low as 26.43 kg. per acre. Those who were able to access fertilizer acquired it from smuggled sources and, therefore, available at a high cost. For similar reasons, the availability of pesticides and weedicides was also limited and inconsistent. Due to the costs and circumstances, farmers were engaged in manual weeding and other labor-intensive techniques of pest management.

Conclusion and Policy Recommendations

This study investigated the relationship between per acre yield and factors affecting maize crops to better assess the potential for food self-sufficiency on fragmented farms in FATA. The project also investigated the cost of production and problems faced by the farmers in enhancing maize production. Survey data was collected from 150 farms in North Waziristan. A *multiple regression model* was applied to quantify the relationship between yield per acre and the factors that affect it. The results indicated that irrigation was the major factor affecting maize per acre yield, followed by fertilizer and seed variety in the area. It is also clear from the findings that fragmented the parcel, lower has been yield per acre, on average.

Irrigation was a major factor affecting per acre yield. Facilitating the installation of tube-wells along with suitable power supply is also highly recommended. One step ahead, the provision of solar tube-wells (and converting the current tube-wells to solar) can adequately improve the irrigation situation. Likewise, where possible, land should be provided with canal access.

This study recommends lifting the ban on fertilizer supply, thus ensuring its availability in local markets with affordable prices for farmers. Farmers would also benefit from the extension services for timely seed availability and pertinent information from the meteorology department to help them in their endeavor. Both resources would help farmers achieve more successful harvests.

Lastly, the existing connectivity of FATA with the rest of the country (or within FATA) is not yet good enough to link farms with their markets and reduce the transportation costs of agricultural products and inputs such as fertilizers and seeds. It is recommended that the government should consider extending the road network. Doing so would increase accessibility to rural areas along with access to minerals and coal resources.

An advanced recommendation would be to start with a land consolidation program to cure ongoing fragmentation by checking its cost-effectiveness and possible success margin. Purely in the interest of the farming community, such a scheme is expected to help with the ineffective land segmentation in FATA.

There are various essential policy implications of the study as most countries that have successfully addressed poverty issues did not directly try to reduce poverty; instead, they were engaged for economic transformation. Thus, a fall in poverty was an indirect result of an increase in productive capacity. Investment rates and capital accumulation in those countries were high and aimed at enterprise development and technological improvement and structural change toward developing the potential non-traditional sectors, including linkages to agriculture and the broader economy.

Given a suitable production environment and hardworking, enthusiastic farmers, the study finds significant potential for producing much more than the current yield for all crops. Addressing the farmers' problems concerning proper seed availability, timely and sufficient irrigation, fertilizer, credit facilities, improved knowledge and information about sowing time and seed quantity, land consolidation scheme, and security issues can help to solve the problem of food-self-sufficiency and food security on one hand, and farmer's prosperity on the other, in FATA.

Annexure-I

QUESTIONNAIRE

FARM FRAGMENTATION AND PRODUCTIVITY IN NORTH WAZIRISTAN AGENCY

1. Information about the Respondent

*Name*_____
*Age*_____
*Village Name*_____
*District*_____
*Farming experience*_____
*Level of Education*_____

2. Land Landownership Characteristics

Owned land	Land type and size		Land rented	Land type and size	
	Type	Area (acres)		Type	Area(acres)
	a. Irrigated			a. Irrigated	
	b. Un–irrigated			b. Un–irrigated	
	Total Owned			Parcel Land	
	a. Rented out				
	b. Rented in				
	Parcel land				

3. Please provide the following information:

1. The maize variety planted
2. Planted Area (in Acres)
3. Total Production (in per 40 KGs)
4. Quantity consumed at home (in per 40 KGs)
5. Quantity marketed (in per 40 KGs)

4. Parcel Size, Fragmentation and location

Size (in acres)	Number of segments	Distance between segments	Distance from market	Distance from residence
< 1				
1 – 3				
3–5				
5<				

5. Source of irrigation

    i. Canal Irrigation
    ii. Tube well
    iii. Others

6. How many, times in a season, you irrigate maize crop

1. Two times
2. Three times
3. Four times
5. Five times

7. From where do you get maize seed?

Sources	Tick
Saved from the last crop	
Bought from local dealers	
Buy from fellow farmers	
Bought from the agricultural Extension office	
Others (please specify)	

8. Please provide the following information about the Input Use in maize

Input/unit	Usage
1. Area (acres)	
2. Quantity of used Seeds (Kg)	
3. Seed cost (in Rs.)	
4. Quantity of Urea applied (Kgs)	
5. Other fertilizers, if applied (kgs.)	
6. Total cost of Fertilizer Rs.	
7. Number of irrigations	
8. Cost paid for irrigation Rs.	
9. Total labor cost	
10. Total cost of land preparation	
11. Total cost of machinery Rs	
12. Total cost of harvesting Rs.	
13. Pesticides cost	
14. Transport cost	
15. other costs	
16. Production (Mounds/Acre)	
17. Market Price per Unit (in Rs.)	

9. Which variety you used and why?

Variety
Reasons

10. Do you prefer to use any modern technology?

    i. Yes
    ii. No

11. If yes, which of the following were used?

Type	Tick (√)
HYVs	
Tractors	
Deep cultivator	
Harvester	
Thresher	
Rotator	
Seeds and spray cultivators	
Others	

12. If no, why?

    1. ....
    2. ....
    3. ....

13. Please give the following information

Training	Yes=1 No=0	Duration (days)	Organization
Seeding			
Land preparation			
Cultivation			
Fertilizer			
Pesticides			
Weeding			
Harvesting			
Production monitoring			

14. Do you leave your land fallow?

    i. *Yes*
    ii. *No*

15. Did you get agricultural credit?

    i. *Yes*

    ii. *No*

17. Source from where you get agriculture credit.

    1. *ZTBL*
    2. *Agriculture office*
    3. *Other*

18. If no why you could not get the loan?

    1. _____
    2. _____
    3. _____

19. Do you practice intercropping in maize cultivation?

    1. *Yes*   *if yes what*_____
    2. *No*

20. Which crop do you cultivate before and after maize?

    1. *Leguminous* ---------------   2. *Non-Leguminous* --------------

Bibliography

Abubakari, Z., Van Der Molen, P., Bennett, R. M., and Kuusaana, E. D. (2016). *Land Consolidation, Customary Lands, and Ghana's Northern Savannah Ecological Zone: An Evaluation of the Possibilities and Pitfalls*. Retrieved February 2017, from http://www.fig.net/resources/monthly_articles/2017/anubakari_etal_februay_2017.asp

Asian Development Bank. (2014). *Project Administration Manual*. Islamic Republic of Pakistan: FATA Water Resources Development Project. Retrieved from, https://www.adb.org/sites/default/files/project-document/151676/47021-002-pam.pdf

Austin, O. C., Ahuchuogu Chijindu, U., and Jamalludin S. (2012). The Link Between Land Fragmentation and Agricultural Productivity. *International Journal of Agriculture and Forestry*, 2(1): 30–34. doi: 10.5923/j.ijaf.20120201.05

Berry, R. A., and Cline, W. R. (1979). *Agrarian Reform and Productivity in Developing Countries*. Baltimore, MD: Johns Hopkins Press.

Blarel et al. (1992, May). The Economics of Farm Fragmentation: Evidence from Ghana and Rwanda. *World Bank Economic Review*, vol. 6 no. 2.

Clay, D. C., Guizlo, M., and Wallace, S. (1994). *Population and Land Degradation.* EPAT/MUCIA Working Paper No. 14. University of Wisconsin, Madison. http://www.wisc.edu/epat/.popenv/.land-deg/.format/.structure.html

Ellis, F. (1989). *Peasant Economics: Farm Households and Agrarian Development.* Cambridge, U.K.: Cambridge University Press.

FATA Development. *Indicators Household Survey (FDIHS) 2013–14.* Planning and Development Department, Bureau of Statistics. FATA Secretariat. Accessed on 15 February 2017, http://govtjobsinpakistan.pk/index.php/fata-development-indicator-household-survey-report-fdihs-2013-14/

FATA Sustainable Development Plan (2007–2015). Civil Secretariat FATA, Peshawar. Accessed on 15 February 2017 at: http://urban.unhabitat.org.pk/Portals/0/Portal_Contents/FATA/Landi%20Kotal/FATA%20Sustainable%20Dev%20Plan%202007-2015.pdf

Government of Pakistan. (2016). *Report of the Committee on FATA Reforms.* Accessed on 15 February 2017, http://202.83.164.29/safron/userfiles1/file/Report%20of%20the%20Committee%20on%20FATA%20Reforms%202016%20final.pdf

Government of Pakistanz. *Comprehensive Multi-Year Plan (2014–2018). Expanded Program on Immunization.* Directorate of Health Services. FATA Civil Secretariat. Accessed on 15 February 2017, http://epi.gov.pk/wp-content/uploads/2014/09/FAT.pdf

Government of Pakistan. (2016). *Pakistan Economic Survey 2015–16.* Finance Division. Accessed on 15 February 2017, http://121.52.153.178:8080/xmlui/handle/123456789/14893

Jha, R., Nagarajan, H. K., and Prasanna, S.. (2005). *Land Fragmentation and Its Implications for Productivity: Evidence from Southern India.* Australia South Asia Research Centre, RSPAS, Division of Economics, Australian National University, Canberra, ACT 0200, Australia ASARC Working Paper 2005/01.

Karki, T. B., Sah, S. K., Thapa, R. B., McDonald, A. J., and Davis, A. S. (2015). Identifying Pathways for Improving Household Food Self-Sufficiency Outcomes in the Hills of Nepal. *PLoS ONE* 10(6): e0127513. doi:10.1371/journal.pone.0127513. Accessed on 3 March 2017, http://journals.plos.org/plosone/article?id=10.1371/journal.pone.0127513

Minot, N., and Pelijor, N. (2010). *Food Security and Food Self-Sufficiency in Bhutan.* Washington, DC: International Food Policy Research Institute. https://www.ifpri.org/publication/food-security-and-food-self-sufficiency-bhutan

Monchuk, D., Deininger, K., and Nagarajan, H. (2010). *Does Land Fragmentation Reduce Efficiency: Micro Evidence from India.* Paper prepared for presentation at the Agricultural & Applied Economics Association 2010 AAEA, CAES, & WAEA Joint Annual Meeting, Denver, Colorado.

Niroula, G. S., and Thapa, G. B. (2007). Impacts of Land Fragmentation on Input Use, Crop Yield and Production Efficiency in the Mountains of Nepal. *Land Degrad. Dev.*, 18: 237–248. doi:10.1002/ldr.771

Niroula, G. S., and Thapa, G. B. (2005). Impacts and Causes of Land Fragmentation, and Lessons Learned From Land Consolidation in South Asia. *Land Use Policy*, 22(4), 358–372. http://doi.org/10.1016/j.landusepol.2004.10.001

Nguyen, T., Cheng, E., and Findly, C. (1996). Land Fragmentation and Farm Productivity in China in 1990s. *China Economic Review* 7(2), 169–180.

Patrik, S., and Anderson, L. (2006). *A Study of the Impacts of Land Fragmentation on Agricultural Productivity in Northern Vietnam.* (Bachelor thesis, Uppsala University).

Rahman, S., and Rahman, M. (2008). Impact of Land Fragmentation and Resource Ownership on Productivity and Efficiency: The Case of Rice Producers in Bangladesh. *Land Use Policy*, 26, 95–103.

Ram, K. A., Tsunekawa, A., Sahad, D. K., and Miyazaki, T. (1999). Sub-division and Fragmentation of Land Holdings and their Implication in Desertification in the Thar Desert. India. *Journal of Arid Environments*, 41, 463–477.

Roussin, R., Wilson, J. E., Ut zig, G., and Lavkulich, L. M. (2015). Assessing the Potential for Pocket Agriculture in Mountainous Regions: A Case Study in West Kootenay, British Columbia, Canada. *Journal of Agriculture, Food Systems, and Community Development*. http://dx.doi.org/10.5304/jafscd.2015.061.016.

Sauer, J., Davidova, S., and Gorton, M. (2012). *Land Fragmentation, Market Integration and Farm Efficiency: Empirical Evidence from Kosovo*. Contributed Paper prepared for presentation at the 86th Annual Conference of the Agricultural Economics Society, University of Warwick, United Kingdom, April 16-18.

Schultz, T. W. (1964). *Transforming Traditional Agriculture*. Chicago, IL: University of Chicago Press, 1983, c1964.

Staatz, J. M. (1991). *Conceptual Issues in Analyzing the Economics of Agricultural and Food Self-Sufficiency*. National and Regional Self-Sufficiency Goals: Implications for International Agriculture. Eds. Fred J. Ruppel, and Earl D. Kellog. Boulder & London: Lynne Reiner Publishers.

Sundqvist, P., and Andersson, L. (2006). *A Study of the Impacts of Land Fragmentation on Agricultural Productivity in Northern Vietnam*. (Unpublished Bachelor thesis, Uppsala University, Sweden).

Thomson, A., and Metz, M. (1998). *Implications of Economic Policy for Food Security: A Training Manual*. Agricultural Policy Support Service Policy Assistance Division. Food and Agricultural Organization of the United Nations and the GTZ, Rome. Accessed on 28th December 2016, http://www.fao.org/docrep/004/x3936e/x3936e00.html

Van Dijk, T. (2003). Scenarios of Central European Land Fragmentation. *Land Use Policy*, 20, 149–158.

Wickramaarachchi, N. C., and Weerahewa, J. (2016). Land Fragmentation and Land Productivity: Empirical Evidence from Land Distribution Schemes of Sri Lanka. *International Academic Research Journal of Business and Management*, 5(1), 11–21.

CHAPTER THIRTEEN

Accelerating Economic Development of Federally Administered Tribal Areas via Improved Transportation and Communication: A Way Forward

DR. MUHAMMAD SABIR AFRIDI
NUST Business School, National University of Sciences and Technology, Islamabad, Pakistan

Introduction

Geographically, the FATA is a massive territory of Pakistan. It lies on the fringes of the approachable Pakistan–Afghanistan border and is recorded as having 27,220 km^2 or 3.4% of Pakistan's region. The FATA region is located northwest of Pakistan bordering Afghanistan. It has seven Agencies and six Frontier Regions, as shown in Figure 13.1. The total population of the FATA is around five million. The area is rich with minerals and coal reserves.

FATA is one of the most underdeveloped regions of Pakistan. Historically, the region has been relegated as a buffer zone between Pakistan and Afghanistan, and the area has been ruled based on British colonial time laws. The area was largely ignored by the government. However, recently after having almost 15 years of extremism and radicalization within Pakistan for which the FATA region was mainly used as a safe haven, the Government of Pakistan finally established a

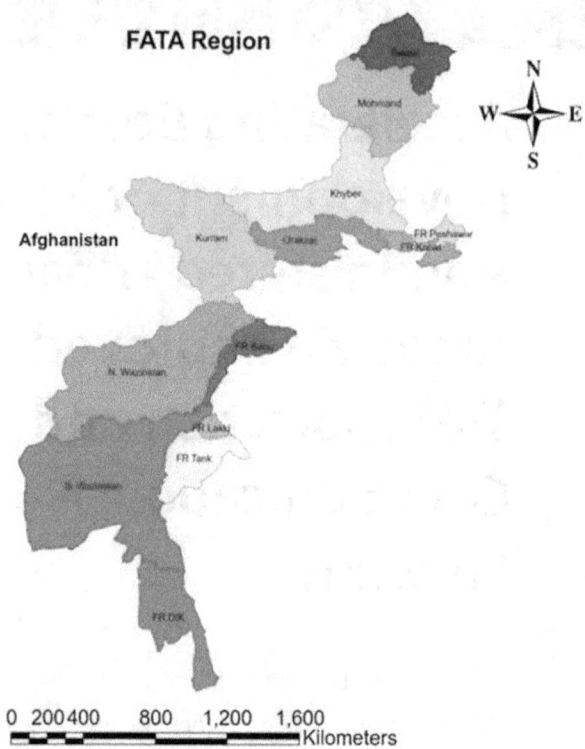

Figure 13.1: Agencies and Frontier regions in FATA.

FATA Reform Committee in 2016 with a mandate to propose various reform options for the future of FATA. Until now, the Reform Committee had not fully completed its consultation with stakeholders nor submitted their report to the government. This report, among others, includes administrative changes for FATA, such as: merging FATA with Khyber Pakhtunkhwa, establishing FATA as a separate province, or giving it a separate special status like Gilgit Baltistan (GB) and Azad Jammu and Kashmir.

Transportation and communication play an undeniable role in economic growth and development. At the national level in Pakistan, development policies lean toward investing in the transportation sector. This is evident in the recent development in motorways constructions, metro bus projects, the China-Pakistan Economic Corridors, and other such projects. However, the situation in the Federally Administrative Tribal Areas (FATA) is one of neglect. This study seeks to fill the missing gap of existing scholarly literature on the most underdeveloped region of Pakistan. The potential impact of transportation and communication on economic growth in the FATA is addressed as well. Lastly, this study proposes a means of intervention in transport and communication that can be helpful for the policymakers addressing the issue.

Literature Review

Transportation is needed for movements of people and freight; it links farmers with markets; connects producers and distributors with customers. Transportation infrastructure is essential for traveling, commuting, enjoying recreational activities, visiting family and friends, and, truly, the freedom of movement. Transportation plays an important part in the economy as well. Goods need to be transported once they are produced and processed so that they may be consumed in diverse locations. Because transportation infrastructure increases production while decreasing travel time, this, in turn, creates a wider range of employment opportunities. It also plays a significant role in reducing regional inequalities between FATA and the main body of Pakistan. It would increase their capacity to be competitive with enterprises existing in the more privileged regions. Improving such infrastructure would enable trade and expand this workforce's access to jobs. The correlation between transport infrastructure and economic development has been the emphasis of increasing examination, debate, and curiosity during the past decades. In a broad sense, as an economy propagates and cultivates, it becomes more dependent upon its transport sector (Robinson and Bamford, 1978).

Dulac (2013) expects that the world will need about 25 million additional kilometers of roads and 335,000 kilometers of rails by 2050 to meet global passenger and freight transportation demand. Accordingly, the estimated cumulative expenditures are about U.S. $45 trillion (0.7% of the global GDP). However, if costs of the upgrades, annual operations and maintenance are also factored in, then these costs might reach up to U.S. $120 trillion by 2050. This sum implies that the infrastructure sector development will gain much more importance in the upcoming years. This includes developing roads, railways, airlines, waterways, and pipelines. Public infrastructure also encompasses access to postal offices, telephone lines, cellular networks, and broadband services, and the like. However, given the scope of this study and topography of the FATA region, the scholarly literature reported herein is confined mainly to road infrastructure. Railways and airlines are discussed to a lesser extent, while waterways and pipelines are ignored because of a limited or lack of infrastructural networks in the FATA.

The connection between transportation infrastructure and economic growth and development has been the focal point of breakdowns, discussions, and interest during the past four decades or so such as: Robinson and Bamford (1978); Mieczkowski (1978); Goodall (1987); Weiss (1999); Felloni, Wahl, and Wandschneider

(1999); Weiss and Figura (2003); Boopen (2006); Fedderke, Perkins, and Luiz (2006); Sahoo and Dash (2012); Ahmed, Abbas, and Ahmed (2013); Beyzatlar, Karacal, and Yetkiner (2014).

According to Mieczkowski (1978), "the transport networks may be compared to the blood flow network in a living organism, without which the organism dies." Transport has always been considered to be a significant aspect of all modern economies. In simple words, as an economy grows and progresses, it becomes more reliant on its transport sector (Goodall, 1987).

Infrastructure and Economic Development

Globally, there is strong evidence indicating that the transport of capital contributes to economic progress. We see this in Sub-Saharan African countries such as Algeria, Kenya, Niger, and Nigeria as well as Small Island Developing States such as Barbados, Cap Verde, Dominican, and Fiji (Boopen, 2006). New road networks reallocate business and industrial activities, reduce the transportation costs and travel time, and link the agricultural minerals and well as natural resources with the market. For instance, Holl (2004b) used microdata for Spanish municipalities between 1980 and 1994, a period when their major road networks were developed. After employing a geographic information system (GIS) analysis, they found that new motorways affected the spatial distribution of manufacturing establishments within these municipalities. New firms moved closer to new infrastructure.

Similarly, in Portugal, studies found that new motorways increased the attractiveness of locations close to the new infrastructure for most of the sectors in Portugal from municipality-level data obtained from 1986 to 1997, a period of significant improvement in Portuguese motorway networks (Holl, 2004a). Wenga et al. (2013) discusses the role of high investment in minerals, iron, and coal industries and then how the construction of roads and railways infrastructure to support these industries further created growth corridors that are now determining the settlement patterns and land use in Africa. These growth corridors linked agricultural productions with the urban markets in African cities that were earlier dependent on imported food. Similar studies looked at changes in the locations of business start-ups and manufacturing plant locations in Portugal (Holl, 2004c).

Investing in road infrastructure generates employment in the form of direct jobs (those building the roads), indirect jobs (employment in industries producing input for road infrastructure such as cement, asphalt, etcetera), and jobs that are created as a result of improved road and communications and overall growth. Schwartz, Andres, and Dragoiu (2009) studied the stimulus plans for

Latin American and Caribbean regions and found that, for U.S. $1 billion investments in infrastructure (transport, water, and energy sector), there will be around 40,000 direct and in-direct job creations in the short-term, keeping all other variables constant. Similar findings were reported regarding Middle Eastern and African countries such as Angola, Cameroon, and Chad (despite the differences across the countries) that a 6% investment of their annual GDP in infrastructure development (transport and energy) can generate about 2.0 million direct, 2.5 million indirect, and infrastructure-related jobs in these countries (Ianchovichina et al., 2013). However, it should be noted that there may be some negative spillover effects from public infrastructure due to moments of input factors from one location to other locations. For instance, Boarnet (1998) used data from California (USA) counties between 1969 and 1988 and found that there exist positive spillovers for street and highway capital within the county, but negative spillovers across distinct counties.

The empirical literature on trade between two regions may be explained by "gravity models." These models state that trade between two regions is inversely proportional to the square of the distance between the two regions when keeping all other variables as constants (Tinbergen, 1962). Improved transportation reduces the distances (travel time, travel costs); thus, it encourages both intra-regional and inter-regional trade. For instance, Akgüngör, Kuştepeli, and Gülcan (2014) explore the relationship between Turkey's highway networks and external trade data with the EU during the period 1970–2008. They confirmed a strong positive correlation between the two variables, both in the long and short run. Storeygard (2016) investigates how transport costs impact the income of Sub-Saharan African cities. Accordingly, when the income of the port cities increases (such as by an increase in oil prices), the elasticity of city economic activity with respect to transport cost is -0.28 for a city 500 kilometers from the port. Therefore, cities that are connected to the port by paved roads are affected less by transport costs compared to cities that are connected by unpaved roads. Limão and Venables (2001) reported that infrastructure is an important determinant of transport costs, particularly for landlocked countries. Accordingly, the elasticity of trade flows for trade transport cost is -3.

Road infrastructure investment is also known to have significant impacts on poverty and income inequalities. For instance, Bakht, Koolwal, and Khandker (2006) studied the impact of rural road investment using household-level panel data from Bangladesh. Their study reported that rural road investment significantly reduces poverty because it influences agricultural production, higher wages, lower input and transportation costs, and higher output prices. This also leads to higher school enrollment. Their study concluded that investing in roads will benefit all economic levels of society. Ahmed, Abbas, and Ahmed (2013) used a dynamic Computable General Equilibrium (CGE) model to study the impact of public infrastructure investment for Pakistan. Their study reveals that public infrastructure investment does have a positive impact on macroeconomic gains, poverty reduction, household consumption, and firms' investments. Transportation infrastructure also contributes to the development of the tourism industry. For instance, Khadaroo and Seetanah (2008), using data from 28 countries, observed bilateral tourism flows between 1990 and 2000, and found that transportation infrastructure is a significant determinant of tourism inflows into a destination.

However, there are additional dimensions of road and infrastructure investment that need to be considered as well. Gachassin, Najman, and Raballand (2015) analyzed the Cameroon National Household Survey and reported that "one-size-fits-all" road investment strategies are irrelevant because the roads are neither systematic nor uniform. The reason is that the impacts of such investment on household well-being through the labor market are not unique but also dependent upon the local characteristics. Beuran, Gachassin, and Raballand (2015) recommended that it would behoove most Sub-Saharan African countries to prioritize investment, better procurement and contract management, and better monitoring to improve the developmental impact of recent road investments. Similarly, Boarnet (1999) debated the gains (for the regions that get the projects) and losses (the regions that pay for it) of highway investments and suggested more decentralized and project-specific highway financing that also includes a role for efficient prices. Ahmed, Abbas, and Ahmed (2013) reported that the public infrastructure investment developed based on internal financing (through taxes, and additional investments in infrastructure) does influence the industrial sector (as it faces major tax burdens) and thus, strains the economic growth in the short run. On the other hand, foreign financing (borrowing) influences the balances with the external sector.

Transportation Infrastructure

The Industrial Revolution of the mid-eighteenth century (around the 1760s) shifted the focus of inland transportation away from animal-pulled wagons, waterways (via canals and rivers), and ships toward trains and railways. This reduced the time needed to traverse vast distances, increased the inland transportation of goods and people, and connected landlocked countries for trade. Inefficiencies occurred in either the high cost of this infrastructure or the travel time in the absence of this infrastructure (Toniolo, 1983). Bignon, Esteves, and Herranz-Loncán (2015) discuss the resources required for the construction of rail infrastructure that depends on government investment. Their empirical studies found that, between 1865 and 1913, all major government revenues in Latin American countries were trade-related. Fremdling (1997) studied the contribution of the German economic growth during 1840–1870 and concluded that the modern German iron industry was due to the railroad's demand for iron products. Tang (2014) studied the relationship between railways and increased firm activity for railroads in Japan in the late nineteenth-century. Tang (2014) reported that firm capitalization increases with increases in rail access. This particularly affected the manufacturing industry. Herranz-Loncán (2011) studied the role of railways in the export-led growth of Uruguay from 1870–1993. He concluded that Uruguay did *not* enjoy the same benefits from railways as other Latin American economies. This was likely due to the small share of railway output in the GDP, its geographical structure, sectoral specializations, and small-scale economy.

Air transport infrastructure and provisions also contribute to a region's economic growth. Marazzo, Scherre, and Fernandes (2010) reported a positive relationship between air transport demand measured by passenger-kilometer and economic growth in Brazil using data from 1966–2006. Chi and Baekb (2013) also reported a positive relationship between air passengers and freight demand with economic growth for the United States. Hakim and Merkert (2016) confirmed a long-run uni-directional relationship between GDP and air transport through data collected for 42 years (1973–2014).

Information and Telecommunication (ICT) Infrastructure

The studies on economic growth and telecommunication infrastructure can be divided into two broad categories. First, studies that are based on country-level data, such as Dholakia and Harlam (1994), Shiu and Pun-Lee (2008). Secondly, studies are based on a regional or global level, such as Dutta (2001) and Lam and Shiu (2010).

The individual-level studies do report mixed results. For instance, Dholakia and Harlam (1994) applied econometric models to state-level statistical data of the United States. They reported that telecommunication had a strong influence on economic development when compared to other inputs such as education, energy, and physical infrastructure. Similarly, Shiu and Pun-Lee (2008) also found that real GDP growth was attributed to telecommunication development in the eastern region of China (which is comparatively more developed); the reverse is true for the western region of China (which is less developed). Shiu and Pun-Lee (2008) also emphasized on the other complementary factors like business environment, transportation infrastructure, education, and human resources training to make the best of national telecommunication infrastructure. The causality debate between telecommunication infrastructure and economic growth is later summarized by Shiu and Pun-Lee (2008) and Tranos (2012).

Global-level studies are also common in the existing body of scholarly literature. For instance, Chavula (2013) explored the impacts of telecommunication expansion with regard to individual living standards in African countries and also its impact on per capita income growth using an endogenous growth model. The study reported a significant impact of telephone, mobile, and internet infrastructure on people's living standards in upper-middle-income citizens of African countries. However, it only reported that mobile phone penetration had a significant impact on growth in both the upper-low-income and low-income African countries. Here, the expansion of mobile technology and infrastructure was the largest among all country groups. Similar findings have been reported by Tranos (2012) on internet infrastructure and regional economic development in Europe's city regions. However, contrary to Shiu and Pun-Lee (2008), Dutta (2001) applied the Granger causality test on telecommunication infrastructure, and economic activity data of fifteen developed and fifteen developing countries (U.S., U.K., Australia, Finland, Italy, Malaysia, Thailand, India, Brazil, and others) from 1970 to 1993. Dutta (2001) found that causality is stronger between telecommunications infrastructure and economic activity than the reverse-causality both for industrialized countries like the U.K., U.S., Australia, and developing countries like Malaysia, Thailand, and India.

The relevant scholarly literature can be summarized in the following bullet points:

I. There is a positive relationship between the development of road infrastructure and economic development; employment generation increases, trade improvements, and industrial re-allocation occur within domestic economies (Arkgüngör, Kuştepeli, and Gülcan, 2014; Goodall, 1987; Holl, 2004a; Mieczkowski, 1978; Robinson and Bamford, 1978; Schwartz, Andres, and Dragoiu, 2009).

II. Roads, railways, and airlines all bear strong links with economic development and growth (Datta, 2012; Fremdling, 1997; Holl, 2004a, 2004b; Marazzo, Scherre, and Fernandes, 2010; Toniolo, 1983; Wenga et al., 2013).

III. Empirical literature (both from developed and developing countries) finds that telecommunication infrastructure plays an important role in the economic development of a region. Where disagreements occur, it is concerning the direction of the causational effects between telecommunication infrastructure and economic growth (e.g., Dutta, 2001 versus Shiu and Pun-Lee, 2008).

Transportation and Communication Infrastructure in the FATA

The total area of FATA is 27,220 km², and it has a total of 7,230 km of road networks showing a road density of 0.26 km² (national road density is 0.33 km²). It should be noted that only 68% of the total road networks in FATA are paved, and the majority of these paved roads are single lane.

Resource Expenditures on Road Infrastructure

Several factors may be linked to the low prevalence of road networks in FATA. Among them, one major reason is the shortage of fund allocations needed to build road infrastructure. From 2013–2016, spending from annual development expenditures of FATA shows that, on average, 22.3% of total annual developmental programs have been spent on infrastructure compared to 27.2% at the federal level during the same period.

Road Infrastructure

The Federally Administered Tribal Areas (FATA) are internally disconnected even though there are many commons among tribes such as shared language, culture, history, and government administrative mechanisms. Currently, no single standard road (highway, motorway, freeway, or paved road) or otherwise internally connects these areas. Travelers within FATA have to travel through the adjoining province of KP. For example, an individual commuting from Khar (Bajaur Agency, the northernmost northern area of FATA) to Torkham (Khyber Agency, which has a border crossing point with Afghanistan) would have to first

Table 13.1. Spending as a Percentage of the Total Annual Developmental Program. Source: Annual Developmental Plans of Pakistan and FATA ADP.

Year	FATA	National
2013–14	22.3%	19.4%
2014–15	24.0%	30.8%
2015–16	20.6%	31.4%
Average	22.3	27.2

travel to Sakhakot and Charsadda and then to Peshawar (all located in KP). This covers about 220 km of distance over about 5 hours (the average speed of travel being 44 km/hr.) before they reach Torkham. A direct link would allow for this passage in a quarter of the length and time. Another issue that arises from the lack of road networks in the region is low government regulation, higher transportation costs of minerals and coal resources (FATA is rich with these resources) to the markets. This situation is worsened by the fact that this population, at the moment, is highly disconnected and uneducated (FATA has the lowest literacy rates in the country). It is far from being integrated with the rest of the country.

Rail Infrastructure

There has been no rail infrastructural development in the FATA since 1947. During the British Rule (before 1947), the Empire built a railway track (Khyber Pass Railway), which connected Peshawar with the Torkham border crossing point into Afghanistan (Khyber Agency). The track was extensively used for travelers and trade. However, in the early-2000s, the track was closed down due to a lack of maintenance and extremism in the Khyber Agency. Today, this link is no longer operational. Presently, the closest working railway track to FATA is the China-Pakistan Economic Corridor (CPEC) between Kalabagh and Mianwali, which taps four railway stations at Mari Indus, Daud Khel, Pai Khel, and Beruli. It stretches 45 km connecting with a touchpoint in Mianwali. With the exception of this track, no railway line exists in FATA, which covers the different localities.

Air Transport

The airports existing in and around FATA are generally non-operational. They are only rarely able to accommodate small-scale ventures. They cannot be used for the massive scale transport of goods or people. Two airports, Zohb and Peshawar, are located in areas neighboring some of FATA's regions, which are operational and are dealing with both civil and military operations. All other airports located either within FATA or nearby are small. When functioning, they can only handle Fokker or ATR planes, but they are typically non-operational. Table 13.2 shows the details about the airports in and around FATA.

Information and Telecommunications

Radio and Television. Currently, FATA does not have a state-owned television structure which can boast of TV stations, towers, or related properties. Rarely,

Table 13.2. Airports in and around FATA

Airport	Location	Current Operational Status
Parachinar	Kurram Agency	Not operational since 2007
Bannu	Bannu	Not operational since 2007
Dera Ismail Khan	D.I. Khan	Operational (only military)
Kohat	Kohat	Operational (only military)
Wana	South Waziristan	Operational (only military)
Zhob	Balochistan	Operational (both civil/military)
Peshawar	KP	Operational (both civil/military)

one might spot a satellite dish. FATA got its first radio network in 2012. The FATA Secretariat fitted radio channel "1" in Khyber and "2" in North Waziristan. The primary A.M. radio station was established to assimilate the individuals of FATA with the rest of the world by keeping them informed about global as well as national and current matters. They sought to endorse healthy and educational content as well. These stations played an important role in notifying the masses about the government's strategies for the FATA. However, later, the stations were shut down due to economic constrictions. The administration plans not only to revive these stations but also to increase the number of stations by including in other agencies of FATA as well.

Landline and Mobile Network. Between 2014 and 2015, there were about 19,733 telephone connections in existence in FATA—with a quantity of 32 people per telephone. The total telephone Exchanges are 52 in number. The majority of cellular facilities are centralized in Khyber. They reach nine locations and are based at seven sites located in the Kurram Agency. The North and South Waziristan Agencies have three and five positions, respectively, all where mobile services are accessible. The Orakzai, Mohmand, and Bajaur Agencies have only two locations where mobile services are accessible. The PTCL covers just one area each in the Bajaur Agency (at Khar) and Mohmand Agency (on the Mohmand Agency Road). There are two zones covered (Kurram and North Waziristan Agency) by infrastructure located in Sadda, Parachinar, and Nizam Bazar, Razmak, respectively. In the Khyber Agency, the areas covered by landline are Landi Kotal, Jamrud, and Bara Road. The Orakzai and South Waziristan Agency do not have any accessible landline services.

Postal Service. Although there are 23,820 postal offices in FATA, seven were destroyed, and only 192 are functioning (Bureau of Statistics, 2015). That means that one post office services every 142 km^2. Due to a lack of data, the exact location where these post offices are located in FATA is uncertain.

Investing in the Future of Transportation and Communications in FATA

Regarding transportation and communications, four aspects of the intervention are vital. These interventions cover adjustments to the institutional framework and financial resource allocations, future transportation and communication project suggestions, and local involvement. These are explained in the following sections.

Institutional Intervention

The Annual Development Plan (ADP) is a mechanism that requires substantial improvements. It is evident that, since 1947, little has changed. Because this region lacks basic transport and communication infrastructure, it remains internally disconnected. FATA desperately needs an institutional intervention that has the capacity to establish procedural mechanisms that determine public spending decisions on economic outcomes rather than based on controlling the region. FATA's reform era will be marked by its merge with the adjacent Khyber Pakhtunkhwa province.

Financial Resource Allocations

Following reforms to the Annual Development Plan itself, fund allocations from ADP for the transport and communications sector development of the FATA should be made deliberately, not by default. Currently, these allocations are not consistent with national policies, as is evident in Table 13.1. There is a need to revisit these policies and increase the share of funds for the transport and communication-related projects within the FATA region. Moving into something of a reform era, it is expected that FATA will be receiving about 3% of its resources from the total divisible pole of resources. Perhaps this is a good time to revisit the existing resource allocation percentages for transport and communications as well as all other sectors and set the priorities for each sector to bring FATA at par with the rest of Pakistan.

Transportation and Communication Proposals

Roads. The proposed motorway shall begin from the Bajaur Agency and end in the Kurram Agency (represented by color in Figure 13.2). This would cover a maximum range of 273.54 km. The motorway would follow a north-south flow and deviate slightly west to accommodate the Orakzai Agency. From the Bajaur Agency, the motorway would unite with the Mohmand Agency via an underpass or tunnel of nearly 1.63 km. This road would continue until the Orakzai Agency and its eventual end in the Kurram Agency. In the Khyber Agency (a factor concerning Ali Masjid), a "flyover" or underpass would join the dual carriageway. This would help manage the flow of traffic of the Peshawar-Torkham Road. At Sadda, Kurram Agency, the proposed motorway would be a part of the existing Parachinar-Wana Highway. Formerly, this highway was constructed by the Federal Government in collaboration with the FATA Secretariat. The bulk of this addition would be beyond the Bajaur Agency running until Wana. It would lie nearly 240 km from the Bajaur Agency and almost 275 km from Parachinar. This would greatly reduce the travel time and would connect all of the agencies internally. In essence, this motorway would act as a central artery, the primary line responsible for transporting people and goods. The result of this circulation would be increased employment opportunities.

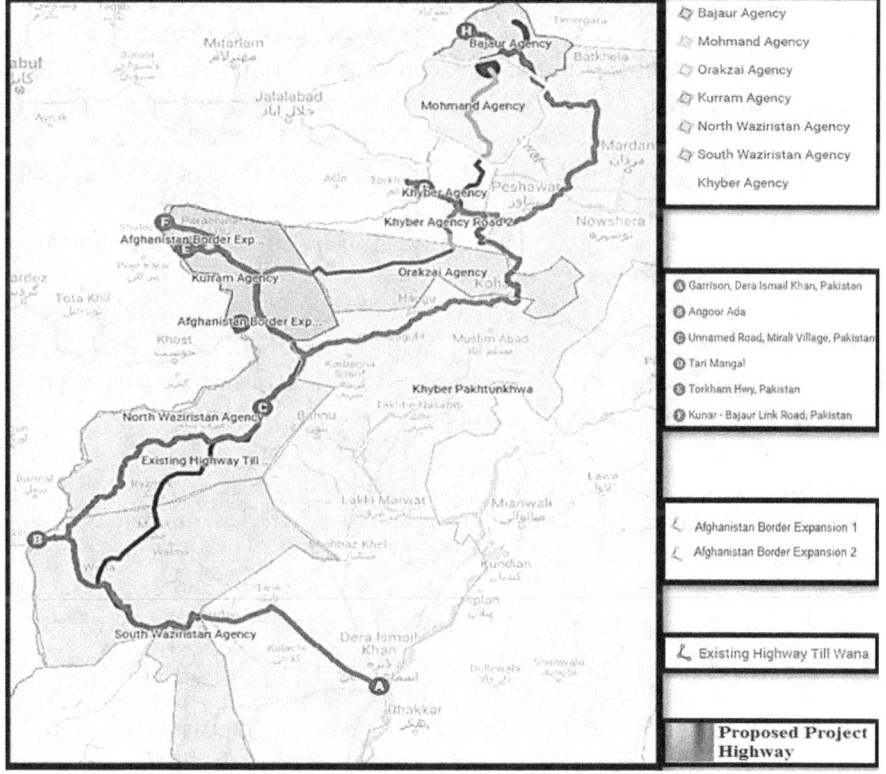

Figure 13.2: Existing and proposed highways in the FATA region.

Railways. The Torkham-Peshawar Railway Track was operational until 1978. This railway line was formerly built by the British Empire, and the surviving segments of it reach into present-day Afghanistan. Today, many sections of the track are damaged, and in much need of repair. From the Peshawar Railway Station to the Karkhano Market is 9.66 km; the track is in decent condition. However, from this point until Jamrud Fort, the track is damaged for the next 6 km. The segment of track from the Landi Kotal Railway Station (about 15 km) is also considerably damaged. The largest obstacle standing in the way of repairing this railway track is that materials from segments of this track were robbed after it fell into disuse. Currently, 45 km of track exists between Kalabagh and Issa Khel, albeit non-functional. Reconstruction of the present line will allow FATA to associate with other regions through Bannu to Mianwali (a key purpose of the CPEC). The cost that would be incurred is on the restoration of the track and stations.

The railway track between Kohat-Thal is nearly 100 km long. By and large, the track is fine except 2.4 km of damaged track stretching between Jawzara and Raisan. Another segment in need of repair exists in the 3.54 km ahead of Hangu. The length of these damaged tracks is small enough that the money spent to repair them should yield far greater financial benefits long-term once the track is fully functioning. For this track specifically, another non-infrastructural barrier exists. Although this railway track would be associated with its major stopping point in Thal, the Pakistan Army has set up a port there, rendering the line inaccessible.

The Kalabagh-Mianwali Railway track runs from Kalabagh to Mianwali. The length of this track is 46 km. This line is completely operational, and the track is sound. It covers the territories of Daudkhel, PaiKhel, and accommodates the needs of nearby regions as well.

The Peshawar-Kohat Railway track would associate Peshawar with Kohat, and it would do so by covering a mere 58 km separation. Likewise, a railway station would also be developed at Mattani. It would create an open door for the brokers of Kohat to be connected with Peshawar.

The Pewar-Issa Khel Railway track is the most vital; if fully functioning, it would join the CPEC track to the outskirts of Afghanistan. This path would coordinate FATA with CPEC through the railway track. This proposed railway track would run a distance of about 255 km. It would start at Pewar (location close in imitation of the Pakistan–Afghanistan border) and end at the Issa Khel Railway Station of Mianwali (the closest touchpoint of CPEC as shown in Figure 13.3). This track would link areas inside FATA with CPEC, including Parachinar, Bannu, Mir Ali, Lakki Marwat, etcetera.

Airports. Simply put, the air terminals which might otherwise operate in the FATA region are non-functional. Even at its former best, it could only accommodate a limited number of passengers. To improve FATA financially, these airplane terminals would need to be revived and expanded so that business planes could

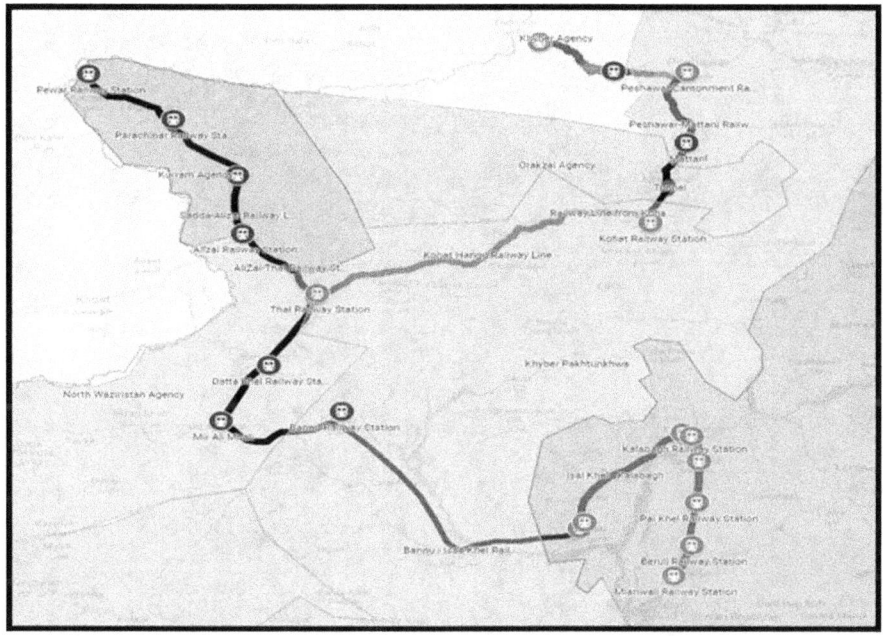

Figure 13.3: Railways in the FATA region.

arrive and depart without hassle. Doing so would expand the economy, tourism, mobility, promote collaboration, and even advance peace. Likewise, the reconstruction of airplane terminals in and around FATA would also offer the population a means of easing into increased communications with the outside world. Prime Minister Nawaz Sharif announced the re-establishment of the air terminal in Bannu (as shown in Figure 13.4) and upgraded it to an international status. Once the terminal is built, people from Bannu and adjoining zones will have the capacity to access both domestic and international flights.

Postal Services. A total of 167 post offices have been proposed to facilitate mail services in FATA. It would be the obligation of each independent mail station to manage the postal facilities that fall in their area. Figure 13.5 shows the Proposed GPO Standard Post Offices, which are organized in FATA as well as the Small Post Offices.

Landline and Mobile Network. An improved Landline Broadband Program would herald the entrance of broadband in those FATA territories which are not currently covered by the Landline and Broadband facilities. Figure 13.6 shows the proposed landline and broadband system in FATA. The phone symbol in the image represents the range that would be accessible by a "green spot" associated with a broadband network. As the primary telecommunication transporter in the

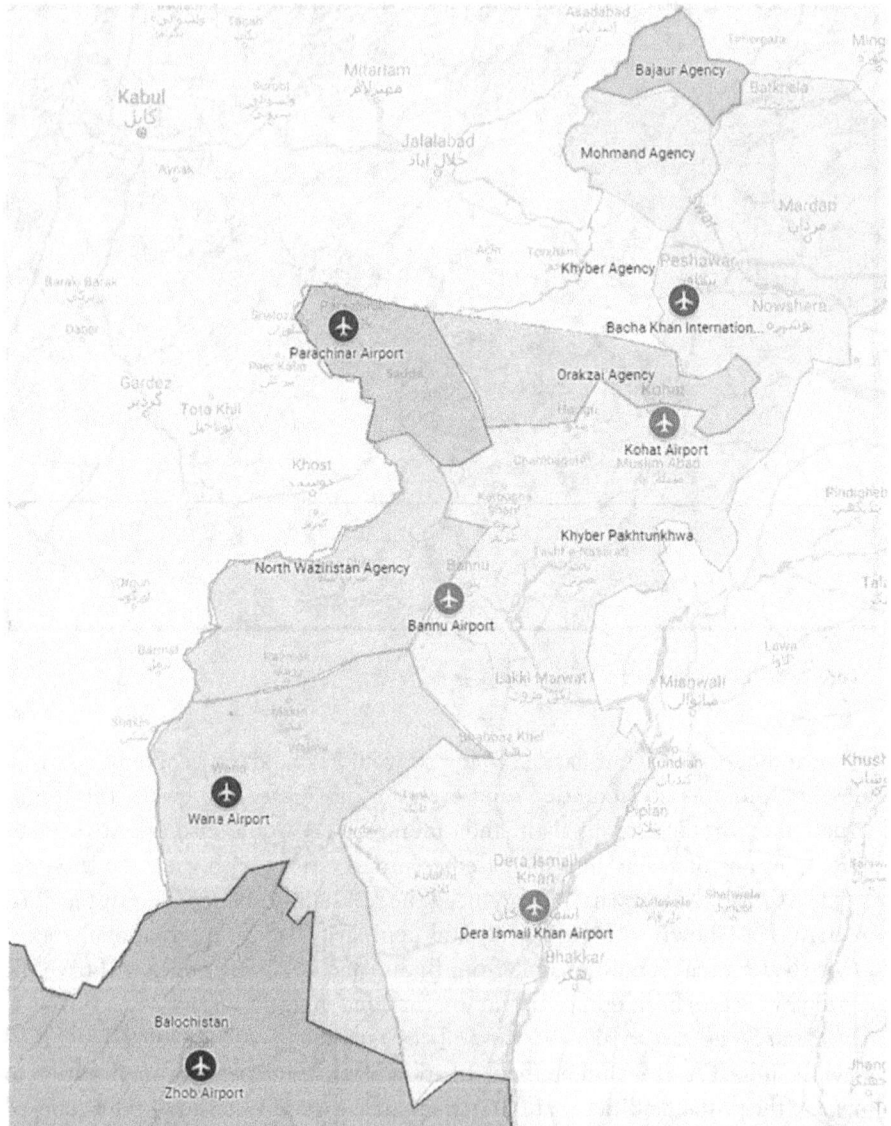

Figure 13.4: Airport locations in the FATA region.

nation, PTCL has access to a large group of interconnection administrations. These can be sub-categorized by how they spatially manage their resources: co-area, interconnection for movement of trade, tower sharing, control, and oversight over other administrations superior to other private companies in FATA. The "co-area" local tower is a contributing factor as to why telecom applications are

ACCELERATING ECONOMIC DEVELOPMENT OF FATA | 213

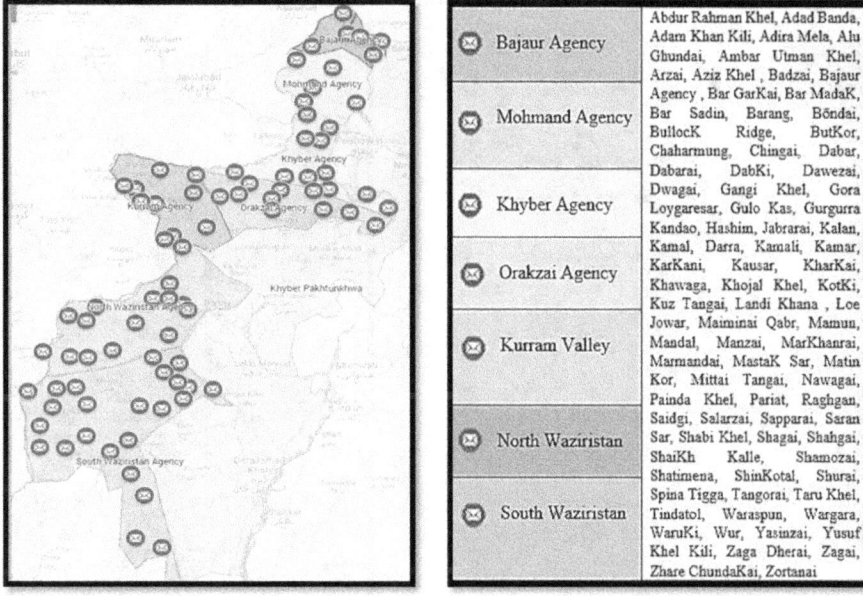

✉ Bajaur Agency	Abdur Rahman Khel, Adad Banda, Adam Khan Kili, Adira Mela, Alu Ghundai, Ambar Utman Khel, Arzai, Aziz Khel, Badzai, Bajaur Agency, Bar GarKai, Bar MadaK,
✉ Mohmand Agency	Bar Sadin, Barang, Bōndai, BullocK Ridge, ButKor, Chaharmung, Chingai, Dabar, Dabarai, DabKi, Dawezai,
✉ Khyber Agency	Dwagai, Gangi Khel, Gora Loygaresar, Gulo Kas, Gurgurra Kandao, Hashim, Jabrarai, Kalan, Kamal, Darra, Kamali, Kamar,
✉ Orakzai Agency	KarKani, Kausar, KharKai, Khawaga, Khojal Khel, KotKi, Kuz Tangai, Landi Khana, Loe Jowar, Maiminai Qabr, Mamun,
✉ Kurram Valley	Mandal, Manzai, MarKhanrai, Marmandai, MastaK Sar, Matin Kor, Mittai Tangai, Nawagai, Painda Khel, Pariat, Raghgan, Saidgi, Salarzai, Sapparai, Saran
✉ North Waziristan	Sar, Shabi Khel, Shagai, Shahgai, ShaiKh Kalle, Shamozai, Shatimena, ShinKotal, Shurai, Spina Tigga, Tangorai, Taru Khel,
✉ South Waziristan	Tindatol, Waraspun, Wargara, WaruKi, Wur, Yasinzai, Yusuf Khel Kili, Zaga Dherai, Zagai, Zhare ChundaKai, Zortanai

Figure 13.5: Post Office locations in the FATA region.

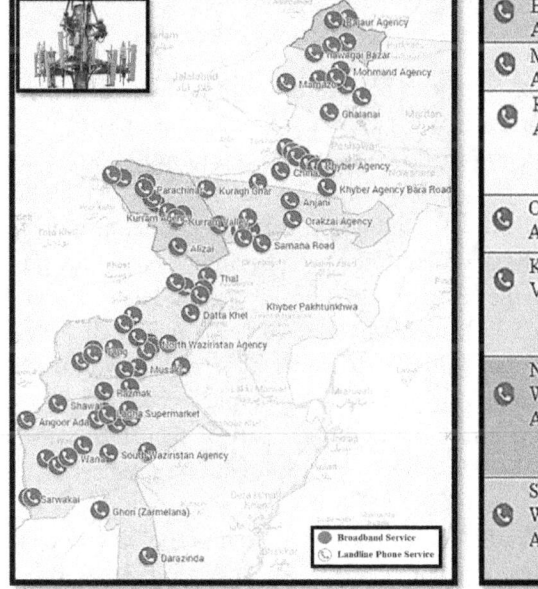

📞 Bajaur Agency	Nawagai Bazar, Pashat, Bajur(larklay), Khar, Markhanai
📞 Mohmand Agency	Ghalanai, Mamazo, Utmanzai, Bazargai, Tarap, Prang ghar
📞 Khyber Agency	Jamrud, Landi Kotal, Torkham, Torkham Road, Landi kotal, Khyber(landikotal), Shaheed sar, Lower dir, Ali Masjid, Jamrud, Abdul khel, China Pakistan, Khyberagency bara Road, Kuragh
📞 Orakzai Agency	Ghiljo Bazar, Samana Road, Khanki Toi, Orakzai Agency Road, Orakzai Forest, Shehzada, Shagai, Anjani
📞 Kurram Valley	Kurram Agency Road, Parachinar, Sadda, Alizai, Badama, Tari Mangal, Tajak, Shakhar, Shublan, Sultan Kallay, Pewar, Tari Mangal, Shalozan, Parachinar, Shublan Kurram(sultan), Shakhar- Shameer, Sadda Kurram Agency, Kurram(alizai) Road, Thal
📞 North Waziristan Agency	Mir Khon Khel, Mir Ali, Datta Khel, Razmak, Ghulam Khan Kalay, Spalga, Shewa, Sidgi, Tang, Musaki, Dosali, Shawal, Kotkai, Jawar, Kachai, Shewa, Ghariom Bazar, Datta khel, Miranshah, Boya, Warana, Razmak, Niram bazar, Miran Shah
📞 South Waziristan Agency	Wana, Azam Warsak, Shin Warsak, Angoor Ada, Ladha Supermarket, Sarwakai, Tiarza Narai, Kaniguram, Darazinda, Walma, Jandola Dadey, Khadar, Gishkor, Mangora, Jandola, Wana, Toor warsak, Shah tora, Khanda kot, Ghori

Figure 13.6: Landline and broadband system in the FATA region.

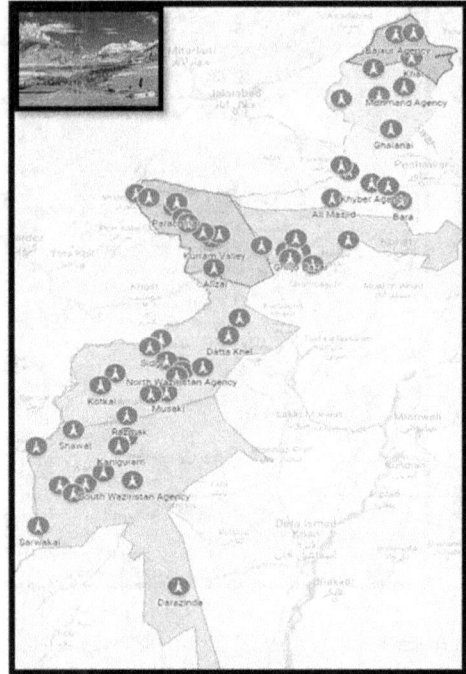

Figure 13.7: Points of interest in each Agency of the FATA region.

most appropriate in this situation. They can be readily used for lodging gear and using other PTCL services. For example, it can coordinate transfer speed and provisioning under one rooftop. Figure 13.6 illustrates the proposed areas for towers (both medium and small).

As noted in Figure 13.7, both points of interest in each Agency define more or less, an "outline" of the FATA. As opposed to the present circumstance, the proposed tower arrangement covers the entirety of the FATA region. No area would be inaccessible. It would connect individuals both inside and outside of FATA and would certainly change the way individuals work. Government workplaces would have the capacity to communicate and collaborate much more efficiently. Business people would be able to direct the dominant part of their business on the internet. Individuals would have the opportunity to educate themselves on current events.

Radio Stations. A system of radio transmission has been proposed crosswise over FATA, which should cover the majority of the Agencies. Figure 13.8 represents the proposed radio scope. On the right side of Figure 13.8, potential city bases for radio transmitters are shown. The area of transmitter-infrastructure is

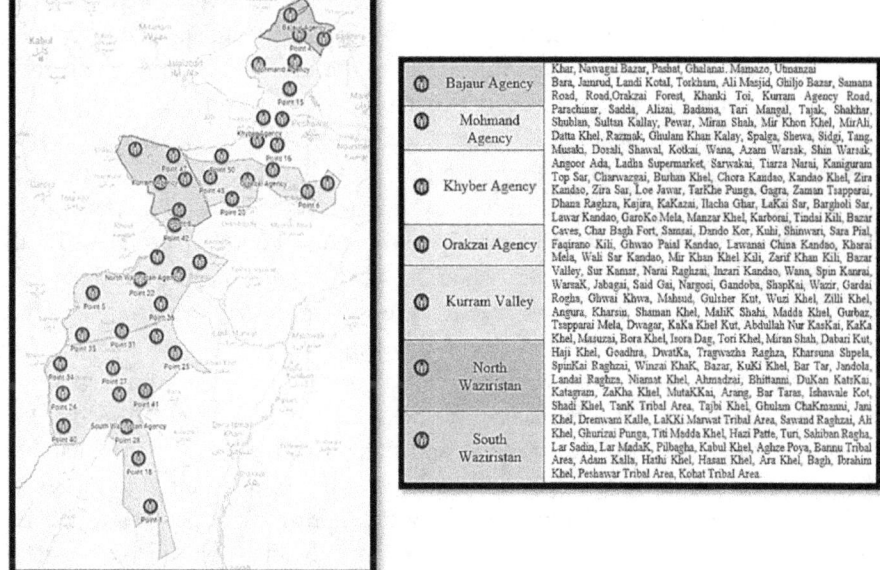

Figure 13.8: Radio stations in the FATA region.

dependent upon the range and scope of each possible unit. Every transmitter is associated with a fiber optic cable line to the radio station. The transmitter delivers the radio frequencies, which can be "caught" by any receiving wire within the range of the transmitter. Along these lines, local locations, scholarly organizations, and rural territories could be connected via radio.

Local Involvement. Although recent estimates from the FATA Directorate indicate that the FATA population is close to five million, few economic activities within the FATA generate significant income and employment opportunities for locals. If the government intends to intervene (in the form of transportation and communication investments), then local people must be involved, not ignored. The FATA can be fully integrated with the rest of Pakistan, *if* appropriate policy interventions put local people first.

Conclusion and Policy Recommendations

Existing infrastructure, particularly the roads and airports, do not bolster business and exchange on the grounds because the necessities of the area were not considered when current infrastructure was set down. Skills development is not demand-based, and the training preparation accessible does not oblige the necessities of the market. Accessible "open doors" of opportunity exist in the form of products and enterprises needed by nearby buyers in Afghanistan. Many neighboring Afghan valleys are geologically closer to the FATA than to Afghanistan's internal market focus. For this reason, exports to fringe territories of Afghanistan will offer a much more aggressive edge to dealers in FATA. Later, circumstances may likewise emerge to set up exchange ties with Central Asia. While business and trade can bring quick financial returns, it provides long-term benefits as well. This division promotes entrepreneurship and creates work for specialists of all levels. Although the private sector should not, in theory, require much capital speculation from the government's bodies, the legislature can help create an ideal administrative environment for business to take place.

Because the private sector assumes the lead role in trade, the administration's role is essentially that of a facilitator. To do this, it will be essential to develop an administrative structure for business and trade with the Tribal Area Chamber of Commerce and Industry. Alongside this, it will be important to continue to advance individual workers' aptitudes. Only by improving the people's skills and attempting to provide alternative job options to individuals who have lost their occupations will there be the hope of rebalancing the economy. It would be wise to build infrastructure and offices for trade among periphery regions as well as to initiate multi-lateral discourse with organizations to expand credit offices to businesses in FATA. Adhering to the above recommendations would significantly improve the framework of the transportation, communications, and monetary systems, respectively, and bring the region closer to lasting economic stability and political peace.

Bibliography

Ahmed, V., Abbas, A., and Ahmed, S. (2013). Public Infrastructure and Economic Growth in Pakistan: A Dynamic CGE-Microsimulation Analysis. In J. Cockburn, Y. Dissou, J.-Y. Duclos, and L. Tiberti, *Infrastructure and Economic Growth in Asia* (pp. 117–143). Springer International Publishing.

Akgüngör, S., Kuştepeli, Y., and Gülcan, Y. (2014). The Impact of Road Network on External Trade: The Case of Turkey and the EU. Historical Methods: *A Journal of Quantitative and Interdisciplinary History*, 47(4), 190–198.

Arbués, P., Baños, J. F., and Matías, M. (2015). The Spatial Productivity of Transportation Infrastructure. *Transportation Research Part A: Policy and Practice*, 75, 166–177.

Bakht, Z. B., Koolwal, G., and Khandker, S. R. (2006). *The Poverty Impact of Rural Roads: Evidence From Bangladesh*. World Bank Policy Research Working Paper 3875.

Beuran, M., Gachassin, M., and Raballand, G. (2015). Are There Myths on Road Impact and Transport in Sub-Saharan Africa? *Development Policy Review*, 33(5), 673–700.

Beyzatlar, M. A., Karacal, M., and Yetkiner, H. (2014). Granger-Causality Between Transportation and GDP: A Panel Data Approach. *Transportation Research Part A: Policy and Practice*, 63, 43–55.

Bignon, V., Esteves, R., and Herranz-Loncán, A. (2015). Big Push or Big Grab? Railways, Government Activism, and Export Growth in Latin America, 1865–1913. *The Economic History Review*, 68(4), 1277–1305.

Boarnet, M. G. (1998). Spillovers and the Locational Effects of Public Infrastructure. *Journal of Regional Development*, 38(3), 381–400.

Boarnet, M. G. (1999). Road Infrastructure, Economic Productivity, and the Need for Highway Finance Reform. *Public Works Management & Policy*, 3(4), 289–303.

Boopen, S. (2006). Transport Infrastructure and Economic Growth: Evidence from Africa Using Dynamic Panel Estimates. *The Empirical Economics Letters*, 5(1), 37–52.

Bureau of Statistics. (2015). *FATA in Figures*. Peshawar: Planning & Development Directorate, FATA Secretariat.

Chavula, H. (2013). Information Technology for Development. *Telecommunications Development and Economic Growth in Africa*, 19(1), 5–23.

Chi, J., and Baekb, J. (2013). Dynamic Relationship Between Air Transport Demand and Economic Growth in the United States: A New Look. *Transport Policy*, 29, 257–260.

Datta, S. (2012). The Impact of Improved Highways on Indian Firms. *Journal of Development Economics*, 99(1), 46–57.

Dholakia, R. R., and Harlam, B. (1994). Telecommunications and Economic Development: Econometric Analysis of the U.S. Experience. *Telecommunications Policy*, 18(6), 470–477.

Dulac, J. (2013). *Global Land Transport Infrastructure Requirements: Estimating Road and Railway Infrastructure Capacity and Costs to 2050*. International Energy Agency. Retrieved January 8, 2017, from https://www.iea.org/publications/freepublications/publication/TransportInfrastructureInsights_FINAL_WEB.pdf

Dutta, A. (2001). Telecommunications and Economic Activity: An Analysis of Granger Causality. *Journal of Management Information Systems*, 17(4), 71–95.

Fedderke, J. W., Perkins, P., and Luiz, J. M. (2006). Infrastructural Investment in Long-Run Economic Growth: South Africa 1875–2001. *World Development*, 36(6), 1037–1059.

Felloni, F., Wahl, T., and Wandschneider, P. (1999). *Evidence of the Effect of Infrastructure on Agricultural Production and Productivity: Implications for China*. Washington, DC: Chinese Agriculture and the WTO, Proceedings of WCC-101 Seattle.

Fremdling, R. (1997). Railroads and German Economic Growth: A Leading Sector Analysis with a Comparison to the United States and Great Britain. *The Journal of Economic History*, 37(3), 583–604.

Gachassin, M. C., Najman, B., and Raballand, G. (2015). Roads and Diversification of Activities in Rural Areas: A Cameroon Case Study. *Development Policy Review*, 33(3), 355–372.

Goodall, B. (1987). *The Penguin Dictionary of Human Geography*. Harmondsworth: Penguin Books.

Hakim, M. M., and Merkert, R. (2016). The Causal Relationship Between Air Transport and Economic Growth: Empirical Evidence from South Asia. *Journal of Transport Geography*, 56, 120–127.

Herranz-Loncán, A. (2011). The Role of Railways in Export-Led Growth: The Case of Uruguay, 1870–1913. *Economic History of Developing Regions*, 26(2), 1–32.

Holl, A. (2004a). Transport Infrastructure, Agglomeration Economies, and Firm Birth: Empirical Evidence from Portugal. *Journal of Regional Science*, 44(4), 693–712.

Holl, A. (2004b). Manufacturing Location and Impacts of Road Transport Infrastructure: Empirical Evidence from Spain. *Regional Science and Urban Economics*, 34(3), 341–363.

Holl, A. (2004c). Start-ups and Relocations: Manufacturing Plant Location in Portugal. *Regional Science*, 83(4), 649–668.

Holl, A. (2007). Twenty Years of Accessibility Improvements. The Case of the Spanish Motorway Building Program. *Journal of Transport Geography*, 15(4), 286–297.

Ianchovichina, E., Estache, A., Foucart, R., Garsous, G., and Yepes, T. (2013). Job Creation Through Infrastructure Investment in the Middle East and North Africa. *World Development*, 45, 209–222.

Khadaroo, J., and Seetanah, B. (2008). The Role of Transport Infrastructure in International Tourism Development: A Gravity Model Approach. *Tourism Management*, 29(5), 831–840.

Lam, P.-L., and Shiu, A. (2010). Economic Growth, Telecommunications Development and Productivity Growth of the Telecommunications Sector: Evidence Around the World. *Telecommunications Policy*, 34(4), 185–199.

Limão, N., and Venables, A. J. (2001). Infrastructure, Geographical Disadvantage, Transport Costs, and Trade. *The World Bank Economic Review*, 15(3), 451–479.

Marazzo, M., Scherre, R., and Fernandes, E. (2010). Air Transport Demand and Economic Growth in Brazil: A Time Series Analysis. *Transportation Research Part E: Logistics and Transportation Review*, 46(2).

Mieczkowski, B. (1978). *Transportation in Eastern Europe: Empirical Findings*. Boulder, CO: East European Monographs.

Robinson, H., and Bamford, C. (1978). *Geography of Transport*. Plymouth, UK: MacDonald and Evans.

Sahoo, P., and Dash, R. K. (2012). Economic Growth in South Asia: Role of Infrastructure. *The Journal of International Trade & Economic Development*, 21(2), 217–252.

Schwartz, J., Andres, L., and Dragoiu, G. (2009). Crisis in Latin America Infrastructure Investment, Employment and the Expectations of Stimulus. *Journal of Infrastructure Development*, 1(2), 111–131.

Shiu, A., and Pun-Lee, L. (2008). Causal Relationship Between Telecommunications and Economic Growth in China and Its Regions. *Regional Studies*, 42(5), 705–718.

Storeygard, A. (2016). Farther on Down the Road: Transport Costs, Trade and Urban Growth in Sub-Saharan Africa. *Review of Economic Studies*, 83(3), 1263–1295.

Tang, J. P. (2014). Railroad Expansion and Industrialization: Evidence from Meiji Japan. *The Journal of Economic History*, 74(3), 863–886.

Tinbergen, J. (1962). *Shaping the World Economy: Suggestions for an International Economic Policy*. New York: Twentieth Century Fund.

Toniolo, G. (1983). Railways and Economic Growth in Mediterranean Countries: Some Methodological Remarks. In G. Toniolo, *Railways and the Economic Development of Western Europe, 1830–1914* (pp. 227–236). United Kingdom: Palgrave Macmillan.

Tranos, E. (2012). The Causal Effect of the Internet Infrastructure on the Economic Development of European City Regions. *Spatial Economic Analysis*, 7(3), 1742–1780.

Weiss, J. (1999). Infrastructure and Economic Development. *African Development Bank*, 50(1999), 1–37.

Weiss, M., and Figura, P. (2003). *A Provisional Typology of Highway Economic Development Projects*. Washington, DC: U.S. Department of Transportation, Highway Administration.

Wenga, L., Boedhihartonoa, A. K., Dirksa, P. H., Dixonb, J., Lubis, M. I., and Saye, J. A. (2013). Mineral Industries, Growth Corridors and Agricultural Development in Africa. *Global Food Security*, 2(3), 195–202.

CHAPTER FOURTEEN

Employment and Economic Development in FATA

SAEED AHMED

Introduction

The Federally Administered Tribal Areas (FATA) have long been under economic and social stress. Lack of economic opportunities resulting in a lack of quality employment creates social unrest. Though the overall employment situation in Pakistan has been turbulent over the past decades, FATA has suffered explicitly due to neglect by the successive governments and changing geopolitical situation. Currently, economic opportunities are limited to subsistence agriculture, informal service sectors, retail, transport, and government service. Most of these sectors offer low-quality working conditions and insecure employment with few career prospects. Hence, the majority of FATA's youth are looking for employment opportunities outside the country. Given the overall employment opportunities in the country elsewhere and the low level of human capital in FATA youth, not many end up in having good quality jobs even if they migrate to other parts of the country. Those who opt for immigrating to other countries for work also typically end up having low quality unskilled employed with little return and a very high burnout rate.

Until recently, this increasing number of youth was considered to be a burden on the economy. However, experience from developed and emerging economies suggests that youth are drivers of economic growth, and they should, therefore, be the focus of policymakers for increasing productivity. Currently, the economy of Pakistan has low productivity, which means the economy has a lot more potential for employment generation compared to the ongoing trend. This productivity can be increased by taking advantage of the increasing number of youth in the population by giving them economic opportunities, which is not happening because the low skills and knowledge negatively affect the economic development of the Pakistan. Economic growth affects both the demand and supply side of the labor market, meaning the greater the growth, the greater the demand will be for labor by the employers. Thus, the greater this employer demand is, the greater would be the number of workers willing to compete for the best jobs available.

Employment is one of the vital steps needed to enhance and improve one's life, both economically and socially. When youth cross into the working-age, which typically starts from 15, the youth begin to expect employment opportunities based on their knowledge and skills. They dream about living an accomplished, independent, and fulfilling life. They are buzzing with the excitement of endless prospects to better themselves by engaging in productive and gainful activities. The economic and social welfare of the youth, thus, highly depends on whether they successfully get employed or not, both in the short and long-term. If the transition to work is smooth, the youth not only support themselves and their families but also positively connect with state and society, which in turn reinforces this social cohesion. Continued unemployment not only harms individuals economically but also causes drastic long-term effects on "freedom, initiatives, and skill" (Sen, 1999).

Transition to work is not smooth in Pakistan in general and specifically in FATA if we keep in mind the current labor market growth and entry of over 4 million young adults into working age every year (Bureau of Emigration and Overseas Employment, 2015). Pakistan needs to generate 1.5 to 2 million jobs every year for the next 20 years (Pakistan Bureau of Labor Statistics, 2013). This, however, does not mean that the current rates of unemployment and labor force participation are sustainable. These rates need to be improved if the economy wants to benefit from the increasing number of youth in the working-age population, which is 15–64. The ongoing demographic transition is one of the key reasons why the labor market of Pakistan has not been able to absorb the existing youth. Research shows that unemployment has damaging effects on psychological health as well (Flatau et al., 2000; Lucas et al., 2004; Mckee-Ryan et al., 2005; Theodossiou, 1998; Winkelmann & Winkelmann, 1998). It is linked to lower psychological and physical welfare. The psychological impressions of unemployment have even been found to be present after the individual is employed later on in life.

Increasing Trend of Unemployment

Unemployment amongst the youth demographic has been unceasingly growing since 1990 except the period between 2003 and 2008. After 2008, youth unemployment has increased drastically, and joblessness is currently at the highest it has been in 25 years. The GDP growth rate has also been stagnant over the same period, which proposes that job creation has been harmfully affected by the recent slowdown in economic growth. This phenomenon is coupled with the rising number of youth entrants into the labor force due to the demographic transition. Youth bulge increases the number of people in the working-age population (15–64) of a country, resulting in a demographic dividend. Pakistan is currently going through a youth bulge where the proportion of the working-age population is at an all-time high. Pakistan needs to reduce the unemployment rate if it wants to transform this youth bulge into a demographic dividend.

Comparing the unemployment trends of different cohorts in the working-age population, joblessness is significantly higher amongst the youth demographic, has remained higher over time, and this increase is severer than the increase in the unemployment of the working-age population. Unemployment amidst young adults (15–19) presently stands at 7.5% as opposed to the unemployment rate of the working-age population (15–64), which is about 5%. This situation is worse in FATA for the unemployment rate of age 10–64 population; the rates for the FATA and FR are 7.36% and 12.6%, respectively. The Bajaur Agency has the highest unemployment rate (11.2%) as compared to all other agencies. The rate of unemployment in the adult population (15–64) within the FATA is 7.1%, which is far higher than overall Pakistan (5%), Punjab (5.6%), Sindh (4.9%), and Balochistan (4%) while lower than KP (7.9%). When unemployment by age groups is plotted, the graph produces a "U-shaped curve," which means that unemployment in the earlier working-age groups is greater than unemployment in older working-age groups. It only begins to diminish between the ages of 25–29-years-old before it starts rising again in the later age brackets. The same pattern can be observed in the FATA and FR, as high unemployment rates in overall FATA occur between the ages of 15–19-years-old and 20–24 years; comparatively, in FR, it occurs in the age group 20–24 years.

Another disparity exists between the levels of unemployment in rural and urban areas where it is higher in urban areas for both genders and all age cohorts. Furthermore, women's unemployment is more significant than men across all age groups in both urban and rural areas. On the other hand, the joblessness of urban young men has reached its pinnacle in the past two and a half decades and is pointedly higher than rural young men. In the past 7 years, unemployment has diverged across the urban-rural divide. Additionally, the rural economy is currently retaining more than half of young adults (53%) as opposed to the urban economy. Those living in rural areas derive their employment from agriculture and rural non-farm activities, where the latter is predominantly services related to the agriculture sector. Agriculture is based on the availability of cultivable land, which is limited in quantity and capacity, whereas the population that needs employment is rapidly increasing. This suggests that the relatively higher rate of the employment generation in the rural areas will diminish gradually in the near future, hence increasing labor migration toward urban centers. However, urban centers have thus far failed to serve as an engine of growth in the economy. If this situation continues, the current slow rate of employment creation will further deteriorate, which would further slow down economic growth.

Equity issues in employment require immediate attention as joblessness is not uniform across the country. One out of every three young girls and one out of every ten young men are unemployed in Khyber Pakhtunkhwa alone. Punjab faces higher unemployment in young men compared to both Baluchistan and Sindh. Continued periods of unemployment will only worsen the already frail situation of law and order. Similarly, FATA gives a very bleak picture given the available data. Provincial disproportions in employment will either take the youth further away from positive engagement with society or increase rural-to-urban labor migration.

The reasons behind unemployment are multi-dimensional and multi-faceted because Pakistan has a uniquely varied economic and cultural environment; therefore, particular region and gender policies and schemes are needed to improve the employment rate. Youth unemployment in urban regions is a pressing issue that needs to be addressed immediately by making and implementing urban-specific policies because urban areas should not lag behind in employment generation but instead, should function as the engines of economic growth for the economy of Pakistan. On the other hand, rural areas and their potential for creating sufficient employment opportunities should not be overlooked, which can be done by raising labor productivity in agriculture, which in turn would improve the standard of living. Area-specific strategies are needed because often, resource management is not very efficient. The unemployment rates for both young men and women in Khyber Pakhtunkhwa, FATA, and Baluchistan are drastic. The dynamics of the FATA and other provinces are different regarding unemployment. Young women in Khyber Pakhtunkhwa and FATA are specifically disadvantaged because of the cultural norms, values, and the unstable, always changing security situation.

Low Labor Force Participation

One of the key issues within labor force participation is the alarmingly low level of women's participation in the labor market. Although women's labor force participation has almost doubled over the past 25 years and is currently touching 30%, the participation of young women in the labor market is the lowest in FATA, as the total women's labor force participation within the 10–64-year-old age bracket is only 8.6%. Either because of familial constraints, cultural practices, or out of their own free will, young women who are not studying or employed, or they are also not in training are a lost resource, particularly in the ongoing youth bulge.

Data for the participation of different age groups suggests that women's participation in the labor force peaks within the 35–44-year-old age bracket (30%), but then it begins to fall again in subsequent age cohorts. However, this trend is a bit different in the FATA, where young women's labor force participation peaks between the ages of 20–24-years-old (10.8%), it then starts to fall after that. The participation of young men in the labor force is well above 95% and has been steady and constant over time. Bridging this gap between men's and women's participation is not only going to affect the economy positively. It will also ameliorate the standards of living of families across Pakistan, which would, in turn, empower them to invest appropriately in the human development of the next generation.

If compared, labor force participation of young women residing in urban areas is lower than in rural areas, and the gap is broadening over time. However, men's participation is almost the same across the rural-urban divide. A key issue for urban employment is the increasing urbanization in Pakistan, where additional housing is provided to migrants. Once settled, migrants present a resource burden on the already stressed labor market of urban centers. This is happening particularly in Punjab, Khyber Pakhtunkhwa, and urban Sindh, which are favorite destinations for labor migrants from FATA.

Another important issue that needs attention is the increasing level of education among women without substantial improvement in their labor force participation. The secondary education attainment of young women has recorded a sharper increase in the past 25 years compared to the attainment of young men in urban Pakistan. The attainment of young women converges with that of young men, and the gap has significantly narrowed down over the past 7 years. However, the gap in their labor force participation has consistently been wide, with no visible signs of convergence in the near future. This busts the myth that by only increasing educational attainment will enhance women's participation in the labor force. This will instead take more than education, such as providing women with transportation and accommodation services, access to good quality employment, improvement in their working conditions, and removing other structural barriers. This should be taken as a precaution while designing FATA interventions, as education alone cannot increase women's labor force participation.

Some of the barriers to increasing women's participation in the labor market are discrimination, segregation of work, unfair treatment of women and girls at the workplace, the non-availability of secure transportation and accommodation facilities in the current socio-cultural and security situation, and lack of local employment opportunities. An equally important factor is the fertility rate in Pakistan, falling at a very slow rate. The connection between fertility rate and labor force participation has been highlighted by multiple studies and its relationship in two ways (Angrist & Evans, 1998; Bloom et al., 2009; Vailey, 2006). The fertility rate needs to decline at a faster pace to ensure labor force participation of women as a higher fertility rate means less time to engage in economically productive activities. Without the optimal contribution of women in the labor force, the currently high dependency ratio would get higher and economic productivity will stay stagnated

The Deteriorating Quality of Employment

Higher unemployment and low labor force participation are not the only issues hampering economic development. A significant proportion of those who are employed, especially youth, have to participate in the labor force for survival because they cannot afford not to engage in economic activities due to high poverty levels in developing countries (Arif & Chaudhry, 2008), and this is evident from over 95% participation of young men in Pakistan. The quality of employment in FATA has also pictured somehow a dismal state where 50% are engaged in sectors where unskilled labor is needed. This is followed by semi-skilled (17%), those who can run plants, machines and can work as operators. A considerable section of the labor force is working in the informal service sector and retail sector. A negligible 1% work as senior officials, managers, and legislators.

The decision to accept low quality employment is motivated by aspirations of economic and social mobility (Cling et al., 2015) in their later age, even if they are not satisfied with their current employment. However, many remain either in poor quality employment or in hidden unemployment with very low levels of mobility as the trend continues without much improvement throughout their remaining working age. The share of vulnerable employees was reported as 59% by the Pakistan Bureau of Statistics (2013) for the working-age population. A high-quality job market expands individual choice. Employment expands choices, but the current level of employment quality does not contribute much in expanding choices and life satisfaction for youth, given that 94% of the dissatisfied youth were those who did not have a choice in employment selection according to the youth perception survey. This makes the poor quality of employment an even more significant challenge for the economic and social well-being of youth.

Quality of employment has been deteriorating for all employed populations irrespective of their age group; however, youth are the worst affected by the process of casualization, although their educational attainment is increasing. Based on the analysis of Labor Force Surveys (1990 to 2013), the highest number of employed youth are reported to be working as unpaid family workers. Though this trend has been declining since 2009, the share of youth working as unpaid family workers out of the total employed youths is still above 35%. Unpaid family workers tend to be contributing little, if not zero, in terms of tangible contributions to the household income. Without economic contribution, these workers also contribute little in terms of increasing productivity at the macro level. However, this phenomenon can be explained as a means of skill development, given the low levels of contribution to skills development by schooling and formal training. This argument is supported by the share of unpaid family workers and self-employed workers out of the working-age population. In the working-age population, the share of self-employed workers is higher than the unpaid family workers. Self-employment may also be associated with low quality of employment in the developing economies (which will be discussed later in this section).

Casualization affects women worse than men, as is evident from the data at federal and provincial levels. It has been noted that young women remain in poor quality jobs during their working life and that 75% do so in unsafe and low-quality employment. The reason behind women being adversely affected by casualization can be explained by the fact that around seven out of ten agricultural workers are women (Pakistan Bureau of Statistics, 2013), and the agricultural sector does not offer good quality employment given the low labor productivity and lack of willingness on behalf of farmers to adopt the latest technologies. As a result, agriculture is one of the lowest-paid sectors (Pakistan Bureau of Statistics, 2013) with seasonality in employment and prone to changing weather conditions and difficult working conditions (Food and Agriculture Organization, 2015). If the same trend of poor quality of work continues, women's participation in the labor market is not going to increase their economic and social status and may rather adversely affect their well-being.

Entrepreneurship is one essential intervention for expanding the formal sector and creating good quality employment, which has historically been neglected in Pakistan, although there have been some efforts from time to time. Entrepreneurship can be a source of improving the quality of new employment opportunities created and, at the same time, will expand the labor market through expansion of related products and services, hence increasing the number of employees as well. Empirically, it is also positively correlated with the reduction of economic and social disparities and poverty alleviation (Bandiera et al., 2013). There have been some efforts from the government in terms of providing loans to youth for business, but there remains much more to be done, especially in the FATA. At a relatively larger scale, the micro-finance sector is providing small loans to the economically active poor, including youth, for initiating small businesses. However, very few areas in FATA are covered by such programs. Another issue is not having a plan to move micro-enterprises to the SME sector, given financial and skills constraints on the part of entrepreneurs. The share of micro-enterprises has also been highlighted by the Harvard Kennedy School's Center for International Development as a "missing middle" in the developing countries (Kwaja, Mian, & Qamar, 2005). The "missing middle" has been explained as the dearth of small and medium enterprises compared to the share of micro-enterprises and large-scale enterprises. The missing small and medium enterprises (SME) sector, because of its capacity for rapid employment generation, has been named as "the missing middle." They argue that, like developed economies, the share of SMEs must be increased not only for employment generation but also for overall economic growth.

Low Human Capital: One of the Key Root Issues

The key ingredients of human capital, education, and vocational skills are very low in Pakistan, but regions like the FATA, KP, and Balochistan are worse off. Pakistan remains far behind its South Asian neighbors on education indicators suggesting that a lot more remains to be done to raise the level of human capital throughout the region. Pakistan was one of the worst-performing countries in terms of net primary enrollment and gross secondary enrollment in South Asia in 2012 (World Bank, 2014).

Education and literacy indicators of women are worse compared to men in Pakistan. The literacy rate in youth is around 70%, below 62% in young women, as opposed to 79% recorded amongst young men (Pakistan Bureau of Statistics, 2014). Out of those who are literate, less than one in four have completed 10 years of education. Higher than secondary education attainment is around 20% in youth, those who have dropped out before completing 10 years of schooling are more than half of the literate youth. In the FATA, these indicators are much lower compared to national data and other provinces. The overall literacy rate in the FATA is 33.3%, as estimated in 2013–2014.

Similarly, the adult literacy rate in the FATA is 28.4%. There is a considerable gender gap in literacy. The male adult literacy rate in FATA is 45%, whereas the same for women is a mere 7.8%. The Gross Enrollment Rate (GER) at the primary level (6–10 years of age) is 77.4% for FATA, while the rest of the country stands at 91%. Only a small proportion (2.3%) of currently enrolled children aged between 6 and 15 attend religious schools, while 68.6% go to government schools, and 29.1% are in private schools. The available statistics show that the percentage of the population with 5 years completed education is as low as 26.1% for the entire FATA.

The challenge is that educational attainment is very low amongst Pakistani youth, but the returns to education are positive in Pakistan (Aslam, Bari, & Kingdon, 2008). The positive return on education suggests that a low level of educational attainment is adversely affecting productivity and economic growth. Though total labor market returns are much higher for men in Pakistan, returns to education were found to be even higher for women in Pakistan (Aslam, 2009). Nonetheless, educational attainment and access to better jobs were found to be significantly positively correlated both for men and women. These findings are also consistent with the World Bank's (2012) analysis of the South Asian labor market, where they found that education was the most important determinant of access to good quality jobs.

We also find in the labor force survey, discussed earlier in the chapter, that educational attainment (beyond the level of higher secondary education in young women) was positively associated with their labor force participation. Research on the return to education provides enough rationale for increasing public spending on all levels of education for young men and women. Doing so would enhance access to quality employment in the future, improve economic and social well-being, and increase the overall productivity of the economy.

Although higher levels of education are associated with access to better jobs and mobility (World Bank, 2012), unemployment among youth with higher levels of education is also high. This puts them at a disadvantage and undermines the benefits of education, especially at the start of a working career. This is consistent with the World Bank's (2012) analysis of the South Asian labor market, which suggests that education does not necessarily increase employment in the absence of related policy interventions. An analysis from the labor force survey shows that both young women and men who completed a level of schooling beyond higher secondary education have the highest unemployment rate in the age bracket of 20–24 years. There are visible differentials in young women and men, and between rural and urban areas; however, the overall trend by education attainment is the same across all areas and for both genders. The second group by education attainment with the highest unemployment rate comprises youth with secondary to higher secondary education, while those with no formal education have the lowest unemployment rates. An ILO report on global youth employment (ILO, 2015) finds similar trends for Asia and the Pacific; it concludes that unemployment among youth with tertiary education is three times higher compared to those with primary or lower education levels in the region.

The overall scenario of unemployment rates by education attainment suggests that higher education attainment is associated with a higher expectation of crisis. This could be either because of the quality of education, the profile of the economy, or both. A little over half of the employed workers' education is well matched with their employment, and the rest are either over-educated or under-educated for the work they do (ILO, 2015). Being over-educated creates an aspiration crisis among youth while being under-educated has lower productivity and lower mobility as crucial challenges for workers and the labor market. There are high expectations associated with higher education, and this came under discussion in our youth consultations where young men and women opined that higher education must help them in having highly paid and secure jobs at the start of their careers. Having higher expectations keeps fresh graduates searching for good quality jobs for a few years. They ultimately settled down in the labor market by doing informal apprenticeship or skill acquisition through formal and informal ways. Many fresh graduates settle for jobs below their expectations after a few years of unsuccessful struggle for good quality jobs.

Vocational training is expected to offset the educational deficit in youth. However, this has not been happening as training attainment has historically been very low. Between 1990 and 2009, youth vocational training attainment rates remained around or below 5%. It showed some improvements in the last few years but is still hovering around 10% with a significant gender differential. There have been efforts in recent years to provide employable skills to youth from the FATA. These efforts, however, are not sufficient given the sheer size of the youth and the skills provided are often rendered as "unemployable." As years of skill training are found to be positively correlated with increased income (Nasir, 2002), low levels of vocational training attainment are adversely affecting the quality of employment, productivity, and growth.

Vocational training attainment is correlated with the level of education and therefore excludes youth with little to no education attainment. Among these youths, the group benefiting the most from vocational training are those with higher secondary education or beyond. However, attainment among university graduates is low as most of their skills have been stigmatized, while the expectations of university graduates are high. Although there can be many reasons for excluding illiterate persons and drop-outs, one primary reason is the educational qualification condition for entry into these training programs. The minimum education qualification required by vocational training programs is 8 years of education, whereas close to 40% of the FATA youth are illiterate. There are also no training programs for basic skills such as reading and numeracy. The dearth of skills will continue to constrain the prospects of economic development and re-building of FATA if the current trends in educational and vocational training attainment continue.

An essential issue to flag is the employability of vocational training content and its relevance to the current labor market. Many of these training courses are either outdated or are delivered in a way that does not *actually* contribute much to skills enhancement. Some training courses also do not appeal to many educated youths because of stigmas attached to the skills that these courses teach. The real challenge is to recognize the value of investing in people and change the mindset through education so that skills are considered as a critical driver of economic and social returns both by the policymakers and labor market entrants.

Conclusion

FATA is in the process of re-building where government and development partners are pooling their resources for sustainable economic, infrastructure, and human development. This re-building process can only succeed with a particular focus on employment, especially for the youth with equitable participation for both genders. Currently, the economic structure of the area and human capital of workers makes it very difficult to engage people in economically productive activities within FATA sustainably. These two key reasons—human capital and labor market structure—are pushing people out of the labor force. Those who participate in the labor force have to wait before finding employment opportunities. Those who are employed cannot move up the social and economic ladder and are hence discouraged to continue contributing to social goods.

A key area of intervention is an investment in education and skills to make existing workers and new labor market entrants ready to take on today's jobs. Basic literacy and numeracy must be improved by removing barriers to access education at the local level. Many schools need to be rebuilt, existing schools need to be improved, and new schools need to be constructed. Girls' education requires particular focus so that the gender gap of those employed can be narrowed. Similarly, skill-training centers need to be opened at the local level with market-oriented skills and teaching methodology so that out-of-school adolescents can be brought into the skilled labor force. These centers can be opened in existing schools and colleges in the afternoon, where regular morning students can also benefit from this infrastructure.

The second significant area is creating employment opportunities by optimizing local resources. Agriculture can be facilitated by providing irrigation infrastructure, the latest technology with necessary capacity building, seeds and fertilizers, and market access to enhance the productivity of this vital sector. Natural resources need to be managed sustainably by introducing technology, especially in the mining sector. The mining sector in some areas can alone provide a significant number of employment opportunities to youth in FATA. Other sectors need to be developed via local resources, trade, the retail sector, dairy, fisheries, and forestry.

Entrepreneurship is another answer to both the quantity and quality of employment in the FATA. With the current technological advancement in Pakistan and the exposure of Pakistani youth to more international best practices, success stories are beginning to emerge. Such success models should be replicated in the FATA with the provision of basic requirements. One basic requirement is the *entrepreneurship ecosystem*, including access to mentorship, incubation centers, finances, skills, and access to the formal market. Another critical step in this direction would be awareness raising of FATA youth so that self-employment and entrepreneurship becomes a priority. The current situation in the FATA requires a large number of good quality jobs in a short time, which can be achieved through entrepreneurship.

Bibliography

Ahmad, R., and Azim, P. (2010). Youth Population and the Labor Market of Pakistan: A Micro Level Study. *The Pakistan Development Review*, 48(2), 183–208.

Amjad, R., and Yusuf, A. (2014). *More and Better Jobs for Pakistan: Can the Manufacturing Sector Play a Greater Role*. MPRA Paper No. 59518: Munich Personal RePEc Archive.

Amjad, R. (2005). Skills and Competitiveness: Can Pakistan Break Out of the Low-Level-Skills Trap? *The Pakistan Development Review*, 44 (4 Part I), 387–409.

Amjad, R. (2006). *Why Pakistan Must Break-Into the Knowledge Economy*. MPRA Paper No. 34448: Munich Personal RePec Archive.

Angrist, J., and Evans, W. (1998). Children and Their Parents' Labor Supply: Evidence from Exogenous Variation in Family Size. *The American Economic Review*, 88(3), 450–477.

Arif, G. M., and Chaudhry, N. (2008). Demographic Transition and Youth Employment in Pakistan. *The Pakistan Development Review*, 47(1), 27–70.

Aslam, M. (2009). Education Gender Gaps in Pakistan: Is the Labor Market to Blame? *Economic Development and Cultural Change*, 57(4), 747–784. doi:10.1086/598767.

Aslam, M., Bari, F., and Kingdon, G. (2008). *Returns to Schooling, Ability and Cognitive Skills in Pakistan*. RECOUP Working Paper No. 20: Research Consortium on Educational Outcomes and Poverty.

Bandiera, O., Burgess, R., Das, N., Gulesci, S., Rasul, I., and Sulaiman, M. (2013). *Can Basic Entrepreneurship Transform the Economic Lives of the Poor?* IZA Discussion Paper No. 7386. http://ssrn.com/abstract=2266813.

Bloom. D. E., Canning, D., Fink, G., and Finlay, J. E. (2009). Fertility, Female Labor Force Participation, and the Demographic Dividend. *Journal of Economic Growth*, 14(2), 79–101. doi:10.1007/s 10887-009-9039-9.

Bureau of Emigration and Overseas. (2015). *Workers Registered for Overseas Employment During the Period 1981–2015 (Up to July)*. http://www.beoe.gov.pk/migrationstatistics/1971-2015%20(upto%20Feb)/Province-wise-1981-2015.pdf.

Cheema, A. (2015). *Pakistan's Demographic Transition: Young Adults, Human Capital and Jobs*. NHDR Background Paper. Islamabad: UNDP.

Cling J. P., Lagree S., Razafindrakoto M., and Roubaud F. (2015). *The Informal Economy in Developing Countries*. New York: Routledge.
Cling, J. P., Razafindrakoto, M., and Roubaud, F. (2015). *UNDP Human Development Reports*. Informality and Human Development. http://hdr.undp.org/en/informality-and-hd.
Cruz, M., Foster, J., Quillin, B., and Schellekens, P. (2015). *Ending Extreme Poverty and Sharing Prosperity: Progress and Policies*. Washington DC: The World Bank Group.
Durrant, V. L. (1998). Community Influences on Schooling and Work Activities of Youth in Pakistan. *The Pakistan Development Review*, 37(4), 915–937.
Flatau, P., Galea, J., and Petridis, R. (2000). Mental Health and Wellbeing and Employment. *The Australian Economic Review*, 33(2): 161–181. doi:10.1111/1467-8462.00145.
Food and Agriculture Organization of the United Nations. (2010). *Rural Youth Employment in Developing Countries: A Global View*. Rome, Italy: Food and Agriculture Organization of the United Nations.
Food and Agriculture Organization of the United Nations. (2015). *Women in Agriculture in Pakistan*. Islamabad: Food and Agriculture Organization of the United Nations.
Goldin, C. (2006). *The Quiet Revolution That Transformed Women's Employment, Education and Family*. Working Paper 11953. Cambridge, MA: National Bureau of Economic Research. http://www.nber.org/papers/w11953.
Goldin, C. (1994). *The U-Shaped Female Labor Force Function in Economic Development and Economic History*. Working Paper No. 4707. Cambridge, MA: National Bureau of Economic Research.
Haque, N. (2007). *Entrepreneurship in Pakistan*. Working Paper 29. Islamabad: Pakistan Institute of Development Economics.
International Labor Organization. (2004). *Bonded Labor in Agriculture: A Rapid Assessment in Sindh and Balochistan, Pakistan*. Geneva, Switzerland: International Labor Organization of the United Nations.
International Labor Organization. (2006). *Stimulating Youth Entrepreneurship: Barriers and Incentives to Enterprise Start-ups by Young People*. Series on Youth Entrepreneurship. Geneva, Switzerland: International Labor Organization of the United Nations.
International Labor Organization. (2014). *Promoting Youth Employment Through Activation Strategies*. Employment Working Paper No. 163. Geneva, Switzerland: International Labor Organization.
International Labor Organization. (2015). *Global Employment Trends for Youth 2015*. Geneva, Switzerland: International Labor Organization of the United Nations.
Khan, S. R., and Irfan, M. (1985). Rates of Returns to Education and the Determinants of Earnings in Pakistan. *The Pakistan Development Review*, XXIV (3&4), 671–683.
Klugman, J. (2015). *Women: Still Lacking Justice at Work, Still Lacking Safety at Home*. United Nations Development Programme, Human Development Reports. Retrieved from, http://hdr.undp.org/en/content/women-still-lacking-justice-work-still-lacking-safety-home
Kwaja, A., Mian, A., & Qamar. (2005). *Identifying Business Networks in Emerging Economies*. Harvard Kennedy School, Center for International Development. https://epod.cid.harvard.edu/publications/identifying-business-networks-emerging-economies
Lucas, R. E., Clark, A. E., Georgellis, Y., and Diener, E. (2004). Unemployment Alters the Set Point for Life Satisfaction. *Psychological Science*, 15(1): 8–13.
McKee-Ryan, F., Song, Z., Wanberg, C. R., and Kinicki, A. J. (2005). Psychological and Physical Well-Being During Unemployment: A Meta-Analytic Study. *Journal of Applied Psychology*, 90(1), 53–76.

Nasir, Z. M. (2002). Returns to Human Capital in Pakistan: A Gender Disaggregated Analysis. *The Pakistan Development Review*, 41(1), 1–28.

Organisation for Economic Co-operation and Development. (2009). *Promoting Pro-poor Growth: Employment*. Paris, France: Organisation for Economic Co-operation and Development.

Pakistan Bureau of Statistics. (2007). *Time Use Survey 2007*. Islamabad: Pakistan Bureau of Statistics.

Pakistan Bureau of Statistics. (2013). *Labor Force Survey 2012–13*. Islamabad: Statistics Division, Government of Pakistan.

Pakistan Bureau of Statistics. (2013). *Pakistan Employment Trends 2013*. Islamabad: Statistics Division, Government of Pakistan.

Pakistan Bureau of Statistics. (2014). *Pakistan Social and Living Measurement Survey 2013–14*. Islamabad: Statistics Division, Government of Pakistan.

Qayyum, W. (2007). Causes of Youth Unemployment in Pakistan. *The Pakistan Development Review*, 46(4), 611–621.

Robalino, D., and Cho, Y. (2012). *Labor Market Policies Under a Youth Bulge*. World Bank Policy Paper Series on Pakistan. The World Bank.

Sen, A. (1999). *Development As Freedom*. New York: Oxford University Press.

Sparreboom, T., and Shahnaz, L. (2007). Assessing Labor Market Vulnerability Among Young People. *The Pakistan Development Review*, 46(3), 193–213.

Theodossiou, I. (1998). The Effects of Low-Pay and Unemployment on Psychological Wellbeing: A Logistic Regression Approach. *Journal of Health Economics*, 17(1), 85–104.

United Nations Population Division. (n.d.) *World Population Prospects 2015 Revision*. http://esa.un.org/unpd/wpp/DataQuery/.

Vailey, M. J. (2006). More Power to the Pill: The Impact of Contraceptive Freedom on Women's Lifecycle Labor Supply. *The Quarterly Journal of Economics*, 121(1), 289–320.

Winkelmann, L., and Winkelmann R. (1998). Why Are the Unemployed So Unhappy? Evidence from Panel Data. Economica, 65(257), 1–15. doi:10.1111/1468-0335.00111.

World Bank, The. (2003). *Trends in Youth Labor Market in Developing and Transition Countries*. Social Protection Discussion Paper Series, Washington DC: The World Bank.

World Bank, The. (2003). *Youth Employment in Developing and Transition Countries: Prevention As Well As Cure*. Social Protection Discussion Paper Series. Washington DC: Human Development Network, The World Bank.

World Bank, The. (2007). *The Knowledge Economy and Education and Training in South Asia*. Washington, DC: The World Bank.

World Bank, The. (2007). *World Development Report 2007: Development and the Next Generation*. Washington, DC: The World Bank.

World Bank, The. (2012). *More and Better Jobs in South Asia*. South Asia Development Matters. Washington, DC: The World Bank. doi:10.1596/978-0-8213-8912-6.

World Bank, The. (2012). *World Development Report 2012: Gender Equality and Development*. Washington, DC: The World Bank.

World Bank, The. (2014). *Striving for Better Jobs*. Washington DC: The World Bank.

World Bank, The. (2014). *Student Learning in South Asia: Challenges, Opportunities and Policy Priorities*. Washington, DC: The World Bank.

CHAPTER FIFTEEN

Justification for Construction of Dams: An Economic Viability of the Jabba Dam in FATA

DR. ZALAKAT KHAN MALIK
Professor of Economics, University of Peshawar

ASFANDYAR
Economic Analyst, FATA Development Authority, Pakistan

Introduction

Over 45,000 times in the last century, people decided to build a dam. Dams were built to provide water for irrigated agriculture, domestic or industrial use, to generate hydropower or help control floods. Decisions to build dams are being contested increasingly as human knowledge and experience expand, as we develop new technologies, and as decision-making becomes more open, inclusive, and transparent. The World Commission on Dams (2009) considers that the end of any dam project must be the sustainable improvement of human welfare.

It is pertinent to mention that a greater water supply scheme covering four possible locations—Warsak Dam, Bara Dam, Munda Dam, and Jabba Dam—is underway to provide water supply to the district of Peshawar with a population of nearly 1.6 million people (Urban Policy Unit, Khyber Pakhthunkhwa, 2014). Extensive water withdrawals from Peshawar and adjoining areas for drinking and irrigation purposes has lowered the water level in the last few decades by as much as 30 to 40 feet. The existing water availability in Peshawar is not adequate to meet the expected future supply needs. Therefore, a dire need is felt for the supply and provision of water through a water supply scheme (FATA Feasibility Study of Jabba Dam, 2012).

With the construction of the proposed dam, it is claimed that most of the population in Peshawar could be served through surface run-off water. This will also lead to the preservation of ground water aquifer through the life of the Jabba Dam. These aquifers will act as an asset for the next generation. The preliminary feasibility study conducted by the FATA Development Authority (2012) concludes that constructing a water supply reservoir, such as the Jabba Dam to supply water for the future needs of Peshawar metropolitan areas and the Jamrud Khyber Agency, is comparatively a better option than the other water supply schemes underway which involves huge operation and maintenance costs as compared to gravity supplies of the Jabba Dam.

The planning of the dam and its feasibility is underway in the Khyber Agency just downstream of the confluence of Chora Khwar and Khyber Khwar near Jabba village, and that is the justification for calling this a Jabba Dam. The dam site is about 12 km away from Tehsil headquarters at Jamrud. The longitude and latitude of the dam are 33° 58', 25″ N & 71° 19' 12″ E, respectively. The other nearest villages are Ganj Gahri and Jamal Khel. The plan of the dam is the outcome of the FATA Development Authority scheme under its Annual Development Program regarding a feasibility study completed in June, 2012 by the joint venture of two firms—BAK and AGES—consultants hired by the Authority for the purpose as per its mandate because the Authority is responsible for small dams initiation and construction in the entire FATA through its small dams section (see Figure 15.1).

Based on the feasibility study, it was determined that the construction of the Jabba Dam is technically feasible. The dam will involve nearly Rs. 3240 million as cost (see Annexure I). The life of the dam is expected to be 50 years. The reservoir area at the full supply level is 847 acres. The dam can be constructed in nearly 6 years. Nearly 33 million US gallons per day and 50 cusecs per year can be the direct benefits in the shape of drinking water supply. Regarding other salient features, the dam will have a gross storage capacity of 37,746 A-ft (46.5 million m^3) at elevation 621 m, the full supply level. Live storage elevation 594 m and 621 m will be 29,159 A-ft (35.98 million m^3). The dead storage capacity is fixed to be 8,587 A-ft (10.59 million m^3) (FATA Development Authority draft feasibility report, 2012).

The Khatiya Khel tribesmen opposed the construction of the Jabba Dam in the Khyber Agency, and referred to it as a project designed to displace a population of 10,000 people from their ancestral abode. Speaking at a joint press conference at the Peshawar Press Club, elders of the Kulli Khel and Mundri Khel tribesmen, two sub-clans of Khatiya Khel, said they considered it against the interests of the tribesmen living in the area (DAWN, Feb. 15, 2009).

JUSTIFICATION FOR CONSTRUCTION OF DAMS | 235

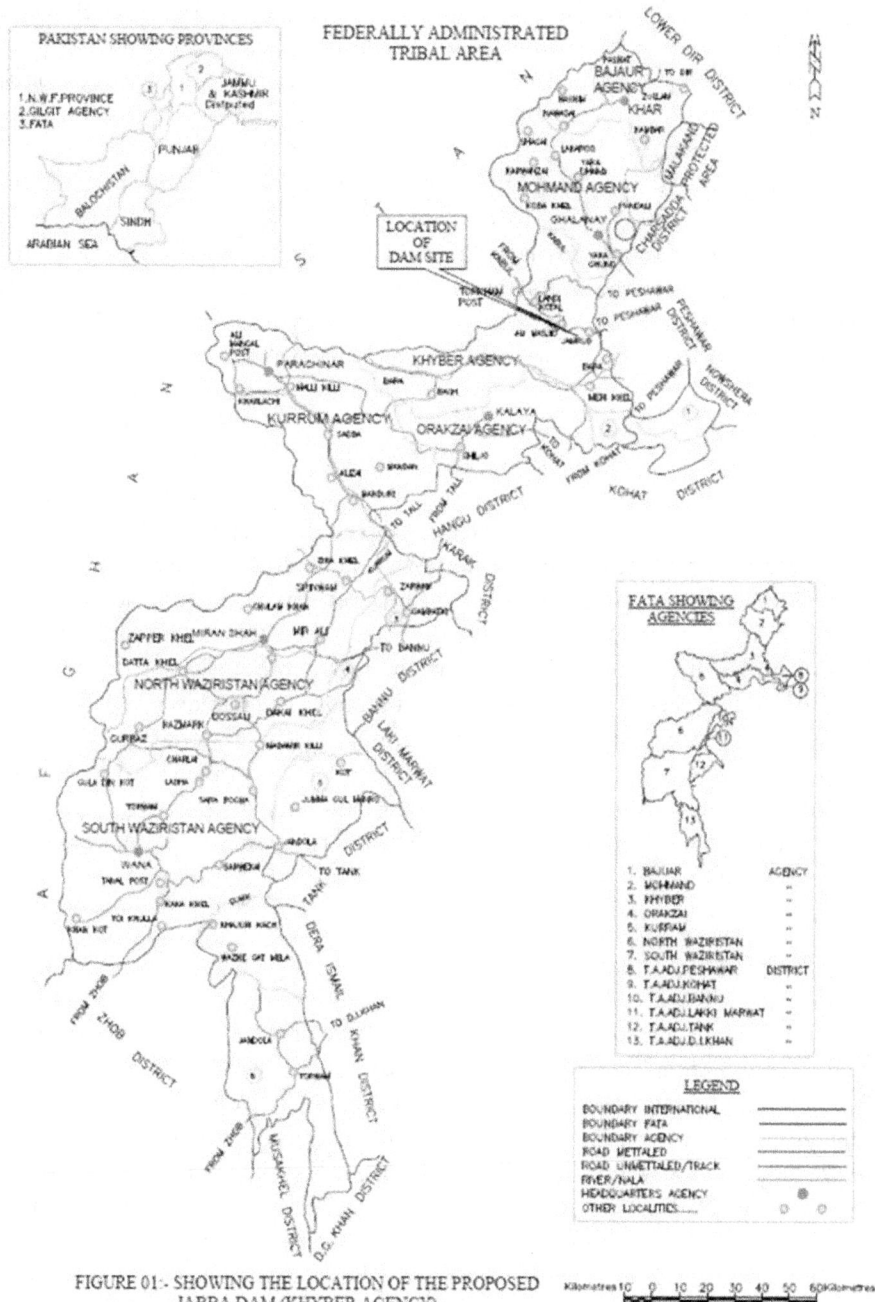

FIGURE 01:- SHOWING THE LOCATION OF THE PROPOSED
JABBA DAM (KHYBER AGENCY)

Figure 15.1: Map of the proposed Jabba Dam in Khyber Agency, Pakistan.

To address the aspirations of the people to be affected by the dam, although a sufficient amount as compensation along with a resettlement plan has been assured even then some are propagating that this dam is not a better economic option, and we must go for smaller dams elsewhere in FATA rather than focusing on this huge investment.

Although the World Bank, in its remarkable book *Pakistan's Water Economy: Running Dry* (2005), has made it very clear that Pakistan has to invest soon in costly and contentious new large dams but the implementing agencies must fulfill the concerns of the people to be affected by the dam and must chart out a complete compensation and resettlement plan for sustainable development because the World Commission on Dams states that at the end of any dam project, there must be the sustainable improvement of human welfare and not just the dam itself.

It is pertinent to assess the economic viability of the Jabba Dam based on estimates from the feasibility report conducted so far to ascertain whether to undertake the investment. A research question can be shaped as "Is Jabba Dam an economically feasible venture for the government to undertake? This will help the policymakers and planners in the FATA Development Authority, the provincial government, the federal government, and other stockholders to base their decision on scientific lines rather than just guesses, apprehensions, hue and cries.

This study proceeds with the subsequent sections wherein Section II presents an overview of the analysis of dams and similar feasibility studies undertaken in this regard. Section III focuses on the methodology adopted in the analysis. Section IV discusses the analysis, calculations, and numerical values to arrive at a clear cut decision. Section V draws conclusions and recommendations based on the analysis undertaken.

I. Analysis of Dams—An Overview

This study focuses on the economic analysis of the proposed Jabba Dam using a traditional approach. Therefore, a relevant and focused review of the literature was chosen along with their critical examination and adherence/nonadherence to the same principles or otherwise. This was also accompanied by other relevant feasibility studies and surveys undertaken in this regard on the dams in other areas.

Since the 1930s in the industrial countries and from the 1970s in developing countries, financial and economic profitability have become necessary, if not the dominant, decision criteria in water projects. Consequently, the approval of many large dam projects was contingent upon estimates of their predicted profitability. The measures typically used to assess profitabilities are the internal financial rate of return (FIRR) and the internal economic rate of return (EIRR) as determined through cost-benefit analyses. The FIRR tells the project owner if the project is profitable, while the EIRR is intended to tell society if the project improves the overall economic welfare (or well-being) of the nation (World Commission on Dams, 2009).

The Economic and Development Resource Center (EDRC, 1997) mentions that four basic steps are involved in analyzing the viability of a project, identification of cost and benefits, quantification of these benefits, valuation of costs and benefits, and comparison of benefits with costs. The same steps have also been followed while undertaking analysis in this study.

The World Commission on Dams (WCD, 2001) conducted a large survey on the costs of dams throughout the world and its findings for dams analysis can be summarized as direct costs that can be divided into four main categories: (1) construction costs; (2) resettlement costs; (3) environmental mitigation costs; and (4) operation and maintenance costs (O&M). In the study, all were considered, but point number three has not been attempted in this analysis, due to its limitations.

Aylward et al. (2001) stated that traditionally, a Cost-Benefit Analysis is performed using a limited set of chosen parameters. In most cases, the costs were restricted to direct capital investments, construction costs, and operational costs. Likewise, only direct (measurable) benefits, such as power generation, irrigation benefits, and tourism, may be taken into account. The analysis in the study used an economic valuation of direct costs and benefits. It overlooked indirect benefits even though nowadays, social and environmental effects are increasingly considered in the planning of dams, through the application of an extended CBA.

Apart from the international level, on Pakistan's level, the analysis of dams is subject to economic analysis in the government sector as well. The Planning Commission of Pakistan (2008), in its published book that also works as a guideline for development projects in Pakistan, points out that the rationale behind the project appraisal is to provide the decision-makers with financial and economic yardsticks for the selection/rejection of projects from among competing alternative proposals for investment. If the project is found technically sound, financially and economically viable, and socially desirable, only then will the project be approved.

The Planning Commission of Pakistan (2008) informs the development practitioners that a comprehensive project appraisal is carried out in the Commission at the approval stage. All the parameters, including Benefit-Cost Ratio, Net Present Worth, and Internal Rate of Return, etcetera, are worked out from financial and economic standpoints for productive and infrastructure projects.

Fraser et al. (2014), in a paper presented to a conference, examines the economics of the proposed Ruataniwha Dam in New Zealand. Three conclusions were drawn from their analysis. The first is that the dam requires a substantial subsidy for its implementation. The second finding refers to the facilitation of dairy units, subsidizing maize silage or palm kernel exfoliator (PKE) being a simpler and more flexible option. The third finding is that the dam should be constructed through farmer-owned and underwritten venture options.

To address the central question of "from where the idea of Jabba Dam originated," it is stated that "A perspective planning of small dam in FATA" was undertaken by the NESPAK and BAK consultants. It was for the first time conceived that the dam could be an option to irrigate approximately 300 acres of barren land just downstream of the proposed dam site near the Shahkas Khyber Agency.

It was revealed from the earlier records that a plan was put forward by the NESPAK consulting firms to irrigate the barren Shakas land from the Barra river canal system by using the Besai tunnel. The consultant NESPAK carried out the feasibility study of the Barra Dam in 2008. The plea of the NESPAK was to irrigate these barren lands from the proposed Barra Dam, which include remodeling of the existing irrigation system. The NESPAK's plan failed to achieve the objectives. Consequently, to proceed with the idea of irrigating the barren land of Shakas along with considering the fulfillment of future water requirements of Peshawar, another dimension of the multi-purpose dam emerged. The Feasibility Study was launched in 2012 by the FATA Development Authority, and the initial feasibility report supports the project to be feasible from an engineering point of view. The detailed design is still underway and has not been finalized.

II. Methodology

This section presents the methodology adopted in undertaking an economic analysis of the proposed Jabba Dam for the entire life of the dam using chosen techniques so that decision-makers are provided with specific tools on whether to undertake a project or not. Out of the few available techniques for evaluation of projects, this analysis prefers to use the NPV, BCR and IRR techniques that are commonly used for the same purpose while leaving opportunity, cost, payback period and initial risk assessment. It is pertinent to mention here that Dams are not an exception to be judged based on these three selected parameters.

The analysis is based on the traditional approach and available data concerning cost based on the FATA's preliminary feasibility study of 2012 and not detailed design, yet not finalized so far. The analysis takes into consideration only direct benefits that will accrue from the dam and overlooks indirect benefits; thus, a proper detailed economic and financial analysis would have an added advantage in case revised costing and revised benefits are known at a detailed design stage in the future.

Prior to conducting the analysis, it is necessary to have information regarding the project's life, expected project costs, and expected project revenue—a Dam in this case. The project's life is expected to be 50 years. The capital costs for the Jabba Dam is estimated to be Rs. 3236 million, which is the first component-initial investment/outlay in the construction of the dam during the proposed 7 years. The second major component is that of the annual operating and maintenance costs after completion of the dam amounting to Rs. 28 million. The cost to be incurred in constructing the dam has been calculated/estimated including the components of the main Dam, Coffer Dam, Clay Blanket, Spillway, Diversion Tunnel, intake tower, delivery pipes, site office, access roads, environmental and resettlement costs, and some other minor costs while that of O&M has been estimated at 1% of the total capital cost as per practices adopted in the sector.

The assumed benefits of the project consist of the gains to the society that can be measured in monetary terms. Two direct benefits are considered in the analysis. The first is the benefits of water supply, and the second is fisheries' benefits. While the indirect benefits like employment opportunities, the saving of electricity, preservation of ground water, flood mitigation control, and improvement in the socioeconomic life of people may be much higher, it has been overlooked at this stage. Both the costs and benefits are discounted through a discount rate of 12% as per the Planning Commission's instructions for the entire life of the dam.

The project would supply drinking water for different uses measured in US gallons per year based on some discharge levels. The minimum discharge level of 50 cfs has been used despite the fact that the dam can have a 60 cfs discharge at maximum to avoid over-estimation. A market value/price is allotted to 1,000 gallons of water due to the reason that water being a scarce resource has a price and is not a free good.

The water rates of Rs. 40, 50, 60, 80 and 100 are applied to perform calculations of NPV, BCR, and IRR accordingly. Thus the direct benefit in monetary terms is calculated by multiplying different water rates per 1,000 gallons with discharge quantity in gallons to obtain total expected revenue/benefits in quantifiable terms in Pakistani rupees in millions per annum and then converted to its economic value using a Standard Discounting Factor (SCF) of 0.9. The procedure involved in the analysis is in line with current practice, adopted by practitioners in the field and also abides by the guidelines of evaluation by the Planning Commission of Pakistan.

On the cost side, the following points were considered while undertaking this analysis:

i. Composite schedule rate (CSR) 2009 of the Khyber Pakhtunkhwa with 20% premium and 2% of area factor has been used for scheduled items.

ii. The rates for non-scheduled items are calculated based on a similar project like the Bazai irrigation scheme in the close vicinity of the project area.
iii. Contingencies, administration, supervision, and escalation cost has also been added to the total cost as per practice adopted for the dam.
iv. Land acquisition cost is based as per discussions with locals, survey, and likely agreements with the local and political administration of the Khyber Agency.

The detailed calculations of water benefits and fisheries benefits along with notes for calculations are in Appendix II and III, respectively.

III. Analysis

The analysis has been undertaken using Microsoft Excel (2007 version). Five scenarios were created for estimation of the total benefits for the entire 50-year lifespan of the dam. The water rates of Rs. 40, 50, 60, 80 and 100 per 1,000 gallons are assumed on 50 cusec feet discharge of the dam. The chosen discount rate while undertaking the analysis is assumed to be 12%. Detailed calculations have been performed through various Excel worksheets keeping in view the chosen five scenarios. Table 15.1 summarizes the analysis results based on three parameters of net present value (NPV), benefit cost ratio (BCR) and internal rate of return (IRR).

The table indicates that the proposed dam is not feasible @ Rs. 40 per 1,000 as expected benefits are lower than the estimated costs of constructing the dam because the NPV is negative and the BCR is less than 1. In addition to that, the IRR is also lower than the chosen discount rate of 12% as shown in detailed calculations (see Annexure IV).

However, when the assumed water rate of Rs. 50 per 1,000 gallons is used, the results indicate that construction of the Jabba Dam is a feasible investment as

Table 15.1. Economic Parameters for the Jabba Dam in FATA

Economic Parameters Summary Table for the Jabba Dam in FATA				
Water Rate Rs./ 1,000 Gallons	Discount Rate	Net Present Value (NPV)	Benefit Cost Ratio (BCR)	Internal Rate Return (IRR) (%)
40	12%	-121.52	0.89	11.34
50	12%	277.09	1.10	13.43
60	12%	675.66	1.31	15.32
80	12%	1472.83	1.73	18.68
100	12%	2269.82	2.14	21.60

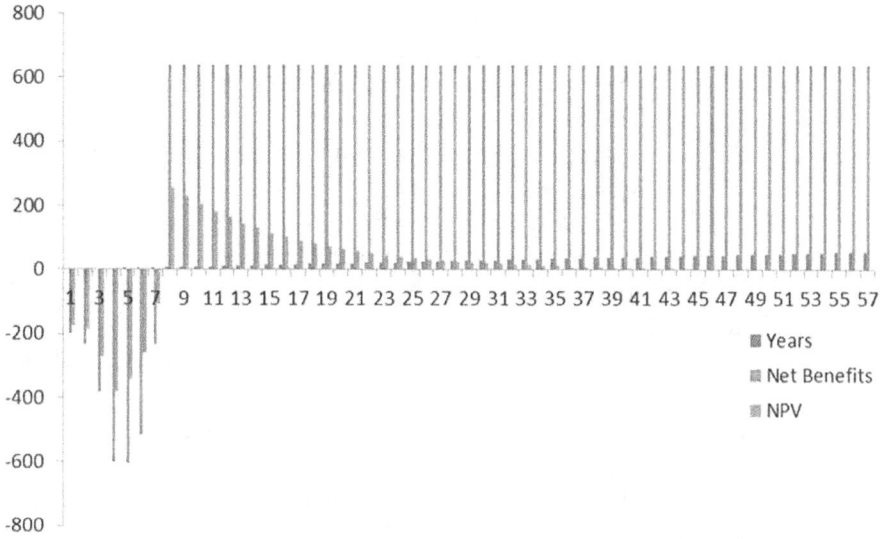

Figure 15.2: NPV and BCR over the entire life of the Jabba Dam.

all the three parameters of NPV, BCR and IRR have positive values greater than one and more than 12%, respectively (see Annexures V to VIII).

Thus, it can easily be concluded that the construction of the Jabba Dam project is feasible if the water rate per 1,000 gallons is Rs.50 or above; in case the water rate is Rs. 40 per 1,000 gallon, the project is not feasible. Thus, the feasibility or non-feasibility of the project depends upon the appropriate water rate to be charged/assumed in the analysis. When the various values of NPV and BCR are plotted against the life period of the dam, the graph indicates that after the completion period of 7 years, the same economic parameters become encouraging as shown in Figure 15.2.

The analysis can be improved further while using detailed design data with revised benefits and costs, incorporating the findings from the Environmental Impact Analysis (EIA) report when received, and the resettlement and compensation plan when prepared accordingly at the proper detailed design and pre-commencement stage of the dam.

IV. Conclusion and Recommendations

The following conclusions can be drawn from the analysis of the Jabba Dam.

i). Based on the 2012 cost estimations and assuming the direct benefits of water and fisheries with a 50-year lifespan, the proposed Jabba Dam is feasible on economic grounds. The dam can also be debated for construction on other grounds like solving the water shortage issue in Peshawar, stopping the drying of the tube wells, creation of tourism opportunities, saving of electricity, preservation of ground water, flood mitigation, avoiding losses caused by heavy floods in the recent past, and improvement in the socioeconomic life of the FATA people.

ii). The specific parameters of NPV, BCR, and IRR indicate the non-feasibility of the dam due to the calculated values of -121.52, 0.89 and 11.34, respectively when the water rate of Rs. 40 per 1,000 gallons is applied in the analysis.

iii). The results of the analysis indicate the feasibility of the dam when a water rate of Rs. 50 per 1,000 gallons is applied in the analysis; resultantly, the values of NPV, BCR, and IRR become 277.09, 1.10, and 113.43, respectively.

iv). The result of this analysis signifies that water usage in FATA (including settles areas) may not be considered a free good or service anymore on economic grounds. The appropriate water rate needs to be charged for utilizing the good without which it would be very difficult for the implementing authorities to have a sustainable water supply system.

v). Paying for water use may have an economic justification for economists. Similarly, the rationale for charging water at an appropriate market rate is to keep the water provision system sustainable. The provision of continuous and improved service at the doorstep may involve costs to the government or an agency, hence paying for the water may have strong economic justifications. However, this may not be considered as a negation of the actual and factual situation of the FATA region that does not pay a single penny for a bill (electricity) due to its peculiar status granted under the Pakistan Constitution. Thus, it is rather an economic explanation and suggestive course of action that may or may not be adopted by the policy makers. This may not be apprehended whereas the construction of the dam will make it compulsory to force people in FATA to pay for water use. The imposition of the water rate and its collection in FATA is a separate issue that may not be confused with assumed economic analysis for calculation purposes.

vi). Construction of the dam will be a tough task for the Government to initiate. On the one hand, the government will have to convince, compensate, and resettle the population to be displaced by the dam; on the other hand, it will have to provide funds of nearly Rs. 4500 million for the dam's construction. However, as the convincing and complete withdrawal of the people from their native lands in FATA would require much time for the government to do so, elongation of time in non-initiation of the dam will increase its costs further, and it would become more difficult for the resource constraints of the government to provide funds for the dam. Thus, the situation would be like the one caught between the devil and the deep blue sea.

vii). The analysis can be improved further during the feasibility and pre-commencement stage by using a detailed design with revised benefits and costs, incorporating the findings of the Environmental Impact Analysis (EIA) report, and the resettlement and compensation plan. In case the project is delayed, which will have a rising impact on the overall costs of the project, the existing analysis conducted on the basis of the assumed cost would require further subsequent revisions to check its economic viability at that stage.

Recommendations

The following recommendations can be forwarded.

i). The proposed Jabba Dam is feasible and is recommended for initiation as being a feasible water sector project. With the construction of the proposed Jabba Dam, the drinking water requirement of the Peshawar and Jamrud area will be fulfilled. The proposed Jabba Dam will supply nearly 11,800 million US gallons per year (50 cusecs) along with some fisheries benefits.

ii). Regarding the question of which Department may start construction of the dam, it is to clarify that although ground work in the form of a feasibility study has been initiated by the FATA Development Authority. Its overall annual development program has been found historically between the ranges of 1500 to 1700 million while the Jabba Dam construction would require a bare minimum amount of above five billion which is beyond the means of FATA Development Authority. Hence, the Dam cannot be implemented by this Authority unless and until some funds beyond its routine annual development program are allocated. Therefore, it is recommended that the FATA Development Authority only undertake its detailed design that will nearly cost her Rs. 120 million as an additional cost and the implementation may be made by the Irrigation/Public Health Engineering Departments of the provincial government of Khyber Pakhtunkhwa or any other relevant department of the Federal Government of Pakistan.

iii). As the Dam Reservoir would be in FATA and the major beneficiaries would be in the settled areas of Khyber Pakhtunkhwa, mostly Peshawar and adjacent areas, it is logical that both provincial governments and political administrations closely communicate and coordinate, including other relevant stockholders like the FATA Development Authority, to facilitate other preliminary requirements, such as conducting feasibility studies, commencing detailed design and land acquisition, etcetera as this dam seems to be a project that will involve many administrative arrangements, facilitation, and likely operational issues in the future.

iv). In case the provincial government is facing scarcity of funds and capacity, the donor's agencies in general and the World Bank and Asian Development Bank, in particular, may be contacted for financial and technical support. As the benefits of the dam are diverse and the direct benefits of water and fisheries i.e., like saving of electricity by stoppage of tube wells, flood control, employment opportunities, preservation of ground water for future generations, recreational facilities along with other environmental benefits may be accrued through this project, which will easily qualify it for assistance from donors.

v). As the Jabba village along with other neighboring lands may be submerged in the reservoir area in the Khyber Agency, proper detailed assessments, compensation surveys, and resettlement plans may be made an integral part of the detailed design, and due care should be made for the aspirations of locals to be addressed accordingly. In case the locals are not willing or reluctant to vacate their land, aggressive sensitization and awareness campaigns may be initiated at the earliest so that the public opinion is molded accordingly. The local elders, *Maliks*, and political representatives may be involved to offset the negative perception and sentiments of the local people.

vi). A rough re-assessment for the year 2016 may indicate that the construction cost may increase and may probably be above five billion when the cost of materials and other components are adjusted for expected inflation, and other factors like escalations and consultancy are taken into consideration. The sooner the construction of the proposed Jabba Dam, the lower the financial burden of construction on the government. Therefore, the early initiation greatly matters for this dam so that its fate does not become like that of the Kala Bagh Dam.

Acknowledgment

The authors of this study acknowledge using some of the data, information and a map, mentioned in the draft feasibility report on Jabba Dam, available from the FATA Development Authority (FATA DA) in unpublished form.

Annexure-I

General Abstract of Cost for Jabba Dam Khyber Agency

S. No	Description	Total Amount (Rs) in Million
A.	**PRELIMINARY ITEMS**	
A.1	Land Acquisition	205.26
	SUB TOTAL	205.26
B.	**WORK ITEMS**	
B.1	Main Dam & Coffer Dam	683.41
B.2	Clay Blanket & Grounting	188.49
B.3	Spillway	1161.76
B.4	Diversion Tunnel	262.67
B.5	Intake Tower, Shaft & Access Bridge	24.45
B.6	Delivery Pipe	134.27
B.7	Access Road (For Dam)	45.21
B.8	Site Office/ Inspection Hut	1.47
	SUB TOTAL	2501.73
	Unforseen items @ 2% of B.1-B.9	50.03
	SUB TOTAL(B)	2551.76
C.	**GENERAL ITEMS**	
C.1	Detail Design & Tender Documents	102.07
C.2	Geo-Technical Investigations for Detail Design Stage	5.00
C.3	Hydraulic Model Testing of Spilway	8.00
C.4	Construction Supervision Charges @ 5% for items B1 To B6	127.59
C.5	Contingencies @ 2% on items B-1 to B-7	51.04
C.6	Managerial Staff	19.64
	SUB TOTAL	313.34
	TOTAL PROJECT BASE COST (A+B+C)	3070.36
D	Escalation @ 6.5% for Items B-1 to B-7	165.86
	TOTAL PROJECT COST (INCLUDING D)	3236.22

Annexure-II

Water Supply Benefits for the Jabba Dam based on 50 and 60 C.F.s Discharge

Discharge cfs	Discharge per Day (US gallons)	Discharge per Year	Water Rate (per 1000 gallon)	Total Benefits (Rupees)	Total Benefits Rs. Million	Total Economic Benefits (Rs. Million)
50	32,300,000	11,789,500,000	40	471,580,000	471.58	424.42
50	32,300,000	11,789,500,000	50	589,475,000	589.48	530.53
50	32,300,000	11,789,500,000	60	707,370,000	707.37	636.63
50	32,300,000	11,789,500,000	80	943,160,000	943.16	848.84
50	32,300,000	11,789,500,000	100	1,178,950,000	1,178.95	1,061.06
60	38,708,460.27	14,128,588,000	40	565,143,520	565.14	508.63
60	38,708,460.27	14,128,588,000	60	847,715,280	847.72	762.94
60	38,708,460.27	14,128,588,000	80	1,130,287,040	1,130.29	1,017.26
60	38,708,460.27	14,128,588,000	100	1,412,858,800	1,412.86	1,271.57

Annexure-III

Fisheries Benefits of Jabba Dam		
Description	Unit	Quantity
Reservoir area (for fisheries)	Acre	847
Fertility	Moderate	
Fish fingering stocking rate	Per Acre	650
Total seed stocking	No.	550550
Mortality	%	40%
Growth @ 1 Kg/year	Kg	330330
Fishing efforts	%	50
Fishing catch	Prer Kg	165165
Average Market rate	Rs. /Kg	200
Total financial value	Rupees in million	33.03
Total economical value (SCF=0.9)	Rupees in million	29.73

Annexure-IV

Economic Analysis of Jabba Dam Khyber Agency @ Rs. 40/1000 Gallons

Discount Rate	0.12								(Rs. Million)
		Costs			Benefits				
Year	Cost	O&M Cost	Total Cost	P.V. of cost	Water benefits	Fishries Benefits	Total Benefits	P.V. of benefits	Net Benefits	NPV
1	198.50	0.00	198.50	177.23	0	0	0.00	0.00	-198.50	-177.23
2	233.20	0.00	233.20	185.91	0	0	0.00	0.00	-233.20	-185.91
3	380.30	0.00	380.30	270.69	0.00	0.00	0.00	0.00	-380.30	-270.69
4	599.10	0.00	599.10	380.74	0.00	0.00	0.00	0.00	-599.10	-380.74
5	604.90	0.00	604.90	343.24	0.00	0.00	0.00	0.00	-604.90	-343.24
6	514.20	0.00	514.20	260.51	0.00	0.00	0.00	0.00	-514.20	-260.51
7	233.10	0.00	233.10	105.44	0.00	0.00	0.00	0.00	-233.10	-105.44
8		27.63	27.63	11.16	424.42	29.73	454.15	183.42	426.52	172.26
9		27.63	27.63	9.96	424.42	29.73	454.15	163.77	426.52	153.81
10		27.63	27.63	8.90	424.42	29.73	454.15	146.22	426.52	137.33
11		27.63	27.63	7.94	424.42	29.73	454.15	130.56	426.52	122.61
12		27.63	27.63	7.09	424.42	29.73	454.15	116.57	426.52	109.48
13		27.63	27.63	6.33	424.42	29.73	454.15	104.08	426.52	97.75
14		27.63	27.63	5.65	424.42	29.73	454.15	92.93	426.52	87.27
15		27.63	27.63	5.05	424.42	29.73	454.15	82.97	426.52	77.92
16		27.63	27.63	4.51	424.42	29.73	454.15	74.08	426.52	69.57
17		27.63	27.63	4.02	424.42	29.73	454.15	66.14	426.52	62.12
18		27.63	27.63	3.59	424.42	29.73	454.15	59.06	426.52	55.46
19		27.63	27.63	3.21	424.42	29.73	454.15	52.73	426.52	49.52

20	27.63	27.63	2.86	424.42	29.73	454.15	47.08	426.52	44.22
21	27.63	27.63	2.56	424.42	29.73	454.15	42.04	426.52	39.48
22	27.63	27.63	2.28	424.42	29.73	454.15	37.53	426.52	35.25
23	27.63	27.63	2.04	424.42	29.73	454.15	33.51	426.52	31.47
24	27.63	27.63	1.82	424.42	29.73	454.15	29.92	426.52	28.10
25	27.63	27.63	1.63	424.42	29.73	454.15	26.71	426.52	25.09
26	27.63	27.63	1.45	424.42	29.73	454.15	23.85	426.52	22.40
27	27.63	27.63	1.30	424.42	29.73	454.15	21.30	426.52	20.00
28	27.63	27.63	1.16	424.42	29.73	454.15	19.01	426.52	17.86
29	27.63	27.63	1.03	424.42	29.73	454.15	16.98	426.52	15.94
30	27.63	27.63	0.92	424.42	29.73	454.15	15.16	426.52	14.24
31	27.63	27.63	0.82	424.42	29.73	454.15	13.53	426.52	12.71
32	27.63	27.63	0.74	424.42	29.73	454.15	12.08	426.52	11.35
33	27.63	27.63	0.66	424.42	29.73	454.15	10.79	426.52	10.13
34	27.63	27.63	0.59	424.42	29.73	454.15	9.63	426.52	9.05
35	27.63	27.63	0.52	424.42	29.73	454.15	8.60	426.52	8.08
36	27.63	27.63	0.47	424.42	29.73	454.15	7.68	426.52	7.21
37	27.63	27.63	0.42	424.42	29.73	454.15	6.86	426.52	6.44
38	27.63	27.63	0.37	424.42	29.73	454.15	6.12	426.52	5.75
39	27.63	27.63	0.33	424.42	29.73	454.15	5.47	426.52	5.13
40	27.63	27.63	0.30	424.42	29.73	454.15	4.88	426.52	4.58
41	27.63	27.63	0.27	424.42	29.73	454.15	4.36	426.52	4.09

Continued

Economic Analysis of Jabba Dam Khyber Agency @ Rs. 40/1000 Gallons

Discount Rate	0.12								(Rs. Million)
	Costs				Benefits				
Year	Cost	O&M Cost	Total Cost	P.V. of cost	Water benefits	Fishries Benefits	Total Benefits	P.V. of benefits	Net Benefits	NPV
42		27.63	27.63	0.24	424.42	29.73	454.15	3.89	426.52	3.65
43		27.63	27.63	0.21	424.42	29.73	454.15	3.47	426.52	3.26
44		27.63	27.63	0.19	424.42	29.73	454.15	3.10	426.52	2.91
45		27.63	27.63	0.17	424.42	29.73	454.15	2.77	426.52	2.60
46		27.63	27.63	0.15	424.42	29.73	454.15	2.47	426.52	2.32
47		27.63	27.63	0.13	424.42	29.73	454.15	2.21	426.52	2.07
48		27.63	27.63	0.12	424.42	29.73	454.15	1.97	426.52	1.85
49		27.63	27.63	0.11	424.42	29.73	454.15	1.76	426.52	1.65
50		27.63	27.63	0.10	424.42	29.73	454.15	1.57	426.52	1.48
51		27.63	27.63	0.09	424.42	29.73	454.15	1.40	426.52	1.32
52		27.63	27.63	0.08	424.42	29.73	454.15	1.25	426.52	1.18
53		27.63	27.63	0.07	424.42	29.73	454.15	1.12	426.52	1.05
54		27.63	27.63	0.06	424.42	29.73	454.15	1.00	426.52	0.94
55		27.63	27.63	0.05	424.42	29.73	454.15	0.89	426.52	0.84
56		27.63	27.63	0.05	424.42	29.73	454.15	0.80	426.52	0.75
57		27.63	27.63	0.04	424.42	29.73	454.15	0.71	426.52	0.67
Total	2763.30			1827.549	11459.34	802.71	12262.05	1631.67	8752.74	-121.52
Economic Internal Rate of Return (EIRR)										11.34%
NPV at 12% Discount Rate										-121.52
Benefit Cost Ratio at 12% Discount Rate										0.89

Annexure-V

Economic Analysis of Jabba Dam Khyber Agency @ Rs. 50/1000 Gallons

(Rs. Million)

Discount Rate	0.12									
		Costs				Benefits				
Year	Cost	O&M Cost	Total Cost	P.V. of Cost	Water Benefits	Fisheries Benefits	Total Benefits	P.V. of Benefits	Net Benefits	NPV
1	198.50	0.00	198.50	177.23	0	0	0.00	0.00	-198.50	-177.23
2	233.20	0.00	233.20	185.91	0	0	0.00	0.00	-233.20	-185.91
3	380.30	0.00	380.30	270.69	0.00	0.00	0.00	0.00	-380.30	-270.69
4	599.10	0.00	599.10	380.74	0.00	0.00	0.00	0.00	-599.10	-380.74
5	604.90	0.00	604.90	343.24	0.00	0.00	0.00	0.00	-604.90	-343.24
6	514.20	0.00	514.20	260.51	0.00	0.00	0.00	0.00	-514.20	-260.51
7	233.10	0.00	233.10	105.44	0.00	0.00	0.00	0.00	-233.10	-105.44
8		27.63	27.63	11.16	530.53	29.73	560.26	226.28	532.63	215.12
9		27.63	27.63	9.96	530.53	29.73	560.26	202.04	532.63	192.07
10		27.63	27.63	8.90	530.53	29.73	560.26	180.39	532.63	171.49
11		27.63	27.63	7.94	530.53	29.73	560.26	161.06	532.63	153.12
12		27.63	27.63	7.09	530.53	29.73	560.26	143.80	532.63	136.71
13		27.63	27.63	6.33	530.53	29.73	560.26	128.40	532.63	122.07
14		27.63	27.63	5.65	530.53	29.73	560.26	114.64	532.63	108.99
15		27.63	27.63	5.05	530.53	29.73	560.26	102.36	532.63	97.31
16		27.63	27.63	4.51	530.53	29.73	560.26	91.39	532.63	86.88

Continued

Economic Analysis of Jabba Dam Khyber Agency @ Rs. 50/1000 Gallons

Discount Rate	0.12								(Rs. Million)
	Cost	Costs			Benefits				
Year		O&M Cost	Total Cost	P.V. of Cost	Water Benefits	Fisheries Benefits	Total Benefits	P.V. of Benefits	Net Benefits	NPV
17		27.63	27.63	4.02	530.53	29.73	560.26	81.60	532.63	77.57
18		27.63	27.63	3.59	530.53	29.73	560.26	72.86	532.63	69.26
19		27.63	27.63	3.21	530.53	29.73	560.26	65.05	532.63	61.84
20		27.63	27.63	2.86	530.53	29.73	560.26	58.08	532.63	55.22
21		27.63	27.63	2.56	530.53	29.73	560.26	51.86	532.63	49.30
22		27.63	27.63	2.28	530.53	29.73	560.26	46.30	532.63	44.02
23		27.63	27.63	2.04	530.53	29.73	560.26	41.34	532.63	39.30
24		27.63	27.63	1.82	530.53	29.73	560.26	36.91	532.63	35.09
25		27.63	27.63	1.63	530.53	29.73	560.26	32.96	532.63	31.33
26		27.63	27.63	1.45	530.53	29.73	560.26	29.43	532.63	27.97
27		27.63	27.63	1.30	530.53	29.73	560.26	26.27	532.63	24.98
28		27.63	27.63	1.16	530.53	29.73	560.26	23.46	532.63	22.30
29		27.63	27.63	1.03	530.53	29.73	560.26	20.94	532.63	19.91
30		27.63	27.63	0.92	530.53	29.73	560.26	18.70	532.63	17.78
31		27.63	27.63	0.82	530.53	29.73	560.26	16.70	532.63	15.87
32		27.63	27.63	0.74	530.53	29.73	560.26	14.91	532.63	14.17
33		27.63	27.63	0.66	530.53	29.73	560.26	13.31	532.63	12.65
34		27.63	27.63	0.59	530.53	29.73	560.26	11.88	532.63	11.30

35	27.63	27.63	0.52	530.53	29.73	560.26	10.61	532.63	10.09
36	27.63	27.63	0.47	530.53	29.73	560.26	9.47	532.63	9.01
37	27.63	27.63	0.42	530.53	29.73	560.26	8.46	532.63	8.04
38	27.63	27.63	0.37	530.53	29.73	560.26	7.55	532.63	7.18
39	27.63	27.63	0.33	530.53	29.73	560.26	6.74	532.63	6.41
40	27.63	27.63	0.30	530.53	29.73	560.26	6.02	532.63	5.72
41	27.63	27.63	0.27	530.53	29.73	560.26	5.38	532.63	5.11
42	27.63	27.63	0.24	530.53	29.73	560.26	4.80	532.63	4.56
43	27.63	27.63	0.21	530.53	29.73	560.26	4.29	532.63	4.07
44	27.63	27.63	0.19	530.53	29.73	560.26	3.83	532.63	3.64
45	27.63	27.63	0.17	530.53	29.73	560.26	3.42	532.63	3.25
46	27.63	27.63	0.15	530.53	29.73	560.26	3.05	532.63	2.90
47	27.63	27.63	0.13	530.53	29.73	560.26	2.72	532.63	2.59
48	27.63	27.63	0.12	530.53	29.73	560.26	2.43	532.63	2.31
49	27.63	27.63	0.11	530.53	29.73	560.26	2.17	532.63	2.06
50	27.63	27.63	0.10	530.53	29.73	560.26	1.94	532.63	1.84
51	27.63	27.63	0.09	530.53	29.73	560.26	1.73	532.63	1.65
52	27.63	27.63	0.08	530.53	29.73	560.26	1.55	532.63	1.47
53	27.63	27.63	0.07	530.53	29.73	560.26	1.38	532.63	1.31
54	27.63	27.63	0.06	530.53	29.73	560.26	1.23	532.63	1.17
55	27.63	27.63	0.05	530.53	29.73	560.26	1.10	532.63	1.05

Continued

Economic Analysis of Jabba Dam Khyber Agency @ Rs. 50/1000 Gallons

Discount Rate	0.12								(Rs. Million)
	Costs			Benefits					
Year	Cost	O&M Cost	Total Cost	P.V. of Cost	Water Benefits	Fisheries Benefits	Total Benefits	P.V. of Benefits	Net Benefits	NPV
56		27.63	27.63	0.05	530.53	29.73	560.26	0.98	532.63	0.93
57		27.63	27.63	0.04	530.53	29.73	560.26	0.88	532.63	0.83
Total	2763.30			1827.549	14324.31	802.71	15127.02	2012.91	11617.71	277.09

Economic Internal Rate of Return — 13.43%
NPV at 12% Discount Rate — 277.09
Benefit Cost Ratio at 12% Discount Rate — 1.10

Annexure-VI

Economic Analysis of Jabba Dam Khyber Agency @ Rs. 60/1000 Gallons

(Rs. Million)

Discount Rate	0.12									
		Costs			Benefits					
Year	Cost	O&M Cost	Total Cost	P.V. of Cost	Water Benefits	Fisheries Benefits	Total Benefits	P.V. of Benefits	Net Benefits	NPV
1	198.50	0.00	198.50	177.23	0	0	0.00	0.00	-198.50	-177.23
2	233.20	0.00	233.20	185.91	0	0	0.00	0.00	-233.20	-185.91
3	380.30	0.00	380.30	270.69	0.00	0.00	0.00	0.00	-380.30	-270.69
4	599.10	0.00	599.10	380.74	0.00	0.00	0.00	0.00	-599.10	-380.74
5	604.90	0.00	604.90	343.24	0.00	0.00	0.00	0.00	-604.90	-343.24
6	514.20	0.00	514.20	260.51	0.00	0.00	0.00	0.00	-514.20	-260.51
7	233.10	0.00	233.10	105.44	0.00	0.00	0.00	0.00	-233.10	-105.44
8		27.63	27.63	11.16	636.63	29.73	666.36	269.13	638.73	257.97
9		27.63	27.63	9.96	636.63	29.73	666.36	240.30	638.73	230.33
10		27.63	27.63	8.90	636.63	29.73	666.36	214.55	638.73	205.65
11		27.63	27.63	7.94	636.63	29.73	666.36	191.56	638.73	183.62
12		27.63	27.63	7.09	636.63	29.73	666.36	171.04	638.73	163.95
13		27.63	27.63	6.33	636.63	29.73	666.36	152.71	638.73	146.38
14		27.63	27.63	5.65	636.63	29.73	666.36	136.35	638.73	130.70
15		27.63	27.63	5.05	636.63	29.73	666.36	121.74	638.73	116.69
16		27.63	27.63	4.51	636.63	29.73	666.36	108.70	638.73	104.19

Continued

Economic Analysis of Jabba Dam Khyber Agency @ Rs. 60/1000 Gallons

Discount Rate	0.12									(Rs. Million)
	Cost	Costs			Benefits				Net Benefits	NPV
Year		O&M Cost	Total Cost	P.V. of Cost	Water Benefits	Fisheries Benefits	Total Benefits	P.V. of Benefits		
17		27.63	27.63	4.02	636.63	29.73	666.36	97.05	638.73	93.03
18		27.63	27.63	3.59	636.63	29.73	666.36	86.65	638.73	83.06
19		27.63	27.63	3.21	636.63	29.73	666.36	77.37	638.73	74.16
20		27.63	27.63	2.86	636.63	29.73	666.36	69.08	638.73	66.22
21		27.63	27.63	2.56	636.63	29.73	666.36	61.68	638.73	59.12
22		27.63	27.63	2.28	636.63	29.73	666.36	55.07	638.73	52.79
23		27.63	27.63	2.04	636.63	29.73	666.36	49.17	638.73	47.13
24		27.63	27.63	1.82	636.63	29.73	666.36	43.90	638.73	42.08
25		27.63	27.63	1.63	636.63	29.73	666.36	39.20	638.73	37.57
26		27.63	27.63	1.45	636.63	29.73	666.36	35.00	638.73	33.55
27		27.63	27.63	1.30	636.63	29.73	666.36	31.25	638.73	29.95
28		27.63	27.63	1.16	636.63	29.73	666.36	27.90	638.73	26.74
29		27.63	27.63	1.03	636.63	29.73	666.36	24.91	638.73	23.88
30		27.63	27.63	0.92	636.63	29.73	666.36	22.24	638.73	21.32
31		27.63	27.63	0.82	636.63	29.73	666.36	19.86	638.73	19.04
32		27.63	27.63	0.74	636.63	29.73	666.36	17.73	638.73	17.00
33		27.63	27.63	0.66	636.63	29.73	666.36	15.83	638.73	15.17
34		27.63	27.63	0.59	636.63	29.73	666.36	14.14	638.73	13.55

35	27.63	27.63	0.52	636.63	29.73	666.36	12.62	638.73	12.10
36	27.63	27.63	0.47	636.63	29.73	666.36	11.27	638.73	10.80
37	27.63	27.63	0.42	636.63	29.73	666.36	10.06	638.73	9.64
38	27.63	27.63	0.37	636.63	29.73	666.36	8.98	638.73	8.61
39	27.63	27.63	0.33	636.63	29.73	666.36	8.02	638.73	7.69
40	27.63	27.63	0.30	636.63	29.73	666.36	7.16	638.73	6.86
41	27.63	27.63	0.27	636.63	29.73	666.36	6.39	638.73	6.13
42	27.63	27.63	0.24	636.63	29.73	666.36	5.71	638.73	5.47
43	27.63	27.63	0.21	636.63	29.73	666.36	5.10	638.73	4.89
44	27.63	27.63	0.19	636.63	29.73	666.36	4.55	638.73	4.36
45	27.63	27.63	0.17	636.63	29.73	666.36	4.06	638.73	3.89
46	27.63	27.63	0.15	636.63	29.73	666.36	3.63	638.73	3.48
47	27.63	27.63	0.13	636.63	29.73	666.36	3.24	638.73	3.11
48	27.63	27.63	0.12	636.63	29.73	666.36	2.89	638.73	2.77
49	27.63	27.63	0.11	636.63	29.73	666.36	2.58	638.73	2.48
50	27.63	27.63	0.10	636.63	29.73	666.36	2.31	638.73	2.21
51	27.63	27.63	0.09	636.63	29.73	666.36	2.06	638.73	1.97
52	27.63	27.63	0.08	636.63	29.73	666.36	1.84	638.73	1.76
53	27.63	27.63	0.07	636.63	29.73	666.36	1.64	638.73	1.57
54	27.63	27.63	0.06	636.63	29.73	666.36	1.47	638.73	1.40
55	27.63	27.63	0.05	636.63	29.73	666.36	1.31	638.73	1.25

Continued

Economic Analysis of Jabba Dam Khyber Agency @ Rs. 60/1000 Gallons

(Rs. Million)

Discount Rate	0.12								
	Costs				Benefits				
Year	Cost	O&M Cost	Total Cost	P.V. of Cost	Water Benefits	Fisheries Benefits	Total Benefits	P.V. of Benefits	Net Benefits	NPV
56		27.63	27.63	0.05	636.63	29.73	666.36	1.17	638.73	1.12
57		27.63	27.63	0.04	636.63	29.73	666.36	1.04	638.73	1.00
Total	2763.30			1827.549	17189.01	802.71	17991.72	2394.10	14482.41	675.66

Economic Internal Rate of Return 15.32%
NPV at 12% Discount Rate 675.66
Benefit Cost Ratio at 12% Discount Rate 1.31

Annexure-VII

Economic Analysis of Jabba Dam Khyber Agency @ Rs. 80/1000 Gallons
(Rs. Million)

Discount Rate	0.12									
	Costs				Benefits					
Year	Cost	O&M Cost	Total Cost	P.V. of Cost	Water Benefits	Fisheries Benefits	Total Benefits	P.V. of Benefits	Net Benefits	NPV
1	198.50	0.00	198.50	177.23	0	0	0.00	0.00	-198.50	-177.23
2	233.20	0.00	233.20	185.91	0	0	0.00	0.00	-233.20	-185.91
3	380.30	0.00	380.30	270.69	0.00	0.00	0.00	0.00	-380.30	-270.69
4	599.10	0.00	599.10	380.74	0.00	0.00	0.00	0.00	-599.10	-380.74
5	604.90	0.00	604.90	343.24	0.00	0.00	0.00	0.00	-604.90	-343.24
6	514.20	0.00	514.20	260.51	0.00	0.00	0.00	0.00	-514.20	-260.51
7	233.10	0.00	233.10	105.44	0.00	0.00	0.00	0.00	-233.10	-105.44
8		27.63	27.63	11.16	848.84	29.73	878.57	354.84	850.94	343.68
9		27.63	27.63	9.96	848.84	29.73	878.57	316.82	850.94	306.86
10		27.63	27.63	8.90	848.84	29.73	878.57	282.88	850.94	273.98
11		27.63	27.63	7.94	848.84	29.73	878.57	252.57	850.94	244.62
12		27.63	27.63	7.09	848.84	29.73	878.57	225.51	850.94	218.42
13		27.63	27.63	6.33	848.84	29.73	878.57	201.35	850.94	195.01
14		27.63	27.63	5.65	848.84	29.73	878.57	179.77	850.94	174.12
15		27.63	27.63	5.05	848.84	29.73	878.57	160.51	850.94	155.46
16		27.63	27.63	4.51	848.84	29.73	878.57	143.31	850.94	138.81

Continued

Economic Analysis of Jabba Dam Khyber Agency @ Rs. 80/1000 Gallons
(Rs. Million)

Discount Rate	0.12								
	Cost	Costs			Benefits				
Year		O&M Cost	Total Cost	P.V. of Cost	Water Benefits	Fisheries Benefits	Total Benefits	P.V. of Benefits	Net Benefits	NPV
17		27.63	27.63	4.02	848.84	29.73	878.57	127.96	850.94	123.93
18		27.63	27.63	3.59	848.84	29.73	878.57	114.25	850.94	110.66
19		27.63	27.63	3.21	848.84	29.73	878.57	102.01	850.94	98.80
20		27.63	27.63	2.86	848.84	29.73	878.57	91.08	850.94	88.21
21		27.63	27.63	2.56	848.84	29.73	878.57	81.32	850.94	78.76
22		27.63	27.63	2.28	848.84	29.73	878.57	72.61	850.94	70.32
23		27.63	27.63	2.04	848.84	29.73	878.57	64.83	850.94	62.79
24		27.63	27.63	1.82	848.84	29.73	878.57	57.88	850.94	56.06
25		27.63	27.63	1.63	848.84	29.73	878.57	51.68	850.94	50.06
26		27.63	27.63	1.45	848.84	29.73	878.57	46.14	850.94	44.69
27		27.63	27.63	1.30	848.84	29.73	878.57	41.20	850.94	39.90
28		27.63	27.63	1.16	848.84	29.73	878.57	36.79	850.94	35.63
29		27.63	27.63	1.03	848.84	29.73	878.57	32.84	850.94	31.81
30		27.63	27.63	0.92	848.84	29.73	878.57	29.32	850.94	28.40
31		27.63	27.63	0.82	848.84	29.73	878.57	26.18	850.94	25.36
32		27.63	27.63	0.74	848.84	29.73	878.57	23.38	850.94	22.64
33		27.63	27.63	0.66	848.84	29.73	878.57	20.87	850.94	20.22
34		27.63	27.63	0.59	848.84	29.73	878.57	18.64	850.94	18.05

JUSTIFICATION FOR CONSTRUCTION OF DAMS | 261

35	27.63	27.63	0.52	848.84	29.73	878.57	16.64	850.94	16.12
36	27.63	27.63	0.47	848.84	29.73	878.57	14.86	850.94	14.39
37	27.63	27.63	0.42	848.84	29.73	878.57	13.27	850.94	12.85
38	27.63	27.63	0.37	848.84	29.73	878.57	11.84	850.94	11.47
39	27.63	27.63	0.33	848.84	29.73	878.57	10.57	850.94	10.24
40	27.63	27.63	0.30	848.84	29.73	878.57	9.44	850.94	9.14
41	27.63	27.63	0.27	848.84	29.73	878.57	8.43	850.94	8.17
42	27.63	27.63	0.24	848.84	29.73	878.57	7.53	850.94	7.29
43	27.63	27.63	0.21	848.84	29.73	878.57	6.72	850.94	6.51
44	27.63	27.63	0.19	848.84	29.73	878.57	6.00	850.94	5.81
45	27.63	27.63	0.17	848.84	29.73	878.57	5.36	850.94	5.19
46	27.63	27.63	0.15	848.84	29.73	878.57	4.78	850.94	4.63
47	27.63	27.63	0.13	848.84	29.73	878.57	4.27	850.94	4.14
48	27.63	27.63	0.12	848.84	29.73	878.57	3.81	850.94	3.69
49	27.63	27.63	0.11	848.84	29.73	878.57	3.40	850.94	3.30
50	27.63	27.63	0.10	848.84	29.73	878.57	3.04	850.94	2.94
51	27.63	27.63	0.09	848.84	29.73	878.57	2.71	850.94	2.63
52	27.63	27.63	0.08	848.84	29.73	878.57	2.42	850.94	2.35
53	27.63	27.63	0.07	848.84	29.73	878.57	2.16	850.94	2.10
54	27.63	27.63	0.06	848.84	29.73	878.57	1.93	850.94	1.87
55	27.63	27.63	0.05	848.84	29.73	878.57	1.72	850.94	1.67

Continued

Economic Analysis of Jabba Dam Khyber Agency @ Rs. 80/1000 Gallons

Discount Rate 0.12

(Rs. Million)

Year	Cost		P.V. of Cost	Benefits				Net Benefits	NPV
	O&M Cost	Total Cost		Water Benefits	Fisheries Benefits	Total Benefits	P.V. of Benefits		
56	27.63	27.63	0.05	848.84	29.73	878.57	1.54	850.94	1.49
57	27.63	27.63	0.04	848.84	29.73	878.57	1.38	850.94	1.33
Total	2763.30		1827.549	22918.68	802.71	23721.39	3156.53	20212.08	1472.83

Economic Internal Rate of Return 18.68%
NPV at 12% Discount Rate 1472.83
Benefit Cost Ratio at 12% Discount Rate 1.73

Annexure-VIII

Economic Analysis of Jabba Dam Khyber Agency @ Rs. 100/1000 Gallons

(Rs. Million)

Discount Rate	0.12								
	Cost	Costs			Benefits				
Year	Cost	O&M Cost	Total Cost	P.V. of Cost	Water Benefits	Fisheries Benefits	Total Benefits	P.V. of Benefits	Net Benefits	NPV
1	198.50	0.00	198.50	177.23	0	0	0.00	0.00	-198.50	-177.23
2	233.20	0.00	233.20	185.91	0	0	0.00	0.00	-233.20	-185.91
3	380.30	0.00	380.30	270.69	0.00	0.00	0.00	0.00	-380.30	-270.69
4	599.10	0.00	599.10	380.74	0.00	0.00	0.00	0.00	-599.10	-380.74
5	604.90	0.00	604.90	343.24	0.00	0.00	0.00	0.00	-604.90	-343.24
6	514.20	0.00	514.20	260.51	0.00	0.00	0.00	0.00	-514.20	-260.51
7	233.10	0.00	233.10	105.44	0.00	0.00	0.00	0.00	-233.10	-105.44
8		27.63	27.63	11.16	1061.00	29.73	1090.73	440.53	1063.10	429.37
9		27.63	27.63	9.96	1061.00	29.73	1090.73	393.33	1063.10	383.36
10		27.63	27.63	8.90	1061.00	29.73	1090.73	351.19	1063.10	342.29
11		27.63	27.63	7.94	1061.00	29.73	1090.73	313.56	1063.10	305.62
12		27.63	27.63	7.09	1061.00	29.73	1090.73	279.96	1063.10	272.87
13		27.63	27.63	6.33	1061.00	29.73	1090.73	249.97	1063.10	243.64
14		27.63	27.63	5.65	1061.00	29.73	1090.73	223.18	1063.10	217.53
15		27.63	27.63	5.05	1061.00	29.73	1090.73	199.27	1063.10	194.22
16		27.63	27.63	4.51	1061.00	29.73	1090.73	177.92	1063.10	173.41

Continued

Economic Analysis of Jabba Dam Khyber Agency @ Rs. 100/1000 Gallons

Discount Rate	0.12								(Rs. Million)	
	Cost	Costs			Benefits					
Year		O&M Cost	Total Cost	P.V. of Cost	Water Benefits	Fisheries Benefits	Total Benefits	P.V. of Benefits	Net Benefits	NPV
17		27.63	27.63	4.02	1061.00	29.73	1090.73	158.86	1063.10	154.83
18		27.63	27.63	3.59	1061.00	29.73	1090.73	141.84	1063.10	138.25
19		27.63	27.63	3.21	1061.00	29.73	1090.73	126.64	1063.10	123.43
20		27.63	27.63	2.86	1061.00	29.73	1090.73	113.07	1063.10	110.21
21		27.63	27.63	2.56	1061.00	29.73	1090.73	100.96	1063.10	98.40
22		27.63	27.63	2.28	1061.00	29.73	1090.73	90.14	1063.10	87.86
23		27.63	27.63	2.04	1061.00	29.73	1090.73	80.48	1063.10	78.44
24		27.63	27.63	1.82	1061.00	29.73	1090.73	71.86	1063.10	70.04
25		27.63	27.63	1.63	1061.00	29.73	1090.73	64.16	1063.10	62.54
26		27.63	27.63	1.45	1061.00	29.73	1090.73	57.29	1063.10	55.83
27		27.63	27.63	1.30	1061.00	29.73	1090.73	51.15	1063.10	49.85
28		27.63	27.63	1.16	1061.00	29.73	1090.73	45.67	1063.10	44.51
29		27.63	27.63	1.03	1061.00	29.73	1090.73	40.78	1063.10	39.74
30		27.63	27.63	0.92	1061.00	29.73	1090.73	36.41	1063.10	35.48
31		27.63	27.63	0.82	1061.00	29.73	1090.73	32.51	1063.10	31.68
32		27.63	27.63	0.74	1061.00	29.73	1090.73	29.02	1063.10	28.29
33		27.63	27.63	0.66	1061.00	29.73	1090.73	25.91	1063.10	25.26
34		27.63	27.63	0.59	1061.00	29.73	1090.73	23.14	1063.10	22.55

Continued

35	27.63	27.63	0.52	1061.00	29.73	1090.73	20.66	1063.10	20.13
36	27.63	27.63	0.47	1061.00	29.73	1090.73	18.44	1063.10	17.98
37	27.63	27.63	0.42	1061.00	29.73	1090.73	16.47	1063.10	16.05
38	27.63	27.63	0.37	1061.00	29.73	1090.73	14.70	1063.10	14.33
39	27.63	27.63	0.33	1061.00	29.73	1090.73	13.13	1063.10	12.80
40	27.63	27.63	0.30	1061.00	29.73	1090.73	11.72	1063.10	11.42
41	27.63	27.63	0.27	1061.00	29.73	1090.73	10.47	1063.10	10.20
42	27.63	27.63	0.24	1061.00	29.73	1090.73	9.34	1063.10	9.11
43	27.63	27.63	0.21	1061.00	29.73	1090.73	8.34	1063.10	8.13
44	27.63	27.63	0.19	1061.00	29.73	1090.73	7.45	1063.10	7.26
45	27.63	27.63	0.17	1061.00	29.73	1090.73	6.65	1063.10	6.48
46	27.63	27.63	0.15	1061.00	29.73	1090.73	5.94	1063.10	5.79
47	27.63	27.63	0.13	1061.00	29.73	1090.73	5.30	1063.10	5.17
48	27.63	27.63	0.12	1061.00	29.73	1090.73	4.73	1063.10	4.61
49	27.63	27.63	0.11	1061.00	29.73	1090.73	4.23	1063.10	4.12
50	27.63	27.63	0.10	1061.00	29.73	1090.73	3.77	1063.10	3.68
51	27.63	27.63	0.09	1061.00	29.73	1090.73	3.37	1063.10	3.28
52	27.63	27.63	0.08	1061.00	29.73	1090.73	3.01	1063.10	2.93
53	27.63	27.63	0.07	1061.00	29.73	1090.73	2.69	1063.10	2.62
54	27.63	27.63	0.06	1061.00	29.73	1090.73	2.40	1063.10	2.34
55	27.63	27.63	0.05	1061.00	29.73	1090.73	2.14	1063.10	2.09

Continued

Economic Analysis of Jabba Dam Khyber Agency @ Rs. 100/1000 Gallons

Discount Rate	0.12								(Rs. Million)
	Costs				Benefits				
Year	Cost	O&M Cost	Total Cost	PV. of Cost	Water Benefits	Fisheries Benefits	Total Benefits	PV. of Benefits	Net Benefits	NPV
56		27.63	27.63	0.05	1061.00	29.73	1090.73	1.91	1063.10	1.86
57		27.63	27.63	0.04	1061.00	29.73	1090.73	1.71	1063.10	1.66
Total	2763.30			1827.549	28647.00	802.71	29449.71	3918.78	25940.40	2269.82

Economic Internal Rate of Return   21.60%
NPV at 12% Discount Rate   2269.82
Benefit Cost Ratio at 12% Discount Rate   2.14

Notes to Calculations from Annexure I to VIII:

1. *The total cost mentioned at Annexure–I has been subtracted escalation and then standard conversion factor (SCF) of 0.9 is applied to arrive at economic cost of the dam.*
2. *The operation and maintenance cost (O&M) has roughly calculated @ 1% of the capital cost of the project and then converted into economic costs using SCF of 0.9 accordingly.*
3. *The water benefits has been assumed on the basis of minimum per day discharge of the dam to be as 32.3 million US gallons per day with detailed calculations at Annexure–II for different water rates and calculated economic value thereof.*
4. *Detailed calculations on the basis of total reservoir area of 847 acres, fisheries benefits has been calculated at Annexure–III and then converted into economic benefit using SCF = 0.9.*
5. *The benefits has been valued @ Rs. 40, 50, 60, 80 & 100 per 1,000 US gallons and total revenue calculated by multiplying the unit price per 1,000 US gallons with total discharge (minimum) per year.*

Bibliography

Aylward, B., Berkhoff, J., Green, C., Gutman, P., Lagman, A., Manion, M., Markandya, A., McKenney, B., Naudascher-Jankowski, K., Oud, B., Penman, A., Porter, S., Rajapakse, C., Southgate, D., and Unsworth. R. (2001). *Financial, Economic and Distributional Analysis, Thematic Review III.1* prepared as an input to the World Commission on Dams, Cape Town, www.dams.org.

Berga, L. (2008). *Dams for Sustainable Development*. Paper presented at High-Level International Forum on Water Resources and Hydropower, Beijing, October 17–18.

Curitiba Declaration, The. (1997). *Affirming the Right to Life and Livelihood of People Affected by Dams*. Approved at the First International Meeting of People Affected by Dams, Curitiba, Brasil, March 14.

Dubash, N. (2009). Global Norms Through Global Deliberation? Reflections on the World Commission on Dams. *Global Governance: A Review of Multilateralism and International Organizations*, 15(2), 219–238.

FATA Development Authority. (2012). *Draft Feasibility Report* (unpublished).

Financial Times. (2006). *EIB Accuses China of Unscrupulous Loans*, 28 November.

Fraser, P. J., Ridler, B. J., and W. J. Anderson, Röpere Consulting, N. Z.Grazing Systems Limited, N. Z. (2014). Institute of Agriculture & Environment, Massey University, N. Z. Paper presented at the 2014 NZARES Conference Tahuna, Nelson, New Zealand, August 28–29, 2014.

Fujikura, R., and Nakayama, M. (2009). Lessons Learned from the World Commission on Dams. *International Environmental Agreements: Politics, Law and Economics*, 9(2), 173–190.

International Commission on Large Dams. (1997). *Some Inescapable Facts Which May Put the Issue in Perspective*. Paper presented at the World Bank/IUCN workshop, Large Dams – Learning from the Past, Looking at the Future. Gland, Switzerland, April 10–11.

International Hydropower Association. (1999). *Financial Statements for the Year Ended 31 December 1999*. London: International Hydropower Association.

International Hydropower Association. (2004). *Sustainability Guidelines*. London: International Hydropower Association.

International Hydropower Association. (2008). Hydropower Sustainability Assessment Forum Launched in Washington, In *IHA Connect*, Issue 1.

International Hydropower Association. (2009). *Draft Hydropower Sustainability Assessment Protocol*. London: International Hydropower Association.

International Social and Environmental Accreditation and Labeling Alliance. (2014). *Code of Good Practice for Setting Social and Environmental Standards*. London: ISEAL Alliance. https://www.isealalliance.org/get-involved/resources/iseal-codes-good-practice

IUCN (The World Conservation Union) and The World Bank Group. (1997). *Large Dams, Learning From the Past, Looking at the Future*. Paper presented at the World Bank/IUCN workshop, Large Dams—Learning from the Past, Looking at the Future. Gland, Switzerland.

Planning Commission of Pakistan. (2008). *Guidelines for Project Management*. Retrieved from https://www.pc.gov.pk.

Reinicke, W., and Deng, F. (2000). *Critical Choices, the United Nations, Networks, and the Future of Global Governance*. Ottawa: International Development Research Centre.

Wolfowitz, P. (2005). *Reaching For a Double Dividend*. Remarks made at the Forum on Global Climate Change and Biodiversity. São Paulo, Brazil, December 20.

World Bank, The. (2000). *World Bank Welcomes Commission on Dams Report*. News Release No. 2001/119/S, 16 November 2000.

World Bank, The. (2003a). *Power for Development: A Review of the World Bank Group's Experience with Private Participation in the Electricity Sector*. Washington, DC: World Bank.

World Bank, The. (2003b). *Water Resources Sector Strategy: Strategic Directions for World Bank Engagement*. Washington, DC: World Bank.

World Bank, The. (2005). *Pakistan's Water Economy: Running Dry*. Washington, DC: The World Bank.

World Commission on Dams, The. (2000). *Dams and Development. A New Framework for Decision-making*. London: The Report of the World Commission on Dams.

World Commission on Dams, The. (2001). *Final WCD Forum Report, Responses, Discussions, and Outcomes*. Cape Town: The World Commission on Dams.

World Commission on Dams. (2009). *The Dam Industry, the World Commission on Dams and the HSAF Process*. London: The Report of the World Commission on Dams.

About the Authors

The contributing authors to this project are not only highly acclaimed publishers in their respective fields, but also possess a valuable depth of personal, academic, and career experience within the FATA region. This team of authors includes development specialists, counterterrorism analysts, humanitarians as well as policy, economics, and international relations experts. Moreover, their insights are as globally diverse as their specializations. Prof. Dr. Syed Hussain Shaheed Soherwordi, Chairman, Department of International Relations, former director of the Institute of Peace and Conflict Studies at the University of Peshawar, a former Fulbright Scholar and University of Edinburgh graduate, has been thoroughly involved in foreign and security policies studies with respect to policy, peace and conflict studies in Afghanistan and Pakistan's tribal districts. Dr. Muhammad Nasir is a Senior Research Economist and member of one of Pakistan's leading think tanks. Prof. Dr. Zalakat Khan Malik, currently serving as a Professor and former chairman of the Department of Economics at Peshawar University, has had significant academic experience in both Pakistan and Afghanistan.

Amongst the development specialists that have contributed to this project are Dr. Shaista Naz, Dr. Zainab Azmat, Mr. Asfandyar, and Saeed Ahmad. Dr. Shaista Naz has a depth of insights from her humanitarian work with Save the Children, Sarhad Rural Support Program (SRSP), FATA Secretariat Special projects, and Aware Girls, among other initiatives. Dr. Shahnaz Akhtar is the former Director of the Institute of Business Management Studies at Agricultural University, Peshawar. She also teaches Advanced Quantitative Research

Methods, Advanced Micro-Economics, Macro-Economics, Managerial as well as Environmental and Resource Economics. Ms. Zainab Azmat has run multiple State Department Projects, conducted several formal research studies with UNDP, and has fulfilled leadership roles in other development projects as well. She was also the founder of the Edifies Youth Network (EYN), a youth initiative aimed at youth empowerment and positive engagement. Mr. Asfandyar holds a Ph.D. in Economics and is the Deputy Director of the National Vocation and Technical Training Commission (NAVTTC). Saeed Ahmad has been highly involved in developmental research and has been commissioned by a wide variety of international organizations including USAID, UNFPA, WHO, UNICEF, UNDP, World Bank, and the KP Government.

Dr. Sajid Ali holds a Ph.D. in Policy Studies from the University of Edinburgh, an MEd in Leadership and Policy Studies from Monash University, Australia; and a Master's in Sociology from the University of Karachi; globalization and education policy reforms, privatization of education, and the role of knowledge in shaping policy. Dr. Noreen Naseer, a resident of the Kurram District, is presently serving as a faculty member of the University of Peshawar's Political Science Department. Throughout her work, she emphasizes Peace Studies and Women's Empowerment. Dr. Fazal Wahid holds a Ph.D. from the department of International Relations, University of Peshawar. He served in the Education Corps of the Pakistan Army, and as a staff officer for different Army Formations in Kashmir, Bahawalpur, Abbottabad, and Islamabad. He later taught National and International Affairs to Cadets and Officers of the Pakistan Army for three years until his retirement. Muhammad Sabir, a PhD from Vrije University, Amsterdam and an associate professor, heads the Department of Management Sciences, GIK Institute, Topi, Swabi. He writes extensively on the tribal areas' economic and social development with a special focus on its management. Dr. Noor Shah Jehan, a graduate of the Hull University, UK is a security analyst. Ms. Amina Khan, a research associate at the Institute of Strategic Studies, Islamabad is a prolific writer on FATA issues.

From humanitarian workers to former military-men, from economics to policy experts, and a range of specializations in between, the insights collected here emerge from an interdisciplinary perspective. Here, these professionals have produced the first-ever text featuring the FATA, its unique challenges, its cultural and geopolitical value as a region, and how to integrate the tribal lands with the rest of Pakistani society.

Contributors

Dr. Tahir I. Shad
Dr. Tahir I. Shad is an Associate Professor in the Department of Political Science and International Studies at Washington College in Chestertown, Maryland. He is the Academic Director for the minor in Middle Eastern Studies. He also directs programs in Islamic, Turkish, and Near Eastern studies at the Institute for Religion Politics and Culture at Washington College. He earned his Ph.D. from the University of Pittsburgh; MA from the University of Pittsburgh; P.G.C.E from the University of London, and a BA honors from the school of African Asian studies at the University of Sussex, U.K. As an expert on the Middle East and South Asia, he has lectured/trained students and elected public policymakers in the United States, Philippines, Indonesia, Argentina, Ecuador, and Colombia. He served as a curator of the Goldstein program in public affairs between 2003 in 2010. He brought national figures to campus to meet with students to discuss domestic and international politics. He served as the Associate Dean of the college between 1995 and 1999. Dr. Shad developed and implemented 40 international exchange programs in 30 countries. He has been a commentator on local Delaware TV stations, National Public Radio in Baltimore, Maryland on Breakfast club and Kingston, Jamaica.

Dr. Syed Hussain Shaheed Soherwordi

Dr. Syed Hussain Shaheed Soherwordi is a Professor, Director of the Institute of Peace and Conflict Studies and former Chairman of the Department of International Relations with the University of Peshawar, following a career as researcher and teacher of International Relations, Conflict Resolution, Political Science and Creative Leadership. He completed his M. Phil and Ph.D. from the University of Edinburgh, Scotland. He remained a fellow of the Fulbright, Carnegie, Charles Wallace, Higher Education Commission (HEC), and Edinburgh University. He taught at the Fulbright Commission in Bulgaria for 5 years (2010–2014), where his teaching and training concerned peace and conflict resolution during the 21st century especially in the conflict zones like FATA (Pakistan), Afghanistan, and the Middle East. Dr. Soherwordi has written more than thirty-seven (37) research papers on India, Pakistan, Tribal Areas of Pakistan, War on Terror, Afghanistan, Pak-U.S. relations, Conflict Resolution, and the application of strategies to the prevention of terrorism and amelioration of counterterrorism. He edited a volume titled "Socio-Economic and Political Currents in FATA: A Way Forward" in 2015. His forthcoming books are on "Pak-U.S. Relations: A Comparative Study during Cold War and War on Terror" and "Pakistan, Taliban and the War on Terror," "Enduring Economic Challenges of FATA" (an edited volume), and "Together We Served: An Empirical History of AK Regiment."

Dr. Tahir Abbas

Dr. Tahir Abbas FRSA is currently Assistant Professor in Security Studies at the Leiden University Institute of Security and Global Studies at The Hague in The Netherlands (2018–). His recent books are *Countering Violent Extremism* (IB Tauris, 2021, *forthcoming*), *Islamophobia and Radicalisation* (Oxford University Press, 2019), *Political Muslims* (Syracuse University Press, 2018, co-edited with S Hamid), *Contemporary Turkey in Conflict* (Edinburgh University Press, 2017), and *Muslim Diasporas in the West* (ed., four volumes, Routledge, 2017). Abbas read Economics at Queen Mary University of London. He has a MSocSc in Economic Development and Policy from the University of Birmingham and a PhD in Ethnic Relations from the University of Warwick. His personal website is www.tahirabbas.co.uk.

Dr. Noor Shah Jehan

Dr. Noor Shah Jehan is a Ph.D. Professor from the University of Hull, United Kingdom. He is teaching in the Department of International Relations at the University of Peshawar where his research and teaching is mostly related to security and foreign policy studies.

Dr. Noreen Naseer

Dr. Noreen Naseer is a resident of the Kurram District, erstwhile Federally Administered Tribal Areas (FATA), presently serving as a faculty in the Department of Political Science, University of Peshawar, Khyber Pakhtunkhwa. As a student of Peace Studies, she attended a three-week course/workshop on "Sources of Conflict in South Asia," arranged by the Friedrich Naumann Foundation, at the HikkaduwaSrilanka in 1998. To further her knowledge and expertise in peace studies, she also attended a three-week course developed and organized by the Peace Women Across the Globe, SANGAT and Mediation Support Project, ETH/Zurich in Katmandu, Nepal in 2013. She also participated in the International Visitor Leadership Program, United States Department of State Bureau of Educational and Cultural Affairs in 2014, "Trade Along the New Silk Road: Promoting Regional Integration through Economic Cooperation." Her work entitled "FATA: 'A Permanent War Zone': Breaking Silence" is showcased in "Women and Politics of Peace: South Asia Narratives on Militarization, Power, and Justice," published in December 2016 by Sage Publications.

Dr. Fazal Wahid

Dr. Fazal Wahid completed his Master's Degree in International Relations from the University of Peshawar in 1998. He joined the Education Corps of the Pakistan Army and served as a Staff Officer at different Army Formations at Kashmir, Bahawalpur, and Islamabad. He was the instructor of International Relations at the Pakistan Military Academy, Kakul Abbottabad and taught National and International Affairs to the cadets and officers of the Pakistan Army for 3 years. In 2007, he left the Pakistan Army as Captain and started pursuing his civilian career. In 2013–2014, he resumed his studies again in the Department of International Relations at the University of Peshawar and completed his Ph.D. studies in 2019. His research topic was "The Post 9/11 U.S. Policy Towards Afghanistan with Impact on the Federally Administered Tribal Area of Pakistan."

Dr. Muqtedar Khan

Dr. Muqtedar Khan is a Professor in the Department of Political Science and International Relations at the University of Delaware. He is the Academic Director of the State Department's National Security Institute (2016–2019) at the Institute for Global Studies at the University of Delaware. He was a Senior Nonresident Fellow of the Brookings Institution (2003–2008), a Fellow of the Alwaleed Center at Georgetown University (2006–2007), and a Fellow of the Institute for Social Policy and Understanding (2001–2016). He is currently a Senior Fellow with the Center for Global Policy (2016–present). He earned his Ph.D. in International Relations, Political Philosophy, and Islamic Political Thought, from Georgetown University in May 2000. He founded the Islamic Studies Program at the University of Delaware and was its first Director from 2007–2010. As an expert on governance, Islam and American foreign policy, he has lectured and trained scholars, students, elected leaders and policymakers in the United States, Philippines, Indonesia, Malaysia, Finland, Germany, United Kingdom, France, Turkey, Tunisia, Morocco, Egypt, India, Ireland, Jordan, Saudi Arabia, UAE, Qatar, Singapore, Canada, and Belgium. He was the Academic Director of the U.S. State Departments' National Security Institute, 2018–2019 and the American Foreign Policy Institute, 2019–2021. His most recent book *Islam and Good Governance: Political Philosophy of Ihsan* was published in April 2019 by Palgrave Macmillan. He is also the author of several books: *American Muslims: Bridging Faith and Freedom* (Amana, 2002), *Jihad for Jerusalem: Identity and Strategy in International Relations* (Praeger, 2004), *Islamic Democratic Discourse* (Lexington Books, 2006), *Debating Moderate Islam: The Geopolitics of Islam and the West* (University of Utah Press, 2007). Dr. Khan is a frequent commentator in the international media. His articles and commentaries can be found at www.ijtihad.org. His research can be found at https://udel.academia.edu/MuqtedarKhan

Dr. Zainab Azmat
Dr. Zainab Azmat worked as an Assistant Professor at the Institute of Management Sciences in Peshawar. She has vast experience as a trainer both in the corporate and social sector. She has run multiple girls education projects with the U.S. State Department, managed the women's enterprise sector with USAID's FATA LDP Project, done research studies with UNDP, Summer Camps with Elementary and Secondary Education Department KP, and the IELTS project with the British Council Pakistan. She is the Founder and owner of Edifiers Youth Network (EYN), a youth initiative aimed at youth empowerment and positive engagement. She holds memberships at the Boards of Directors Elementary and Secondary Education Foundation, Private Schools Regulatory Authority, and Youth Development Commission Government of Khyber Pakhtunkhwa. She has represented FATA as a member of the National Commission on Status of Women Pakistan. She is also a member of the Pakistan U.S. Alumni network, Thakra Qabailee Khwenday, and United Nations Women Gender Taskforce.

Dr. Shaista Naz
Dr. Shaista Naz is currently working as a Lecturer in the Rural Development Department of Amir Muhammad Khan Campus, Mardan, University of Agriculture, Peshawar. She is pursuing a doctorate in Rural Development from the Institute of Development Studies (IDS), University of Agriculture, Peshawar. Previously, she served as a humanitarian worker for several years with Save the Children, Sarhad Rural Support Program (SRSP), FATA Secretariat Special Projects, and Aware Girls. In her journey with these organizations, she empowered

rural women of Peshawar, Charsadda, Buner, and FATA in the field of kitchen gardening and political participation. Being a Rural Development Specialist, she has published several research articles mainly focusing on women's empowerment in the under-privileged areas of Khyber Pakhtunkhwa like the FATA.

Noor Paio Khan
Professor Khan is a Professor at the Institute of Development Studies, The University of Agriculture, Peshawar.

Dr. Muhammad Nasir
Dr. Muhammad Nasir works as a Senior Research Economist at the Pakistan Institute of Development Economics (PIDE), a leading think tank in economic research in the country. He has also served as the Head of Research Unit at the Pakistan Centre for Philanthropy. He obtained his Ph.D. from Clark University, USA in 2016. He has over 10 years of experience in applied economic research and teaching. He has more than 20 publications in reputable national and international journals.

Dr. Sajid Ali
Dr. Sajid Ali is an Associate Professor and Interim Director at the Aga Khan University's Institute for Educational Development, Pakistan. He holds a Ph.D. in Policy Studies from the University of Edinburgh, an MEd in Leadership and Policy from Monash University, and a Masters in Sociology from the University of Karachi. Dr. Ali is the recipient of various awards including A.R. Kiyani Gold Medal–1997, Australian Development Award–2003, Commonwealth Youth Leadership Award–2003, Edinburgh Research Award–2006, South Asian Visiting Fellowship at Oxford–2011, and Australian Alumni Excellence Award–2014. Dr. Ali has taught at the Hamdard University, Karachi University, and the University of Edinburgh. He is the General Secretary of the Pakistan Association for Research in Education (PARE). His research interests include globalization and education policy, new forms of educational governance, policy networks, education reforms, privatization of education, and role of knowledge resources in shaping policy.

Amina Khan
Amina Khan is a Senior Research Fellow at the Institute of Strategic Studies in Islamabad. She is a prolific writer on FATA's governance and economics.

Dr. Shahnaz Akhtar
Dr. Shahnaz Akhtar is currently a Professor in the Institute of Development Studies (IDS) at the University of Agriculture, Peshawar-Pakistan. In addition

to her regular job as a professor in IDS-AUP, she has also served as the Director of Institute of Business Management Studies (IBMS), Agricultural University Peshawar, Pakistan in 2013–2014. In the capacity of a Visiting Faculty, she has served in numerous universities and academic institutions in Peshawar and Islamabad. Her teaching specialization is Advanced Quantitative Research Methods, Advanced Microeconomics, Macroeconomics, Managerial, and Environmental & Resources Economics. During 2013–2014, she worked as a Consultant for Editorial and Technical Panel Experts on an FAO publication, "Women in Agriculture in Pakistan" (ISBN 978-92-5-106598-8).

Sher Ayaz
Sher Ayaz is a lecturer of Economics at the Government Degree College, Mir Ali, North Waziristan Tribal District.

Dr. Muhammad Sabir Afridi
Dr. Muhammad Sabir Afridi has a Ph.D. from the Vrije University in Amsterdam and is an Associate Professor. He heads the Department of Management Sciences at the GIK Institute, Topi, Swabi. He writes extensively on the tribal areas' economic and social development with a special focus on its management. Previously, he has worked as an Economist at Planning Commission of Pakistan for about 5 years at various economic sections such as *China Pakistan Economic Corridor, Money, Prices and Fiscal Policy, Plan Coordination* and also as a team member for *New Growth Strategy* for Pakistan.

Saeed Ahmed
Saeed Ahmed has over 10 years of social research experience in the Public and Development sector—having conducted numerous research studies for the Pak/Afghan region, commissioned by a diverse range of international organizations, including USAID, UNFPA, WHO, UNICEF, UNDP, World Bank, and the KP Government. Some of Saeed's policy research work includes a chapter on youth employment in the Pakistan National Human Development Report 2016, meta-analysis for the Common Country Assessment of Pakistan and contributions to the United Nations' Development Assistance Framework (UNDAF), and policy inputs for the United Nations' Population Fund's 5-year plan. Saeed's academic credentials comprise post-graduate studies in Social Research with a concentration on Social Policy and Development from the Australian National University (ANU); while his prior academic pursuits feature an M.B.A in Finance.

Dr. Zalakat Khan Malik

Dr. Zalakat Khan Malik is a Professor and Chairman of the Department of Economics at the University of Peshawar. He completed his Ph.D. in Economics from the University of Peshawar. He started his career as a Lecturer in the Department of Economics in Islamia College Peshawar. He has also worked as Professor and Chairman at the Department of Economics, Kardan University Kabul Afghanistan. Dr. Malik has been a Visiting Civilian Faculty Member of the Command and Staff College Quetta since 2013. He is the author of 30 research papers published in national journals and 14 in international journals.

Asfandyar

Asfandyar is a PhD scholar at Economics Department, University of Peshawar. Presently, he is serving as Economic Analyst, FATA Development Authority, Pakistan. He facilitates the commission on the planning of training activities, selection of the institutes for training, induction of trainees, preparing budgets, monitoring of training activities, and impact evaluation of training. A special feature of this assigned work consists of the implementation of the Prime Minister's Youth Skills Development Programme in the entire province and merged districts (FATA). Prior to this assignment, he served as a Statistical Officer and Senior Planning Officer in the Higher Education Department Khyber Pakhtunkhwa for almost 3 years and effectively dealt with all development matters of the department. He also worked as an Economic Analyst at the FATA Development Authority for 5 years.

Index

A

Abbas, A. 200–202
Abbottabad Commission Inquiry Report 23
Abubakari, Z. 184
Accelerated Development Strategy (ADS) 174
Access, defined 181
Adkin, Mark 36
Adrenocorticotropic hormone (ACTH) 141
Adult literacy rate 226
Adult population unemployment 221
Afghan Civil War 2
Afghan community 81
Afghan guerrilla 51
Afghanistan
   Al-Qaeda operatives 9
   bleeding wound 41
   civil war 37
   covert war in 39
   FATA and 90–91
   free state of Pukhtoonistan 80
   Graveyard of Empires 35, 40
   Islamic extremism 46
   market of violence 43
   militaristic and nationalistic rhetoric 83
   Operation Enduring Freedom 61
   political and social turmoil 8
   Soviet forces 45
   Soviet invasion 34
   special envoy 81
   strategic depth 48
   Taliban 35
   terrain
      and climate 34
      highlands and low lands 35
   U.S. attitude 42
   U.S. operations in 88
   war against Soviet forces 60

war of independence 89–90
Afghanistan–Pakistan Transit Trade Agreement (APTTA) 31
Afghan Muhajideen
  logistics and training 51
Afghan Mujahideen
  assault on Jalalabad 42
  struggle against the invading Soviet forces 81–82
Afghan policy 51
Afghan refugees 64
  Muhajireen 81, 90
Afghan Resistance Force
  Government of Pakistan
    political, moral and diplomatic support 81
  Mujahideen 81, 90
Afghan resistance movement 82
Afghan security forces 84
Afghan war 38, 41
  multidimensional after-shocks 49
Afridi Maleks 81
Afridi, Muhammad Sabir 179–183, 197–216
Aga Khan Rural Support Programme (AKRSP) 156
Agencies 169
Agriculture 222
  extension workers 184
  food security and food self-sufficiency 180
  irrigation infrastructure 229
  lack of irrigation water 187
  lowest-paid sectors 225
Agronomic strategies 183
Ahmad, Khurshid 48
Ahmad, T. I. 126–127, 130–132
Ahmed, A. 8, 18
Ahmed, Eqbal 42–43, 57
Ahmed, Ishtiaq 36
Ahmed, Khaled 50
Ahmed, Mahmood 44
Ahmed, Mahmud 53
Ahmed, Saeed 200–202, 219–230

Ahmed, Samina 57
Ahmed, Shamshad 54, 55
Ahmed, V. 200, 201, 202
Ailaan, Alif 156, 160–161, 163
Air transport in FATA 206
  civil and military operations 206
  infrastructure 203
Akhtar., S. 128, 179–193
Akresh, R. 140
Ali, Arshad 107–108
Ali, Hazrat 82
Ali, Sajid (Dr.) 153–165
Allah 99–100
All India Radio station
  free state of Pukhtoonistan 80
Al-Qaeda 42, 83, 84, 94
  FATA, hub of 86–87
    terrorist activities 87
  financing of Taliban 43
  Tora Bora 87
Al-Salam (Quran 59:23) 100
Altman, J. 115
Al-Zawahiri, Aiman 91
America
  policy interests in South Asia 59
  proxy war against the Soviet Union 39
Analysis of Variance (ANOVA) 186
And fight them until persecution is no more (Quran 8:39) 98
Annual Development Program (ADP) 17, 74, 208, 234
Annual Status of Education Report (ASER) 157
Arab Islam 35, 46
Arab Spring 94, 95
  2011 to 2013, 3
Armitage, Richard 45
ASER survey 160–161, 163
Asfandyar 233–266
Ashton, D. N. 155
Askari-Rizvi, Hasan 49
Austin, O. C. 183
Australian Government
  indigenous communities 115

Ayaz, E. 19, 107, 109
Aylward, B. 237
Azad Jammu and Kashmir 198
Aziz, Mohammad 44, 53
Aziz, Sartaj 55
Aziz, Shahid 85
Azmat, Zainab 105–120

B

Backwardness 3, 135
Bajaur Agencies 10–11, 179, 207, 208, 209
    unemployment rate 221
Bakht, Z. B. 201
Balochistan 32, 106
Barker, D. J. P. 141
Barra Dam 233, 238
Basic Health Units (BHUs) 34
Bazai irrigation scheme 240
B.C. Ministry of Agriculture and Lands 2006 81
Bearden, Milton 40–41, 42–43
Becker, Gary 155
Beg, Mirza Aslam 48
Benefit-Cost Ratio 237
Bennett, R. M. 184
Benz, A. 156–157
Berkhoff, J. 237
Berry, R. A. 181
Betts, R. K. 55
Beuran, M. 202
Beyzatlar, M. A. 200
Bhurtto, Benazir 44, 47
Bhutto, Z.A. 32, 69
    development and economic reforms 170
Bignon, V. 202
Bilsborrow, R. E. 114
Bin Laden, Osama 49–50, 86
Biradar, N. 125, 129, 132
BJP government
    military offensive against the Pakistani intruders 55
Black market 3

Blue-water navigation technologies 35, 46
Boarnet, M. G. 201, 202
Bofors guns 53
Boopen, S. 200
Breadwinners 159
British model of administration 169
British Raj, 1901 169
Brodie, Bernard 38
Brown, R. 140
Brzezinski, Zbigniew 90
Bureau of Emigration and Overseas
    Employment, 2015 220
Bureau of Statistics Planning and
    Development Department Government
    of KP 65–66, 72
Bush, George H.W. 40, 42, 59
    isolationism 60
Butt, Ziauddin 44

C

Camacho, A. 140
Cameroon National Household Survey 202
Caring for country, defined 115
Carr, E. H. 90
Caruso, G. D. 140
Cattle farming
    Ghilzai Powindas 12
Cawthome, R. 36
Central Asia
    oil and gas resources 48
Central Asian Republics (CARs) 13
Central Treaty Organization (CENTO) 80
Centre for FATA Studies 157
Chakma 40
Chamberlin, Peter 90
Chase, Robert 60
Chavula, H. 204
Chayal, K. 131
Cheema, Iqbal 52
Chemical fertilizers 188
Chibber, M. L. 53
Chi, J. 203

Child health indicators
  FATA and KP 138–139
Children
  exposure to terrorism 142, 149
  impact of violence 136–138
China–Pakistan Economic Corridor (CPEC) 4, 157, 198, 206
Chi-square test 126, 130
Civil war 43
Clean drinking water and sanitation in the FATA 65
Cline, W. R. 181
Clinton, William J. 54, 89–90
  failing to take action against bin Laden 59–60
Coalition-Islamic Jamhoori Ittehad (IJI) 48
Coal mining 173
Cobb-Douglas (CD) 183
Cohen, Stephen P. 37–38, 54
Cold War 42, 49, 50
  1947–1991 2
  U.S- led Western victory 46
Combat economy 107
Communal riots in 1947 137
Communication networks 172
  of FATA, telephone infrastructure and post offices 33
Communism
  Pakistan as "Frontline State" in the war against 34
Community Appraisal and Motivation Program (CAMP) 33, 158
Composite schedule rate (CSR) 239
Computable General Equilibrium (CGE) model 201
Conflagration
  war report 86
Constitution of Pakistan 80
Constitution of the Islamic Republic of Pakistan 170
Cooley, John K. 43
Cooperative farming 183
Coping economy 107

Corticotropin-releasing hormone (CRH) 141
Cost-benefit analysis 237
Cottage enterprises 118
Cottage industries 69
Counter-insurgency actions 135
Counterterrorism 110
Country Partnership Strategy (CPS) 110
Cultivable waste 67
Cultural Revolution (1966–1976) 18
Culture and indigenous knowledge 116

D

Daesh 2
Dams *See also* Jabba Dam
  construction 242
  Reservoir 243
  uses 233
Daoud, Muhammad
  coup d'etat 81
  ultra-nationalism 80–81
Data management and analysis
  SPSS software 185
Davis, A. S. 183
Declaration of Jihad 49
Deeni Madaris 159
Democracy 93, 95
Desai, M. 125, 129, 132
Descriptive statistics 184–185
Destruction of the Tribal Code 10
Deteriorating quality of employment 224–226
Developing countries 154
  missing middle 226
Dholakia, R. R. 203
Director General (DG) 44
Dkaka, B. L. 131
Doddamani, M. T. 125, 129, 132
Drug trafficking 32
Dubai chalo 31
Dulac, J. 199
Duque, V. 140

Durand Line 7, 64, 87
  Agreement of 1893 80
  social and cultural bonds 81
Durrani, Asad 44
Dutta, A. 204

E

Easement Rights 80
Econometric models 180
Economic and Development Resource Center (EDRC, 1997) 237
Economic and social mobility 224
Economic conditions of FATA 66–68
  administrative system 66
  agriculture 66
    land used for 67
    production of crops, fruits, and vegetables 67–68
  internal conflict and international warfare 66
  livestock and poultry 68
  remittances or small-scale commerce 66
Economic cost
  of terrorism 107
Economic devastation in FATA 111–112
  indigenous economics 112–116
    in action 113–115
    an integrated approach to sustainable development 112
    basics 112–113
    future aspects 115–116, 118–120
    investment in 117–118
    review 116–117
Economic development in FATA 153
  changing mutual calculus of deterrence 58–59
  conceptual framework of analysis 29–30
  deteriorating quality 224–226
  economic potential 172–173
  future aspects 174–175
  half-hearted reforms 171–172
  high-risks Kargil gamble 52–56

impediments to progress 173–174
increasing trend of unemployment 221–222
indigenous economics and the role of women
  development statistics 108–109
  implications of economic devastation 111–120
  population demographics and the youth bulge 109–110
  restoring the traditional economy 110–111
International Context 59
Kargil's fall-out 56–58
low human capital 226–229
low labor force participation 222–224
nuclear flashpoint, refocusing attention on 50–51
Pakistan
  as "Frontline State" in the war against communism 34
  as "Frontline State" in the war against terror 59–61
  quest for "Strategic depth," 46–50
Pakistan-Afghanistan tribal area 24–29
role of nuclear weapons 51
September 11, 59
social development 30–34
via improved transportation and communication
  air transport 206
  future aspects 208–215
  information and telecommunications 206–207
  infrastructure and 200–204
  literature review 199–200
  policy recommendations 215–216
  rail infrastructure 206
  resource expenditures 205
  road infrastructure 205–206
Zia's Guerrilla Jehad and ISI 34–36
Economic empowerment 171
Economic implications
  of FATA

destruction of the Tribal Code 10
economic potential 10–12
merger with Pakhtunkhwa 10
for Pakistan 12–20
in retrospect 8
U.S. invasion of Afghanistan 9
for Pakistan
  agriculture sector 13–14
  analysis 17–20
  budgetary allocation 17
  conflict resolution 17
  development plan 12–13
  forestry sector 14
  good governance 16
  industrial sector 15–16
  infrastructure development 16
  law and order 16–17
  live stock sector 14–15
  minerals sector 15
  private sector participation 17
  share in National Finance Commission (NFC) Awards 13
  tourism sector 16
  trade sector 13
  transparent financial management 13
Economic Migrants of FATA 74
Economic potential of FATA 171–173
  Bajaur Agency 10–11
  Khyber Agency 11
  Kurram Agency 11–12
  Mohmand Agency 12
  North Waziristan Agency 12
  Orakzai Agency 11
  South Waziristan Agency 12
Economics of fragmentation 183
Economic Take-off Theory 154
Economic viability of Jabba Dam
  analysis of dams 236–238, 240–241
  capital costs 239, 245
  economic analysis 236, 238, 248–266
  fisheries benefits 240, 241, 243, 247
  methodology 238–240

NPV, BCR and IRR techniques 238–239, 241
supply of drinking water 239
water supply benefits 240, 241, 243, 246
Economic well-being of people 156
Economy of Pakistan 220
Economy of war 110
Education facilities in FATA 63–64
Educational Index-District Ranking 161
Education and socioeconomic development of FATA 154–159
  current education status 153, 159–162
  due diligence 153
  improvements 163–165
  modernization theory 154
  quality education provisions 153
  theoretical connections 153
  theory of human capital 154
Education system, improvements in
  curriculum aligned to the local needs 164
  educational provisions 163–164
  education to be linked to employment opportunities in the region 164–165
  facilities for basic education 164
  teacher's pedagogical improvement 164
  vocational training attainment 228
Egypt 93
Electronic media 172
Ellis, F. 181
Employment in FATA
  deteriorating quality 224–226
  economic and social welfare of the youth 220
  equity issues 222
  freedom, initiatives, and skill 220
  increasing trend of unemployment 221–222
  low human capital 226–229
  low labor force participation 222–224
Empowerment *See* Women empowerment
Entrepreneurship 225, 230
  ecosystem 230

INDEX | 285

Environmental Impact Analysis (EIA) 241, 243
Ethnic and sectarian violence 137
Ethnicity 43
Evans, W. 47
Exposure to violence, FATA *See also* Violence
    data and methodology 142–144
    literature review 138–140
    potential channels 141–142
    results and discussion 144–148
    violence and child health 137–138
Extremism 2, 4

F

Falsification test 146
Farm fragmentation 189–193
Farm productivity 182
Farmyard manure 123
    economic, political, and religious issues 1
    peace and stability 1
FATA Development Authority (FATA DA) 234, 236, 238, 243–244
FATA Development Corporation (FATADC) 170
FATA Development Household Indicators Survey (FDIHS) 108, 136, 142–143, 146, 179
FATA-KP
    British imperial power 1
FATA Sustainable Development Plan, 2007–2015 180
FATA Sustainable Development Plan 2007–2015 60
Fedderke, J. W. 200
Federal Government of Pakistan 107, 243
Federally Administered Tribal Agencies
    backwardness 3
    domestic and international security 2
    geostrategic area for Pakistan 1

Federally Administered Tribal Areas (FATA) 198
    access to basic facilities 66
    ADS 174
    agencies and frontier regions 198
    agrarian economy 63
    agriculture 8
    by-products 185
    airport locations 212
    airports in and around 207
    collateral turmoil 3
    communication network 172
        telephone infrastructure and post offices 33
    crude activity rate 108
    current state of affairs 171
    describtion of the area 7
    development indicators 171
    developmental funds 4, 74
    domestic insecurity 3
    domestic security 2, 5
    drug trafficking 32
    economic and social stress 219
    economic developments
        and financial stability 136
        and social development 30–34
        changing mutual calculus of deterrence 58–59
        conceptual framework of analysis 29–30
        economic potential 172–173
        future aspects 174–175
        half-hearted reforms 171–172
        high-risks Kargil gamble 52–56
        impediments to progress 173–174
        Kargil's fall-out 56–58
        nuclear weapons, roles 51
        Pakistan–Afghanistan tribal area 24–29
        Pakistan as "Frontline State," 34, 59–61
        Pakistan's quest for "strategic depth," 46–50

refocusing attention on the nuclear flashpoint 50–61
September 11 and International Context, 59
via improved transportation and communication *See* Economic development in FATA
Zia's Guerrilla Jehad and ISI 34–36
economic development reforms 2
economic growth 136
economic implications
  destruction of the Tribal Code 10
  merger with Pakhtunkhwa 10
  for Pakistan 12–20
  in retrospect 8
  U.S. invasion of Afghanistan 9
economic migrants 74
economic potential 10–12
economic viability of Jabba Dam
  analysis of dams 236–238, 240–241
  cost for 245
  economic analysis 248–266
  economic parameters 240
  fisheries benefits 240, 241, 243, 247
  methodology 238–240
  water supply benefits 240, 241, 243, 246
  education and socioeconomic development 154–159
    current education status 153, 159–162
    improvements 163–165
Education Department 164
education statistics 160
Educational Index-District Ranking 161
educational institutions 32
educational services 159
effect of terrorism 136
electronic media 172
employment and economic development
  deteriorating quality 224–226
  increasing trend of unemployment 221–222
  low human capital 226–229
  low labor force participation 222–224

ethnic and cultural differences 2
excessive explosions 9
existing and proposed highways 209
exposure to violence, human capital, and market development
  data and methodology 142–144
  literature review 138–140
  potential channels 141–142
  results and discussion 144–148
  violence and child health 137–138
FDA funds allocated to the development 75
food self-sufficiency on fragmented farms
  data sources 184–185
  estimations and discussion 186–188
  literature review 181–184
  policy recommendations 188–189
  research methodology 185–186
forests and rivers 73
geo-political and geo-strategic issue 83
geo-political patterns 34
government services to residents 159
"In and Out" of school children 160
industrial statistics in 71
industrial units established in 70
integration 172
international security 2, 5
lack of economic opportunities 219
lack of education 159
lack of funds or mismanagement 4
landline and broadband system 213
learning levels of students 162
literacy rate 63
long-term welfare effects 136
medium-and small-scale industrial enterprises 63
militancy 64
military operations 157
mineral production 173
minerals and coal reserves 197
minerals extracted from FATA (2006–2008) 73
national and international spheres 120
natural and mineral resources 72

natural resources 172, 175
opium cultivation 32
Pakistan armed forces 9
Pashtun tribes 2
points of interest in each Agency 214
policy recommendations 5
political-administrative system 9
political agencies 7
political and religious history 82
population growth rate 109
post-military operations 136
post office locations 213
postural economy 180
potential agriculture output 170
precious and semiprecious gemstones 173
primary exporter of instability 4
Provincial and National Education Scores 161
quality of employment 224, 230
quasi-governmental projects 69
radio stations 215
Reform Bill 1
railways in 211
refined activity rate 108
reform and development 171
Reform Committee 198
religion and politics
    and Afghanistan 90–91
    Afghanistan and Free State of Pukhtoonistan 80–81
    collapsed governance system 88–89
    conflagration 84–86
    hub of *Al-Qaeda* activities 86–87
    religious extremism 91
    schools of thought 82–83
    Soviet invasion of Afghanistan 81–82
    super power politics 83–84
    U.S. Espousal of Political Islam 91
    war of independence in Afghanistan and religious coloration 89–90
religious extremism in 91
ruled by *Riwaj* 79
school, college, and university statistics 64
security issues 105

services sector 73–74
smuggling of goods 31
social and economic development 174–175
social and economic indicators 107–108
    education 108
    employment 108
    foreign remittances 108
    health 108
socioeconomic profile
    access to clean water and sanitation 65
    economic conditions 66–68
    education facilities 63–64
    funds and grants 74–76
    health facilities 64–65
    housing and living conditions 65–66
    tribal women 69–64
special area 170, 174
special constitutional status 63
Taliban
    school buildings for activities 64
trade and commerce 74
Tribal Agencies and Frontier Regions 2
unemployment rates 108
war economy 107
Felloni, F. 199–200
Fetal Origin Hypothesis (FOH) 141
fi al-silm, peace 101
Field survey 184, 189–193
Financial capital 154
Fiscal growth 154
Fish farming 175
Food availability 181
Food security 180–181
Food self-sufficiency (FSS) 180–181, 183, 185, 188
    on fragmented farms in FATA
        data sources 184–185
        estimations and discussion 186–188
        literature review 181–184
        policy recommendations 188–189
        research methodology 185–186
Foreign and civil wars 96
Foreign colonialism 95
Fraser, P. J. 237

Freedom of religion 98
Fremdling, R. 203
Friends of Democratic Pakistan 60
Frontier Corps 16
Frontier Crimes Regulation (FCR) 169
Frontier Regions (FRs) 7, 106, 169
F-statistics 186
Fukuuyama, Francis 46
Funds and grants
    allocated to FATA 74–76

G

Gachassin, M. C. 202
Gaddafi, Muammar 96
Gall, Carlotta 84–85
Gates, Robert 84
GDP growth rate 221
Gender discrimination 148
Gender equality 122, 124, 133
Generalized Linear Model (GLM) 183
Geneva Accords, April of 1988 41
Geo-economics 24, 61
Geographic information system
    (GIS) 200
Geo-politics 94
German economic growth 203
German iron industry 203
Gilgit Baltistan (GB) 156, 198
Gillani, Yousaf Raza 45
Global counterterrorism strategy 60
Global Gender Gap Index 123
Global Terrorism Database (GTD) 142
Global youth employment
    ILO report 227
Godless Soviet Union 82
Gomal River 25, 26
Goodall, B. 199
Goods and exports 31
Gorbachev, Mikhail S. 41
Governance system
    of FATA collapsed 88–89
Government of Pakistan

    failing to afford time and financial
        resources 117
Gravity models 201
Greek armies and art 35, 46
Gross Enrollment Rate (GER) 108, 226
Guerrilla warfare 45
Gul, Hameed 44
Gul, Hamid 42

H

Haider, S.
    Line of Control 52
Hakim, M. M. 203
Hand, Jonathan
    war economy 107
Haq, Mahboobul 155
Haqqani 38
    Afghan "market of violence," 43
    influence of Islam 50
    Jamaat-e-Islami 48
    strategic defiance 48
Hassan, Javed 53
Healthcare services 141
Health facilities in FATA 64–65
Health of children
    effect of violence and terrorism 140
Height-for-age-Z score (HAZ) 136, 140
    child health measurement 143
    descriptive statistics 143
    impact of terrorism 144–146
Herranz-Loncan, A. 203
Heterogeneous effects 147–148
High-quality job market 224
High-risks Kargil gamble 56
    Pakistan
        aggressive form of nuclear
            deterrence 52
        political leadership 53
        tit-for-tat nuclear tests 52
        policy-making process 52
        usage of nuclear weapons 52, 54
Hill, Emily 60

Hoffman, Stanely 57
Holl, A. 200
Holt, F. L. 114
Holy War 9, 87
Holy Warriors 82
Host-communities 105
Housing and living conditions
  in the FATA 65–66
Hoyt, Kargil operation 53
Hujras 64
Human capability theory 163
Human capital 229
  of workers 229
Human capital theory 153, 155
Human development
  good quality of life 155–156
Human development theory 153, 155
Hussein, Saddam 2
Hybrid economic model 106, 111, 115, 116

I

Ibn Arabi 100
Illicit trade and trafficking 3
Improved transportation and
  communication
  economic development of FATA via
    air transport 206
    future aspects 208–215
    information and
      telecommunications 206–207
    infrastructure and 200–204
    literature review 199–200
    policy recommendations 215–216
    rail infrastructure 206
    resource expenditures 205
    road infrastructure 205–206
In-utero exposure 142, 144
Income and employment
  farming 68
India
  Indo-Pakistan dispute over Kashmir 50
  land consolidation 183

mutual calculus of deterrence 58
nuclear delivery vehicles 54
Readiness State 3, 54
India-Pakistan border skirmishes 52
Indian Army 52
  intruders's penetration 53
Indian attacks or invasions 51
Indian blackmailing 83
Indian Buddhism 35, 46
Indian National Congress 80
Indian rule 38
Indian-controlled Kashmir 59
Indigenous Amazonian populations 114
Indigenous economic development
  participatory approaches for 119–220
Indigenous economics
  blending environmental and mixed
    economy objectives 114
  customary management
    responsibilities 115
  defined 105–106
  economic devastation in FATA 112–116
    an integrated approach to sustainable
      development 112
    basics 112–113
    future aspects 115–116, 118–120
    in action 113–115
    investment in 117–118
  encouraging the role of women 119
  hybrid economies 115
  independent model of economics 116
  policy context 118
  research and explorative studies 119
  socio-cultural knowledge 113–114
  sustainable natural resource allocation 115
  women's roles 117
Indigenous entrepreneurship 115–116
  and market linkages 119
Indigenous women
  economic activities or revenue
    generation 119
Individuals
  policymakers 30
  self-fulfilled and self-sustaining citizens 3

Industrial Revolution 202
Industries
   employment opportunities 3
Information and
   telecommunications (ICT)
   infrastructure 203–204
   landline and mobile network 207
   postal service 207
   radio and television 206–207
Infrastructure and economic development
   geographic information system
      (GIS) 200
   gravity models 201
   ICT infrastructure 203–204
   road infrastructure 200
   transportation infrastructure 202–203
Insurgencies and counter-insurgencies 137
Inter-Services Intelligence
   (ISI) 23, 24, 36
   Benazir Bhutto government 44
   powerful arm of the General Zia 44
Interim Islamic Council 42
Internal economic rate of return (EIRR) 236
Internal financial rate of return
   (FIRR) 236–237
Internally displaced persons (IDPs) 108
International community 169
International Fund for Agricultural
   Development 123–124
International newspapers
   Pakistan's Kargil operation 55
International stability and security 60
Invisible guardians 124
Iran
   Islamic Revolution 34
Iranian Islamic Revolution 83
Iranian Revolution 83
Iraq war 91
ISI *See* Inter-Services Intelligence (ISI)
Islam 99, 100
   of *madaris* 88
Islam and Christianity
   marriage of convenience 82
Islamabad 169

mass destruction 40
military and economic aids 40
nuclear capability 53
Islami Jamhoori Ittihad 44
Islamic Caliphate 94
Islamic conception
   of nonviolence and peace 101
Islamic Democratic Alliance 44
Islamic extremism 46
Islamic fundamentalism 43
Islamic guerrilla jihad 38
Islamic Jihad 37
Islamic Madrassa 35
Islamic militancy 137
Islamic peace
   two pillars of 100–101
Islamic political party
   Jamat-i-Islami 36
Islamic resistance 43
Islamic Revolution 34
Islamic schools/*madrassas* 36
Islamic teachings and peace 100
Islamic Ummah 83
Islamists
   Communist ideology 45

J

Jabeen, N. 128
Jahiliyyah 99
Jamaat-e-Islami 35, 48
Jamat-i-Islami 36
Jami'a-e Hafsa 87
Jammu and Kashmir 43
Januszewski Index 183
Jha, R. 182
Jihad 37
Jihadi groups 23
Jihadist ideology 43
Jinnah, Quaid-e-Azam Muhammad Ali 8, 20, 36, 81
Journal of Islamic & Religious Studies, July–December 2017 102

K

Kalashnikov (AK-47) culture 32
Kamal, Nazir 52
Karachi
  political violence 137
Kargil Heights 54
  in 1999 56
Kargil mini-war 56–58
  nuclear blackmail 56
  nuclear deterrence strategy 57
  political and strategic wisdom 56
  self-interest and self-regulation 58
Kargil war
  indirect and direct nuclear threats 55
Karki, T. B. 183
Kashmir policy 50
  Pakistan's aggressive form of nuclear deterrence 52
Kashmir Valley 43, 47
Kashmir War of Independence 81
  in 1948 91
Kayani, Ashfaq 44
Kennedy, Paul 60
Khan, A.Q. 20, 39, 169–176
Khan, F.R. Dera Ismail 179
Khan, Gohar Ayub 47
Khan, Kallu 44
Khan, Muqtedar (Dr.) 93–102
Khan, Noor Paio 121–133
Khasadars 25, 80
Khobar Towers, Saudi Arabia
  terrorists' attack on 60
Khyber Agency 11, 206
  free state of Pukhtoonistan 80
Khyber and Mohmand agencies 82
Khyber and Waziristan Agencies 81
Khyber Pakhtunkhwa (KP) 1–2, 7, 79–80, 83, 91, 106, 111, 164, 173–174, 180
  economic implications of FATA 10
    destruction of the Tribal Code 10
    economic potential 10–12
    for Pakistan 12–20
    in retrospect 8
    U.S. invasion of Afghanistan 9
Khyber tribal agency 82
Kim 27
Kipling, Rudyard 27
Klonis, N. I. 45
Kohler-Rollefson, I. 124
Kristjanson, P. 123
Kuki Khel tribes 81
Kurram and Aurakzai agencies 11–12, 83
Kurram and Khyber Agencies 175
Kurram Tangi Dam 31
Kuusaana, E. D. 184
Kux, Dinnis 48

L

Lakeshore Summit 59
Lal Masjid 87
Lamb, Christina 48
Land consolidation 184
Land fragmentation 181, 182, 183
Landholding 181
Landline and mobile network 207
Land Parcel 181
Land productivity and profitability 182
Latent Class Frontier Method 183
Latin American economies 203
Law Enforcement Agencies (LEAs) 89
Leprosy Centres 34
Liberal utopianism 90
Liberation fighters 82
Line of Control 52–53, 55, 58
Linear regression model 186
Livestock
  and farming 180
  cash profits 123
  nutritional requirements 123
  poor livestock keepers 123
  products 128, 132
  rearing 128

rural economy of Pakistan 123
women empowerment in 126–133
    contributions 125–126
    objectives 124–125
Local empowerment 3
Lodhi, Maleeha
    culture of violence 49
Longi
    head of sub-clans 33

M

Male child
    employment 158
Maleks 9, 88
Maliks 30–31
    head of sub-clans 33
    milking the system 32
Manjunath, L. 125, 129, 132
Mansour, H. 140
Maoist military 37
Marazzo, M. 203
Marwat, Fazal Rehim
    Dubai phenomenon 31
Masood, Talat 84
Maternal and Pediatric Health Centres (MCHC) 34
Maternal mortality ratio (MMR) 65, 108
Matlock, Jack 42
Mawdudi, Mawlana Syid Abu A'ala 36
McDonald, A. J. 183
Menhas, R. 128
Merged Tribal Districts *See* Federally Administered Tribal Agencies
Mian, A. 53
Micro-economies 114
Mieczkowski, B. 199, 200
Militant groups 172
Militant terrorists
    jihadi infrastructure 35
Military insecurity 39
Military operations 135
Military overtures 3

Millennium Development Goals (MDGs) 4, 110, 121
Mineral extraction 73
Minerals in FATA 72
Mixed economies 115, 116
Modernization theory 153, 154–155
Modern politics 19
Mohmand Agency of FATA 11
    livestock to rural livelihoods 124
    soapstone 173
Mohmand and Bajuar agencies 82
Monchuk, D. 183
Mongol conquest 35, 46
Mujahideen 36, 41, 82
Mullah 79, 88
Multiple regression model 185, 188
Multi-stage sampling technique 125
Musharraf, Pervez 32–33, 44, 53–55, 84, 90
    strategic miscalculation 57
Muslim Middle East 93, 95
Muslims
    Assalamu 'Alaykum 99
    civil society 95
    militants's insurgency 58
    "Peace!" (Quran 14:23) 99
    preachers and teachers 100
Muslim societies 94, 95
Muslim world
    injustices and persecution 98

N

Nagarajan, H. K. 182
Najibullah regime 42, 45
Naseer, Noreen (Dr.) 63–66
Nasir, muhammad 135–149
Nasr, V. 8
National Action Plan (NAP) 135
National Assembly of Pakistan 1
National Finance Commission (NFC) 4
National telecommunication
    infrastructure 203

NATO 89
Naz, Shaista 121–133
9/11 terrorist attacks 33, 59, 84–85, 88, 137
Niroula, G. S. 182
North and South Waziristan agencies 82
Northern Alliance 85
North Waziristan Agency 12, 135, 143, 180, 184, 189–193
North West Frontier Province (NWFP) 79–80, 107
Nuclear blackmail 56
Nuclear bombs 54
Nuclear deterrence strategy 57
Nuclear flashpoint
　refocusing attention on 50–61
Nuclear-tipped missiles 54
Nuclear weapons 50
　roles 51
　utility 38

O

"Off-war" cold season 35
OLS methodology 144, 146
"One-size-fits-all" road investment strategies 202
1973 Constitution 170
1988 general elections 44
1979 Soviet invasion of Afghanistan 7
1948 UN Security Council 50
Operation Enduring Freedom 61
Operation Midnight Jacka 44
Operation Zarb-e-Azb 4, 135
Opium cultivation 32
Orakzai Agency 11

P

Pak-Afghan border area 83
Pak-Afghan Transit Trade Agreement (ATTA) 31

Pakistan
　Afghan policy 34, 57
　aggressive form of nuclear deterrence 52
　annual developmental plans 205
　armed forces 36
　crude deterrence for security 56
　domestic and foreign policies 50
　domestic Pakistani manufacturing sector 31
　economic implications
　　agriculture sector 13–14
　　analysis 17–20
　　budgetary allocation 17
　　conflict resolution 17
　　development plan 12–13
　　forestry sector 14
　　good governance 16
　　industrial sector 15–16
　　infrastructure development 16
　　law and order 16–17
　　live stock sector 14–15
　　minerals sector 15
　　private sector participation 17
　　share in National Finance Commission (NFC) Awards 13
　　tourism sector 16
　　trade sector 13
　　transparent financial management 13
　failure to resolve internal and external security problems 57
　FATA 28
　　backward area 33
　foreign policy 23
　foreign policymakers 24
　Frontier Region (FR) 1
　"Frontline State" in the war
　　against communism 34
　　against terror 59–61
　GDP 118, 135
　gender equality 123
　growth rate of population 61
　guerrilla warfare and people's war 37
　independence in 1947 30

294 | INDEX

internal and external security 60
Kashmir policy 50
Khyber Pakhtunkhwa 169
labor force 123
military and intelligence agency (ISI) 51
military and security services 50
Mineral Department 72
mutual calculus of deterrence 58
national security policy 50
nuclear capability 48, 56
nuclear explosive device 40
Pashtun-majority area 48
policy projections for 2025 106
policymakers 34–35
political history 35
political leadership 53
primary net enrollment rate 157
public infrastructure investment 202
quest for "strategic depth," 46–50
religious identity 35
rural and indigenous communities 118
security forces 57, 87
socio-political space 153
Taliban and Jihadi forces in 85
tit-for-tat nuclear tests 52
venial geopolitics 61
wars against India 52
Western-sponsored alliances 80
women
    empowerment 123
    livestock farming 123
Pakistan-Afghanistan border tribal area 24–29, 197
    geography 24–29
    northern portion 26
    policy outputs 30
    southern portion 27
Pakistan Army 8, 87, 88–89
Pakistan-controlled Kashmir 58
Pakistan Dairy Development Company, 2006 124
Pakistan Economic Survey 137
Pakistani Armed Forces 85

Pakistani context
    education and economic development 156
    literacy rate 156
Pakistani Customs Service and Levies 25
Pakistani declaratory policy 24
Pakistani duties or customs tariffs 31
Pakistani independence 169
Pakistani intelligence agencies 60
Pakistani ISI 43
Pakistani military 43
Pakistani policy 51
Pakistani policymakers 24, 51
    compelling action from India 57
    nuclear capability 56
Pakistani politics 36
Pakistani security forces 87
Pakistani society
    FATA-KP 1
Pakistan People's Party (PPP) 44, 170
Pan-Islamic radicalism 49
Parental quality 141
Parsons, Talcott 154
Pasha, Ahmad Shuja (DG-ISI, 2009–2012) 44
Pashtun tribes 107, 111
Patrik, and Andersson (2006) 182
Peace 97, 99–100, 102
    and harmony 98
    Quran on 99–100
"Peace!" (Quran 14:23) 99
Peace accords 135
Peace and nonviolence 96
Peace economy 109
Pearl Harbor 59
Per acre yield
    effect of pouch farming 185
    food self-sufficiency 188
    irrigation 188
Persecution 101
Persecution is worse than killing (Quran 2:217) 98
Persian administration 46

Persian administrative techniques 35
Pesticides 188
Pest management
   labor-intensive techniques 188
Pious Caliph of Islam 82
Planning and Development Department of FATA, 2014 124
Pocket area approach 13–14
Political Agent (PA) 9, 107
Political Agents (PA) 80, 88
Political Islam
   U.S. Espousal of 91
Population demographics 109–110
Population growth rate 109
Portuguese motorway networks 200
Post-9/11 politics 8
Poverty and income inequalities
   road infrastructure investment 201
Power politics 29
Pre-and postnatal vulnerability
   to violence 140
Pregnancy
   chronic maternal stress 141
   econometric methodology 144
   exposure to violence 144
   nutritional deprivation 141
   stress hormones 145
Prenatal and childhood exposure 146
Prenatal vulnerability
   to violence 140
Pressler Amendment 40
Pressler, Larry 40
Private school children
   achievement scores 161
Provincial and National Education Scores 161
Psacharopoulos 155
PSLM 2013–2014 156
Psychological health
   impact on adults 136
Public and private schools 161
Public infrastructure 199
Public Sector Developmental Project (PSDP) funds 17, 74

Q

Qadir, Brigadier
   air power 53
   Indian army 53
Qazi, Javed Ashraf 44
Quality of education 165, 227
Quality of employment 225
Quality of schooling 163
Quran 96
   al-Baqarah 97
   Al-Salam 97
   dar al-Islam 97
   forgiveness and peace 98
   murder and terrorism 101
   peace 97, 99–100, 102
      and harmony 98
   religious domination and repression 98
   use of force by Muslims 97
Qur'ānic sources
   Jihad to Salam for change 97–98
   Quran on peace 99–100
   two pillars of Islamic peace 100–101

R

Radio and television 207–208
Radio stations 214–215
Rahman, Amir Abdul 46
Rahman, M. 182
Rahman, S. 182
Rail infrastructural development 206
Ramana 53
Ram, K. A. 181
Rann of Kutch incident (1965) 52
Rashid, Ahmed 49–50
Readiness State 3, 54
Reagan, Ronald 40
Red Army 42, 81, 90
Rehman, Akhtar Abdur 36
Rehman, F. U. 135
Reidel, Bruce 54

Reiss, Michel 39
Religion and politics of FATA 3
　Afghanistan 90–101
　　and Free State of Pukhtoonistan
　　　80–81
　　and religious coloration 89–90
　　Soviet invasion 81–82
　　war of independence 89–90
　collapsed governance system 88–89
　conflagration 84–86
　hub of *Al-Qaeda* activities 86–87
　religious extremism 91
　schools of thought 82–83
　super power politics 83–84
　U.S. Espousal of Political Islam 91
Religious coloration 89–90
Religious extremism
　in Afghanistan 91
　in FATA 91
Religious tensions 2
Resource expenditures
　on road infrastructure 205
Riwaj 79
Road and infrastructure investment 202
Road infrastructure 200
Robinson, H. 199
Rostow, W. W. 154
Roy, Oliver 45
Ruataniwha Dam 237
Rubin
　Pakistan's quest for "strategic
　　depth," 46–50
　security and economic implications 47
　security issues 43
Rubine
　military damages 45
Rural and urban areas
　unemployment levels 221
Rural economy 221
Rural Health Units (HRC) 34
Rural livelihoods
　contribution of livestock 125–126,
　　128–130
　　theoretical framework 126

　role of women
　　Chi-square test 126, 130
　　managing livestock 124, 126–128,
　　　130–132
　　simple linear regression
　　　analysis 126, 131
　　time allocation 127
Rural living and cottage needs
　mineral excavation and
　　furnishing 69
Rural living enterprises 69
Rural-to-urban labor migration 222
Rural women
　livestock management activities 124
　work hours 123

S

SAHE (2016) 163
Sahib, Sarkano Mullah 82
Sahib, Sheikh Gul 82
Sahoo, P. 200
Sah, S. K. 183
Salaam (peace) 99
Sanitation and hygiene facilities
　in the FATA 65
Saudi Arabia
　multi-billion-dollar arms and funds
　　transactions 44
Saudi General Intelligence
　Department 36
Sauer, J. 183
Schultz, Theodore 155, 181, 182
Schwartz, J. 200
Sectarianism 93
Self-employment 230
Self-sufficiency ratio (SSR) 181
Sen, Amartya 155
September 11 attack, 59
Services sector in FATA 73–74
Shadow economy 107
Shad, Tahir 1–5, 93–102
Shah, King Zahir 81

Shahkas Khyber Agency 238
Sharif, Nawaz 44, 54, 211
　Pakistani army 55
　role in Kargil conflict 59
Sheikh, Arab 86
Shiaism 83
Shinwari, N. A. 17, 158–159
Shiu, A. 203, 204
Siachen Glacier (1984) 52–53
Sibling fixed-effect model 145–147
Siddiqa-Agha
　nuclear weapons 51
　use of nuclear weapons 51
Silent Soldier: The Man behind the Afghan Jehad, General Akjhtar Abdur Rahman Shaheed 36
Simes 42, 46
Simla Agreement 53
Simple linear regression analysis 126–127, 131
Singapore
　economic development 155
　education
　　and economy 155–156
　　and workplace training 155–156
Singer, J. David 29
Skills development 215
Skill-training centers 229
Small and medium enterprises (SME) 226
Smuggling 11
Smuggling of goods 31, 32
Social and environmental system 116
Social Institutions and Gender Index 123
Social mobility 4
Socioeconomic development *See* Education and socioeconomic development in FATA
Socioeconomic development of FATA 153
　prenatal and postnatal violence 3
　theory of human capital 154
Socioeconomic profile in FATA
　access to clean water and sanitation 65
　economic conditions 66–68
　education facilities 63–64

Federally Administered Tribal Areas from 2001–2014 63
　funds and grants 74–76
　health facilities 64–65
　housing and living conditions 65–66
　tribal women 69–74
Soherwordi, Syed Hussain Shaheed 1–5, 7–10
South Asian labor market 227
South Asian military 51
South Asian politics 23
South Asian Terrorism Portal, 2016 135
South East Asian Treaty Organization (SEATO) 80
Southern Afghanistan 85
South Waziristan Agency 12
Soviet-Afghan War 2, 43
Soviet invading forces 91
Soviet invasion
　of Afghanistan 34, 59, 81–82, 83, 90, 107
Soviet Union 46
　interference in Afghanistan 81
　massed forces 47
　strategic depth 47
Spatial and temporal violence 137
Special Services Group (SSG) 37
Staatz, J. M. 181
Stability and security
　economic development 3
　geopolitics 3
State Bank of Pakistan 71
State of Food and Agriculture 123
Statistical Package for Social Sciences (SPSS) 184
Strategic weapon 38
Stress hormones 141
Storeygard, A. 201
Students
　learning achievement 160
　learning levels 162
Study of Terrorism and Responses to Terrorism (START) 142
Sub-Health Centres 34
Sufism 100

Sung, J. 157
Super power politics
  in the FATA 83–84
Surah al-Maidah 99
Surah *Baqrah* 98, 101
Surah *Maidah* 101
Sustainable Development Goals
  (SDGs) 121–122
  indigenous economics 112
  2030 development agenda 122
Sustainable economic model 106
Sustainable improvement of human
  welfare 236
  dam project 233
Suwika. R. L. 131
Syrian Civil War 94

T

Tahreek-e-Taliban Pakistan (TTP) 137
Tajalli 100
Taliban 23, 24, 83
  1992–1996 2
  Kabul, 1996 86
  pan-Islamic war 50
Taliban-controlled Afghanistan
  army strategic depth 51
Talibanization 85
Tarikh key Ayeney Mein (The SSG in the Mirror of History), 2004 37
T.B. Clinics 34
Tehreek-e Taliban Pakistan (TTP) 87, 110, 171–173
Tehrik-e-Taliban movement 60
Tellis, Ashley J. 57
Terror
  Pakistan as "Frontline State" in the war against 59–61
Terrorism 2, 60, 93
  economic cost 107
  height-for-age-Z score (HAZ) 144–146
Terrorist attacks 135, 142
  on September 11, 2001, 101

Terrorist incidents
  2001–2006 138
  2007–2012 139
Terrorist recruitment 112
Thapa, R. B. 183
The Bear Trap: Afghanistan's Untold Story 36
The Daily Times 43
Theory of human capital 154, 163
Theory of modernization 163
The Wrong Enemy, America in Afghanistan 2001–2014 84
Third World 154
Tit-for-tat nuclear tests 52
Torkham 24
Torkham-Peshawar Railway Track 210
Tourism industry 202
Trade and Commerce in FATA 74
Trafficking 3–5
Transportation and communication
  economic development of FATA via
    air transport 206
    future aspects 208–215
    information and
      telecommunications 206–207
    infrastructure and 200–204
    intraregional and inter-regional
      trade 201
    literature review 199–200
    policy recommendations 215–216
    rail infrastructure 206
    resource expenditures 205
    road infrastructure 205–206
    tourism industry 202
Tribal Agencies 106, 111
Tribal Areas 174
Tribal economy
  agriculture 174
Tribalism 43
Tribal people
  Afghan Refugees *(Muhajireen)* 81, 90
  migration to Karachi 31
Tribal regions
  economic development 118

Tribal society
  patterns 31
  social structure 33
Tribal women
  educational and training 19
  in FATA's economy 69–74
    agriculture labor 69
    government banks 71
    honey extraction or
      woodcutting 69
    industries in 69–70
    livestock and poultry 69
    minerals 72
    natural and mineral resources 72
    Taliban's restrictions 69
  livestock management 124
Troops
  moral and religious conduct 36
  satisfactory military performance 36
Tunisia 93
Turkey
  highway networks and external trade
    data 201
Turkic military formations 35, 46
2025 Vision 117

U

U.S.-led NATO forces 84, 87, 89
U.S.–Pakistani relations 23
Uma economy 114, 120
Unemployment 221–222
  psychological health 220
United Kingdom
  education with the economy 155
United Nations
  General Assembly 81
  Security Council 52
United States
  administration 39
  arms and equipment to Pakistan 82
  Army 90
  Assistance Program 40
  bombers 87
  Central Intelligence Agency 36
  Cold War 83
  Congressional Kerry-Lugar Act 60
  counterterrorism policy 61
  Espousal of political Islam 91
  inter-state and intrastate relations 60
  invasion
    Afghanistan 2
    Iraq 2
    of Afghanistan 9
  isolationism 59
  jihadi 83
  Jihadism 90
  military support 37
  multi-billion-dollar arms and funds
    transactions 44
  national security 40
  policy on ISIS and Afghanistan 91
  policymakers 91
  proxy war 40
  September 11 attacks 59, 87, 101
  State Department
    nuclear weapons development
      program 39
  support 42
  war against Taliban 9
  wars of choice 46
Unregistered medical practitioners 65
Upper-low-income and low-income African
  countries 204
Urban economy 222
Urban young men
  joblessness 221
Urbanization 110
USSR 37, 40, 90
Utilization 181

V

Valente, C. 140
Van Der Molen, P. 184
Van Dijk, T. 181

Vel, Jacqueline 113–114, 119–120
Vietnam War 90
Violence
   and child health in FATA 137–138
   childhood exposure 142
   impact on HAZ 145
      heterogeneous effects 148
      robustness 147
   in-utero and vulnerability 140
   in-utero exposure 142
   mental stress 142
   miscarriages or stillbirths 140
   parent's mental health 142
   prenatal and postnatal exposures 136
Vladivostok Speech 41

W

Wage-related livestock work 123
Wage war 107
Wahabi/Salafi school of thought 83
Wahid, Fazal (Dr.) 79–81
Waltz, Kenneth N. 29
War
   against Communism 34
   economy 107, 109
   on Terror 1, 107–108, 110, 137
   wage war 107
Warlords 43
Warruwi women 119
   community development 115
Warsak Dam 233
Washington
   military operations 60
Water supply scheme 233–234, 242
Waziristan Agency 87, 137
Weiss, J. 199
Weiss, M. 200
Wenga, L. 200
Wickramaarachchi, N. C. 183
Women
   agricultural activities 117
   casualization 225
   concern of SDGs 122
   education and literacy indicators 226
   increasing level of education 223
   labor force participation 222–224
   leadership in FATA 119
   livestock management 117
   public socioeconomic spheres 118
   roles in indigenous economics 106
   time allocation to livestock management activities 130–131
   unemployment 221–222
   wage-related livestock work 123
Women empowerment
   livestock management 126–133
      contributions 125–126
      objectives 124–125
   sustainable development goals 124
Woodhall, M.
   research on human capital 155
Working-age population 224
Working-age youth demographics 110
World Bank Group 32, 110, 236
World Commission on Dams 233, 236, 237
World Economic Forum Pakistan
   Global Gender Report 123
World Food Program
   poor agriculture in FATA 68
World Trade Center 46, 49, 60

Y

Yaqoob, M. 128
Ye Khamoshi Kahan Tak 85
Young men and women
   labor force participation 223
Yousaf, Brigadier Mohammad 36, 45
Youth
   economic and social well-being 224
   employment opportunities 219

literacy rate 226
unemployment 222
vocational training attainment 228
Yusufzai, R. 9

Z

Zakha Khel tribes 81
Zia ul Haq
    guerrilla jehad and ISI 35–36
    long rule 47
    low-enriched, non-weapon-grade material 40
    Operation Fair Play 35
    Pakistan's *strategic byways* 39
    strategic depth 47
    USA and Saudi Arabia 44
Zionist strategy
    Gulf War 48

Washington College

Studies in Religion, Politics, and Culture

Joseph Prud'homme
General Editor

Washington College Studies in Religion, Politics, and Culture explores the role of religious belief in political and cultural life, both in the United States and across the world. Special emphasis is placed on theoretical, historical, and legal assessments of the relationship of religion to public life, the meaning and practice of citizenship, and cultural development. Empirical work is also welcome.

For additional information about this series or for the submission of manuscripts, please contact:

Dr. Joseph Prud'homme
Director, Institute for Religion, Politics, and Culture
Washington College
300 Washington Avenue
Chestertown, MD 21620
E-mail: jprudhomme2@washcoll.edu

To order other books in this series, please contact our Customer Service Department:

peterlang@presswarehouse.com (within the U.S.)
orders@peterlang.com (outside the U.S.)

Or browse online by series at www.peterlang.com

www.ingramcontent.com/pod-product-compliance
Lightning Source LLC
Chambersburg PA
CBHW070232230426
43664CB00014B/2277